6

Everyone's Getting Married

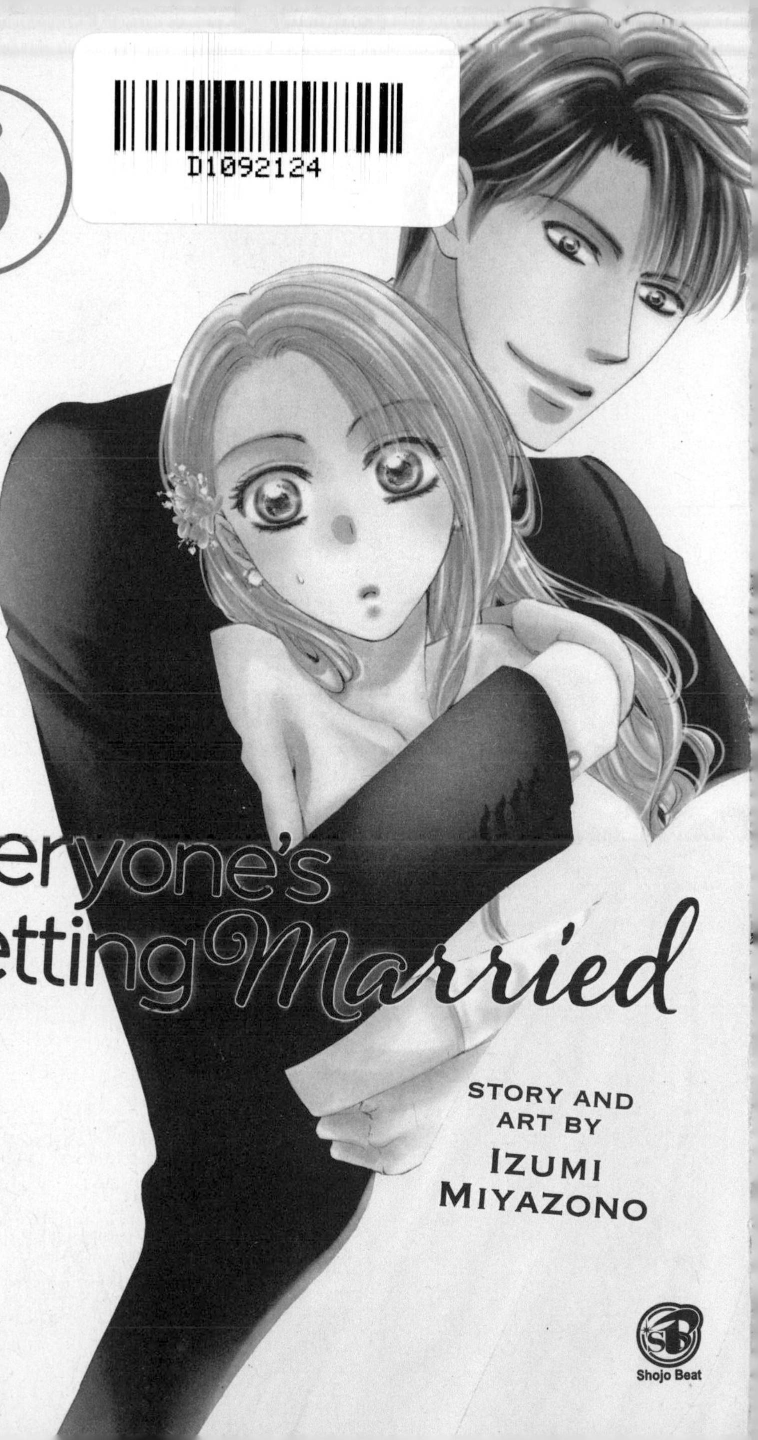

STORY AND ART BY
IZUMI MIYAZONO

Shojo Beat

CHARACTERS

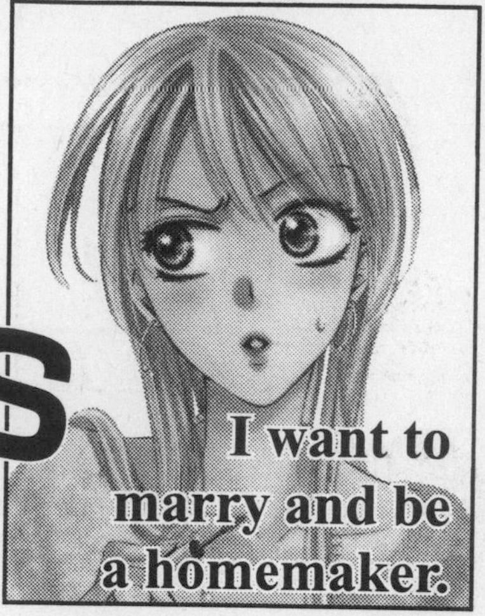
I want to marry and be a homemaker.

THE WOMAN WHO WANTS TO GET MARRIED

Asuka Takanashi
She takes pride in her career at a major bank, but feels strongly about getting married.

COLLEAGUES

VS

THE MAN WHO DOESN'T WANT TO GET MARRIED

Ryu Nanami
The handsome, up-and-coming newscaster at PTV. He's returned from the New York office.

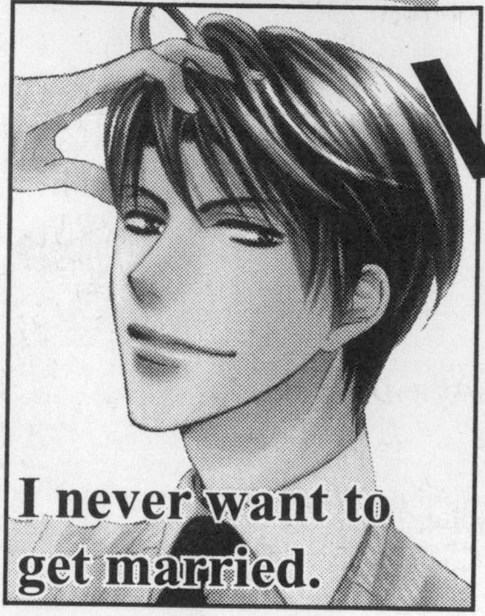
I never want to get married.

WERE INVOLVED IN AN ILLICIT RELATIONSHIP

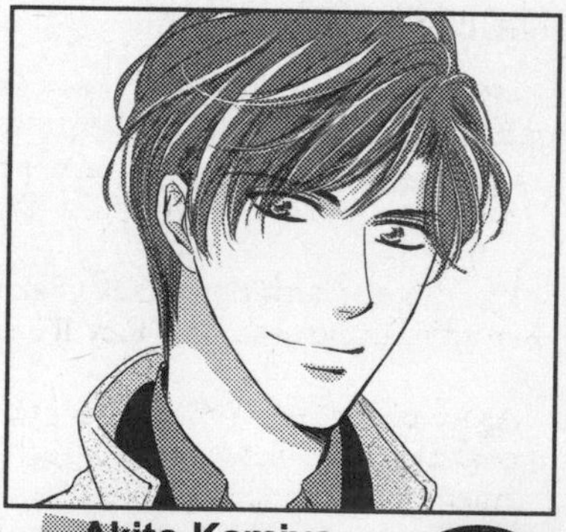

THE MAN WHO WANTS A BENEFICIAL MARRIAGE

Akito Kamiya
The top salesman of a major bank. He's envisioned the woman he wants to be his wife, and he has set his sights on Asuka.

THE WOMAN WHO CLINGS TO MARRIAGE

Yuko Sakura
A former singer turned actress. She will not leave her husband, Uesaki.

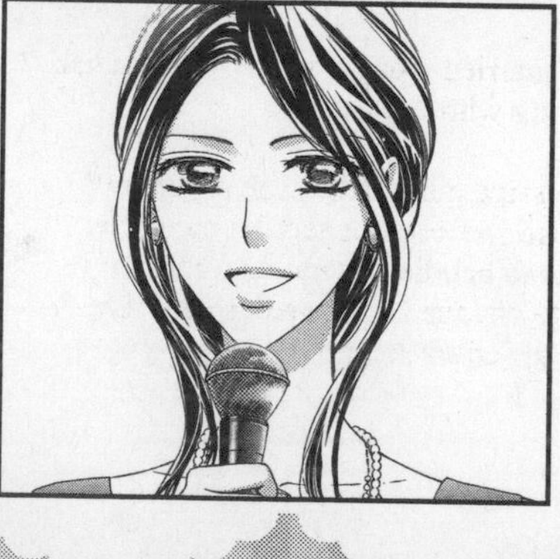

Hiroki Ono
A senior colleague of Asuka and Rio. He's roommates with Nanami.

HE WANTS TO

IN A RELATIONSHIP ♥
(with no plans to marry in the future)

SHE DOESN'T WANT TO

Rio
Asuka's best friend. She's in a relationship with Hiroki.

HE DIDN'T WANT TO

Himuro
A producer at PTV.

COWORKERS

HE DID

Mikami
A news anchor at PTV.

STORY THUS FAR

Inspired by her mother who was a fulltime homemaker, Asuka aspires to get married and create a happy home too. She falls in love with the popular TV host, Ryu, but he is against marriage. The two set aside their differing values and fall in love to the degree that they feel they would never be happy apart...

Ryu is then reunited with Yuko Sakura, a married woman with whom he had an affair in the past. Now they'll be working with each other.

Asuka continues parrying Kamiya's aggressive pursuit, but she realizes it's now more than just his wanting her because she's someone who meets his criteria for marriage. Asuka isn't sure how to handle this change in Kamiya, and she wonders if she would be willing to change her stance on marriage for Ryu. Auska heads for her parents' house, the epitome of the happy home she wishes to create, and...?!

Contents

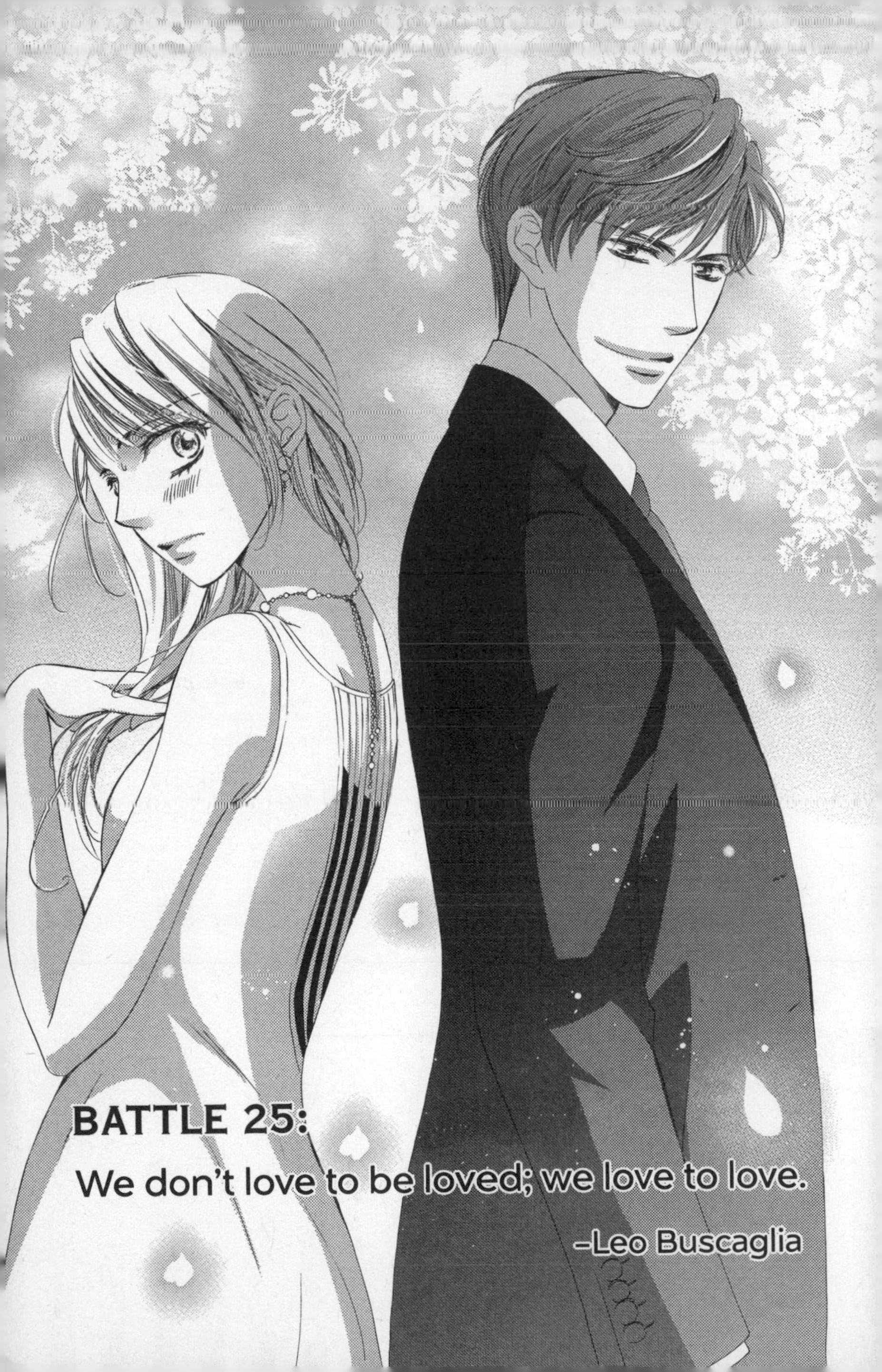
BATTLE 25:
We don't love to be loved; we love to love.
–Leo Buscaglia

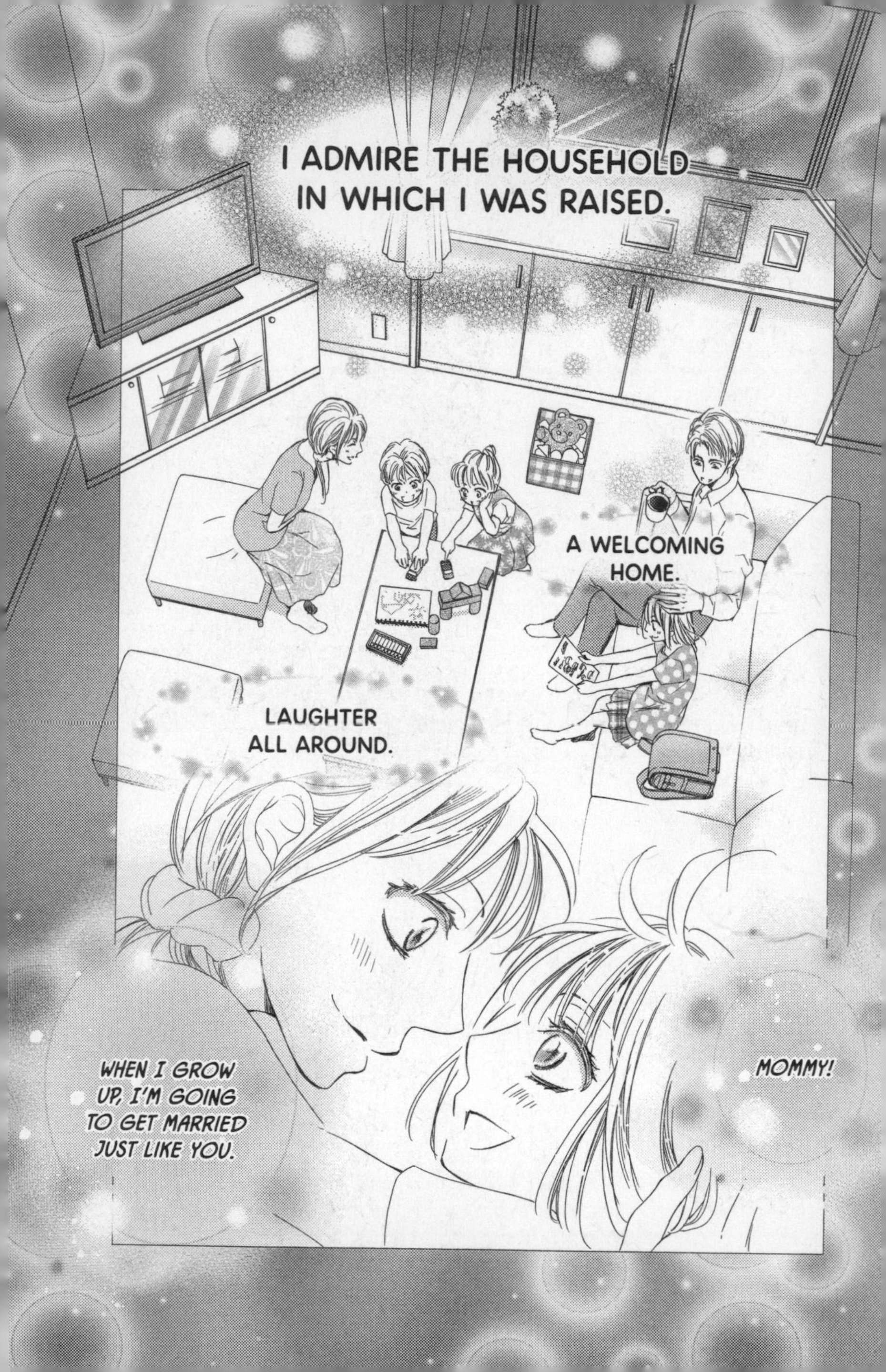
I ADMIRE THE HOUSEHOLD IN WHICH I WAS RAISED.
A WELCOMING HOME.
LAUGHTER ALL AROUND.
MOMMY!
WHEN I GROW UP, I'M GOING TO GET MARRIED JUST LIKE YOU.

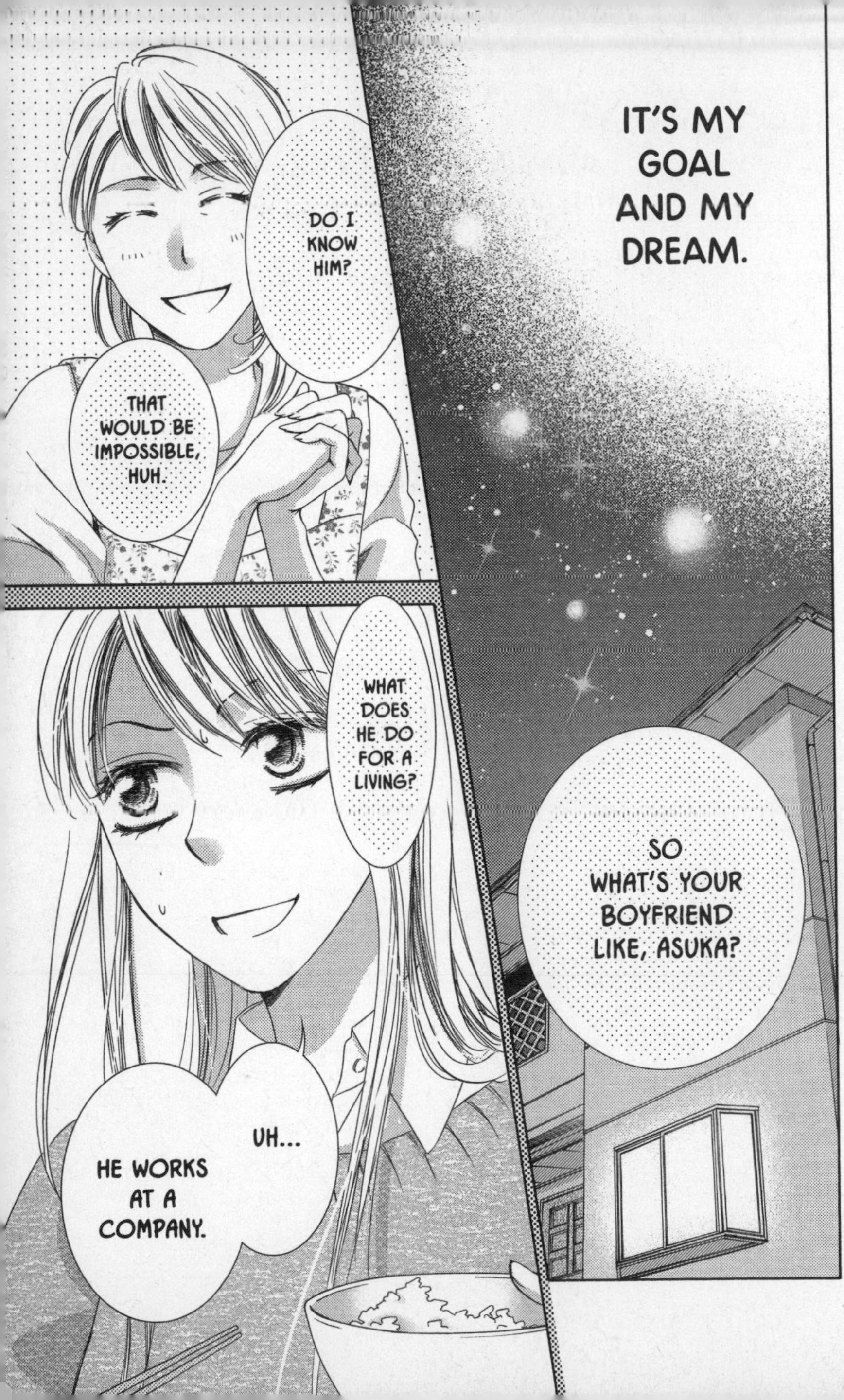
IT'S MY GOAL AND MY DREAM.
SO WHAT'S YOUR BOYFRIEND LIKE, ASUKA?
DO I KNOW HIM?
THAT WOULD BE IMPOSSIBLE, HUH.
WHAT DOES HE DO FOR A LIVING?
UH...
HE WORKS AT A COMPANY.

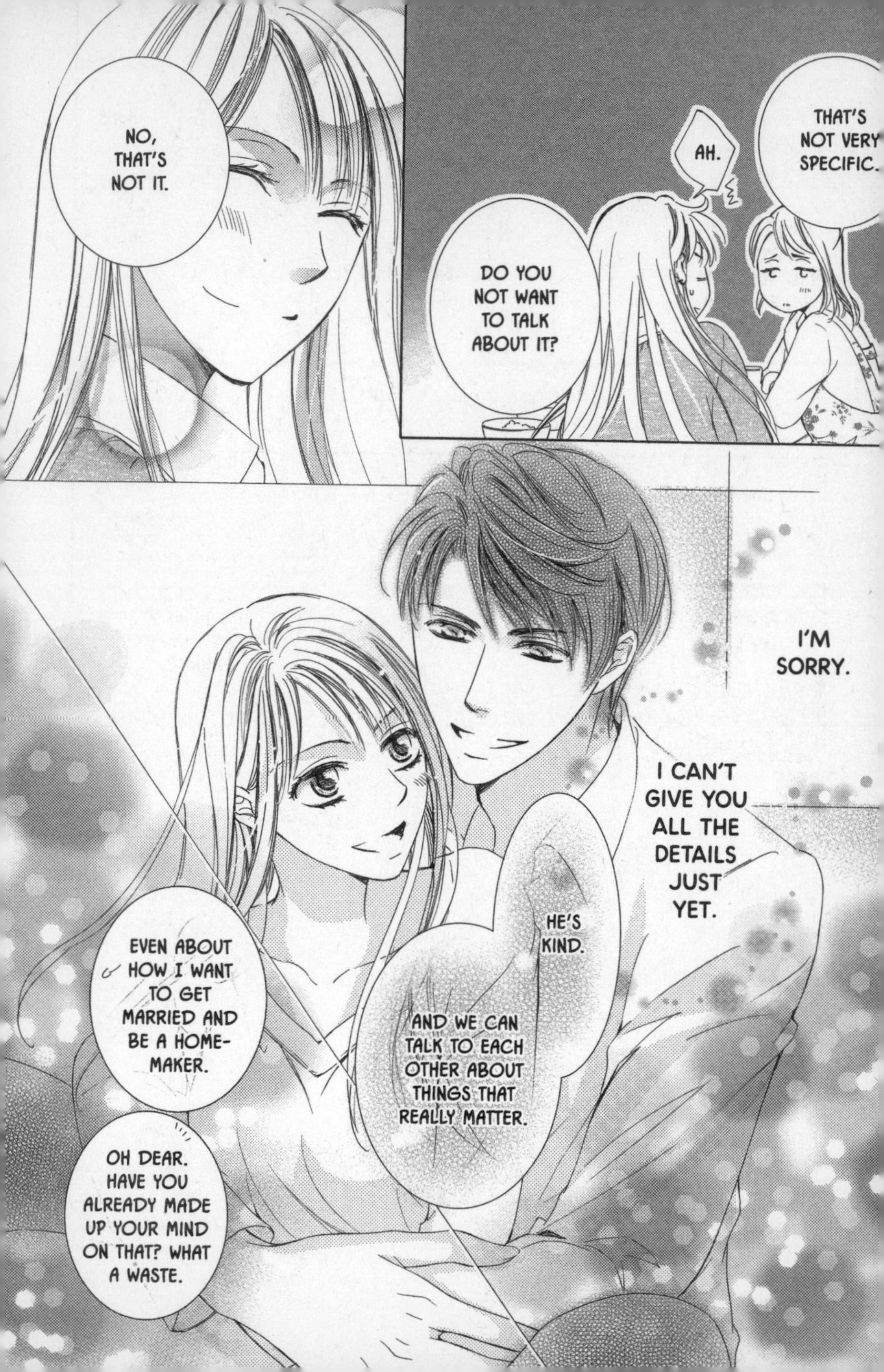
THAT'S NOT VERY SPECIFIC.
AH.
DO YOU NOT WANT TO TALK ABOUT IT?
NO, THAT'S NOT IT.
I'M SORRY.
I CAN'T GIVE YOU ALL THE DETAILS JUST YET.
HE'S KIND.
AND WE CAN TALK TO EACH OTHER ABOUT THINGS THAT REALLY MATTER.
EVEN ABOUT HOW I WANT TO GET MARRIED AND BE A HOME-MAKER.
OH DEAR. HAVE YOU ALREADY MADE UP YOUR MIND ON THAT? WHAT A WASTE.

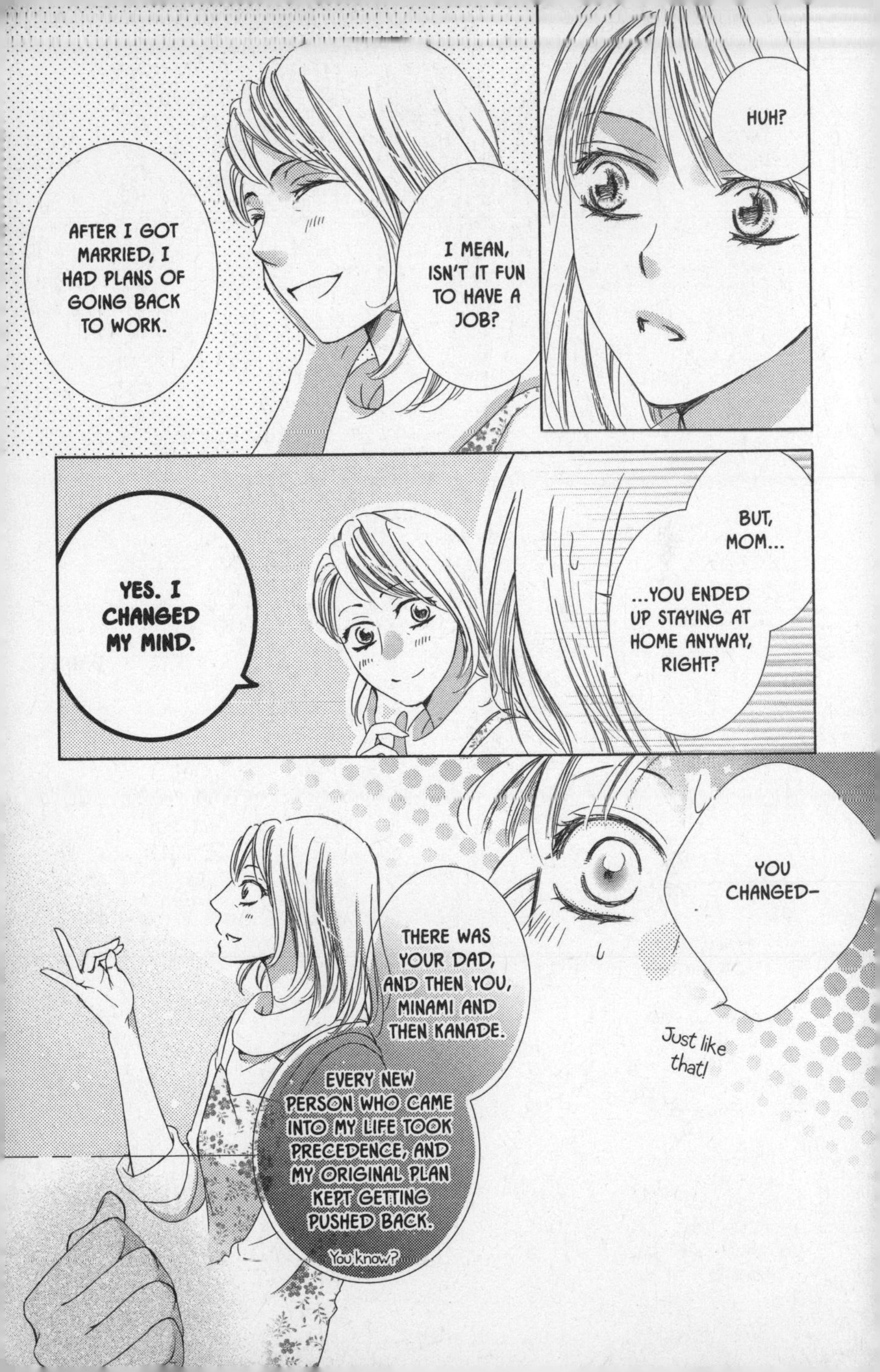
HUH?
I MEAN, ISN'T IT FUN TO HAVE A JOB?
AFTER I GOT MARRIED, I HAD PLANS OF GOING BACK TO WORK.
BUT, MOM...
...YOU ENDED UP STAYING AT HOME ANYWAY, RIGHT?
YES. I CHANGED MY MIND.
YOU CHANGED—
Just like that!
THERE WAS YOUR DAD, AND THEN YOU, MINAMI AND THEN KANADE.
EVERY NEW PERSON WHO CAME INTO MY LIFE TOOK PRECEDENCE, AND MY ORIGINAL PLAN KEPT GETTING PUSHED BACK.
You know?

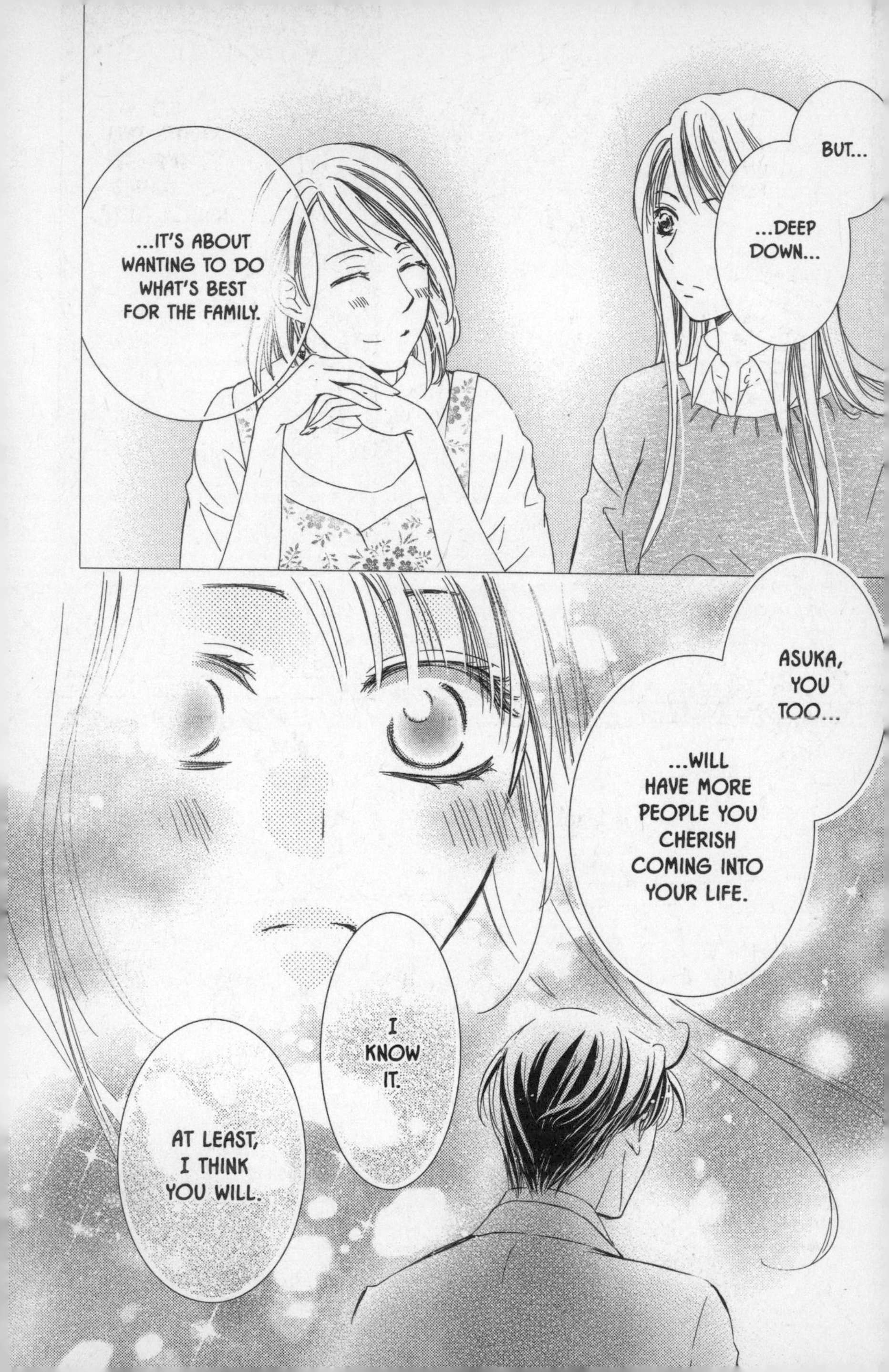
BUT...
...DEEP DOWN...
...IT'S ABOUT WANTING TO DO WHAT'S BEST FOR THE FAMILY.
ASUKA, YOU TOO...
...WILL HAVE MORE PEOPLE YOU CHERISH COMING INTO YOUR LIFE.
I KNOW IT.
AT LEAST, I THINK YOU WILL.

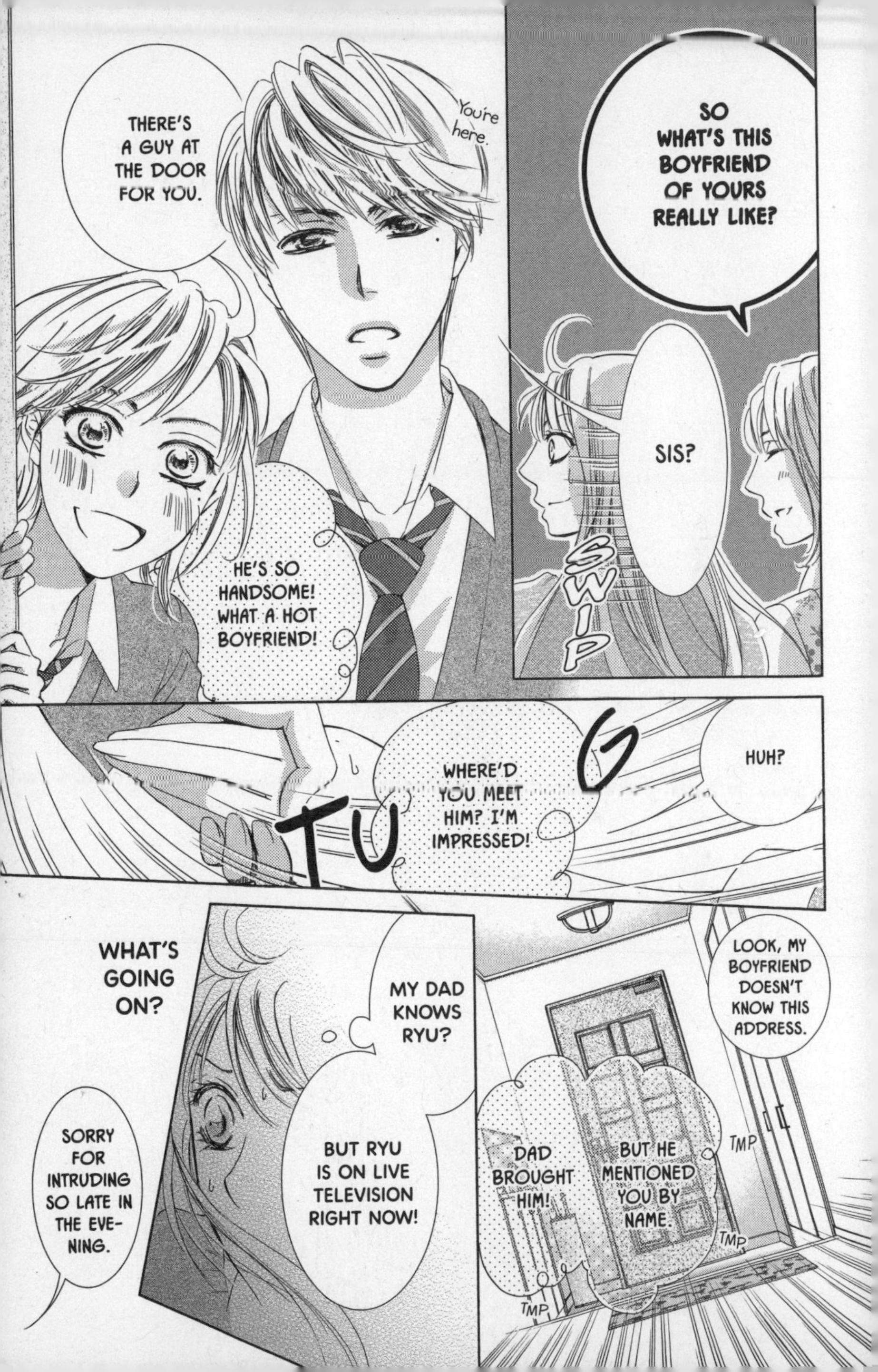
SO WHAT'S THIS BOYFRIEND OF YOURS REALLY LIKE?
SIS?
SWIP
You're here.
THERE'S A GUY AT THE DOOR FOR YOU.
HE'S SO HANDSOME! WHAT A HOT BOYFRIEND!
HUH?
TUG
WHERE'D YOU MEET HIM? I'M IMPRESSED!
LOOK, MY BOYFRIEND DOESN'T KNOW THIS ADDRESS.
TMP
BUT HE MENTIONED YOU BY NAME.
DAD BROUGHT HIM!
TMP
TMP
MY DAD KNOWS RYU?
WHAT'S GOING ON?
BUT RYU IS ON LIVE TELEVISION RIGHT NOW!
SORRY FOR INTRUDING SO LATE IN THE EVE-NING.

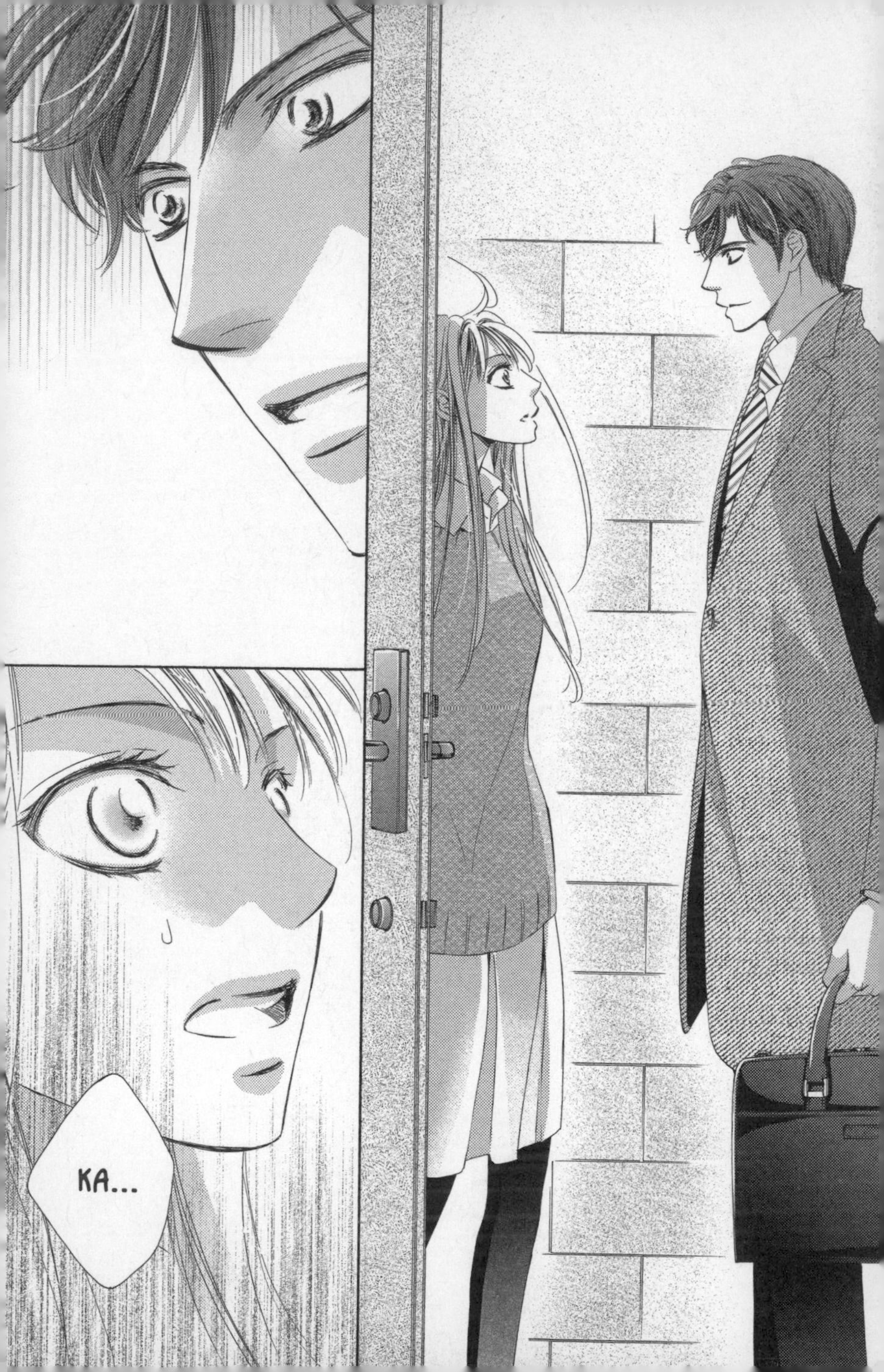
KA...

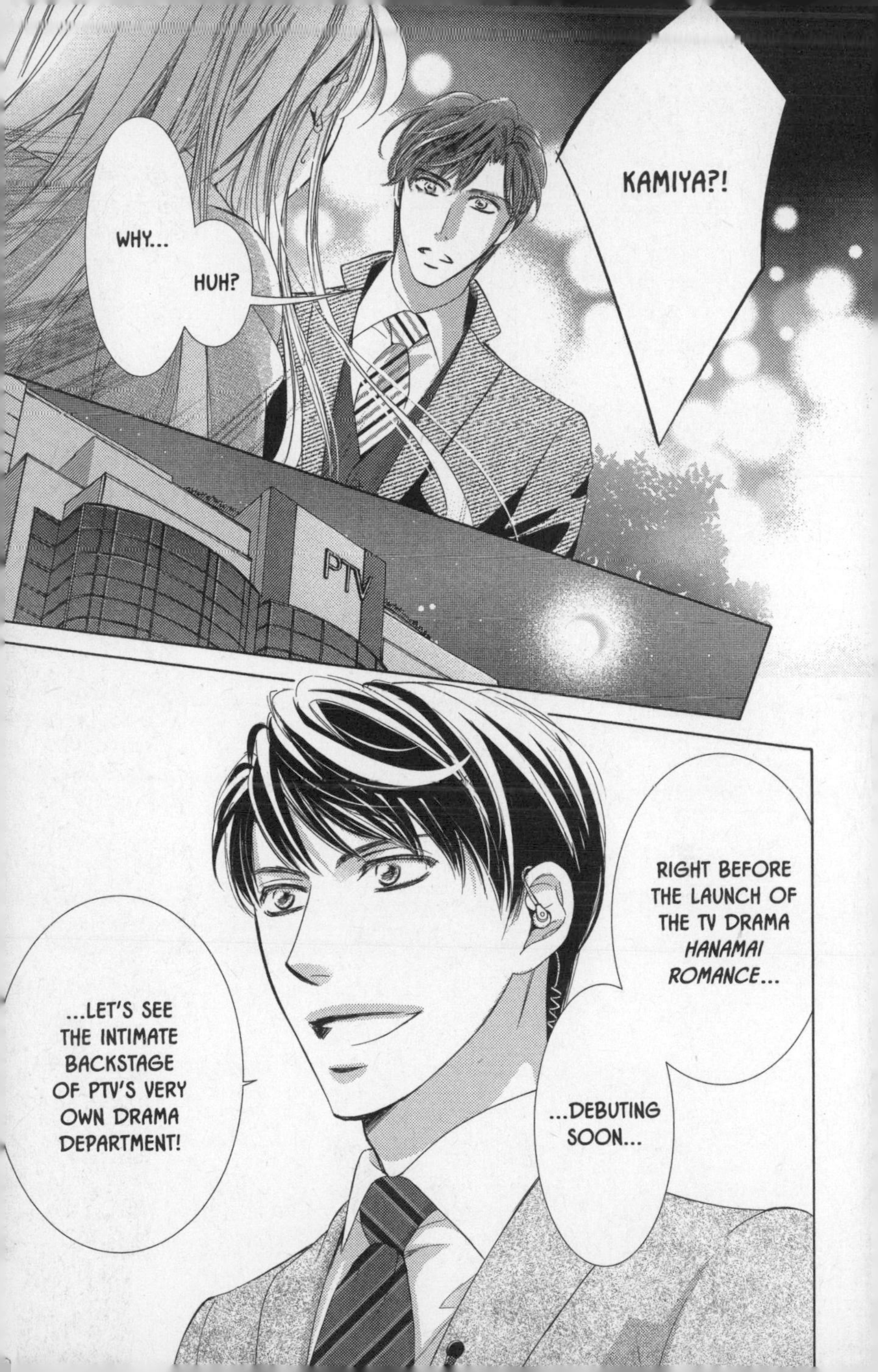
KAMIYA?!
WHY...
HUH?
PTV
RIGHT BEFORE THE LAUNCH OF THE TV DRAMA *HANAMAI ROMANCE*...
...DEBUTING SOON...
...LET'S SEE THE INTIMATE BACKSTAGE OF PTV'S VERY OWN DRAMA DEPARTMENT!

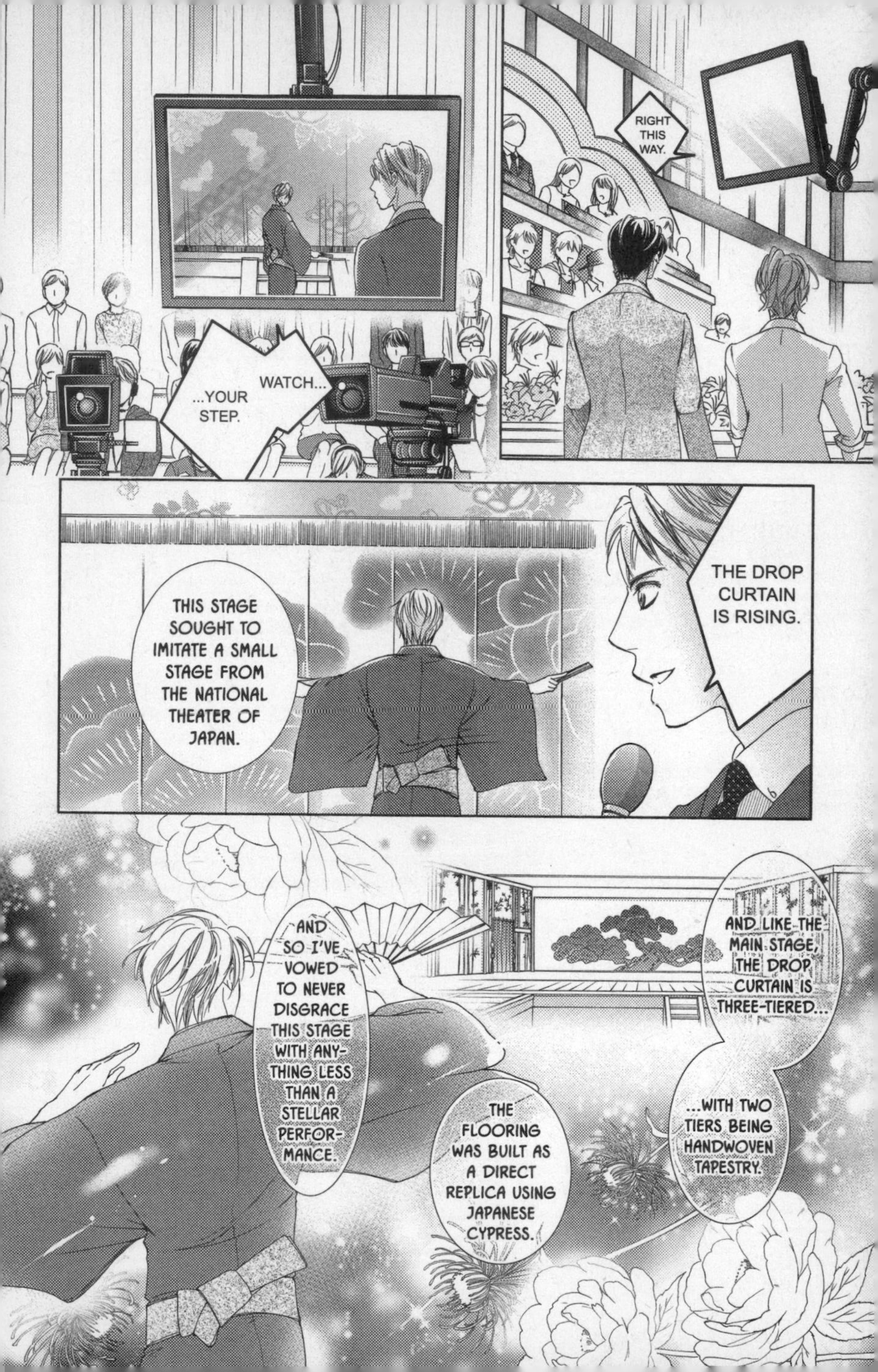
RIGHT THIS WAY.
WATCH...
...YOUR STEP.
THE DROP CURTAIN IS RISING.
THIS STAGE SOUGHT TO IMITATE A SMALL STAGE FROM THE NATIONAL THEATER OF JAPAN.
AND LIKE THE MAIN STAGE, THE DROP CURTAIN IS THREE-TIERED...
...WITH TWO TIERS BEING HANDWOVEN TAPESTRY.
THE FLOORING WAS BUILT AS A DIRECT REPLICA USING JAPANESE CYPRESS.
AND SO I'VE VOWED TO NEVER DISGRACE THIS STAGE WITH ANYTHING LESS THAN A STELLAR PERFORMANCE.

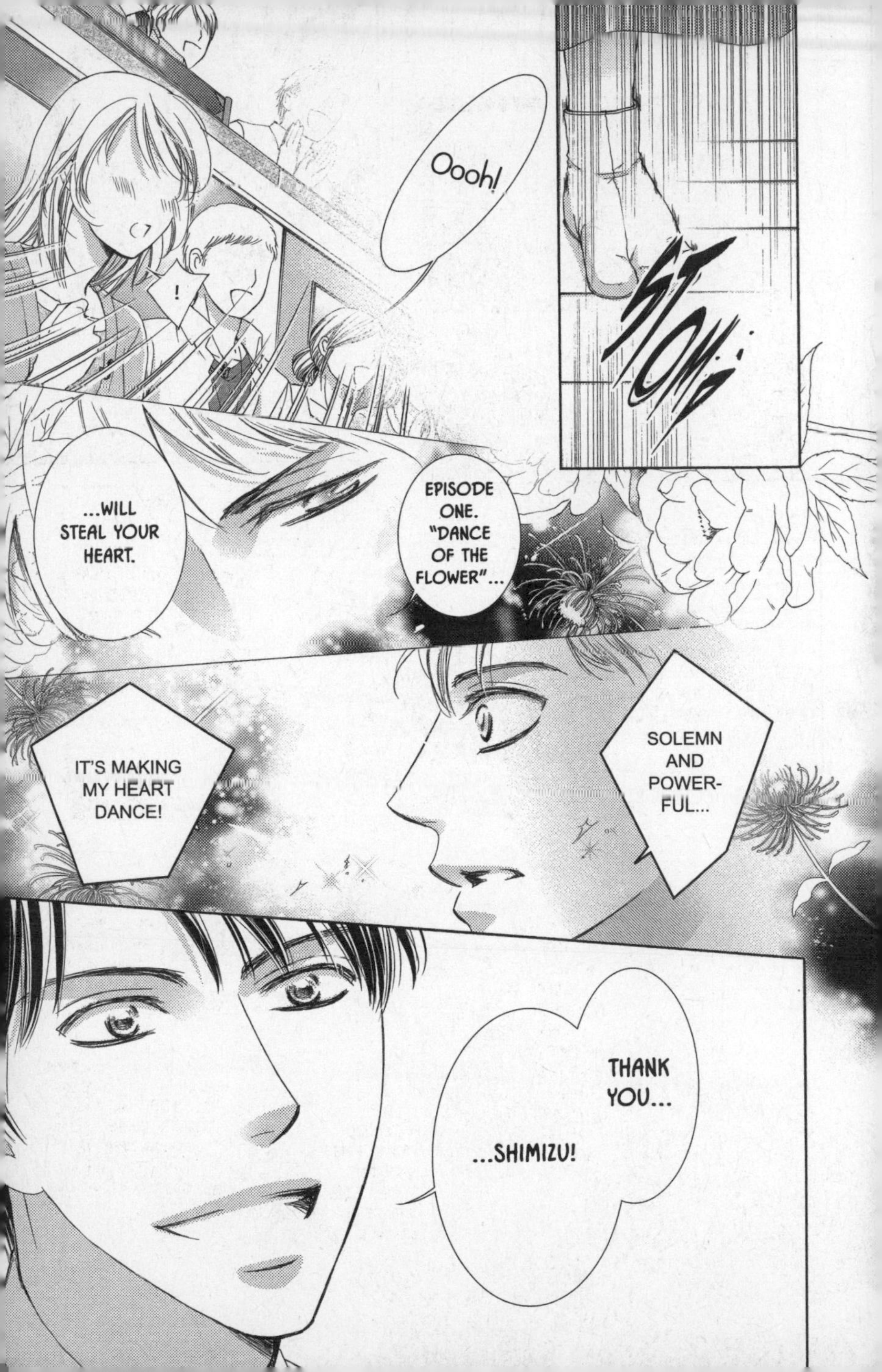
STOMP
Oooh!
!
EPISODE ONE. "DANCE OF THE FLOWER"...
...WILL STEAL YOUR HEART.
SOLEMN AND POWER-FUL...
IT'S MAKING MY HEART DANCE!
THANK YOU...
...SHIMIZU!

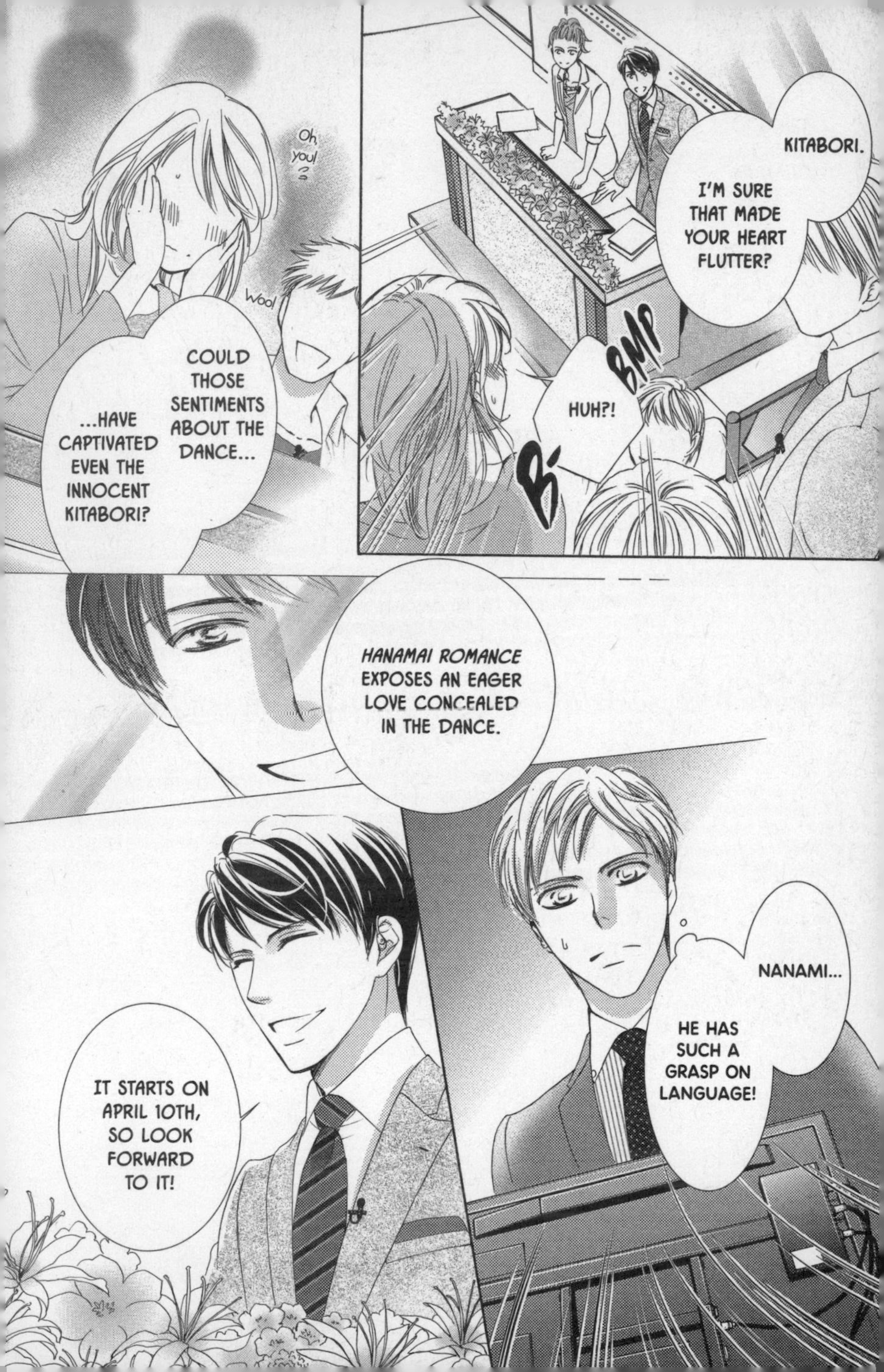
KITABORI.
I'M SURE THAT MADE YOUR HEART FLUTTER?
BMP
HUH?!
B'
Oh, you!
Woo!
COULD THOSE SENTIMENTS ABOUT THE DANCE...
...HAVE CAPTIVATED EVEN THE INNOCENT KITABORI?
HANAMAI ROMANCE EXPOSES AN EAGER LOVE CONCEALED IN THE DANCE.
NANAMI...
HE HAS SUCH A GRASP ON LANGUAGE!
IT STARTS ON APRIL 10TH, SO LOOK FORWARD TO IT!

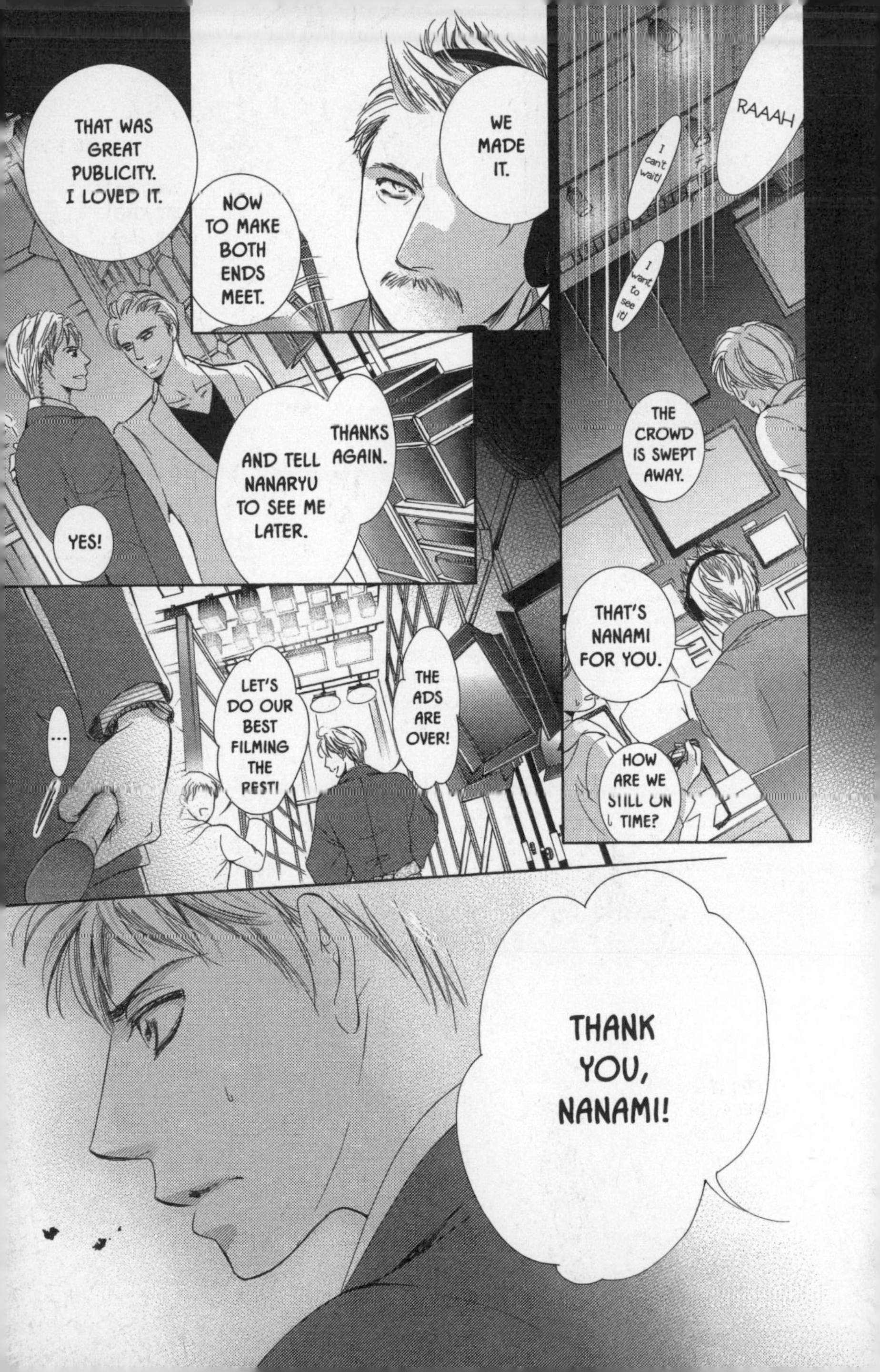
RAAAH
I can't wait!
I want to see it!
THE CROWD IS SWEPT AWAY.
THAT'S NANAMI FOR YOU.
HOW ARE WE STILL ON TIME?
WE MADE IT.
NOW TO MAKE BOTH ENDS MEET.
THAT WAS GREAT PUBLICITY. I LOVED IT.
THANKS AGAIN.
AND TELL NANARYU TO SEE ME LATER.
YES!
THE ADS ARE OVER!
LET'S DO OUR BEST FILMING THE REST!
...
THANK YOU, NANAMI!

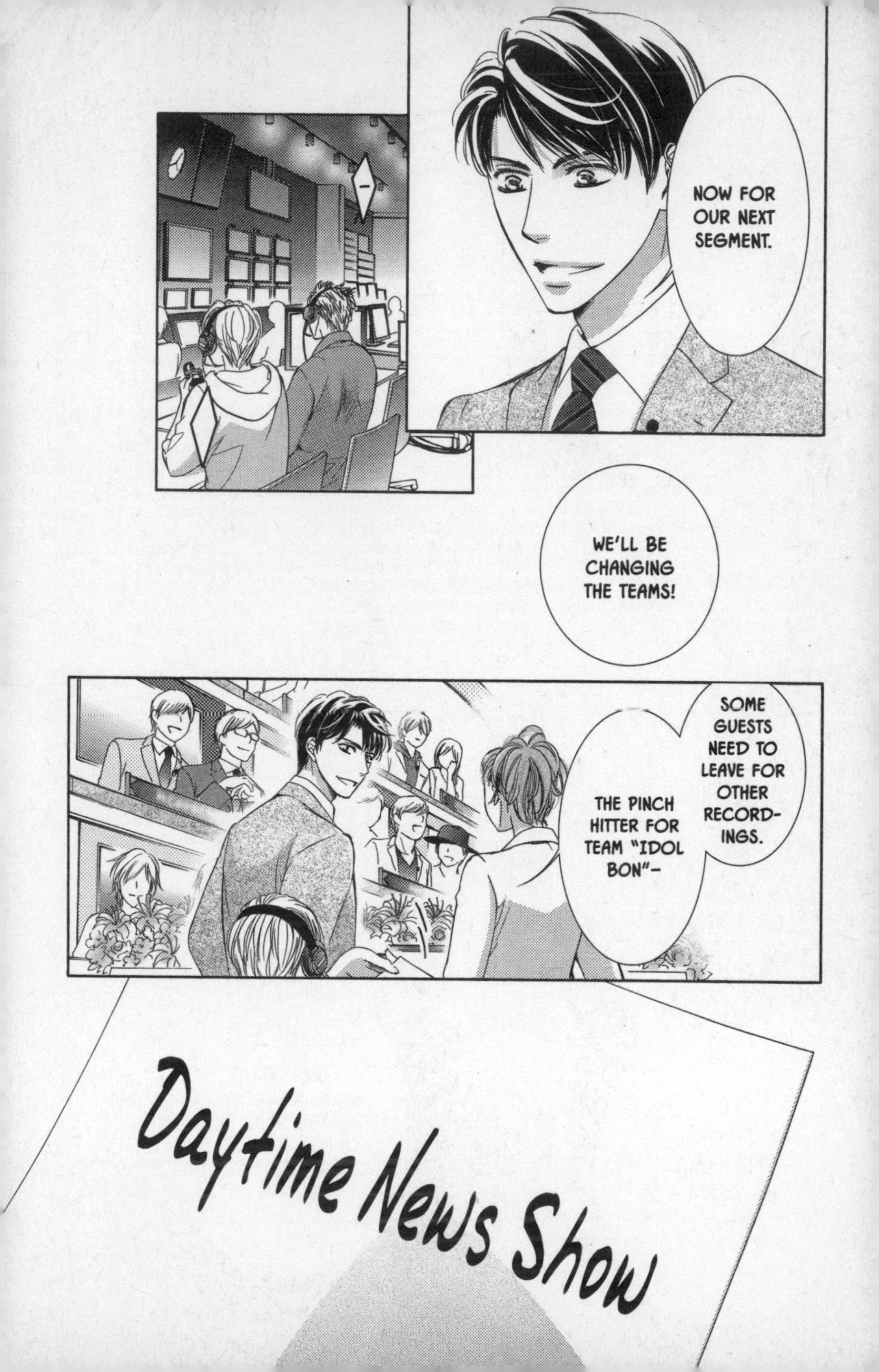
NOW FOR OUR NEXT SEGMENT.
WE'LL BE CHANGING THE TEAMS!
SOME GUESTS NEED TO LEAVE FOR OTHER RECORDINGS.
THE PINCH HITTER FOR TEAM "IDOL BON"–
Daytime News Show

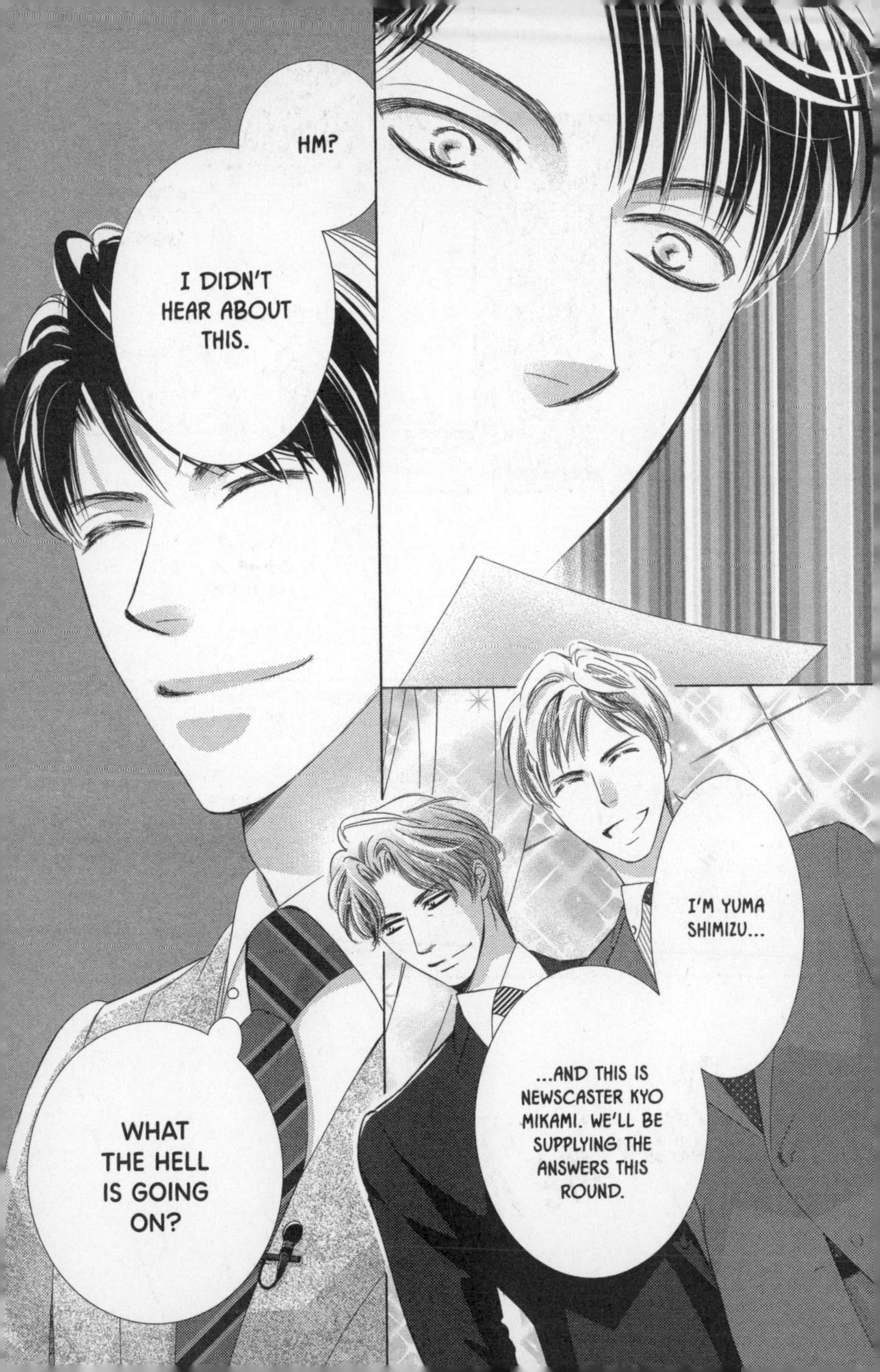
I'M YUMA SHIMIZU...
...AND THIS IS NEWSCASTER KYO MIKAMI. WE'LL BE SUPPLYING THE ANSWERS THIS ROUND.
HM?
I DIDN'T HEAR ABOUT THIS.
WHAT THE HELL IS GOING ON?

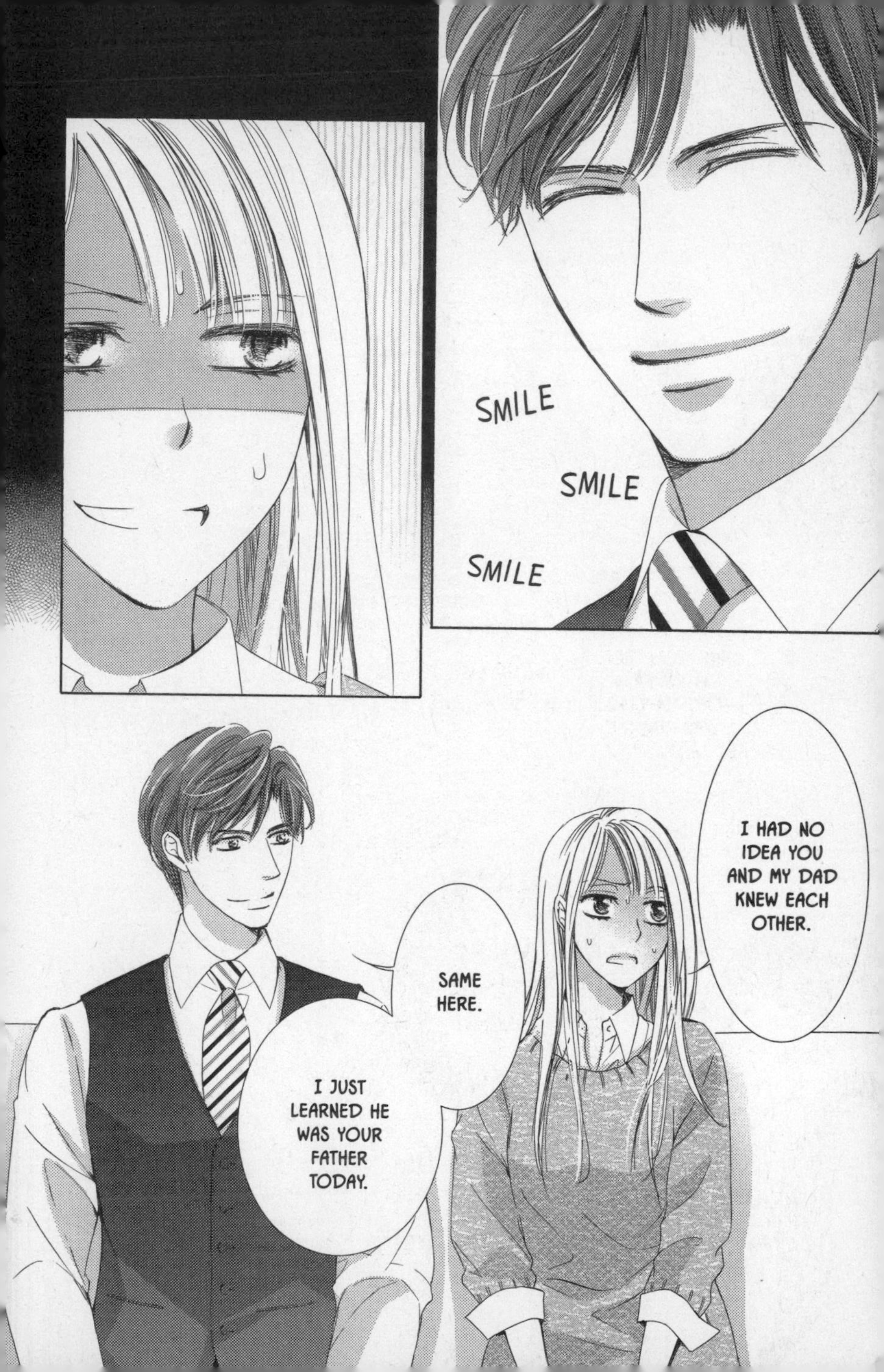
SMILE
SMILE
SMILE
I HAD NO IDEA YOU AND MY DAD KNEW EACH OTHER.
SAME HERE.
I JUST LEARNED HE WAS YOUR FATHER TODAY.

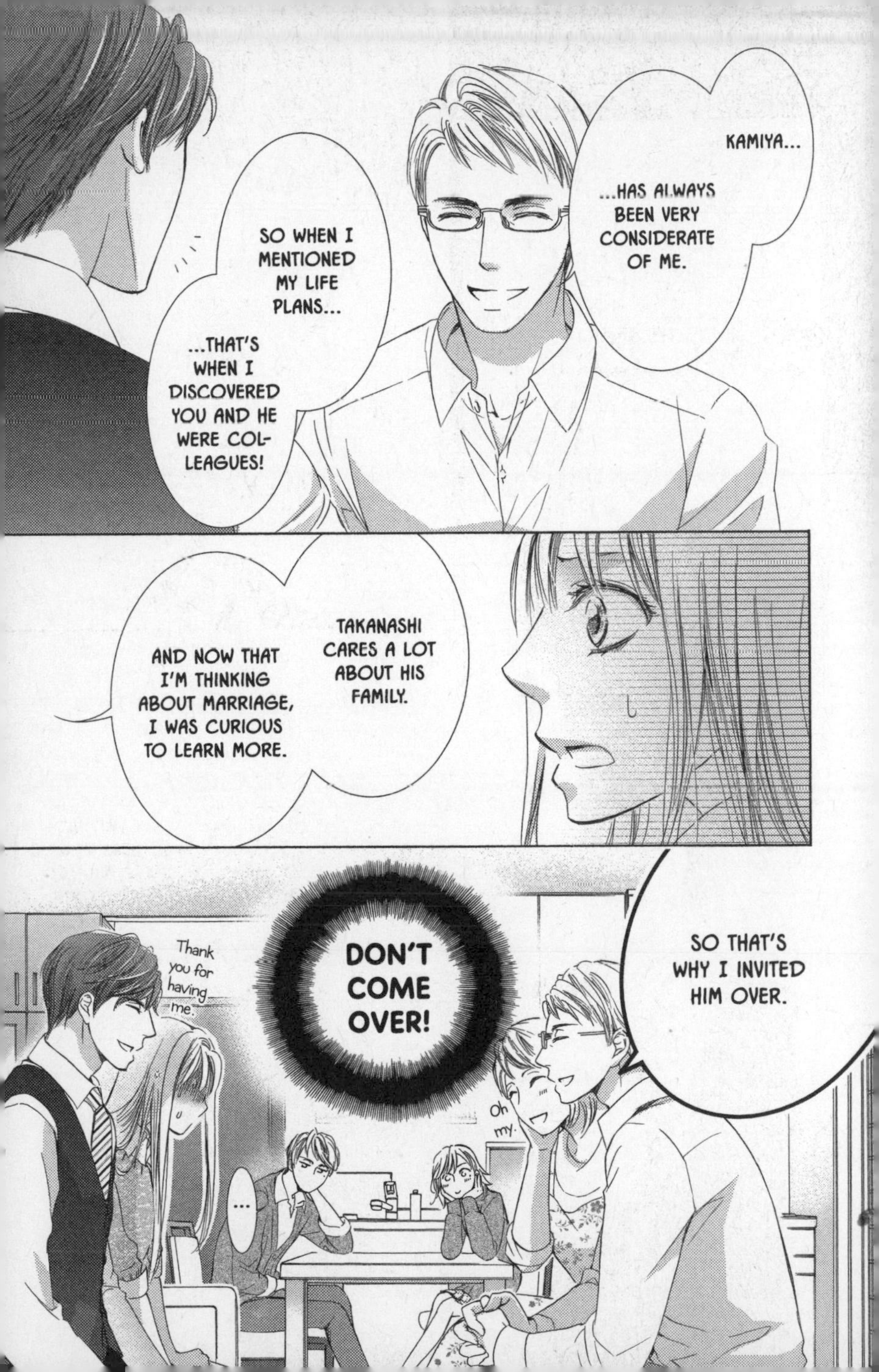
KAMIYA...
...HAS ALWAYS BEEN VERY CONSIDERATE OF ME.
SO WHEN I MENTIONED MY LIFE PLANS...
...THAT'S WHEN I DISCOVERED YOU AND HE WERE COL-LEAGUES!
TAKANASHI CARES A LOT ABOUT HIS FAMILY.
AND NOW THAT I'M THINKING ABOUT MARRIAGE, I WAS CURIOUS TO LEARN MORE.
SO THAT'S WHY I INVITED HIM OVER.
Oh my.
DON'T COME OVER!
Thank you for having me.
...

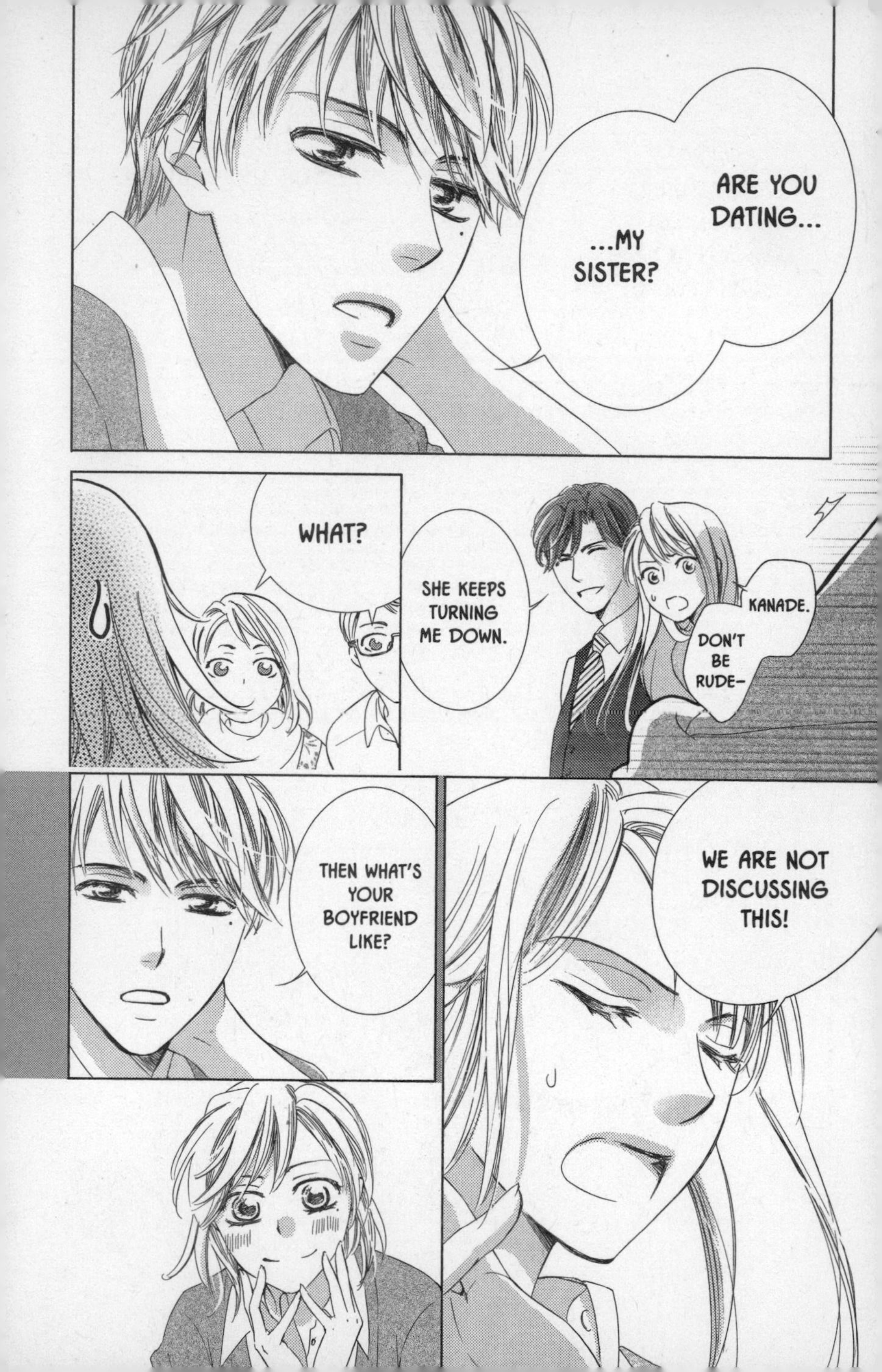
ARE YOU DATING...
...MY SISTER?
KANADE.
DON'T BE RUDE–
SHE KEEPS TURNING ME DOWN.
WHAT?
WE ARE NOT DISCUSSING THIS!
THEN WHAT'S YOUR BOYFRIEND LIKE?

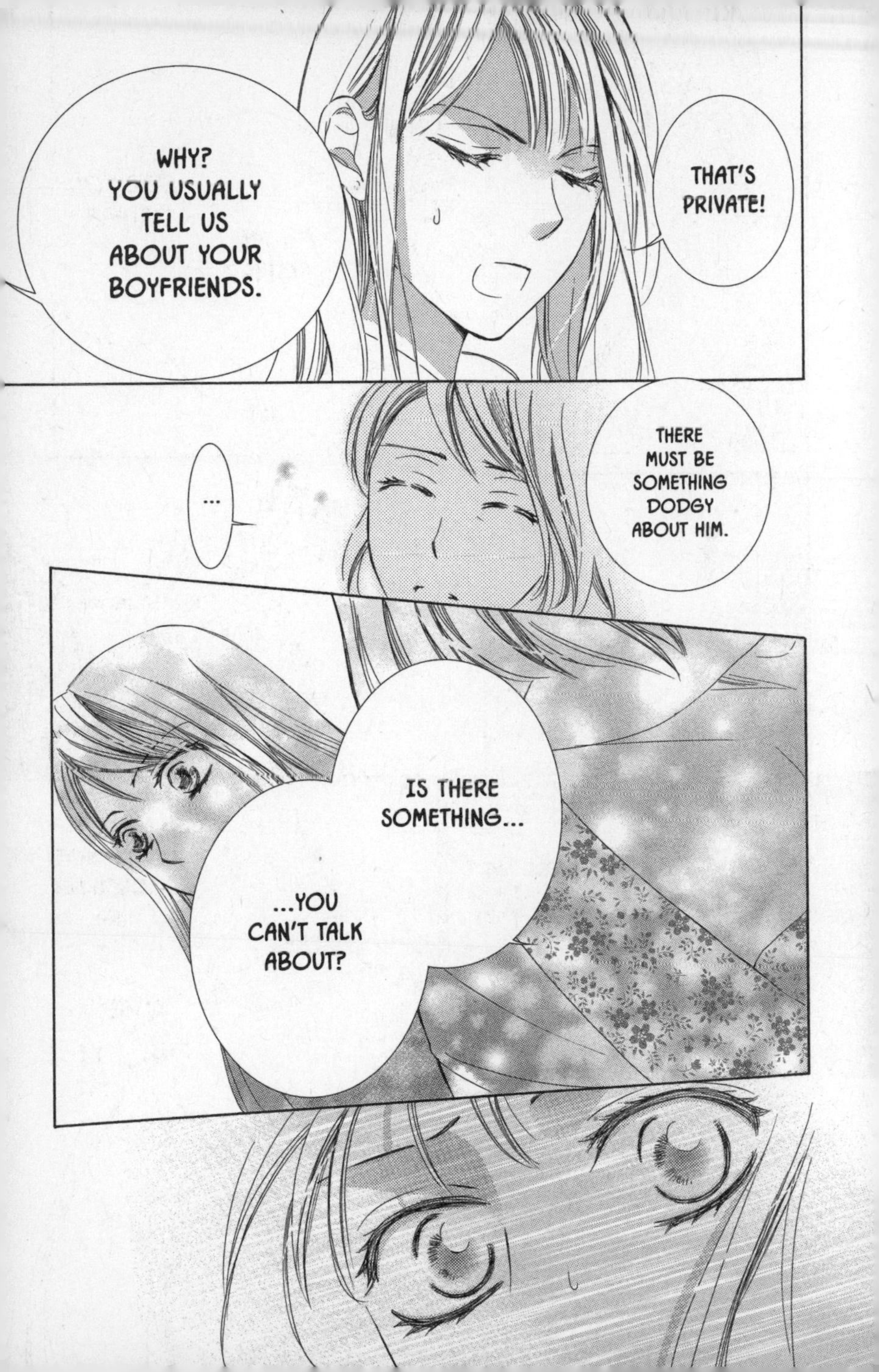
THAT'S PRIVATE!
WHY? YOU USUALLY TELL US ABOUT YOUR BOYFRIENDS.
THERE MUST BE SOMETHING DODGY ABOUT HIM.
...
IS THERE SOMETHING...
...YOU CAN'T TALK ABOUT?

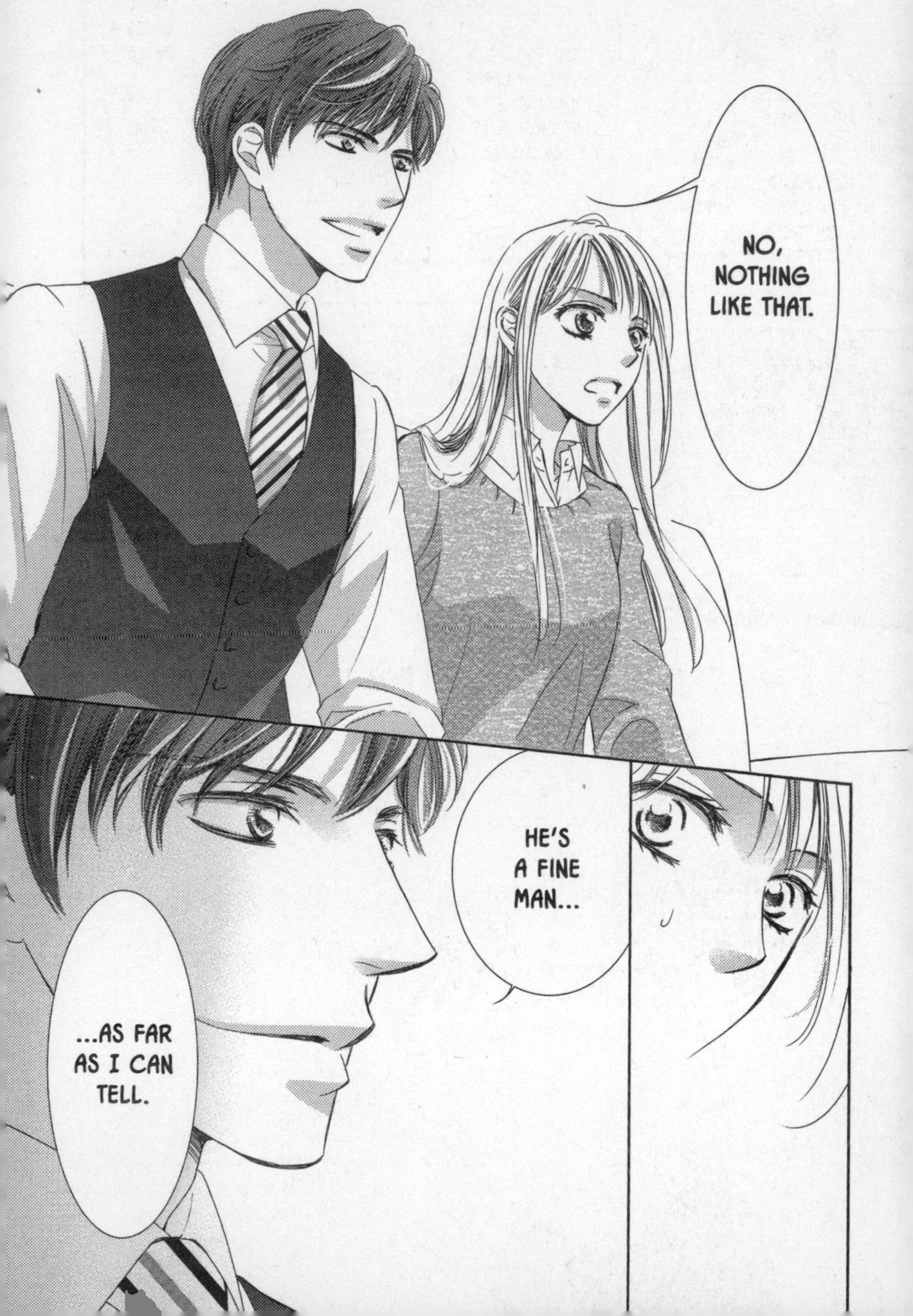
NO, NOTHING LIKE THAT.
HE'S A FINE MAN...
...AS FAR AS I CAN TELL.

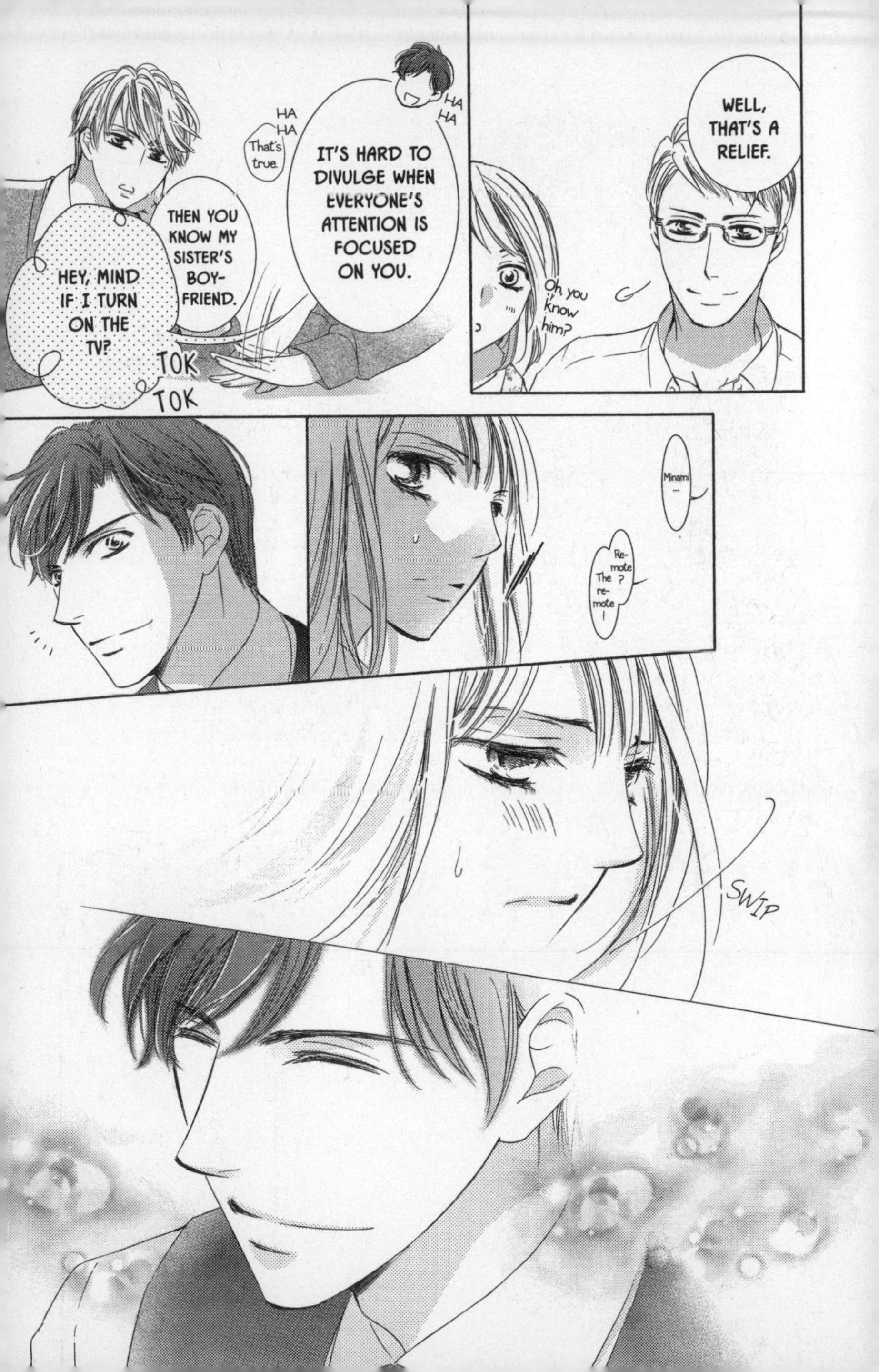
WELL, THAT'S A RELIEF.
Oh, you know him?
HA HA
IT'S HARD TO DIVULGE WHEN EVERYONE'S ATTENTION IS FOCUSED ON YOU.
HA HA
That's true.
THEN YOU KNOW MY SISTER'S BOY-FRIEND.
HEY, MIND IF I TURN ON THE TV?
TOK TOK
Minami...
Remote? The remote!
SWIP

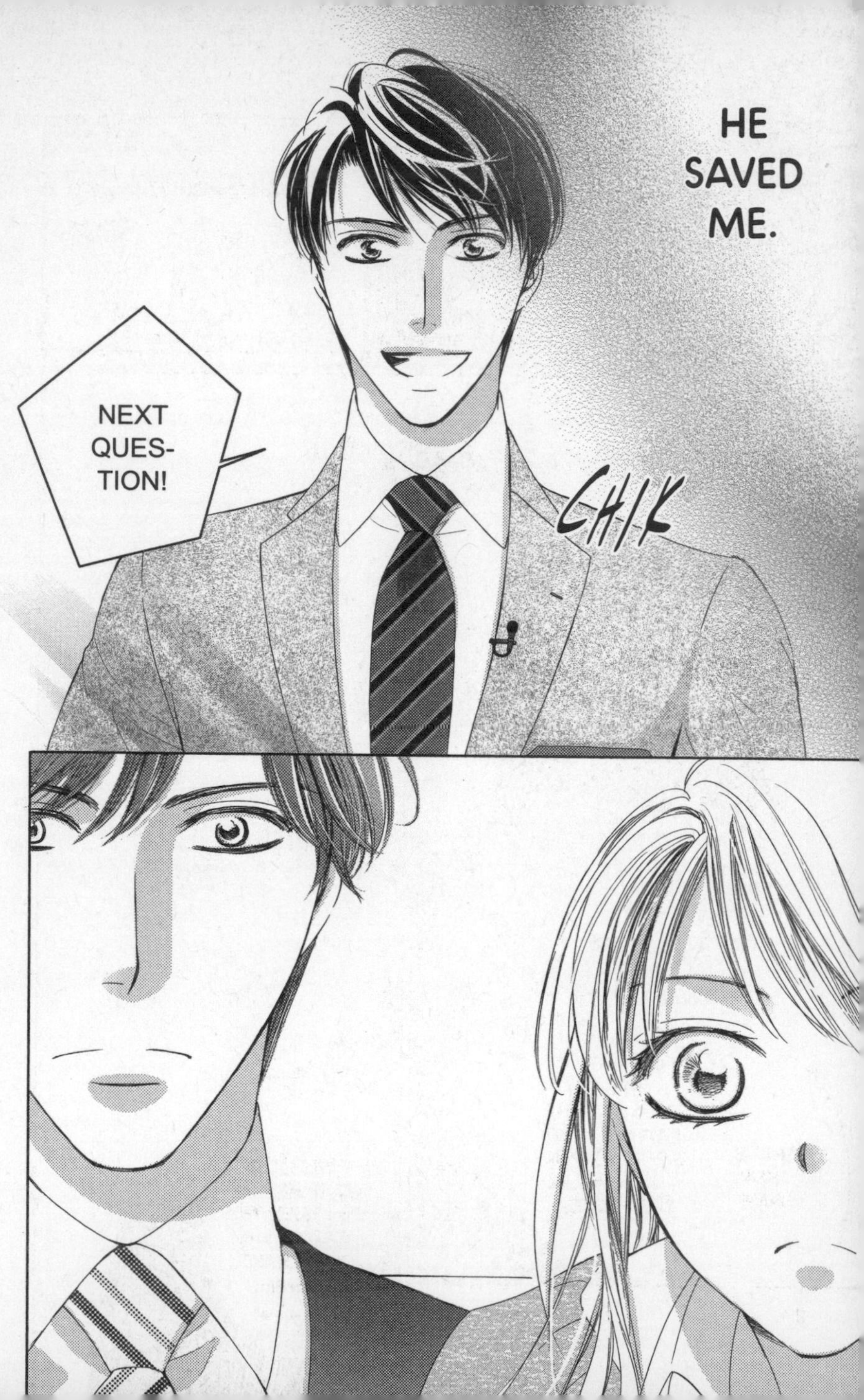
HE SAVED ME.
NEXT QUES-TION!
CHIK

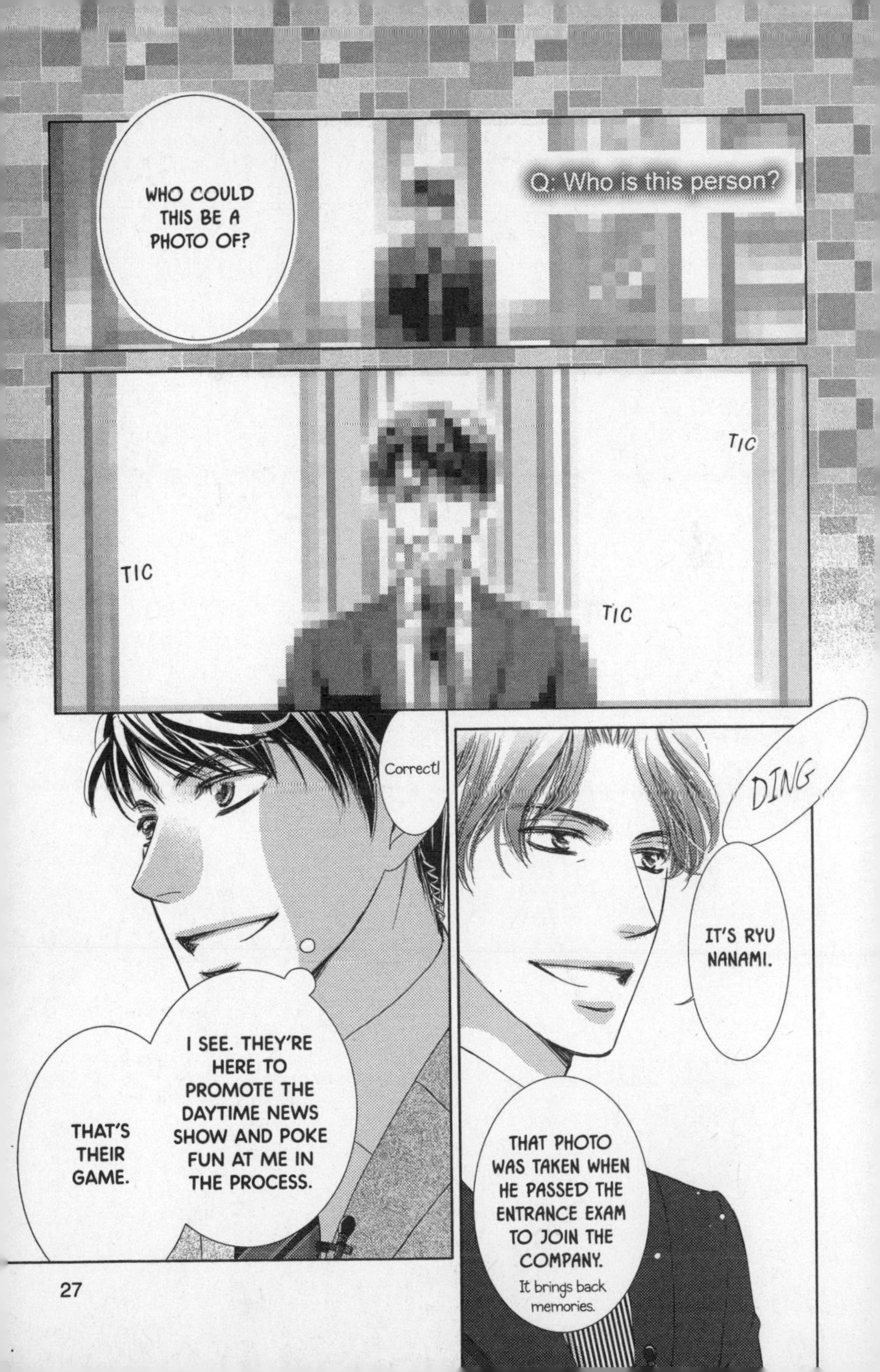
Q: Who is this person?
WHO COULD THIS BE A PHOTO OF?
TIC
TIC
TIC
DING
IT'S RYU NANAMI.
THAT PHOTO WAS TAKEN WHEN HE PASSED THE ENTRANCE EXAM TO JOIN THE COMPANY.
It brings back memories.
Correct!
I SEE. THEY'RE HERE TO PROMOTE THE DAYTIME NEWS SHOW AND POKE FUN AT ME IN THE PROCESS.
THAT'S THEIR GAME.

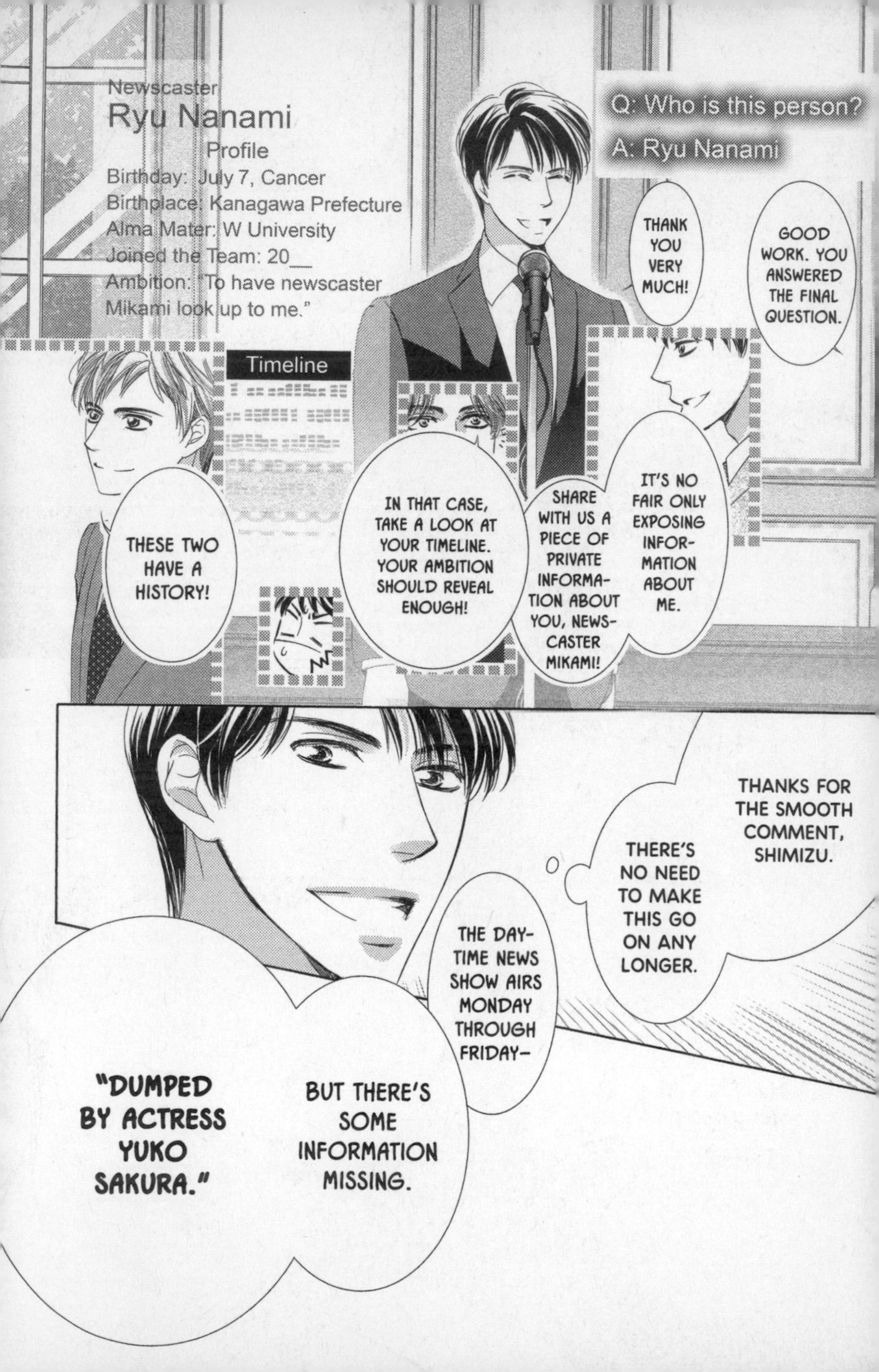
Q: Who is this person?
A: Ryu Nanami
GOOD WORK. YOU ANSWERED THE FINAL QUESTION.
THANK YOU VERY MUCH!
Newscaster
Ryu Nanami
Profile
Birthday: July 7, Cancer
Birthplace: Kanagawa Prefecture
Alma Mater: W University
Joined the Team: 20__
Ambition: "To have newscaster Mikami look up to me."
IT'S NO FAIR ONLY EXPOSING INFORMATION ABOUT ME.
SHARE WITH US A PIECE OF PRIVATE INFORMATION ABOUT YOU, NEWSCASTER MIKAMI!
IN THAT CASE, TAKE A LOOK AT YOUR TIMELINE. YOUR AMBITION SHOULD REVEAL ENOUGH!
Timeline
THESE TWO HAVE A HISTORY!
THANKS FOR THE SMOOTH COMMENT, SHIMIZU.
THERE'S NO NEED TO MAKE THIS GO ON ANY LONGER.
THE DAYTIME NEWS SHOW AIRS MONDAY THROUGH FRIDAY–
BUT THERE'S SOME INFORMATION MISSING.
"DUMPED BY ACTRESS YUKO SAKURA."

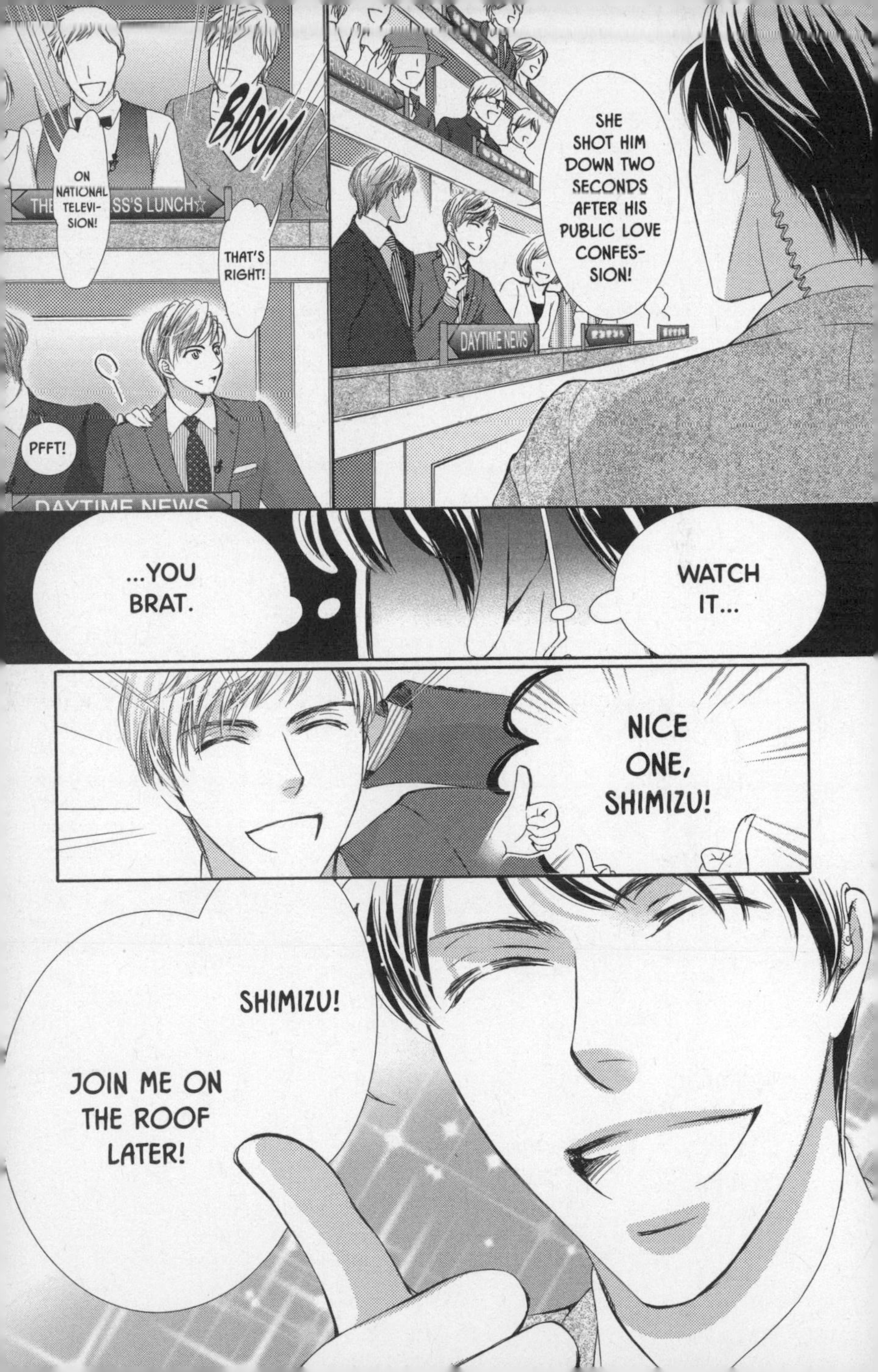
SHE SHOT HIM DOWN TWO SECONDS AFTER HIS PUBLIC LOVE CONFES-SION!
DAYTIME NEWS
BADUM
ON NATIONAL TELEVI-SION!
THAT'S RIGHT!
PFFT!
WATCH IT...
...YOU BRAT.
NICE ONE, SHIMIZU!
SHIMIZU!
JOIN ME ON THE ROOF LATER!

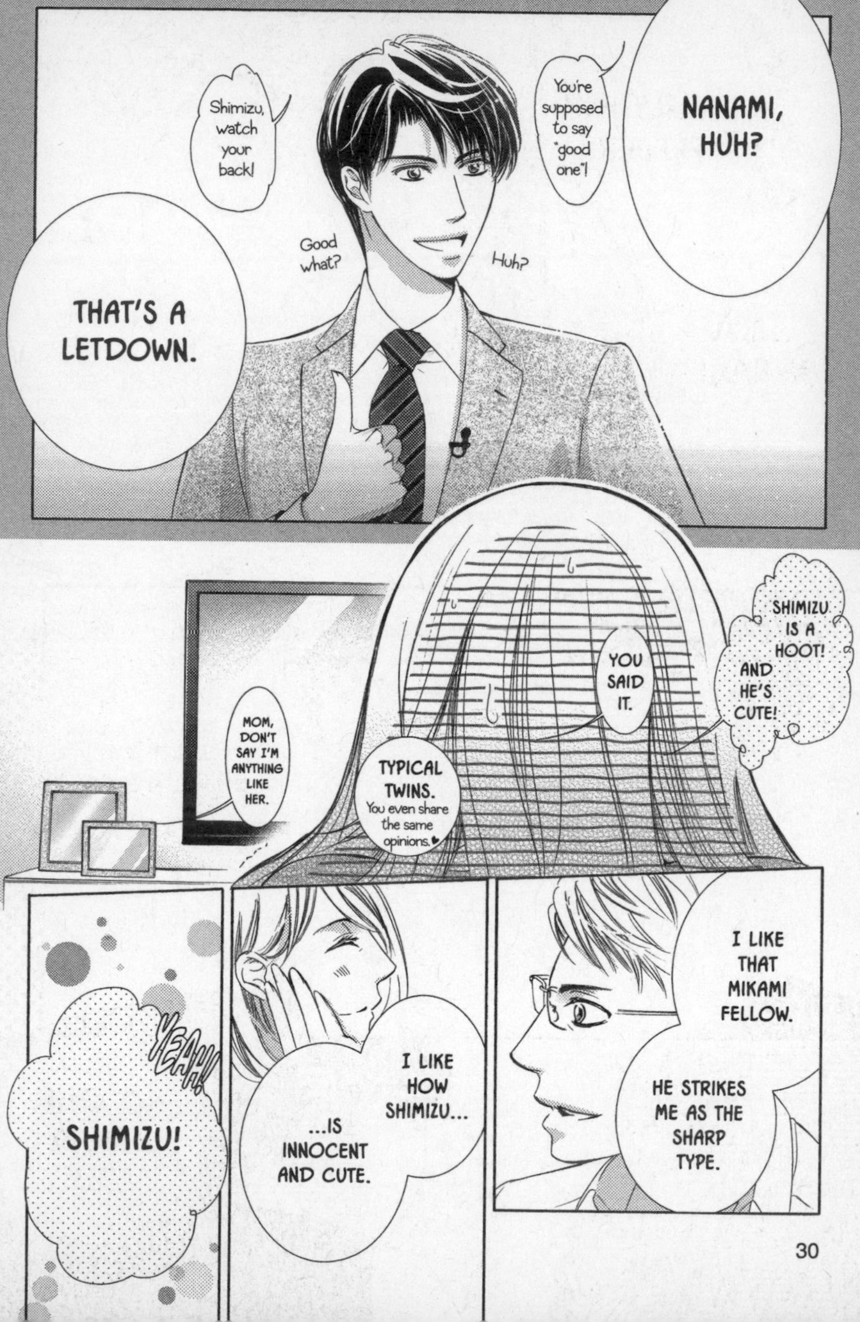
NANAMI, HUH?
You're supposed to say "good one"!
Huh?
Shimizu, watch your back!
Good what?
THAT'S A LETDOWN.
SHIMIZU IS A HOOT! AND HE'S CUTE!
YOU SAID IT.
TYPICAL TWINS. You even share the same opinions.
MOM, DON'T SAY I'M ANYTHING LIKE HER.
I LIKE THAT MIKAMI FELLOW.
HE STRIKES ME AS THE SHARP TYPE.
I LIKE HOW SHIMIZU...
...IS INNOCENT AND CUTE.
YEAH!
SHIMIZU!

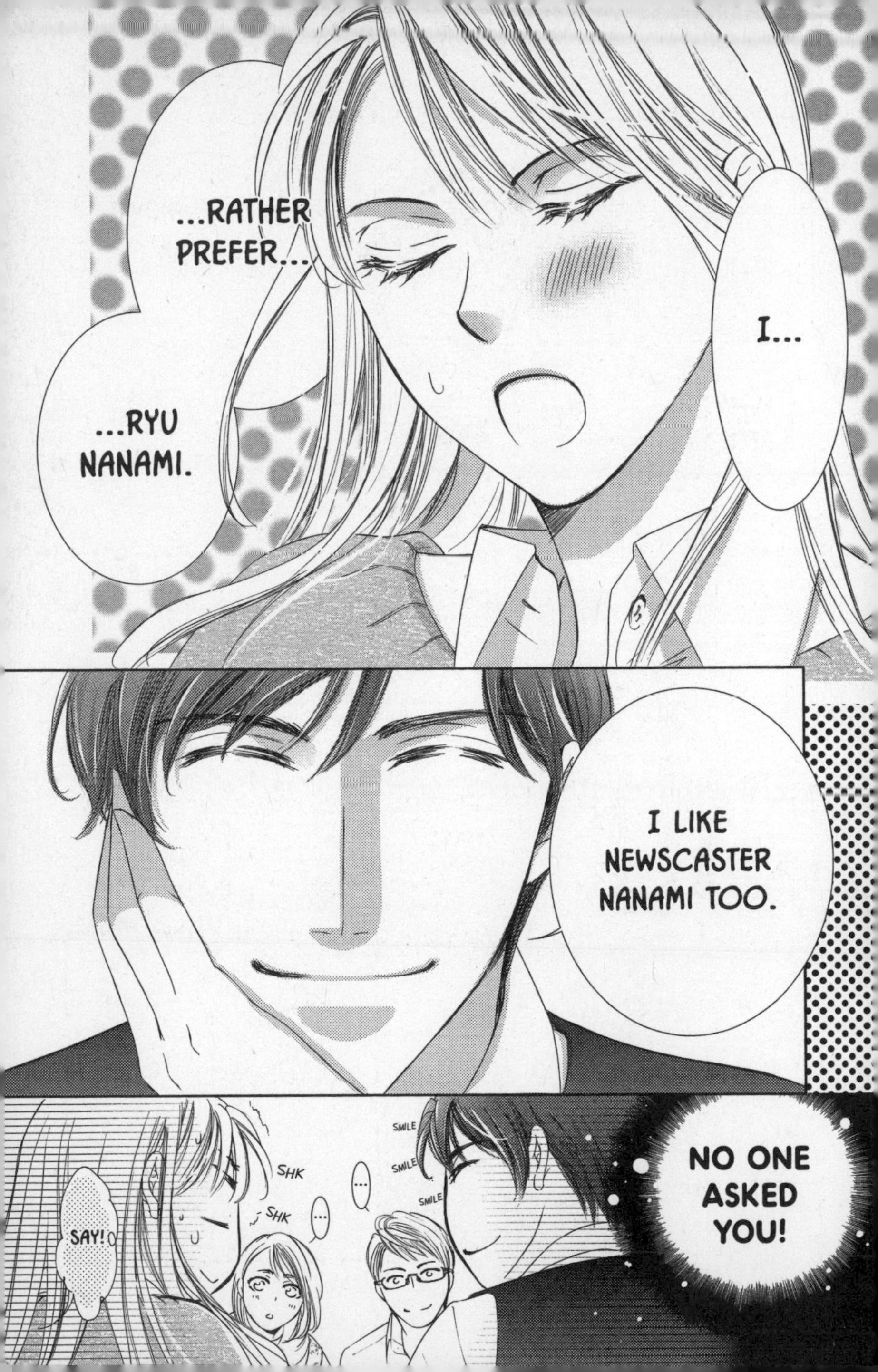
I...
...RATHER PREFER...
...RYU NANAMI.
I LIKE NEWSCASTER NANAMI TOO.
NO ONE ASKED YOU!
SMILE
SMILE
SMILE
...
...
SHK
SHK
SAY!

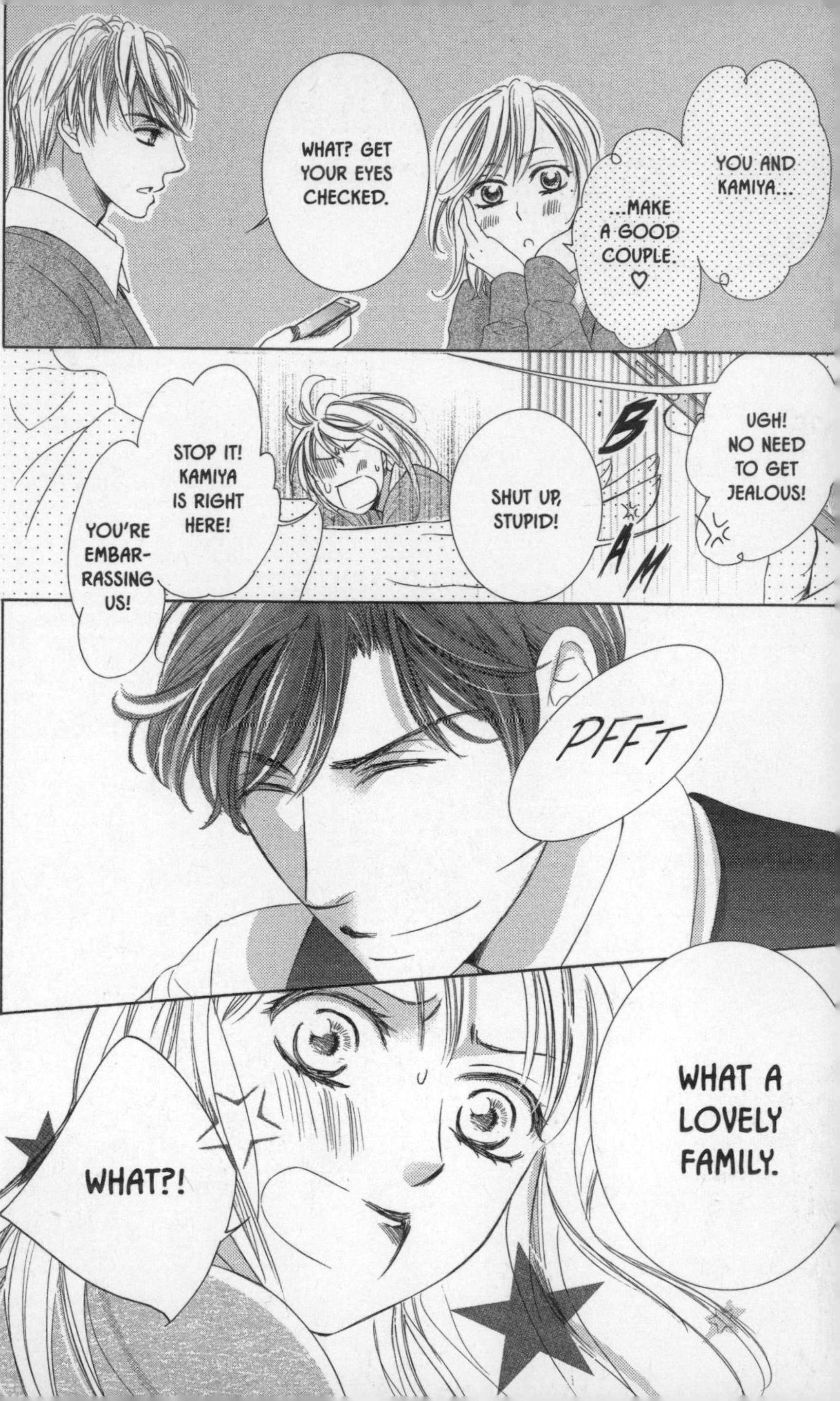
YOU AND KAMIYA...
...MAKE A GOOD COUPLE. ♡
WHAT? GET YOUR EYES CHECKED.
UGH! NO NEED TO GET JEALOUS!
BAM
SHUT UP, STUPID!
STOP IT! KAMIYA IS RIGHT HERE!
YOU'RE EMBAR-RASSING US!
PFFT
WHAT A LOVELY FAMILY.
WHAT?!

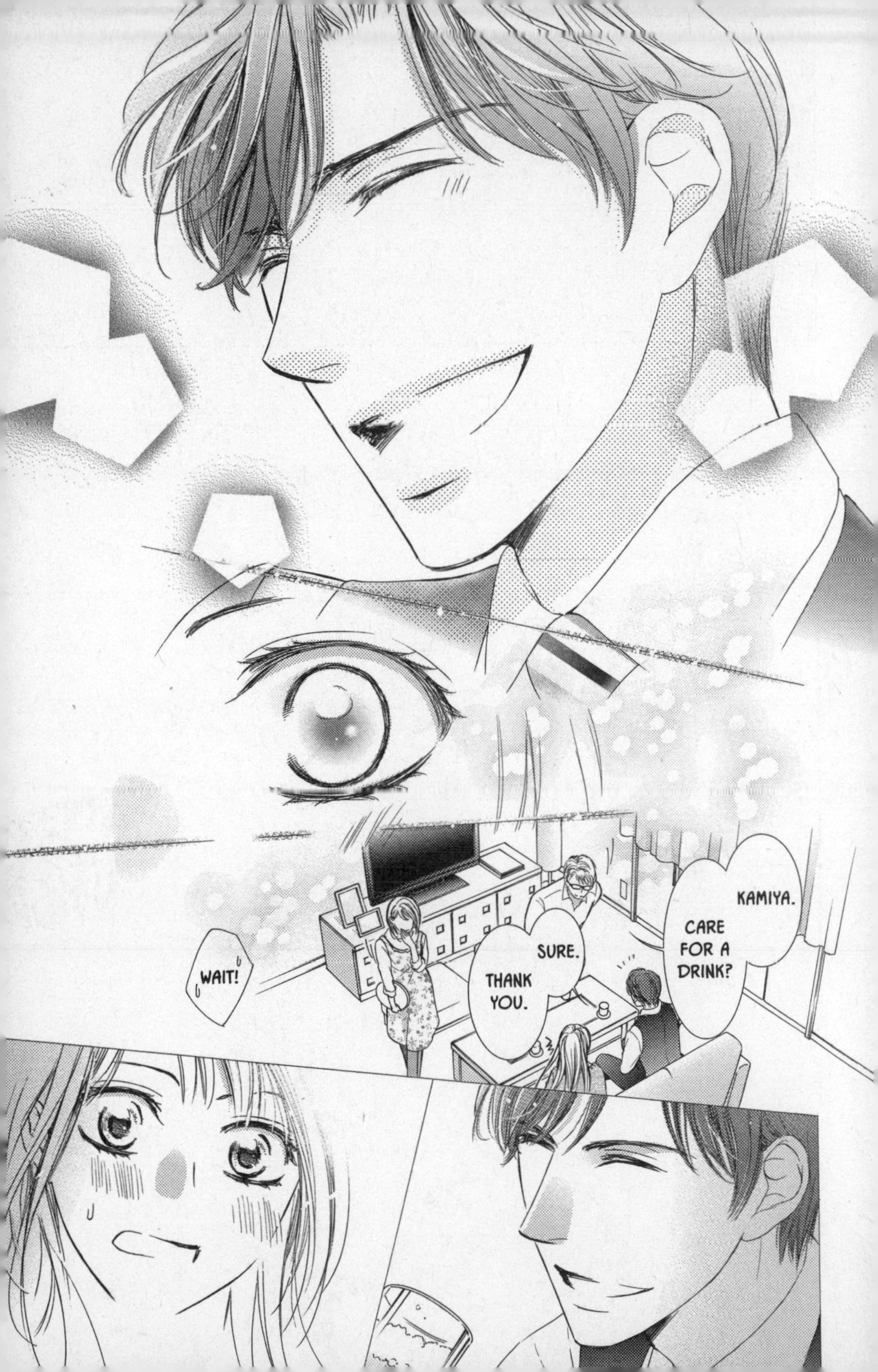
KAMIYA. CARE FOR A DRINK?
SURE. THANK YOU.
WAIT!

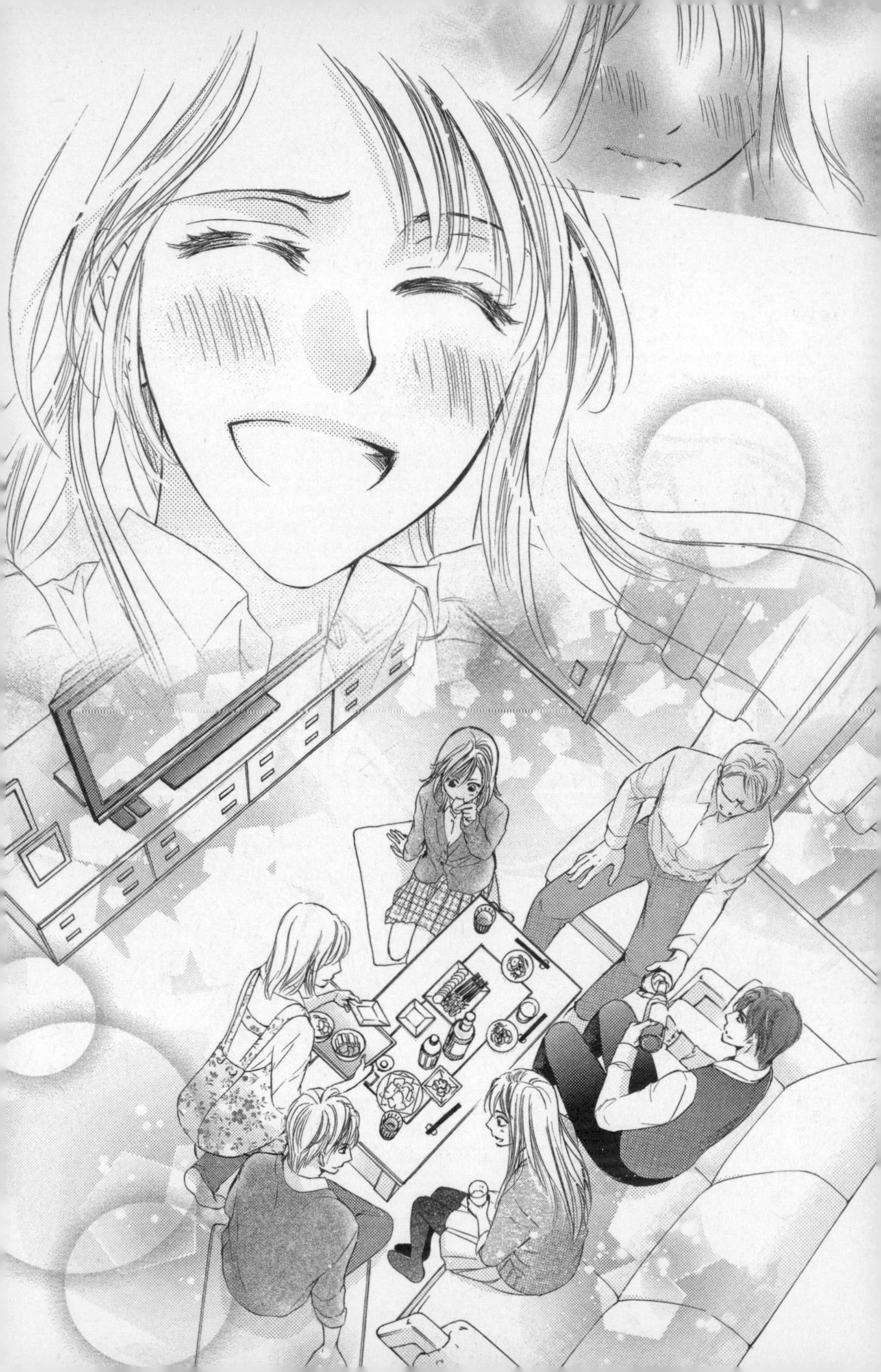

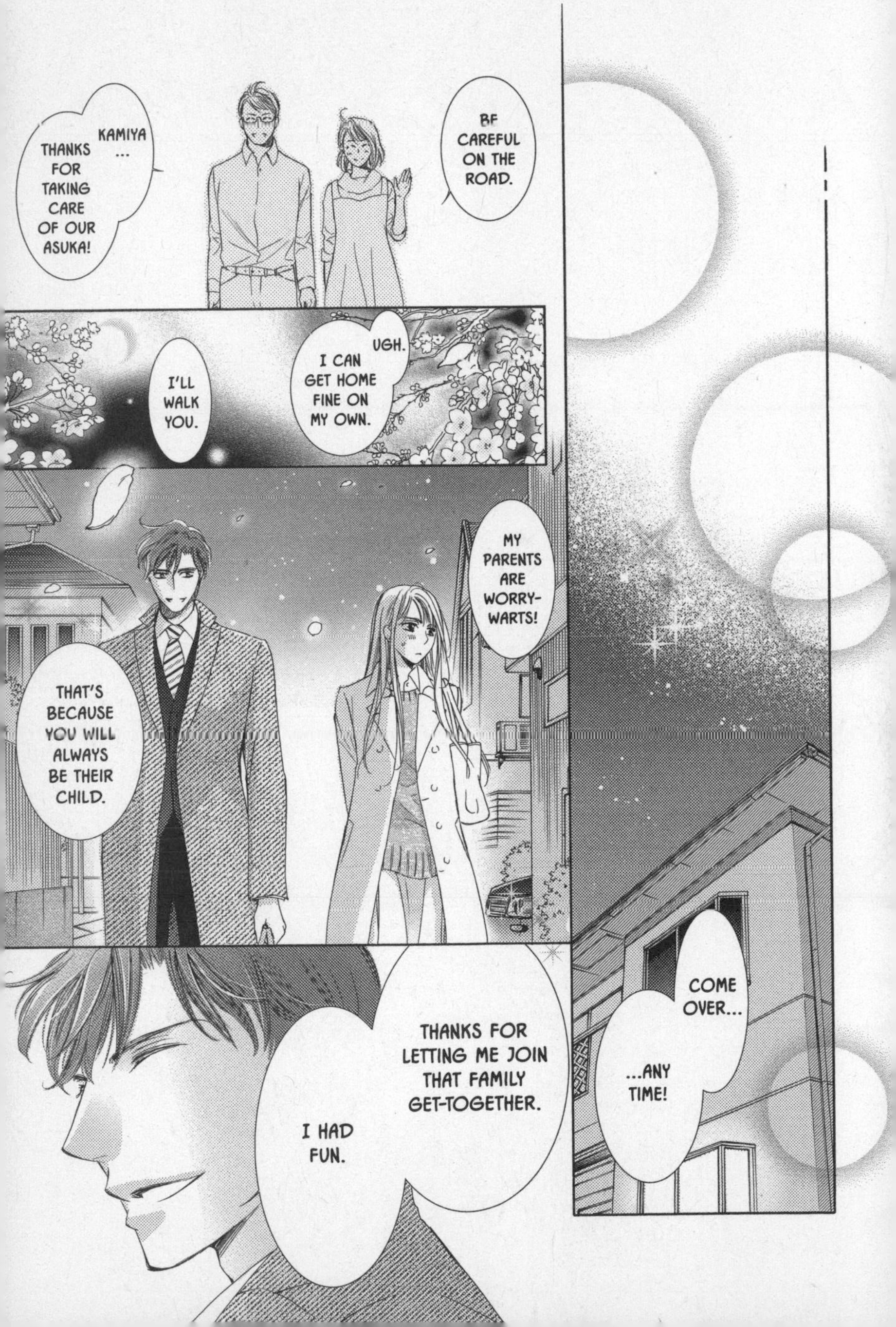
COME OVER...
...ANY TIME!
BE CAREFUL ON THE ROAD.
KAMIYA...
THANKS FOR TAKING CARE OF OUR ASUKA!
UGH.
I CAN GET HOME FINE ON MY OWN.
I'LL WALK YOU.
MY PARENTS ARE WORRY-WARTS!
THAT'S BECAUSE YOU WILL ALWAYS BE THEIR CHILD.
THANKS FOR LETTING ME JOIN THAT FAMILY GET-TOGETHER.
I HAD FUN.

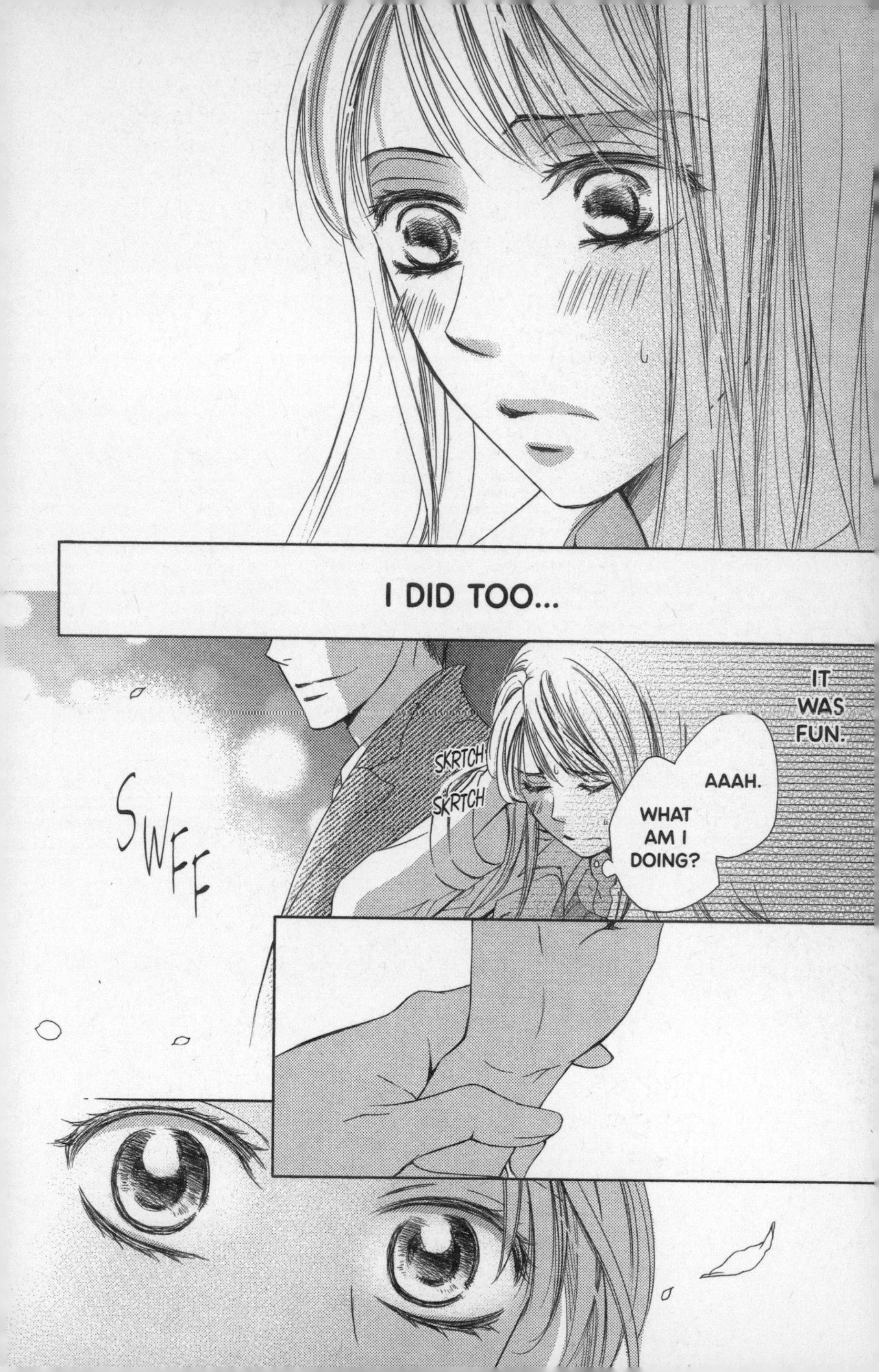
I DID TOO...
IT WAS FUN.
AAAH. WHAT AM I DOING?
SKRTCH SKRTCH
SWFF

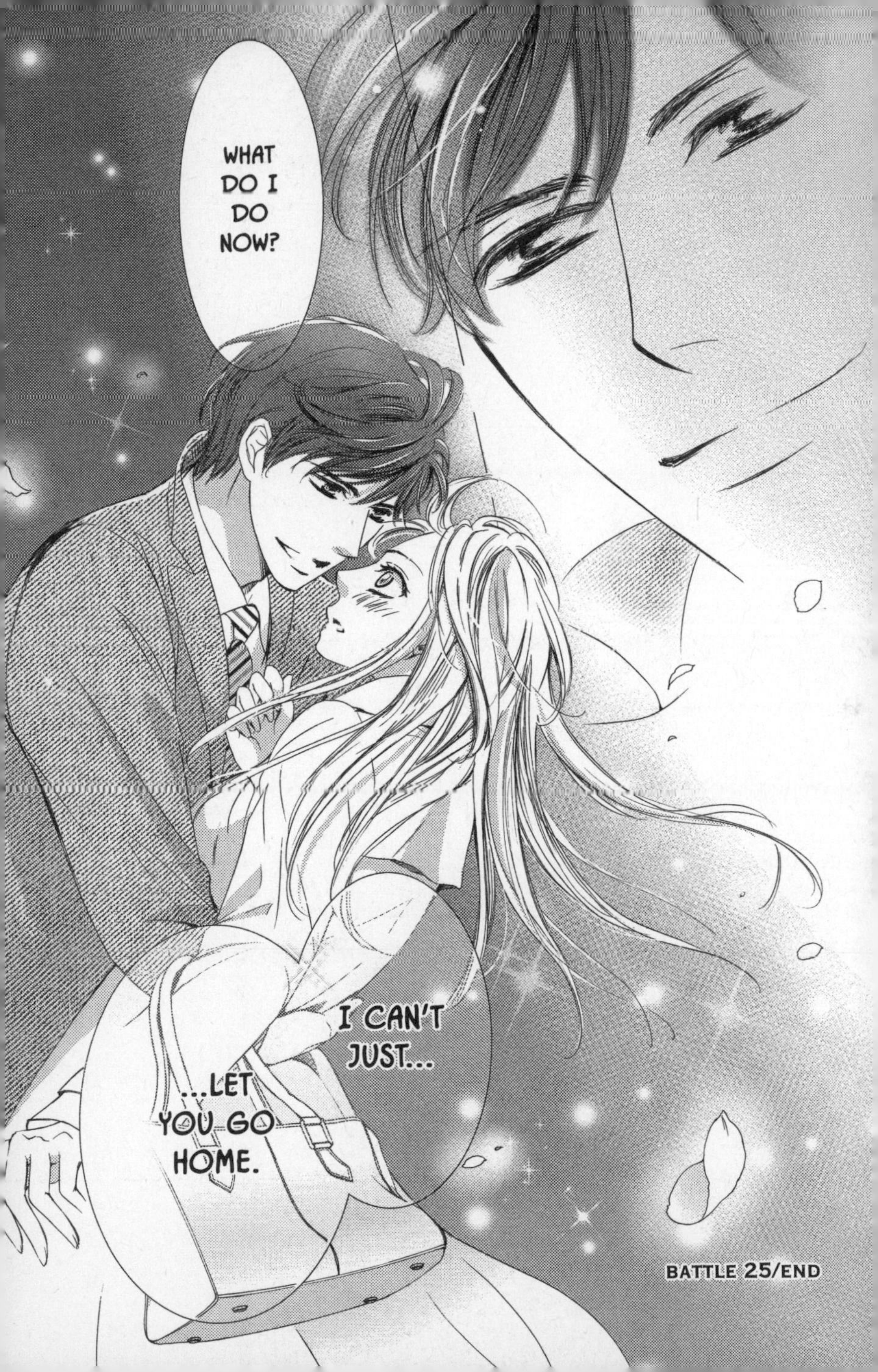
WHAT DO I DO NOW?
I CAN'T JUST...
...LET YOU GO HOME.
BATTLE 25/END

What if I changed
my mind?

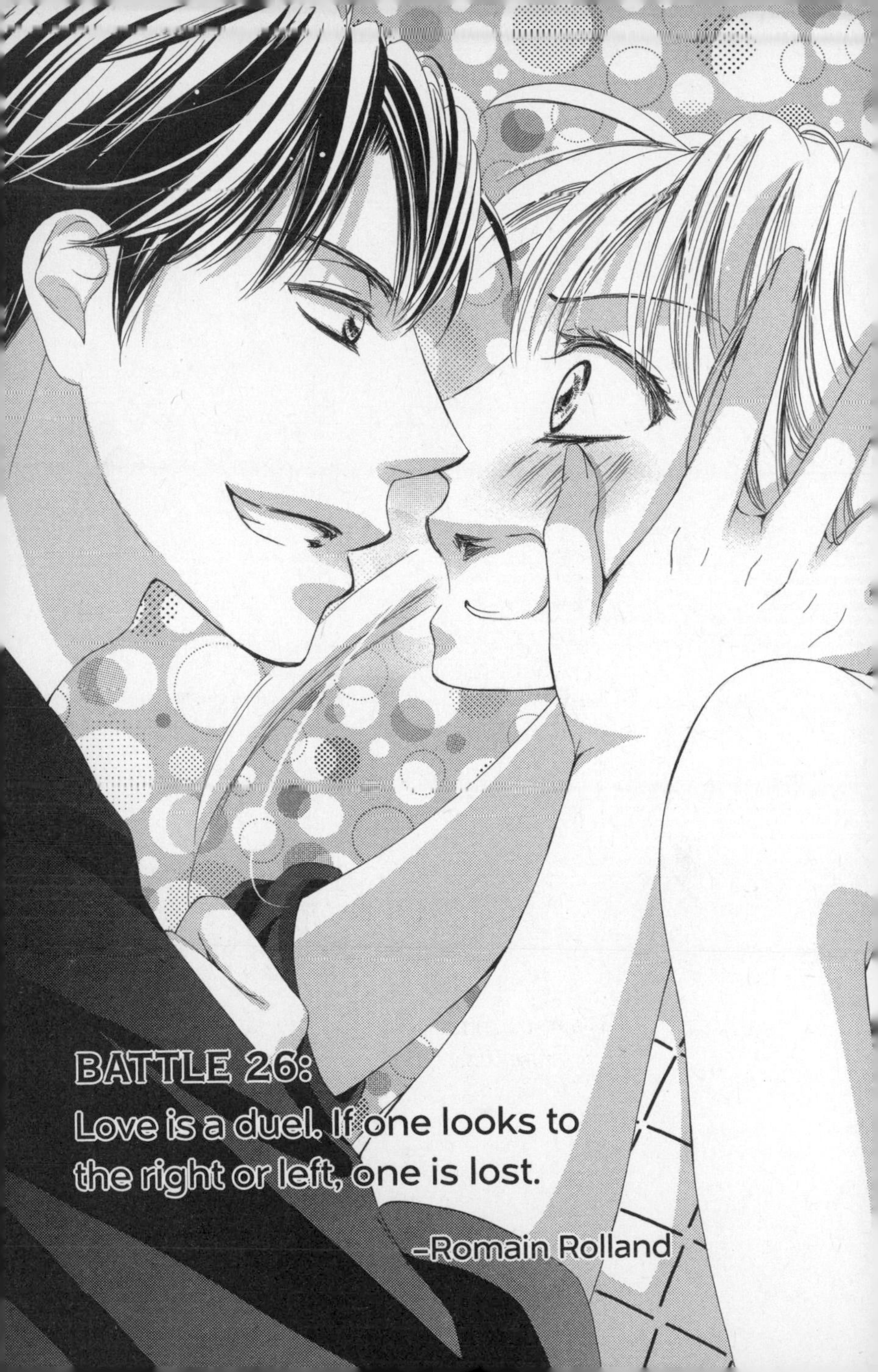
BATTLE 26:
Love is a duel. If one looks to the right or left, one is lost.
–Romain Rolland

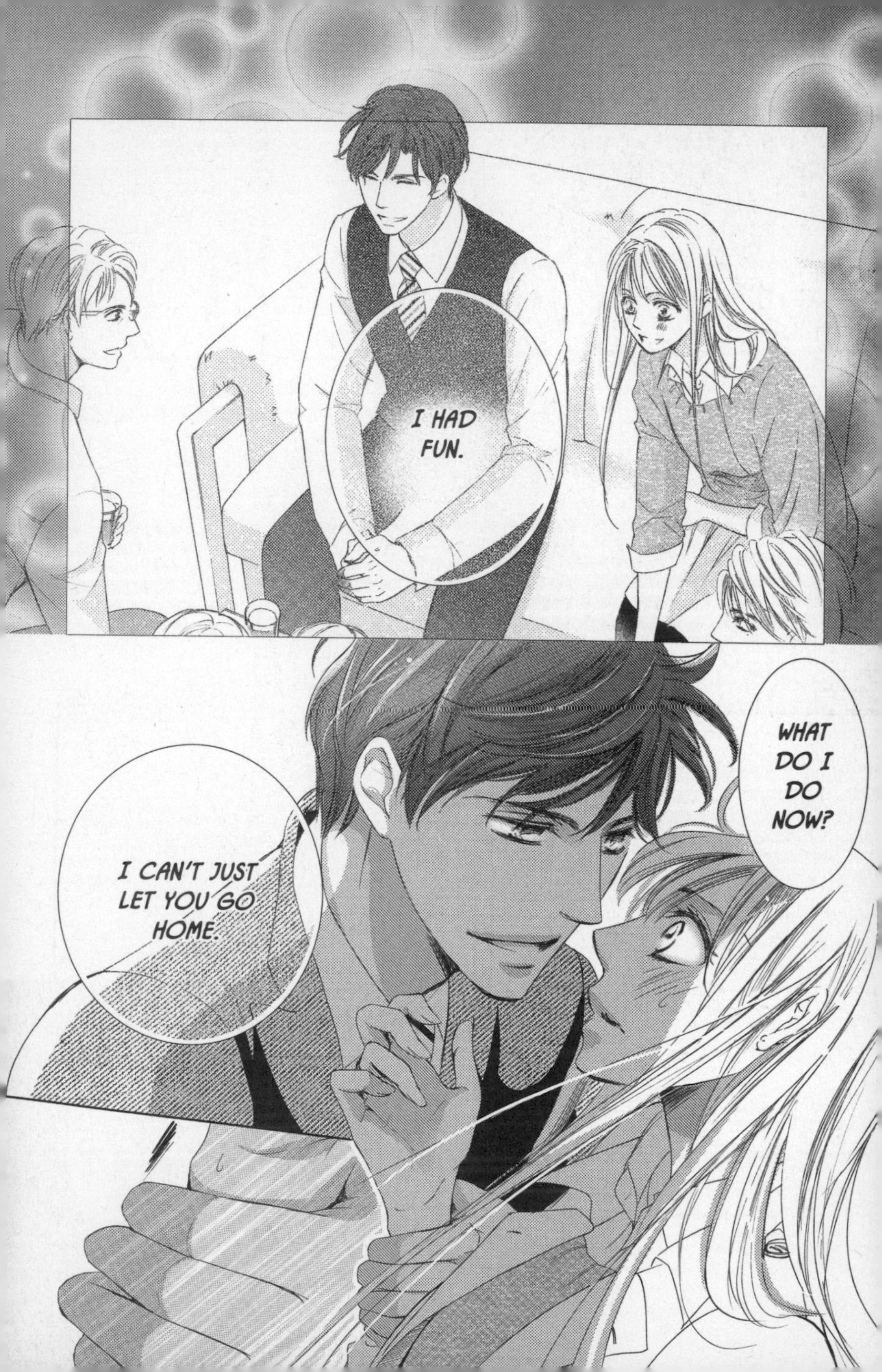
I HAD FUN.
WHAT DO I DO NOW?
I CAN'T JUST LET YOU GO HOME.

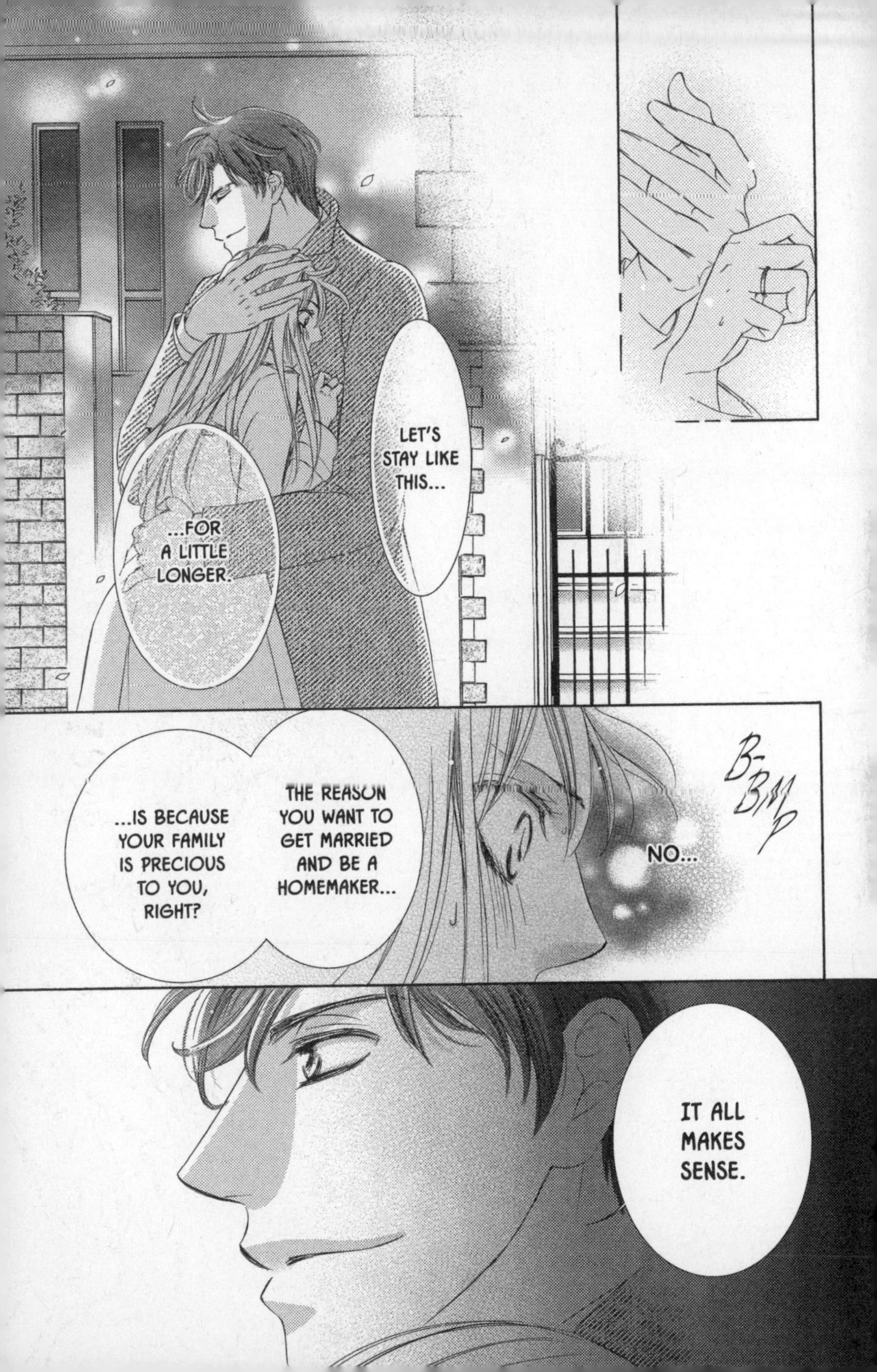
LET'S STAY LIKE THIS...
...FOR A LITTLE LONGER.
B-BMP
NO...
THE REASON YOU WANT TO GET MARRIED AND BE A HOMEMAKER...
...IS BECAUSE YOUR FAMILY IS PRECIOUS TO YOU, RIGHT?
IT ALL MAKES SENSE.

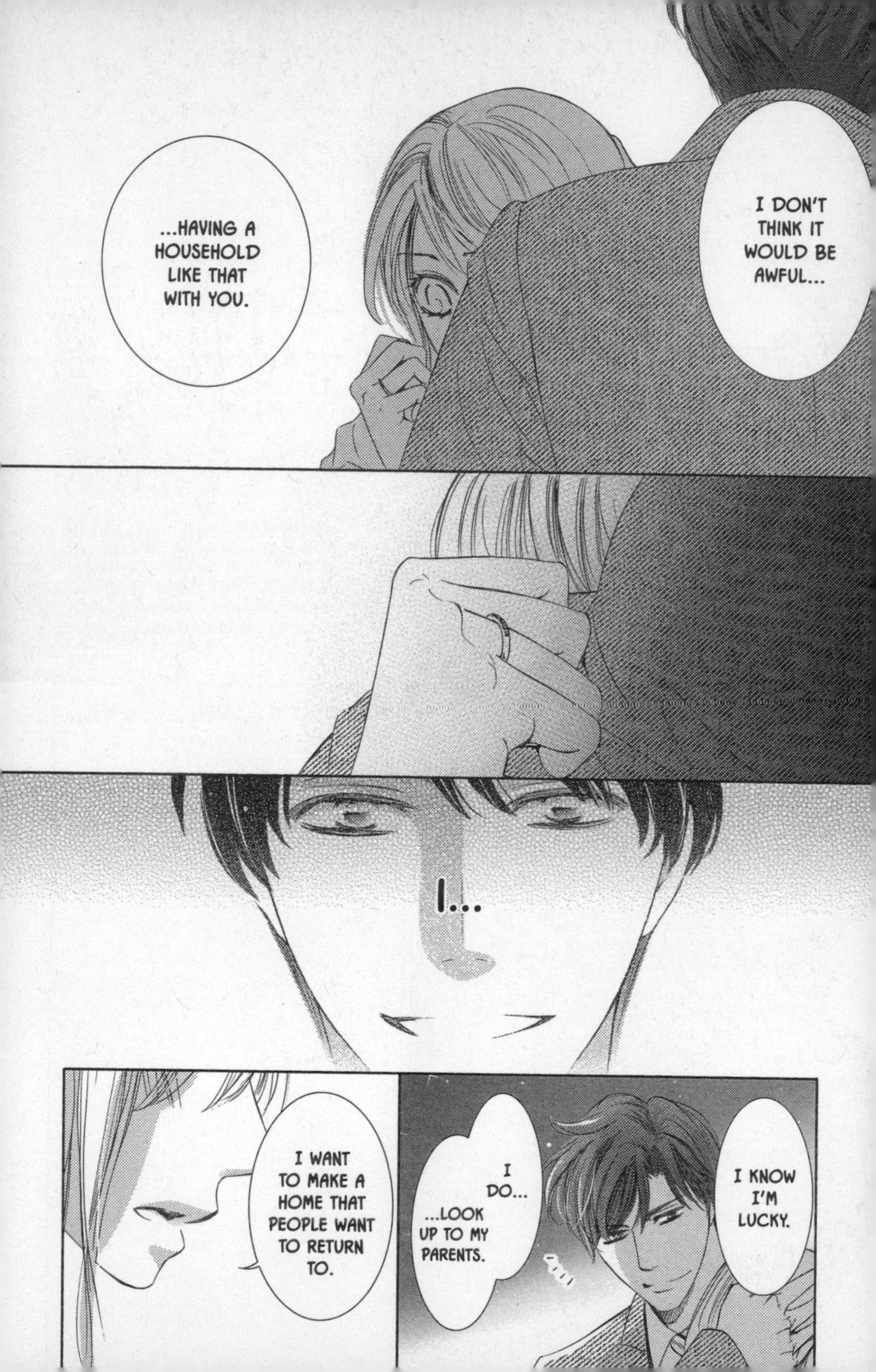
I DON'T THINK IT WOULD BE AWFUL...
...HAVING A HOUSEHOLD LIKE THAT WITH YOU.
I...
I KNOW I'M LUCKY.
I DO...
...LOOK UP TO MY PARENTS.
I WANT TO MAKE A HOME THAT PEOPLE WANT TO RETURN TO.

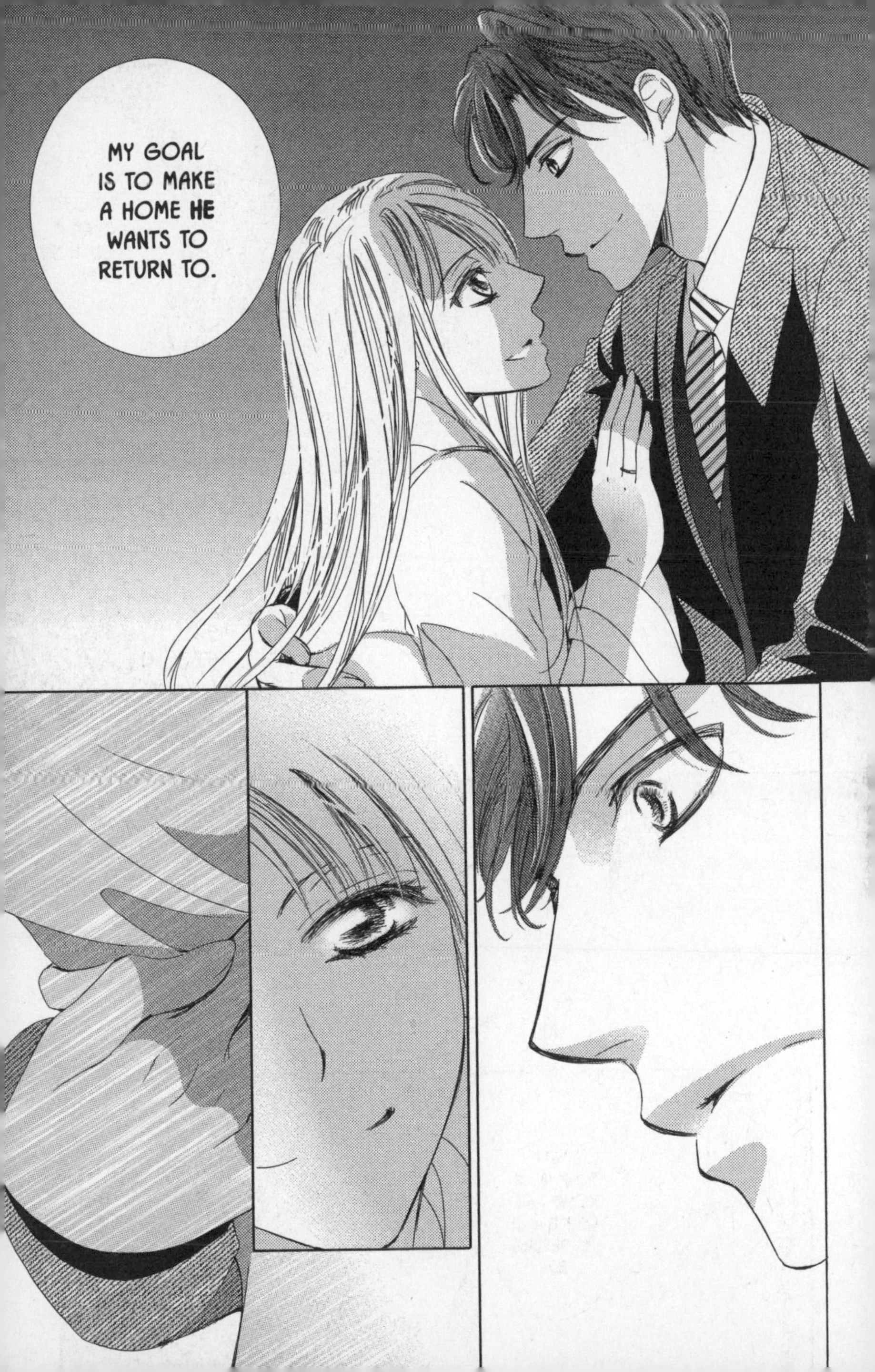
MY GOAL IS TO MAKE A HOME **HE** WANTS TO RETURN TO.

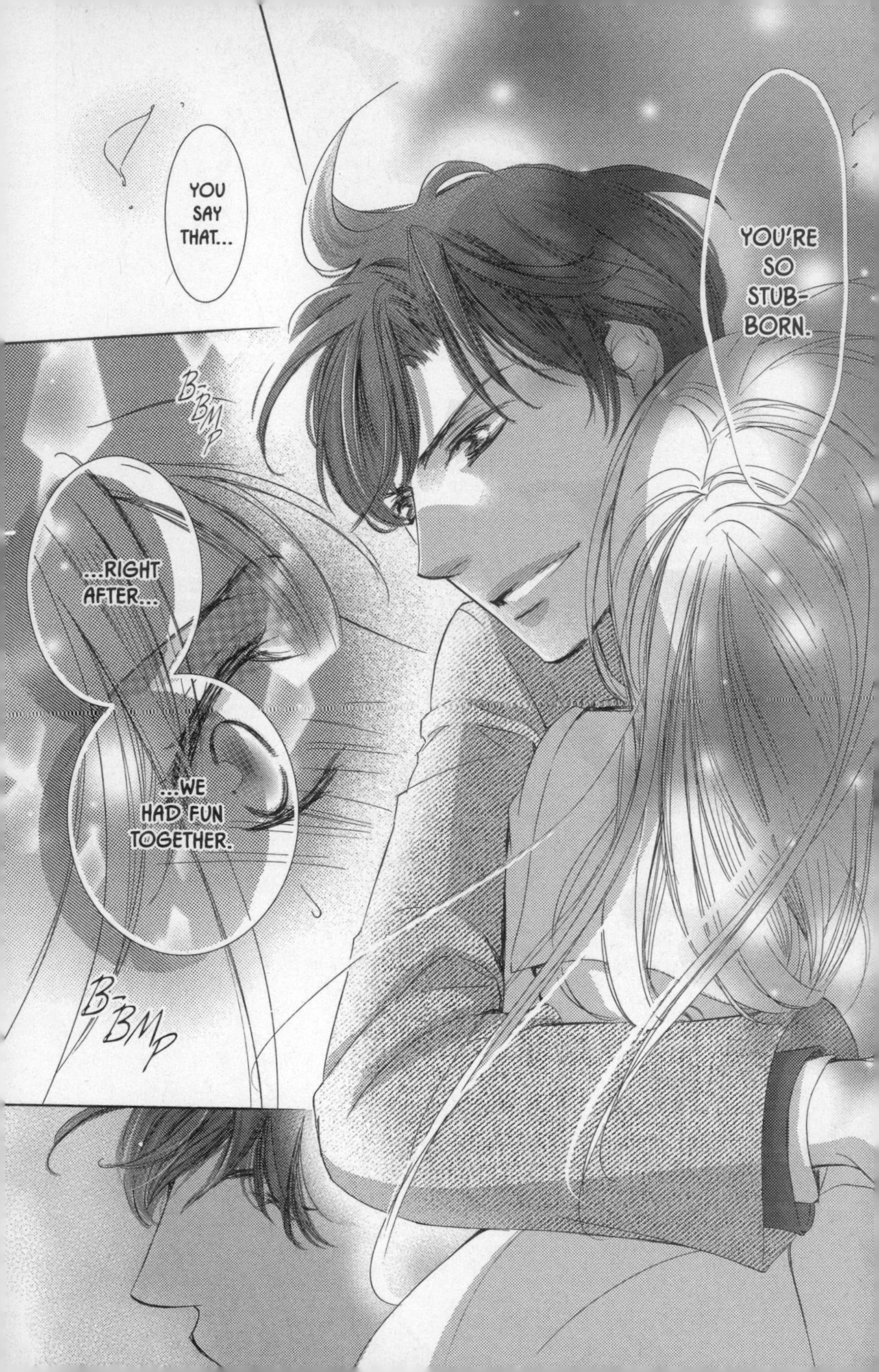
YOU'RE SO STUB-BORN.
YOU SAY THAT...
B-BMP
...RIGHT AFTER...
...WE HAD FUN TOGETHER.
B-BMP

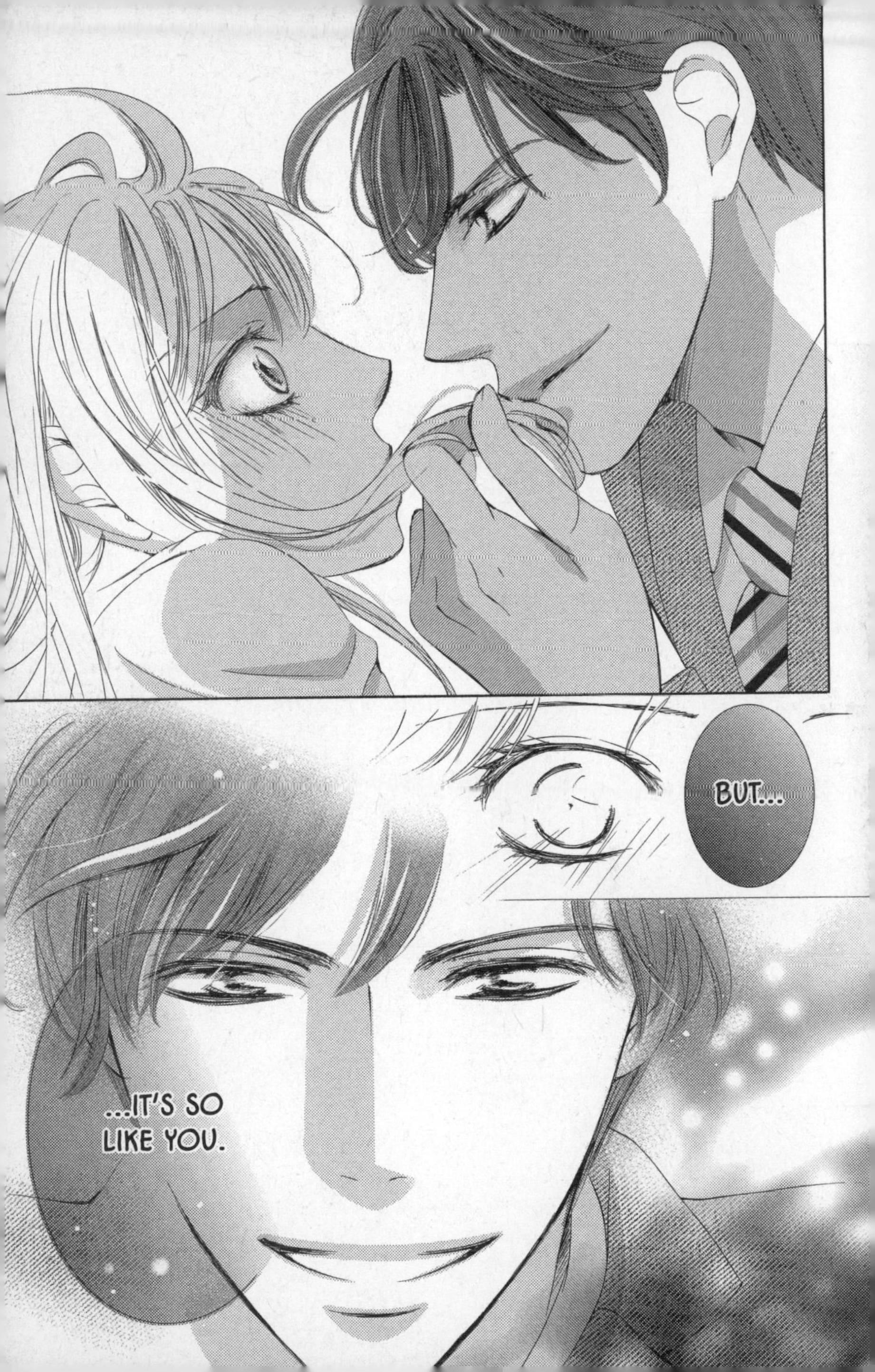
BUT...
...IT'S SO LIKE YOU.

RYU.

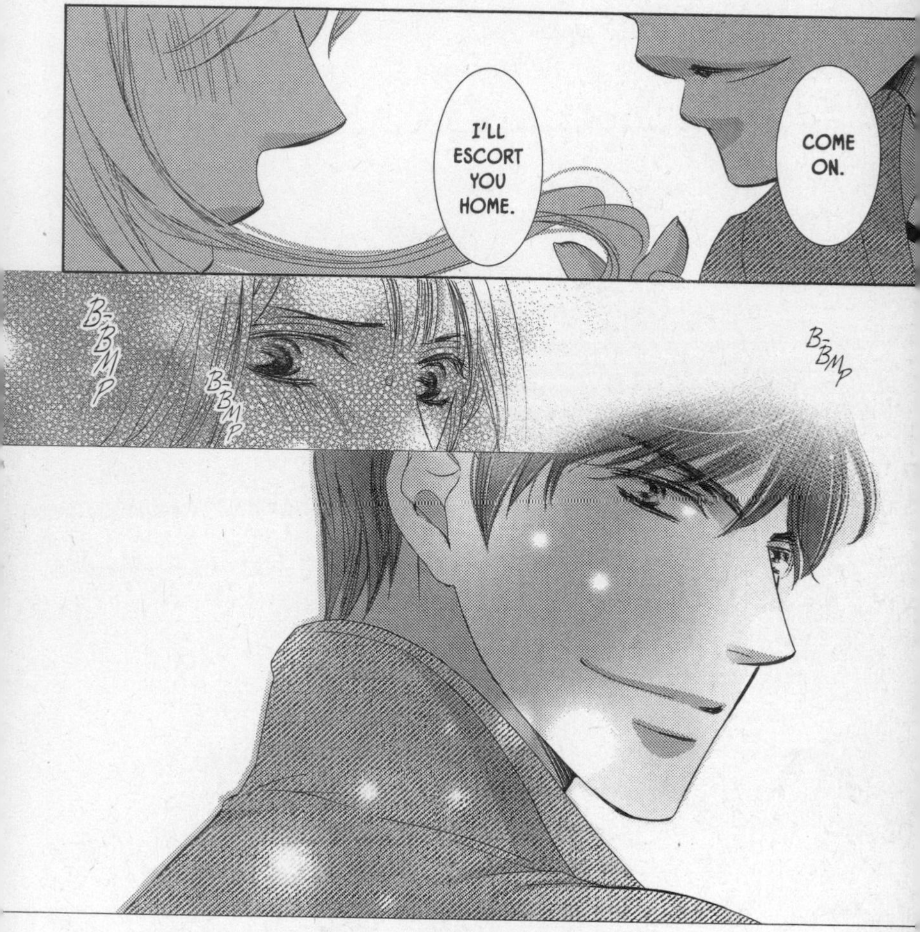
COME ON.
I'LL ESCORT YOU HOME.
B-BMP
B-BMP
B-BMP

RYU, I MISS YOU.

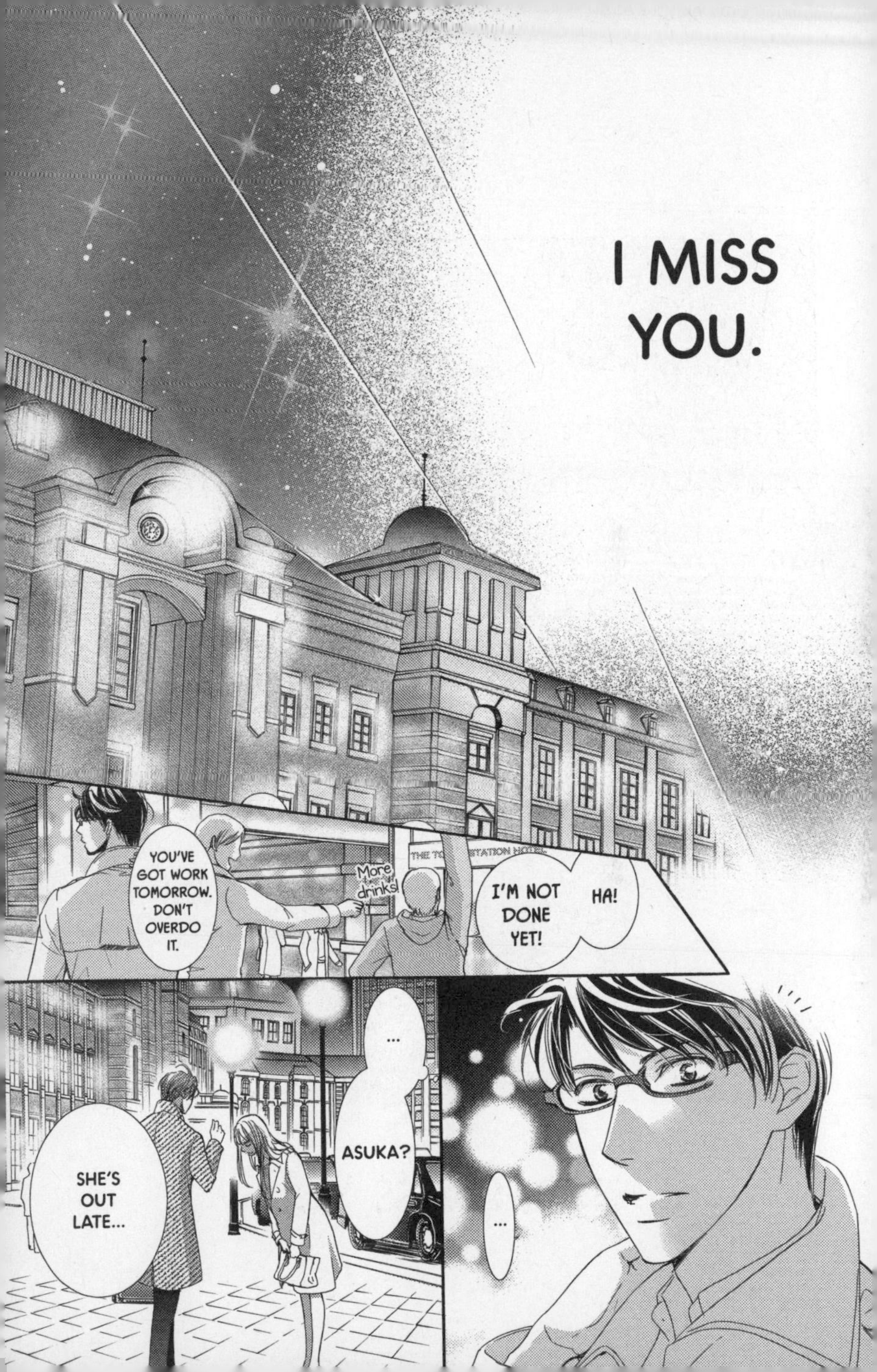
I MISS YOU.
HA!
I'M NOT DONE YET!
More drinks!
YOU'VE GOT WORK TOMORROW. DON'T OVERDO IT.
...
...
ASUKA?
SHE'S OUT LATE...

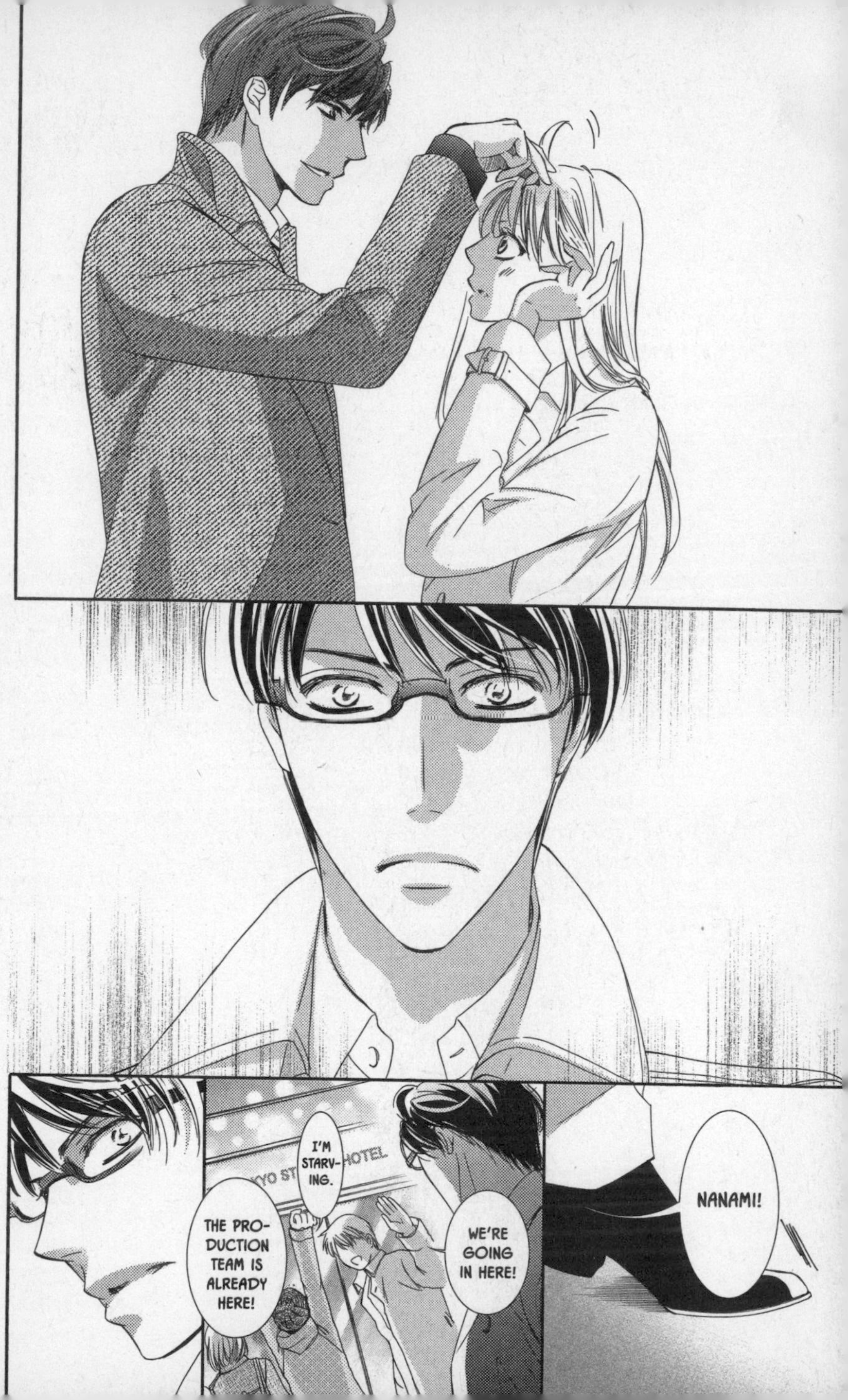
NANAMI!
I'M STARV-ING.
WE'RE GOING IN HERE!
THE PRO-DUCTION TEAM IS ALREADY HERE!

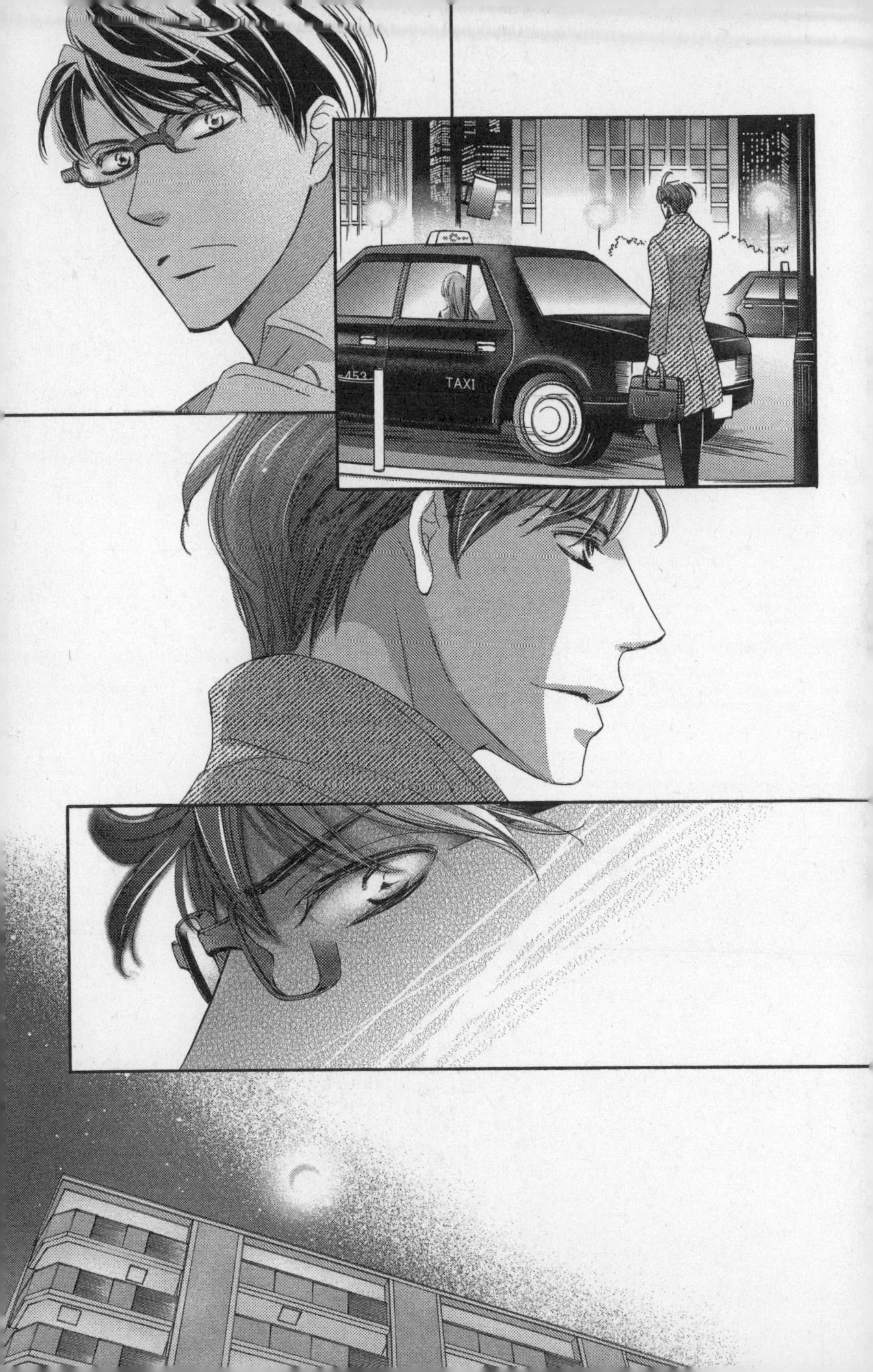
TAXI

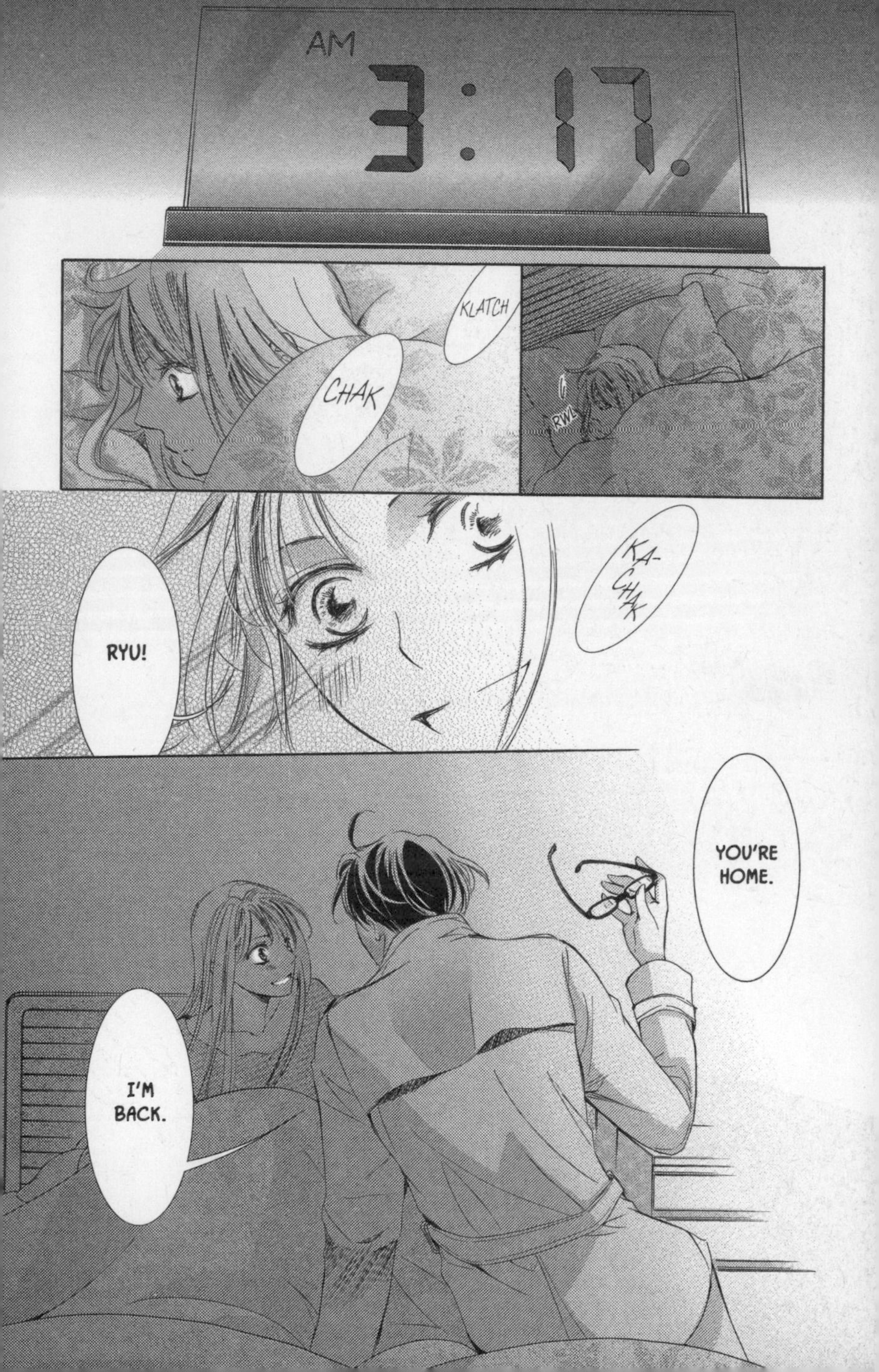
AM
3:17.
RWL
KLATCH
CHAK
KA-CHAK
RYU!
YOU'RE HOME.
I'M BACK.

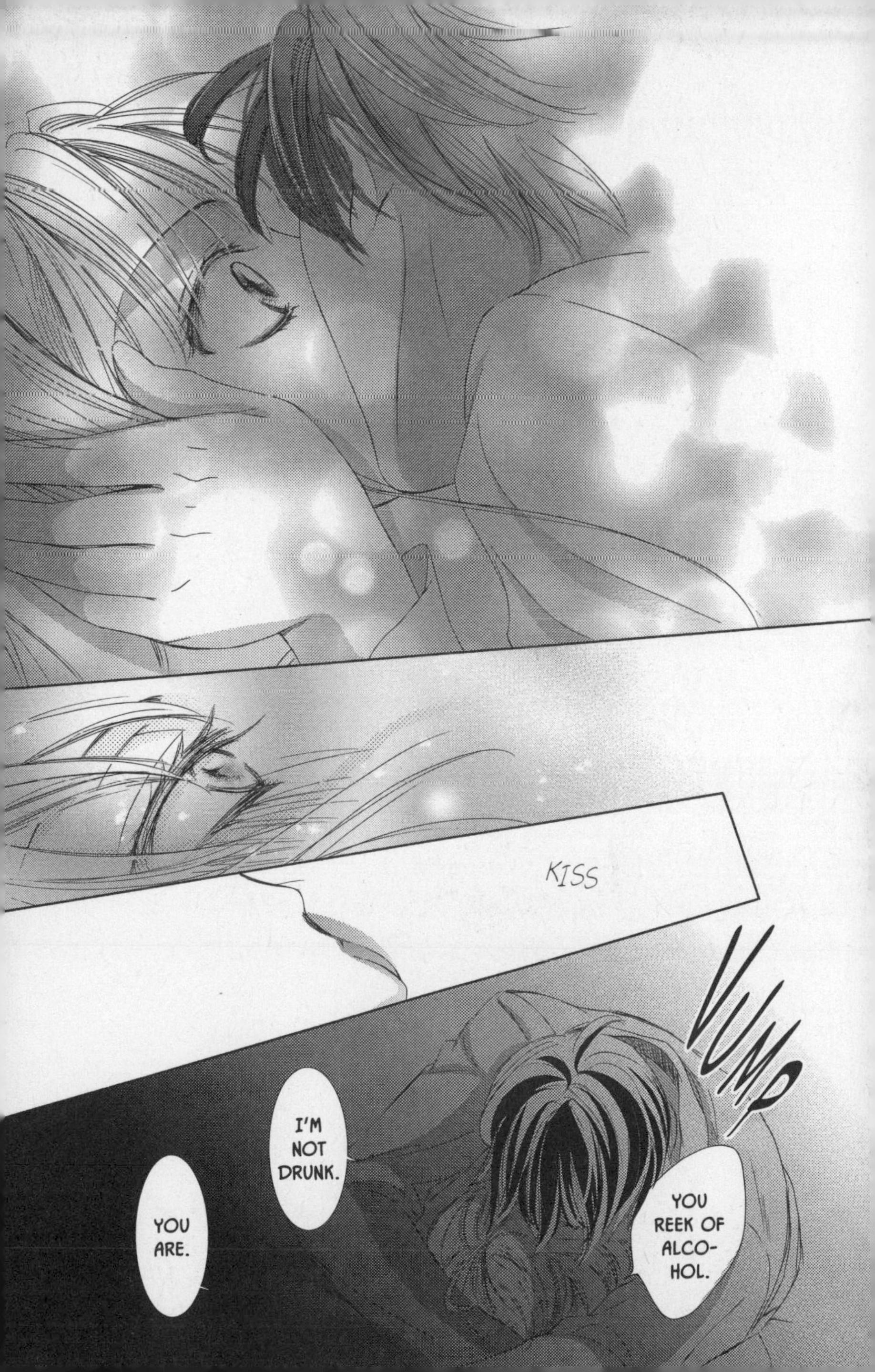
KISS
VUMP
YOU REEK OF ALCO-HOL.
I'M NOT DRUNK.
YOU ARE.

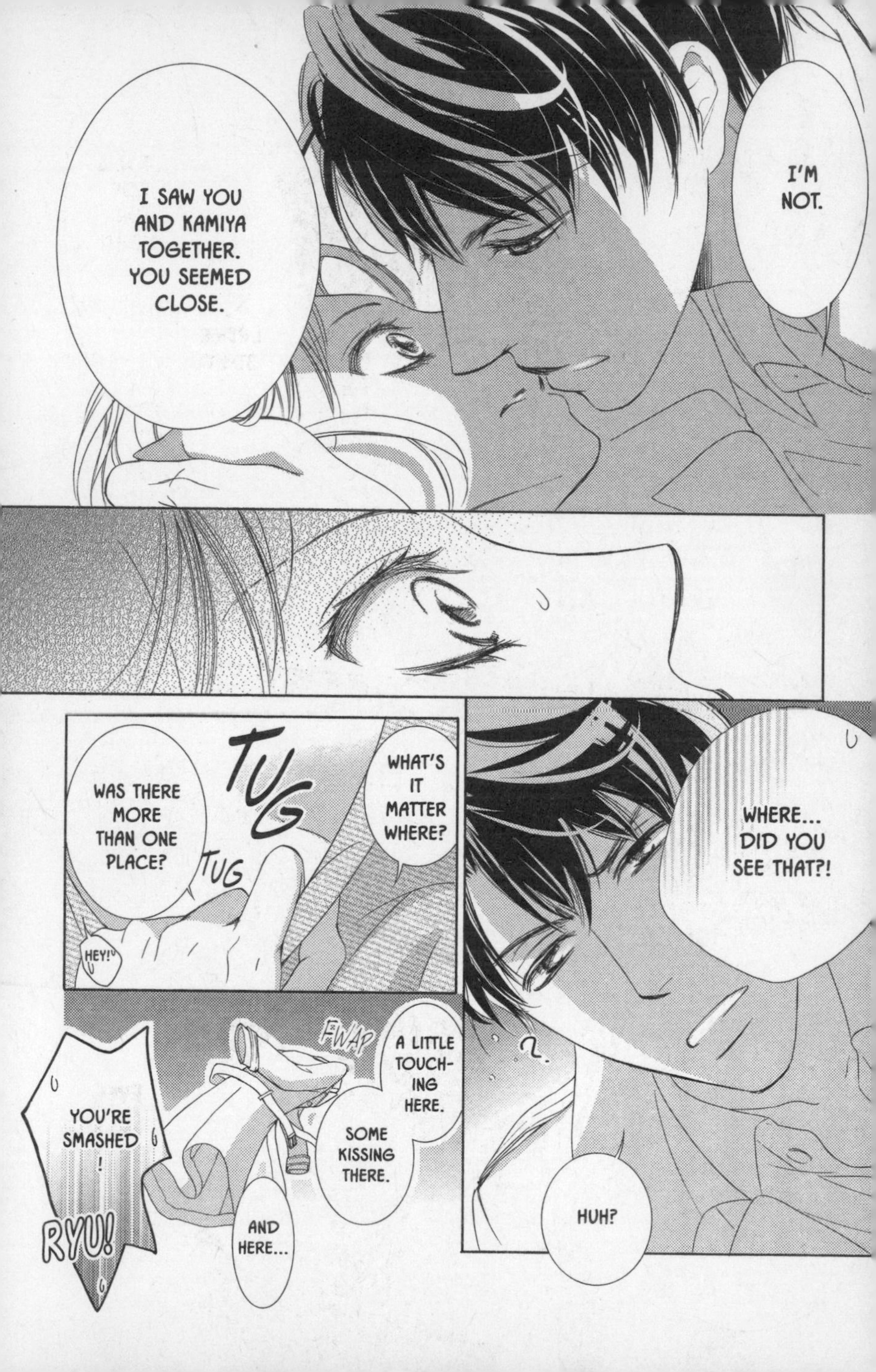
I'M NOT.
I SAW YOU AND KAMIYA TOGETHER. YOU SEEMED CLOSE.
WHERE... DID YOU SEE THAT?!
HUH?
WHAT'S IT MATTER WHERE?
TUG
WAS THERE MORE THAN ONE PLACE?
TUG
HEY!
FWAP
A LITTLE TOUCHING HERE.
SOME KISSING THERE.
AND HERE...
YOU'RE SMASHED!
RYU!

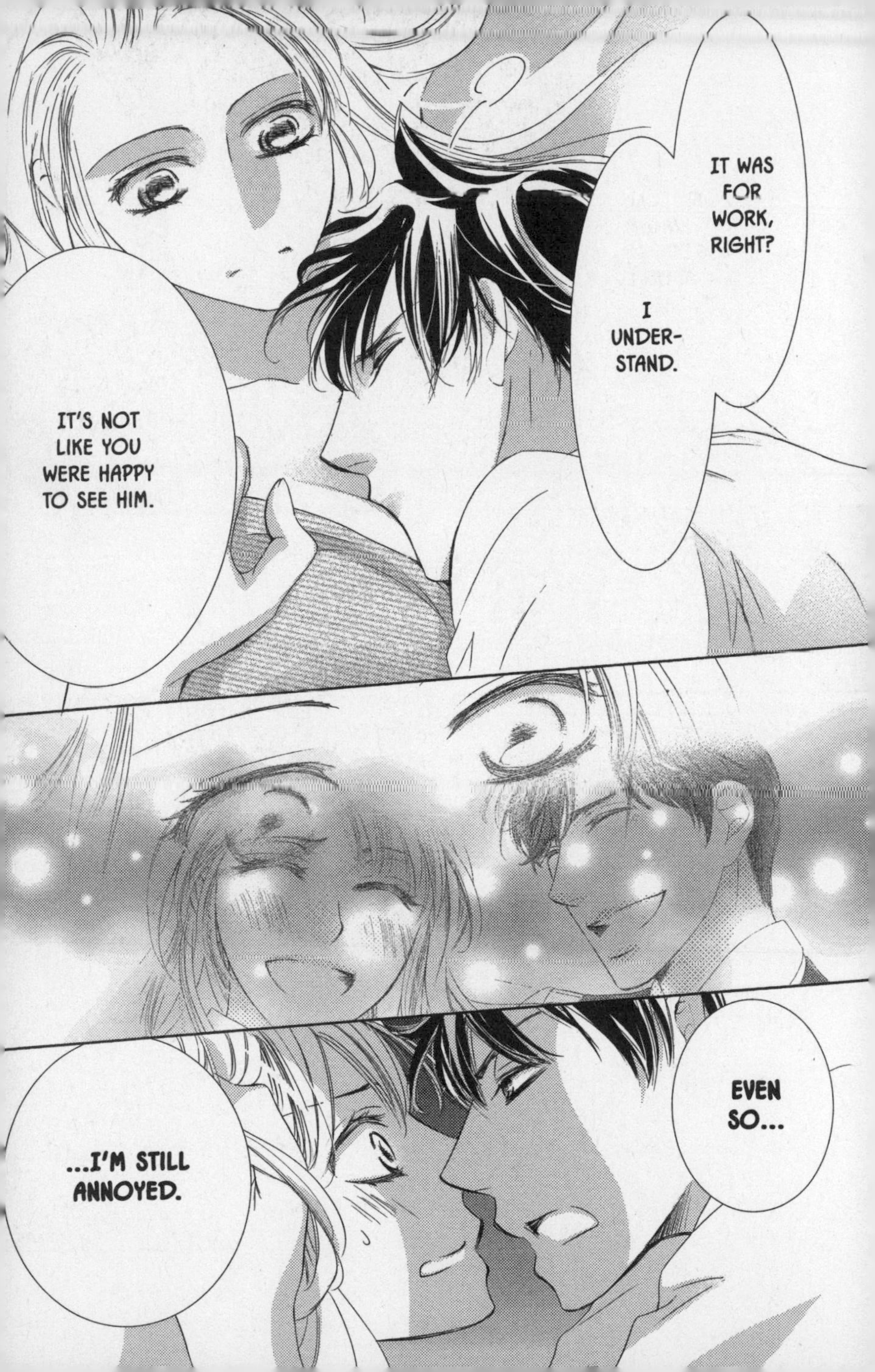
IT WAS FOR WORK, RIGHT?
I UNDER-STAND.
IT'S NOT LIKE YOU WERE HAPPY TO SEE HIM.
EVEN SO...
...I'M STILL ANNOYED.

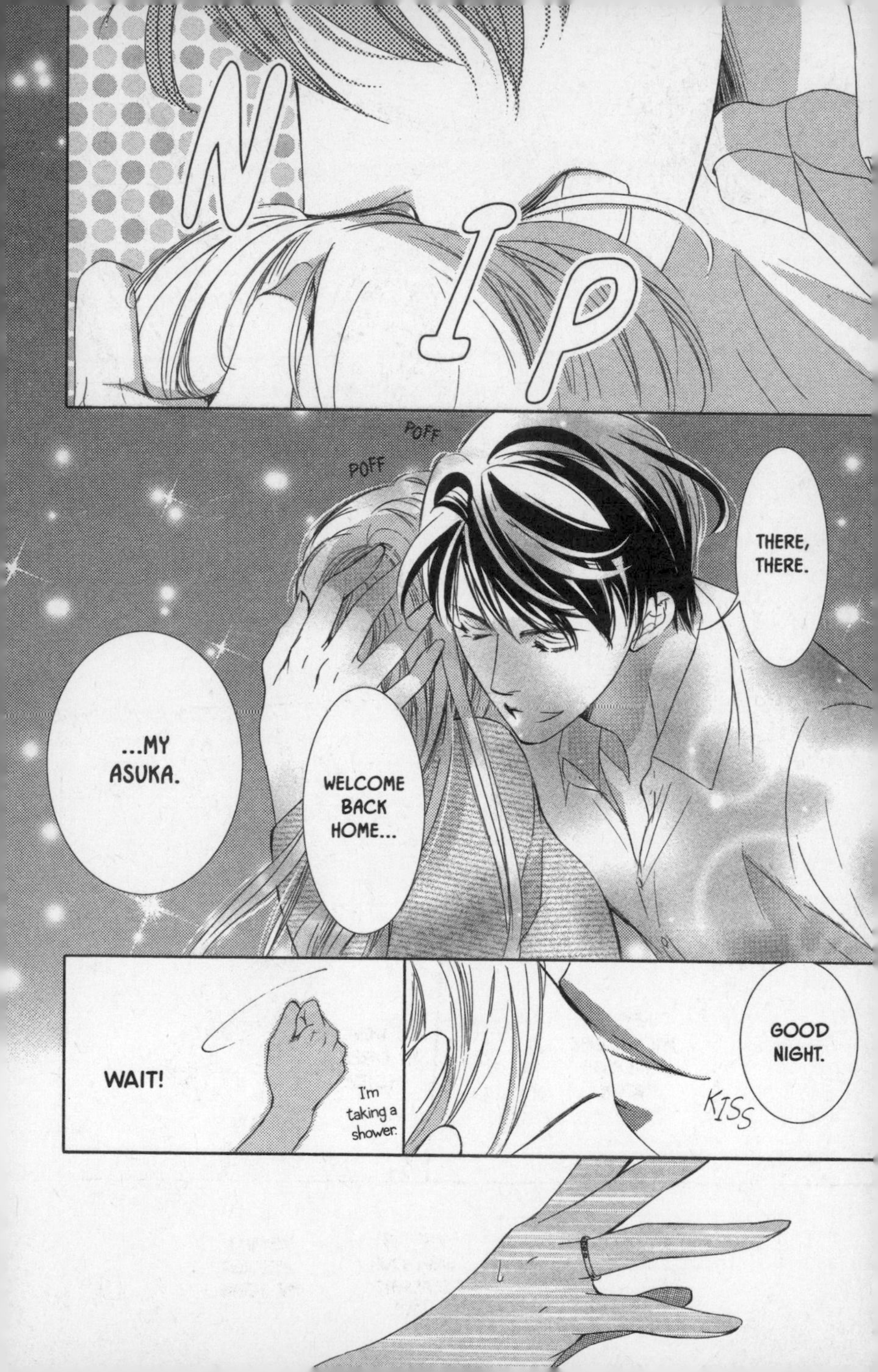
NIP
POFF
POFF
THERE, THERE.
WELCOME BACK HOME...
...MY ASUKA.
GOOD NIGHT.
KISS
I'm taking a shower.
WAIT!

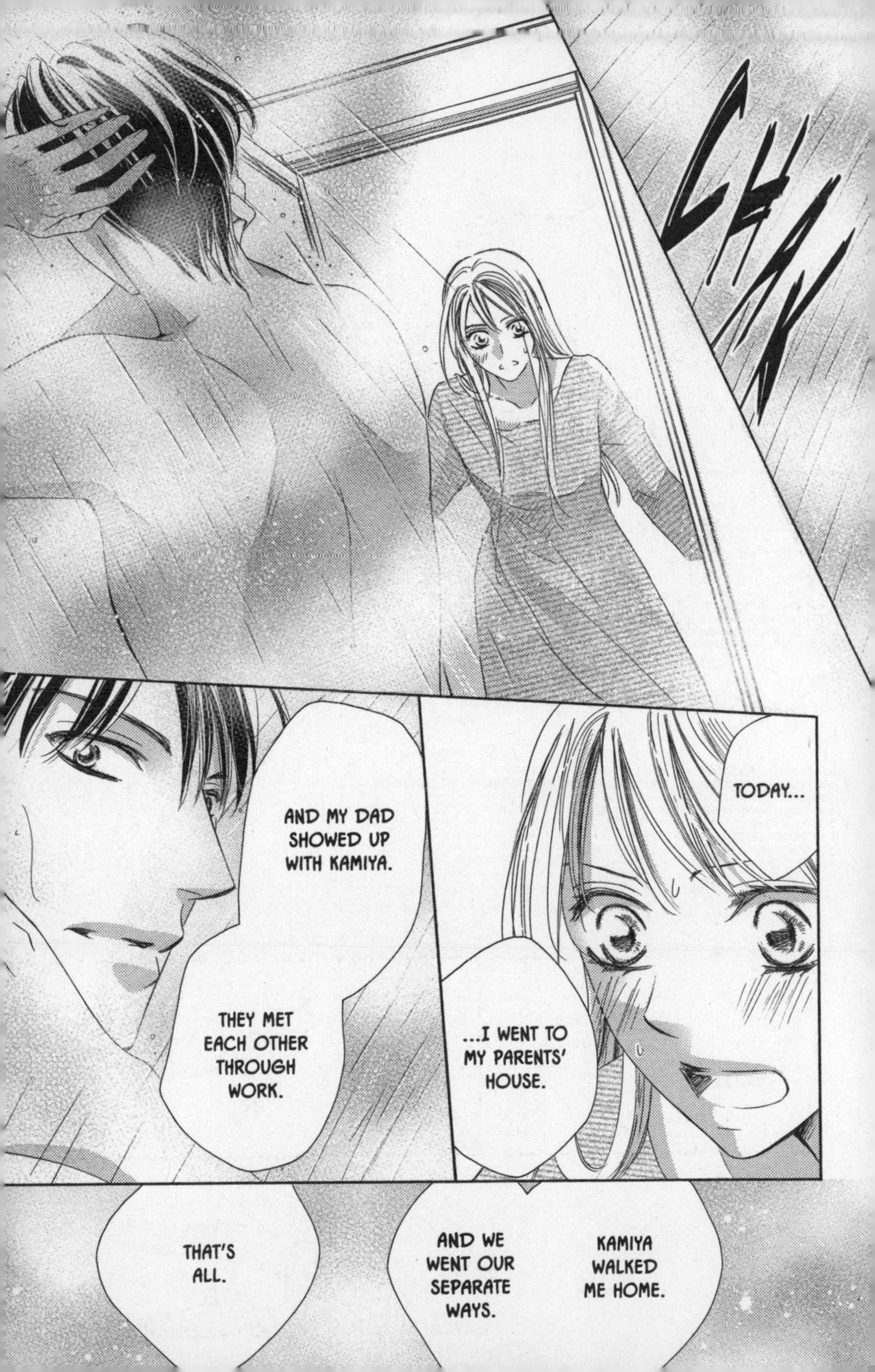
CHAK
TODAY...
...I WENT TO MY PARENTS' HOUSE.
AND MY DAD SHOWED UP WITH KAMIYA.
THEY MET EACH OTHER THROUGH WORK.
KAMIYA WALKED ME HOME.
AND WE WENT OUR SEPARATE WAYS.
THAT'S ALL.

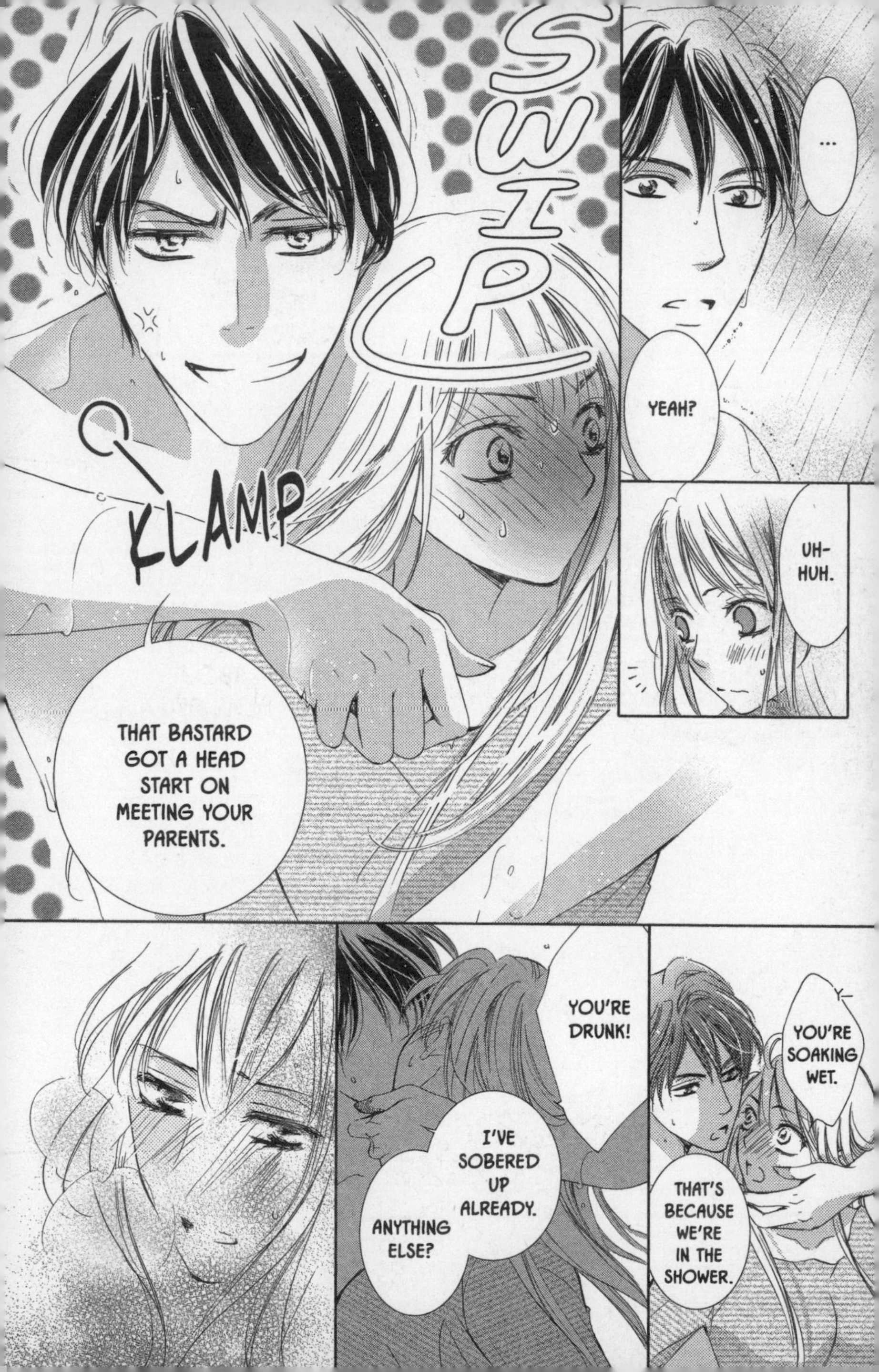
...
YEAH?
UH-HUH.
SWIP
KLAMP
THAT BASTARD GOT A HEAD START ON MEETING YOUR PARENTS.
Y—
YOU'RE SOAKING WET.
THAT'S BECAUSE WE'RE IN THE SHOWER.
YOU'RE DRUNK!
I'VE SOBERED UP ALREADY.
ANYTHING ELSE?

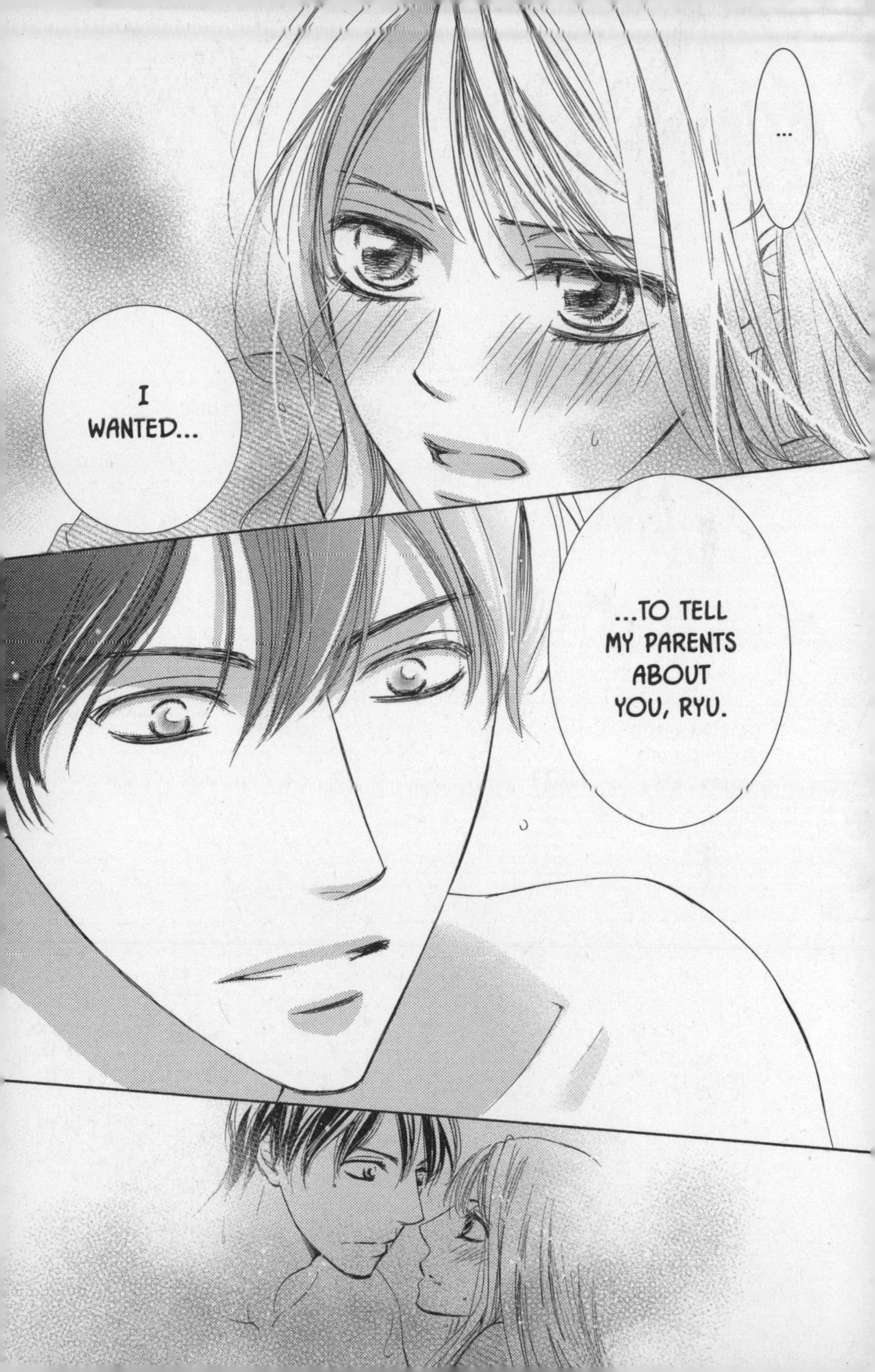
...
I WANTED...
...TO TELL MY PARENTS ABOUT YOU, RYU.

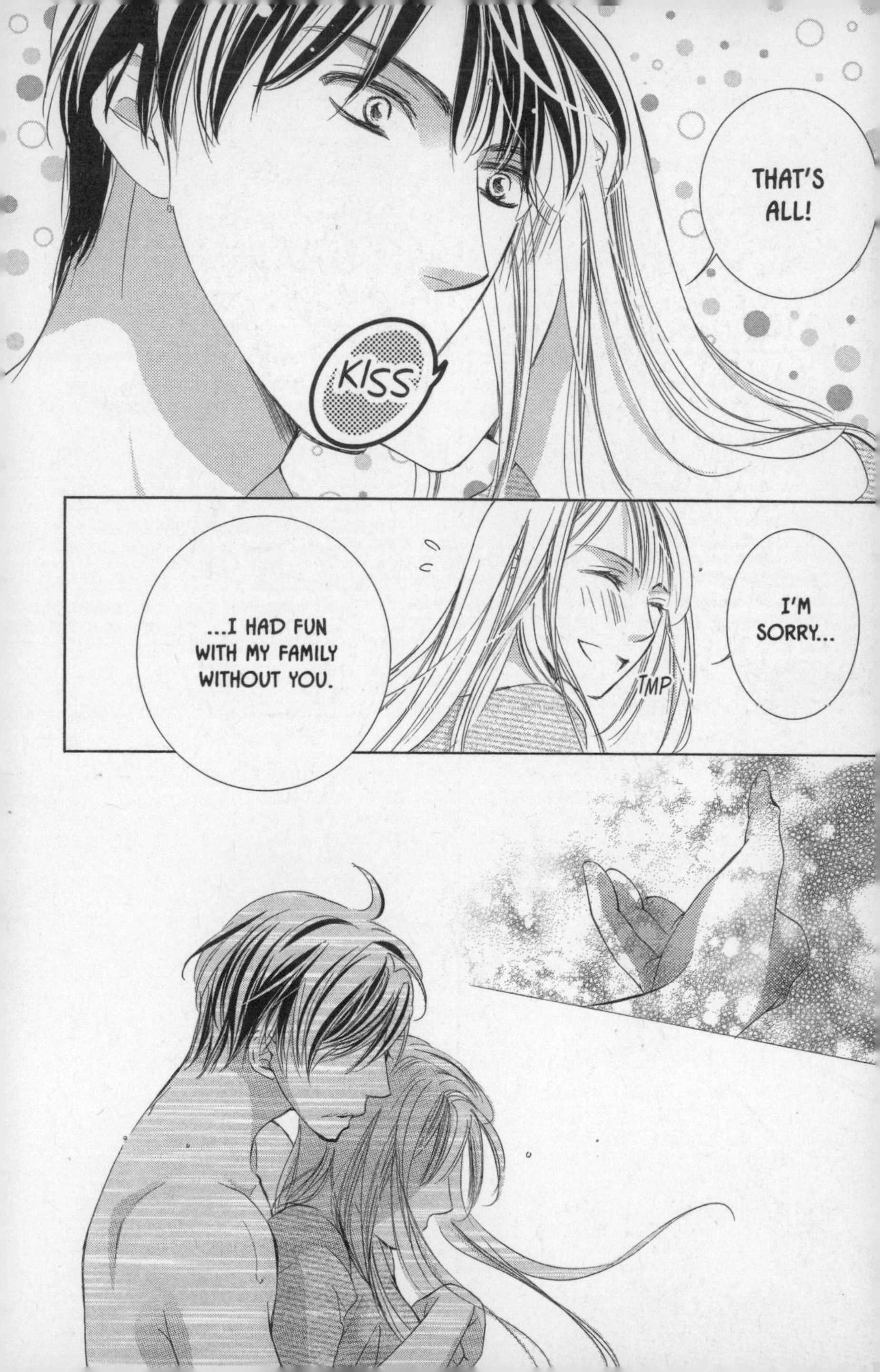
THAT'S ALL!
KISS
I'M SORRY...
TMP
...I HAD FUN WITH MY FAMILY WITHOUT YOU.

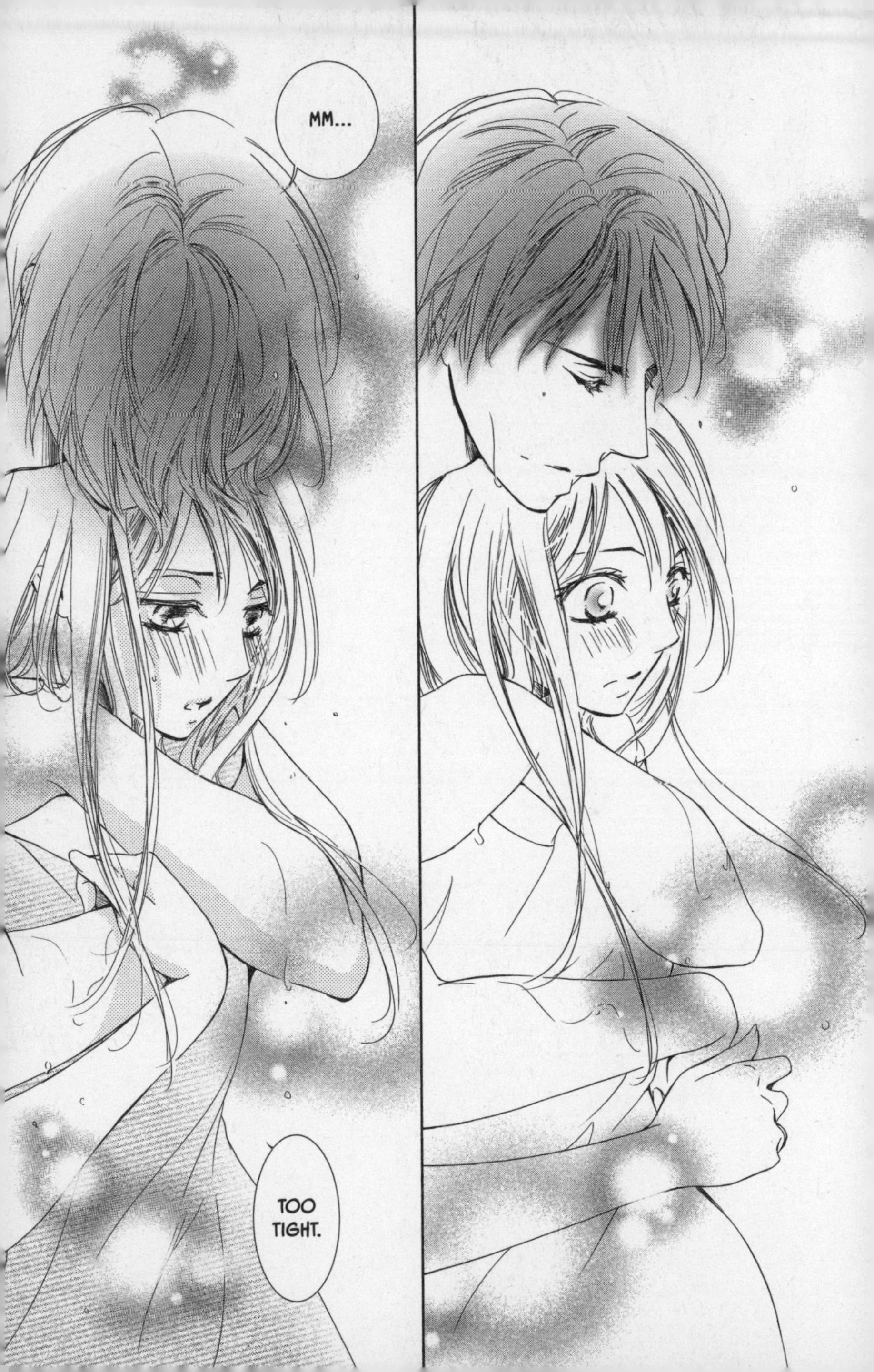
MM...
TOO TIGHT.

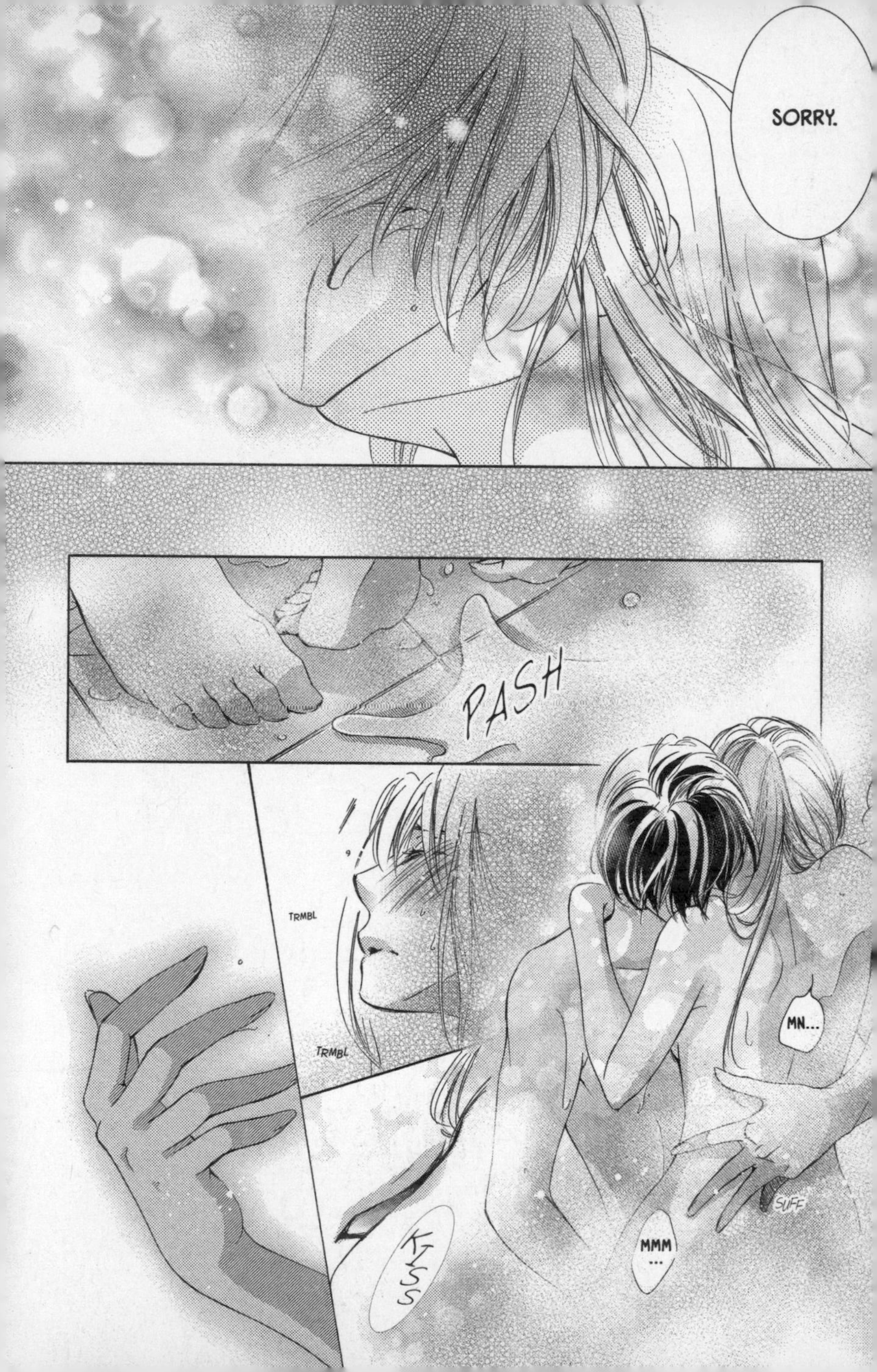
SORRY.
PASH
MN...
SUFF
MMM...
KISS
TRMBL
TRMBL

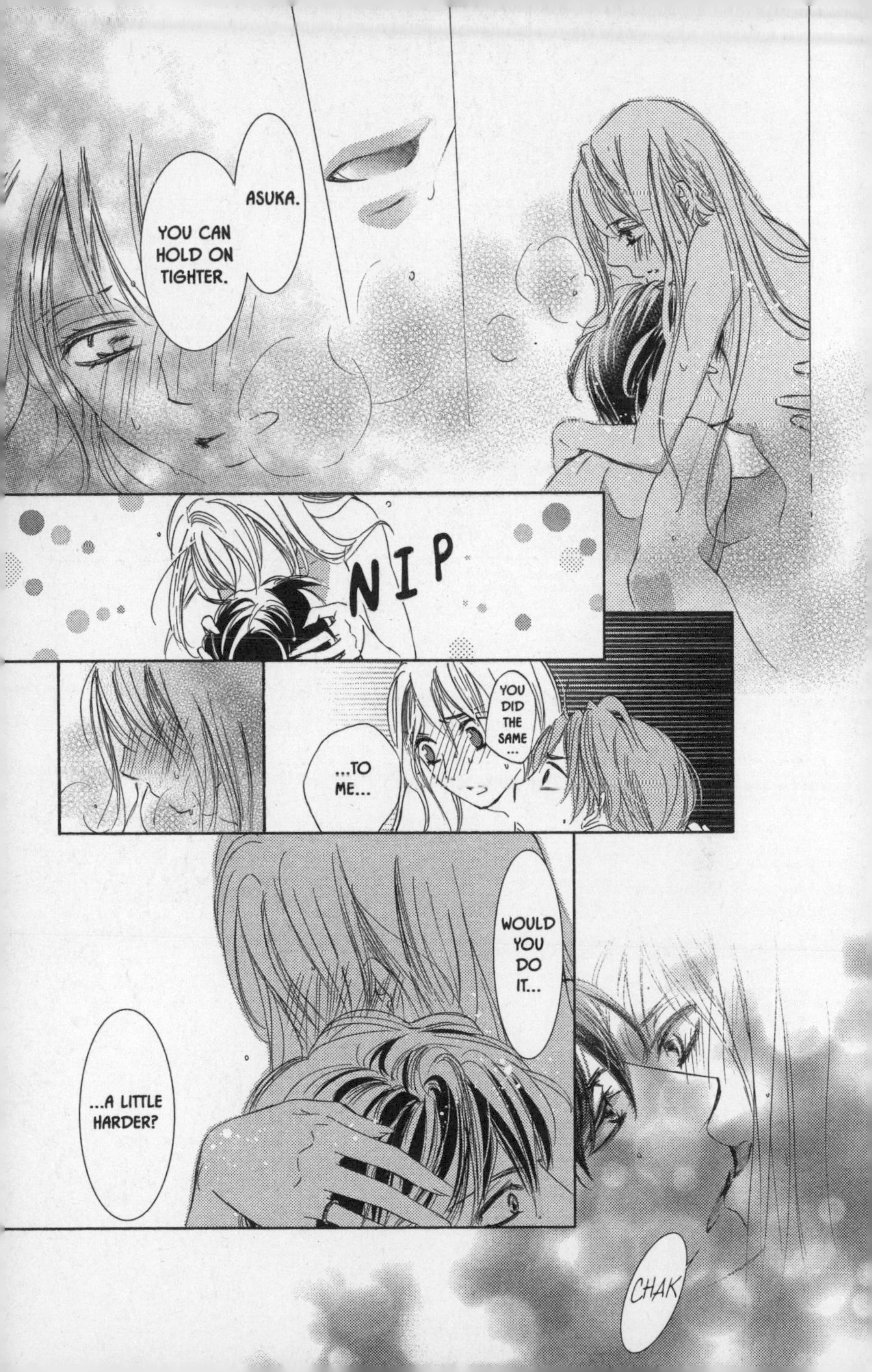
ASUKA.
YOU CAN HOLD ON TIGHTER.
NIP
YOU DID THE SAME...
...TO ME...
WOULD YOU DO IT...
...A LITTLE HARDER?
CHAK

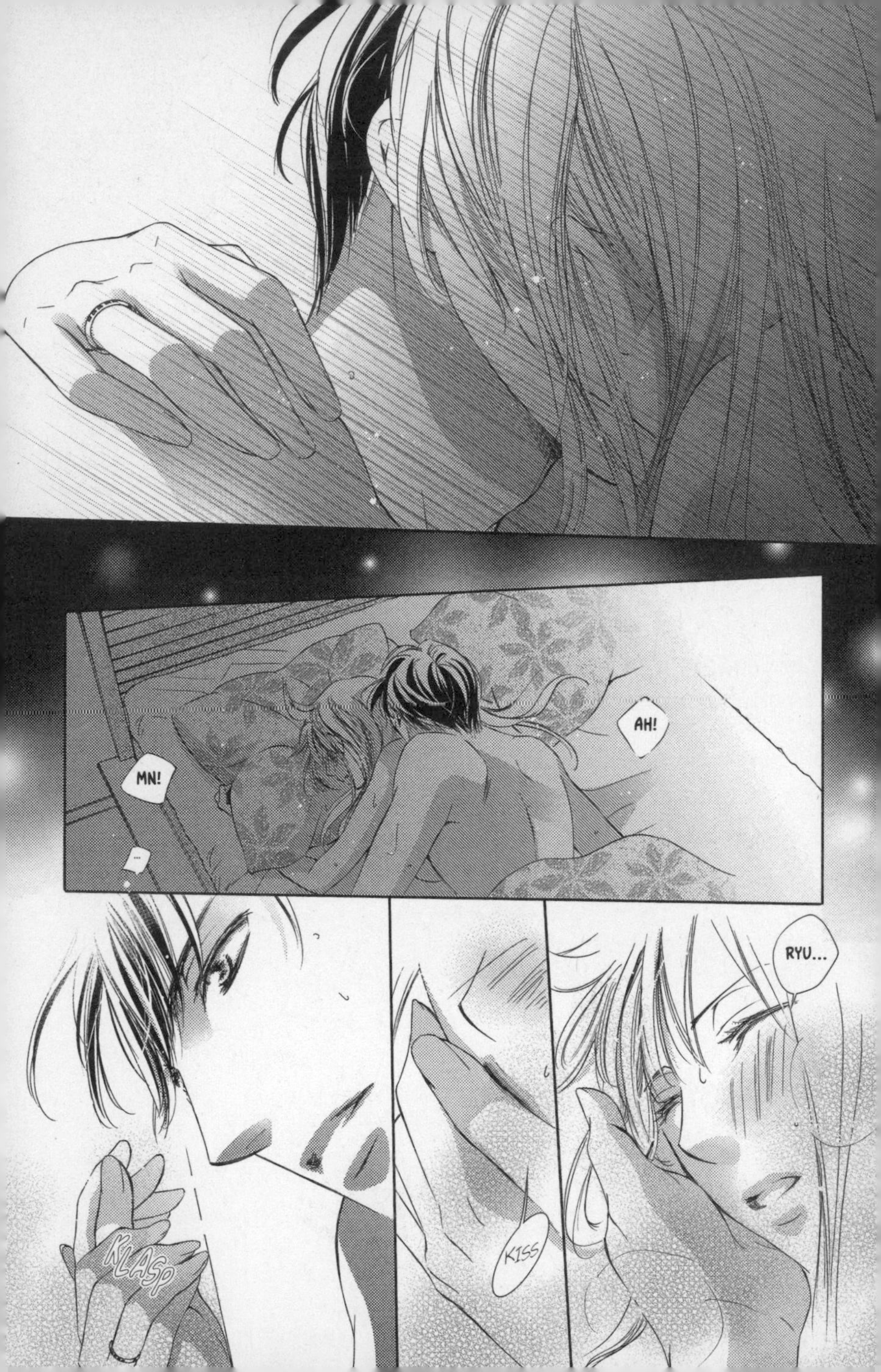
AH!
MN!
...
RYU...
KISS
KLASP

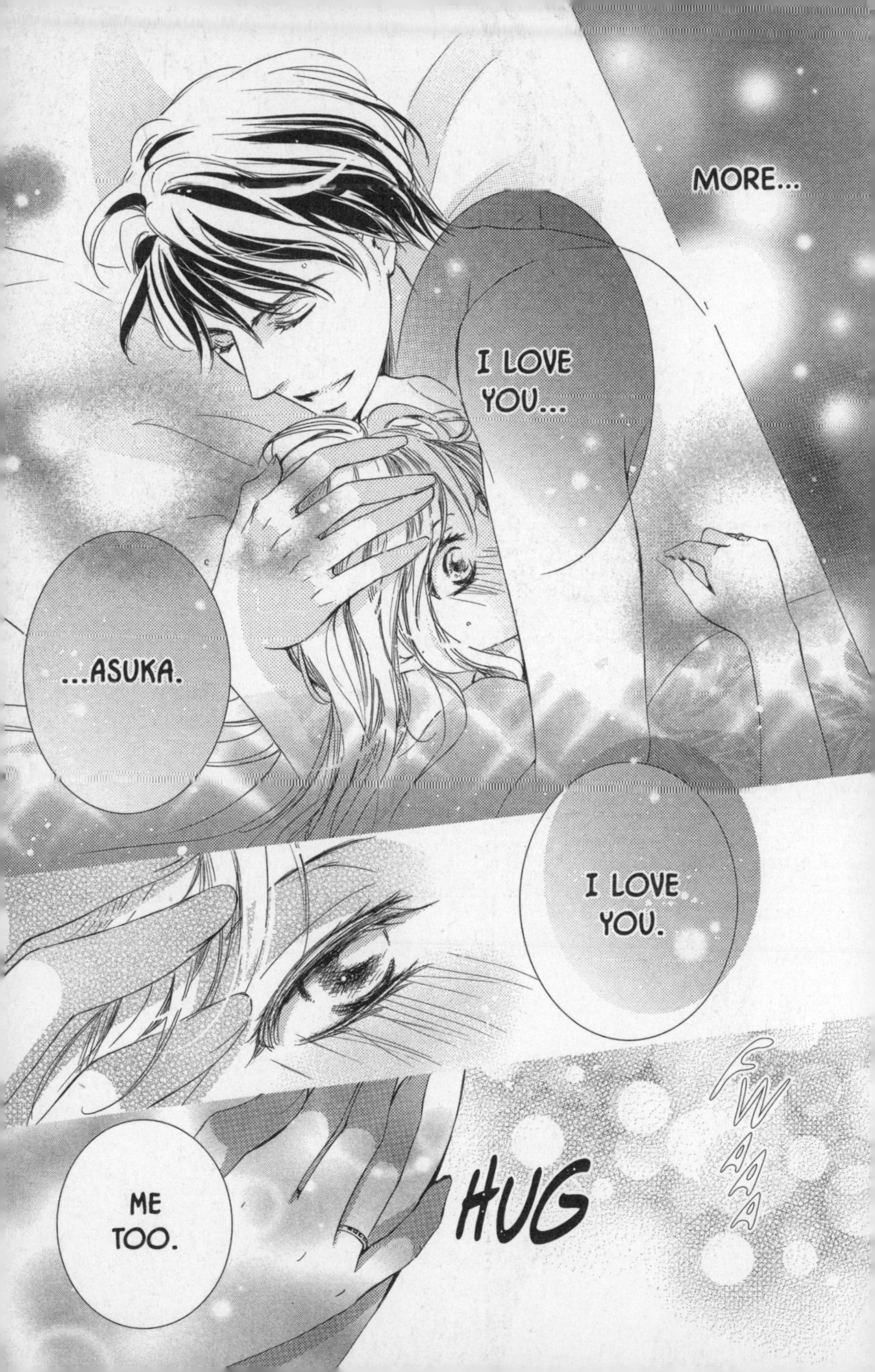
MORE...
I LOVE YOU...
...ASUKA.
I LOVE YOU.
FWAAA
HUG
ME TOO.

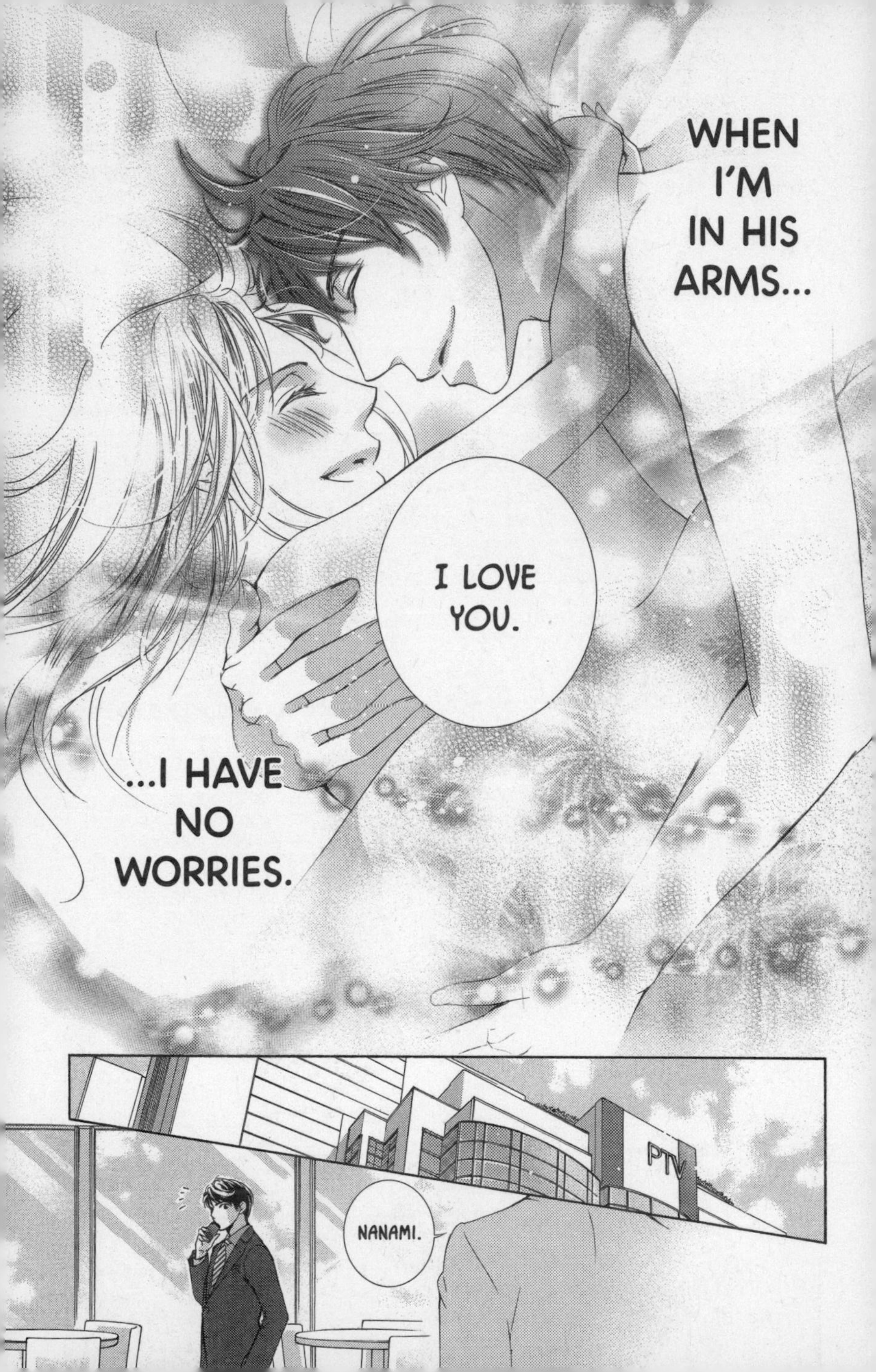
WHEN I'M IN HIS ARMS...
I LOVE YOU.
...I HAVE NO WORRIES.
PTV
NANAMI.

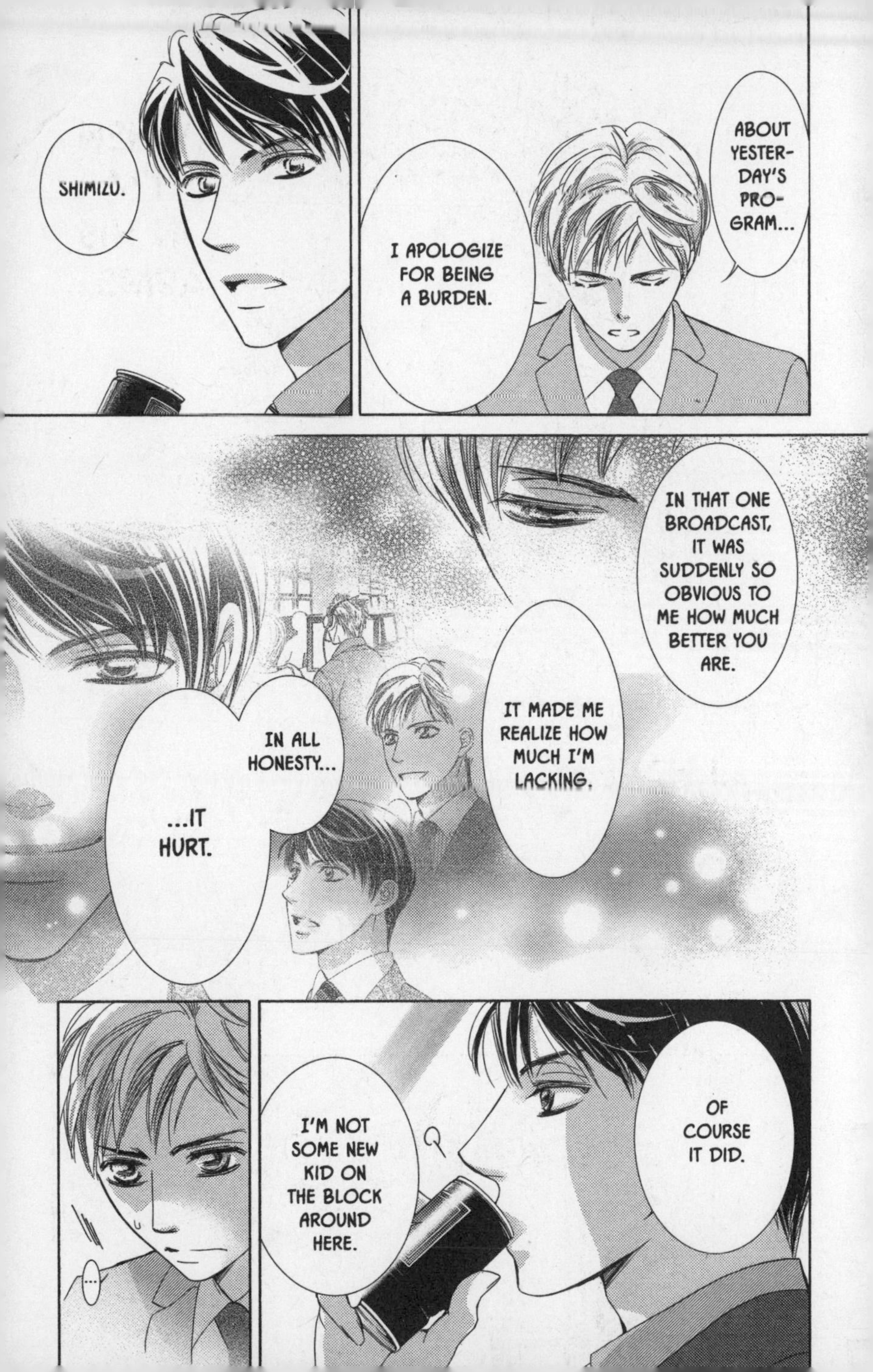
ABOUT YESTER-DAY'S PRO-GRAM...
I APOLOGIZE FOR BEING A BURDEN.
SHIMIZU.
IN THAT ONE BROADCAST, IT WAS SUDDENLY SO OBVIOUS TO ME HOW MUCH BETTER YOU ARE.
IT MADE ME REALIZE HOW MUCH I'M LACKING.
IN ALL HONESTY...
...IT HURT.
OF COURSE IT DID.
I'M NOT SOME NEW KID ON THE BLOCK AROUND HERE.
...

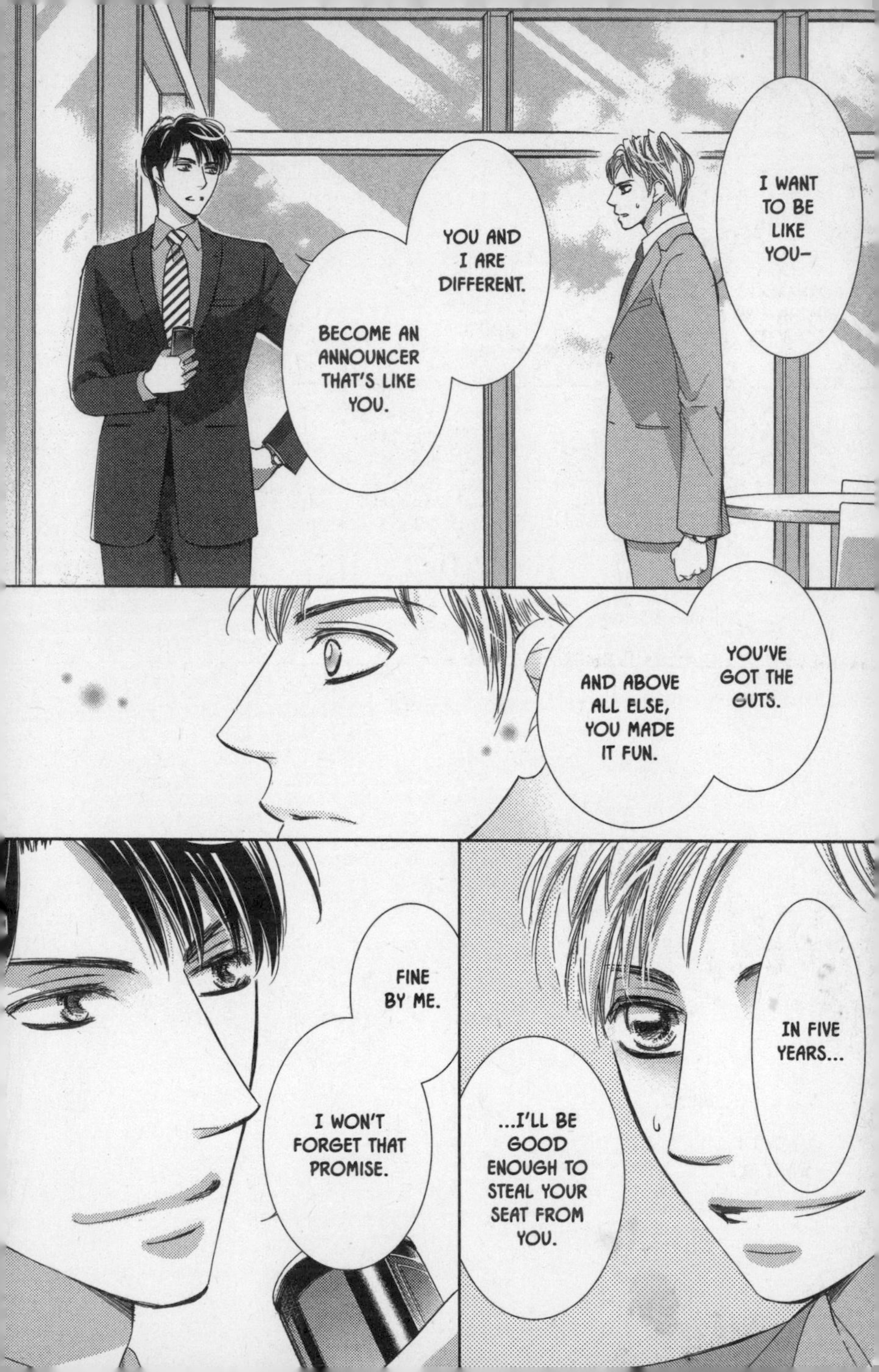
I WANT TO BE LIKE YOU–
YOU AND I ARE DIFFERENT.
BECOME AN ANNOUNCER THAT'S LIKE YOU.
YOU'VE GOT THE GUTS.
AND ABOVE ALL ELSE, YOU MADE IT FUN.
IN FIVE YEARS...
...I'LL BE GOOD ENOUGH TO STEAL YOUR SEAT FROM YOU.
FINE BY ME.
I WON'T FORGET THAT PROMISE.

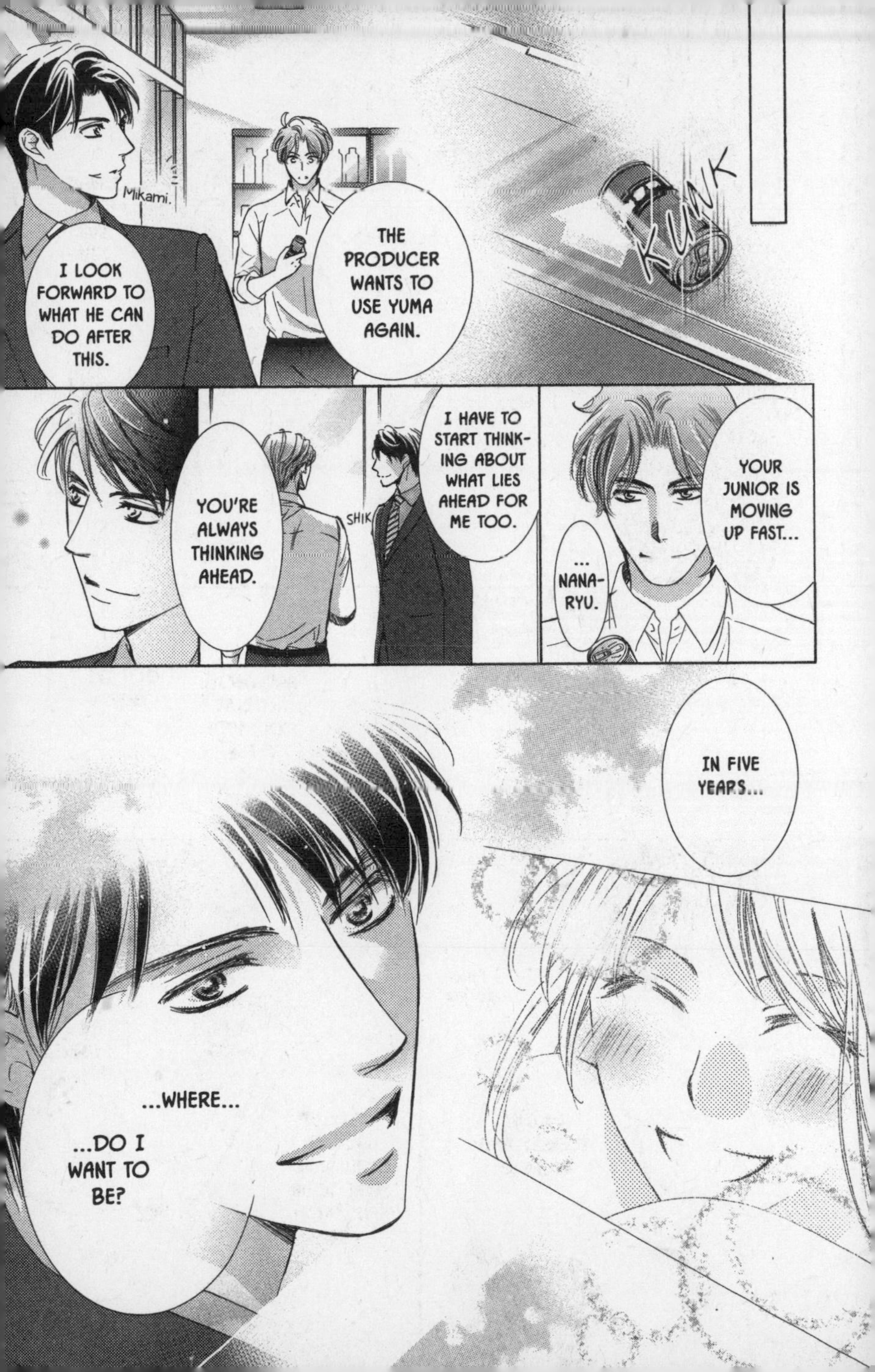
KUNK
THE PRODUCER WANTS TO USE YUMA AGAIN.
Mikami.
I LOOK FORWARD TO WHAT HE CAN DO AFTER THIS.
YOUR JUNIOR IS MOVING UP FAST...
...NANA-RYU.
I HAVE TO START THINKING ABOUT WHAT LIES AHEAD FOR ME TOO.
SHIK
YOU'RE ALWAYS THINKING AHEAD.
IN FIVE YEARS...
...WHERE...
...DO I WANT TO BE?

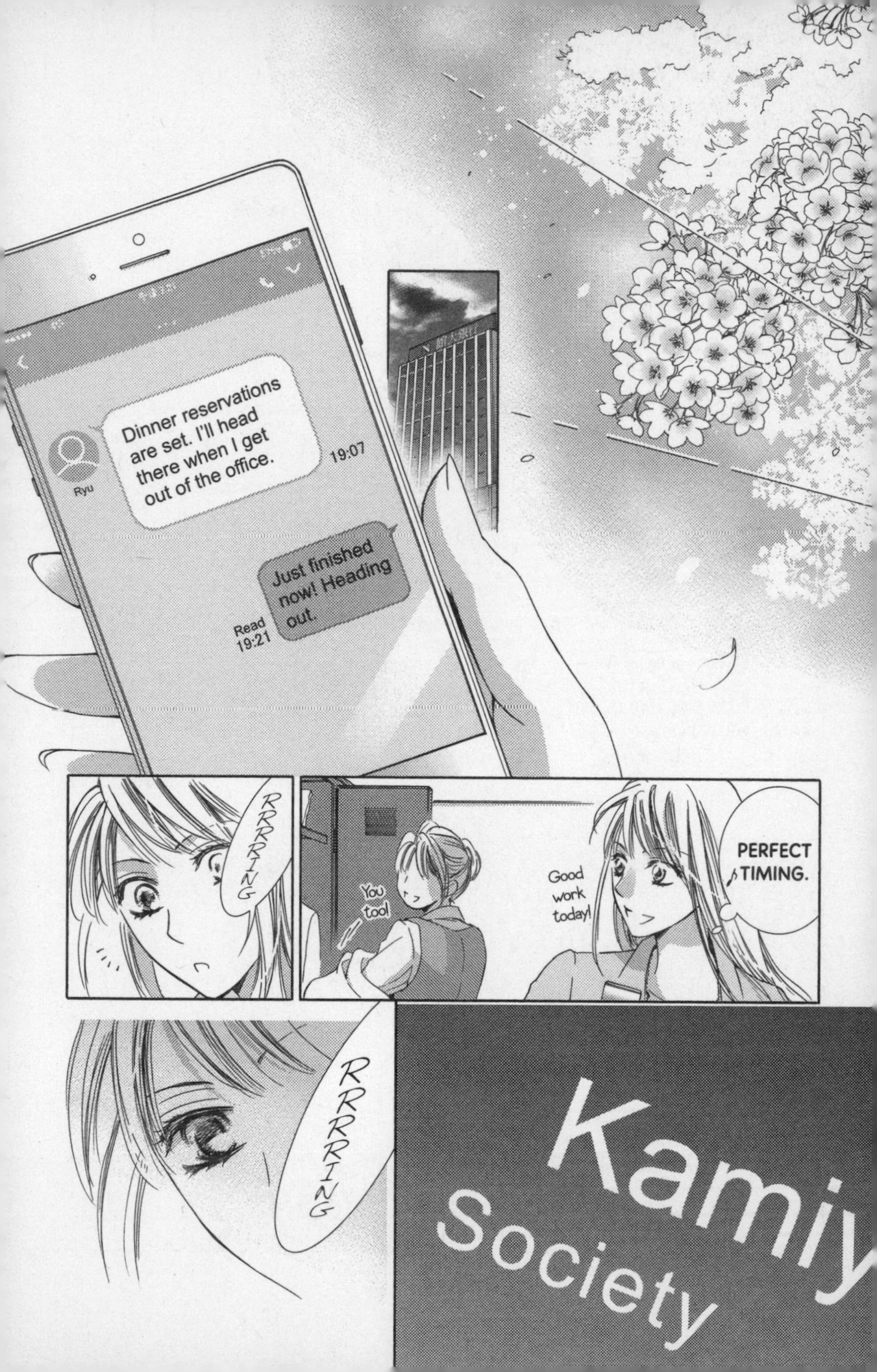
Ryu
Dinner reservations are set. I'll head there when I get out of the office.
19:07
Just finished now! Heading out.
Read 19:21
PERFECT TIMING.
Good work today!
You too!
RRRRING
Kamiy
Society
RRRRING

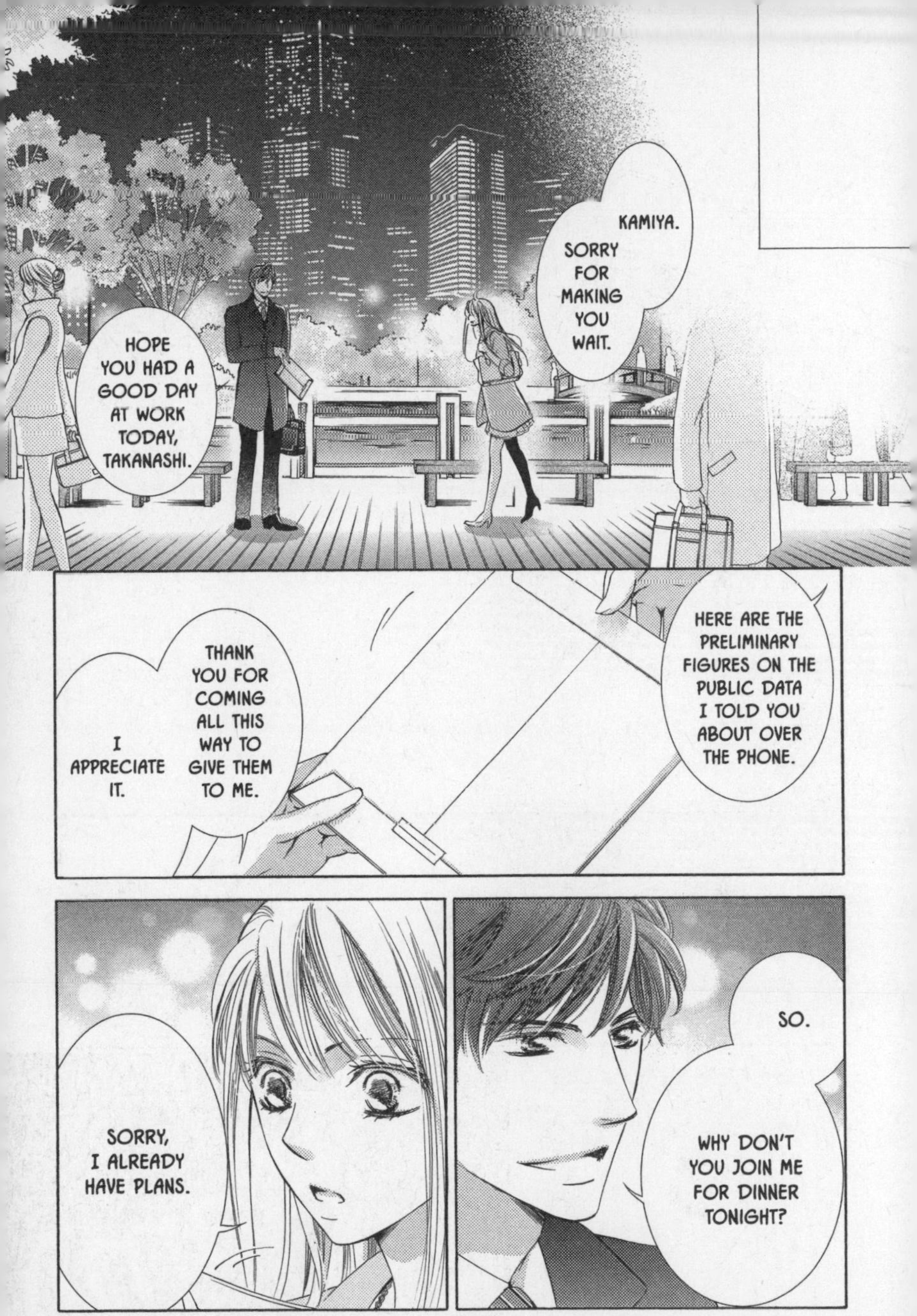
KAMIYA. SORRY FOR MAKING YOU WAIT.
HOPE YOU HAD A GOOD DAY AT WORK TODAY, TAKANASHI.
HERE ARE THE PRELIMINARY FIGURES ON THE PUBLIC DATA I TOLD YOU ABOUT OVER THE PHONE.
THANK YOU FOR COMING ALL THIS WAY TO GIVE THEM TO ME.
I APPRECIATE IT.
SO.
WHY DON'T YOU JOIN ME FOR DINNER TONIGHT?
SORRY, I ALREADY HAVE PLANS.

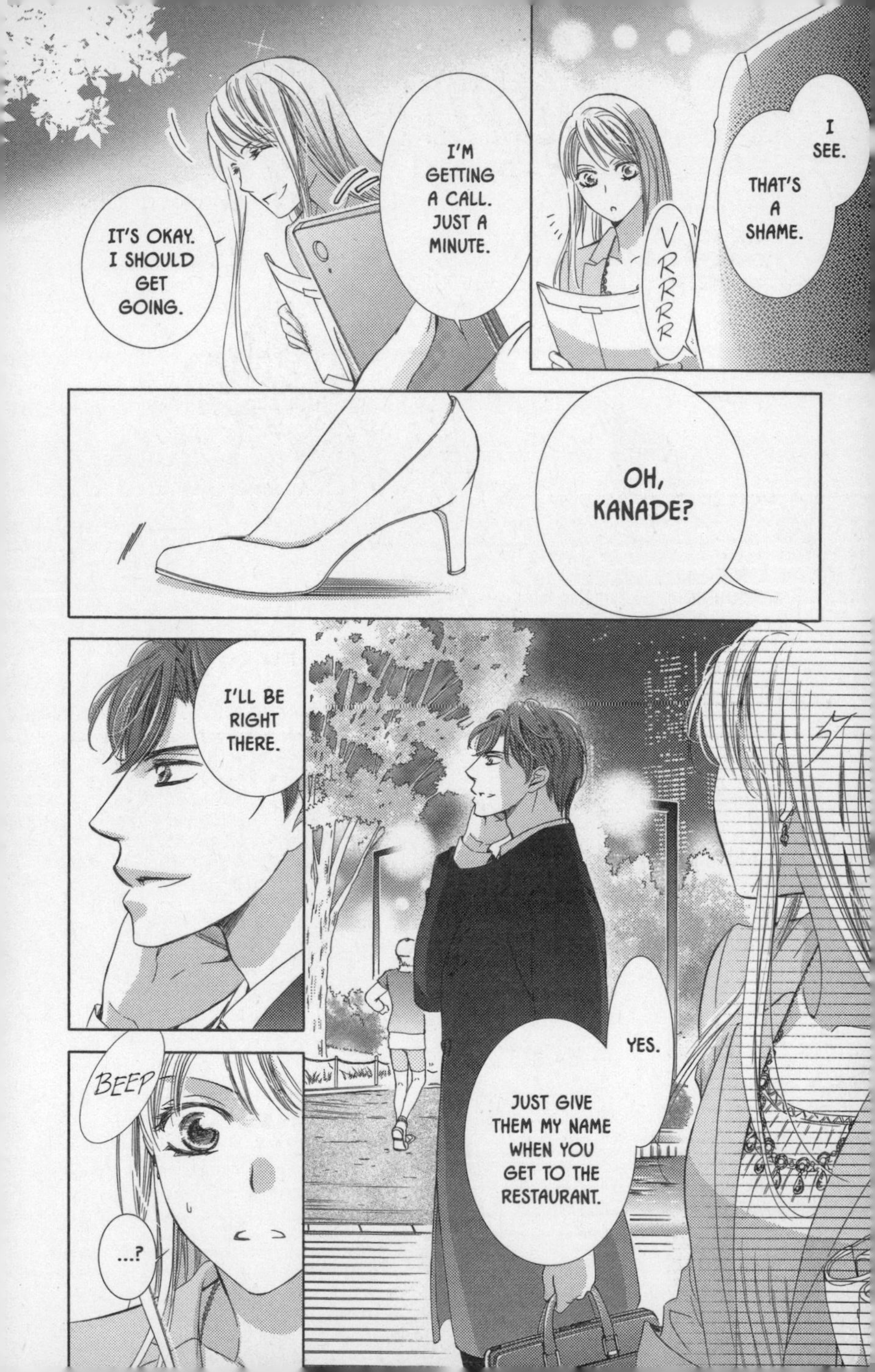
I SEE.
THAT'S A SHAME.
VRRRR
I'M GETTING A CALL. JUST A MINUTE.
IT'S OKAY. I SHOULD GET GOING.
OH, KANADE?
YES.
JUST GIVE THEM MY NAME WHEN YOU GET TO THE RESTAURANT.
I'LL BE RIGHT THERE.
BEEP
...?

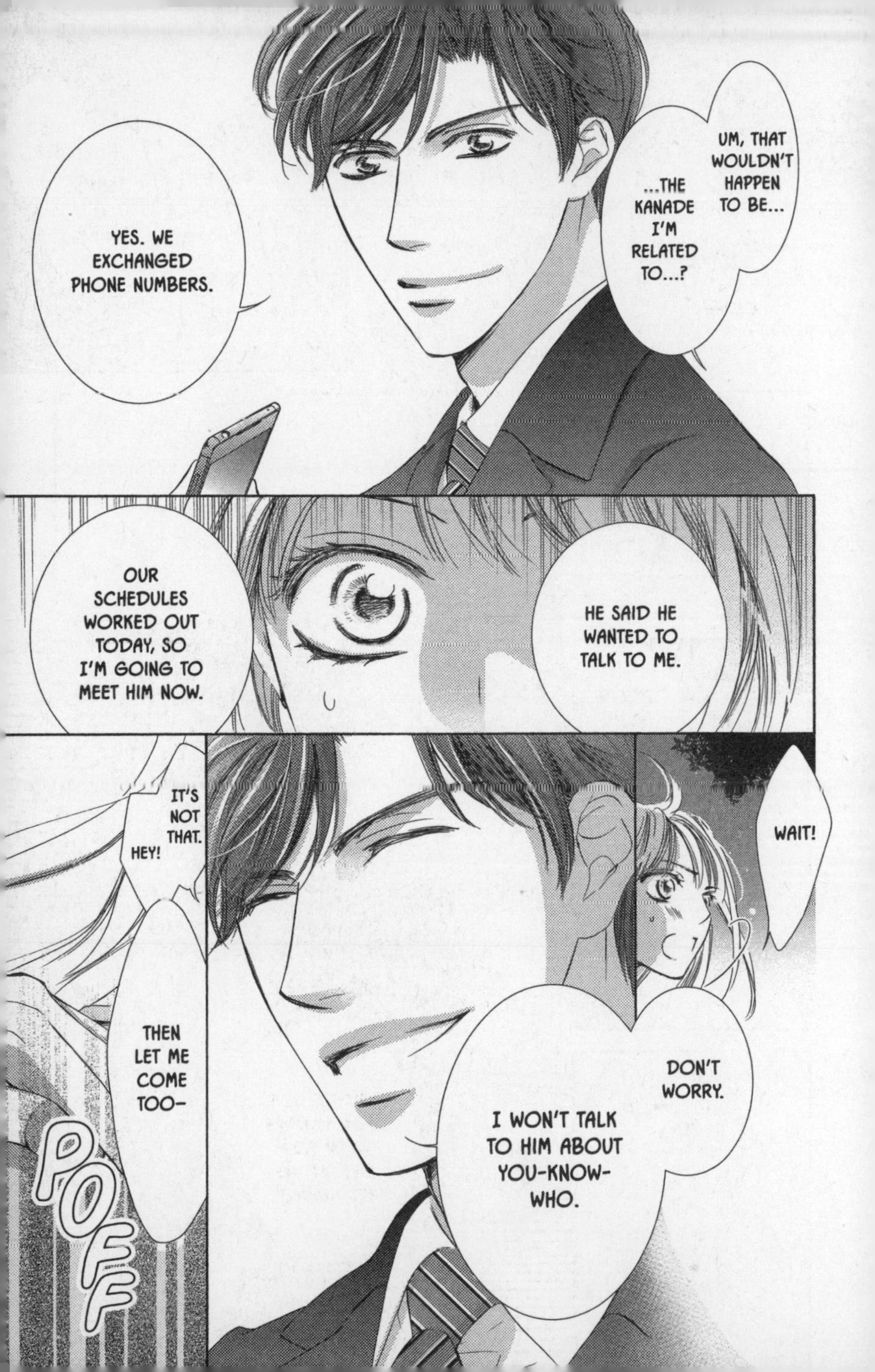
UM, THAT WOULDN'T HAPPEN TO BE...
...THE KANADE I'M RELATED TO...?
YES. WE EXCHANGED PHONE NUMBERS.
HE SAID HE WANTED TO TALK TO ME.
OUR SCHEDULES WORKED OUT TODAY, SO I'M GOING TO MEET HIM NOW.
WAIT!
DON'T WORRY.
I WON'T TALK TO HIM ABOUT YOU-KNOW-WHO.
IT'S NOT THAT.
HEY!
THEN LET ME COME TOO—
POFF

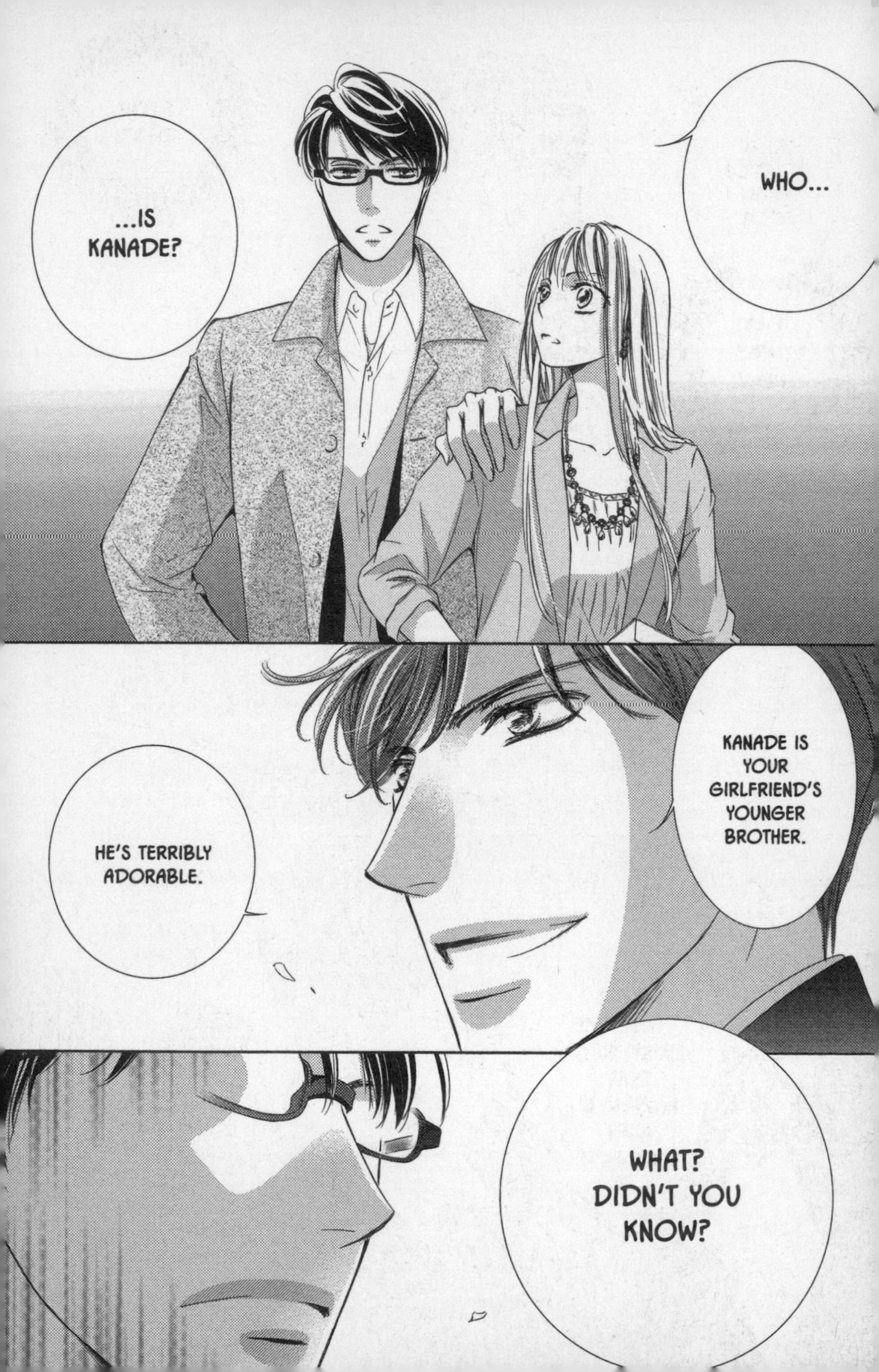
WHO...
...IS KANADE?
KANADE IS YOUR GIRLFRIEND'S YOUNGER BROTHER.
HE'S TERRIBLY ADORABLE.
WHAT? DIDN'T YOU KNOW?

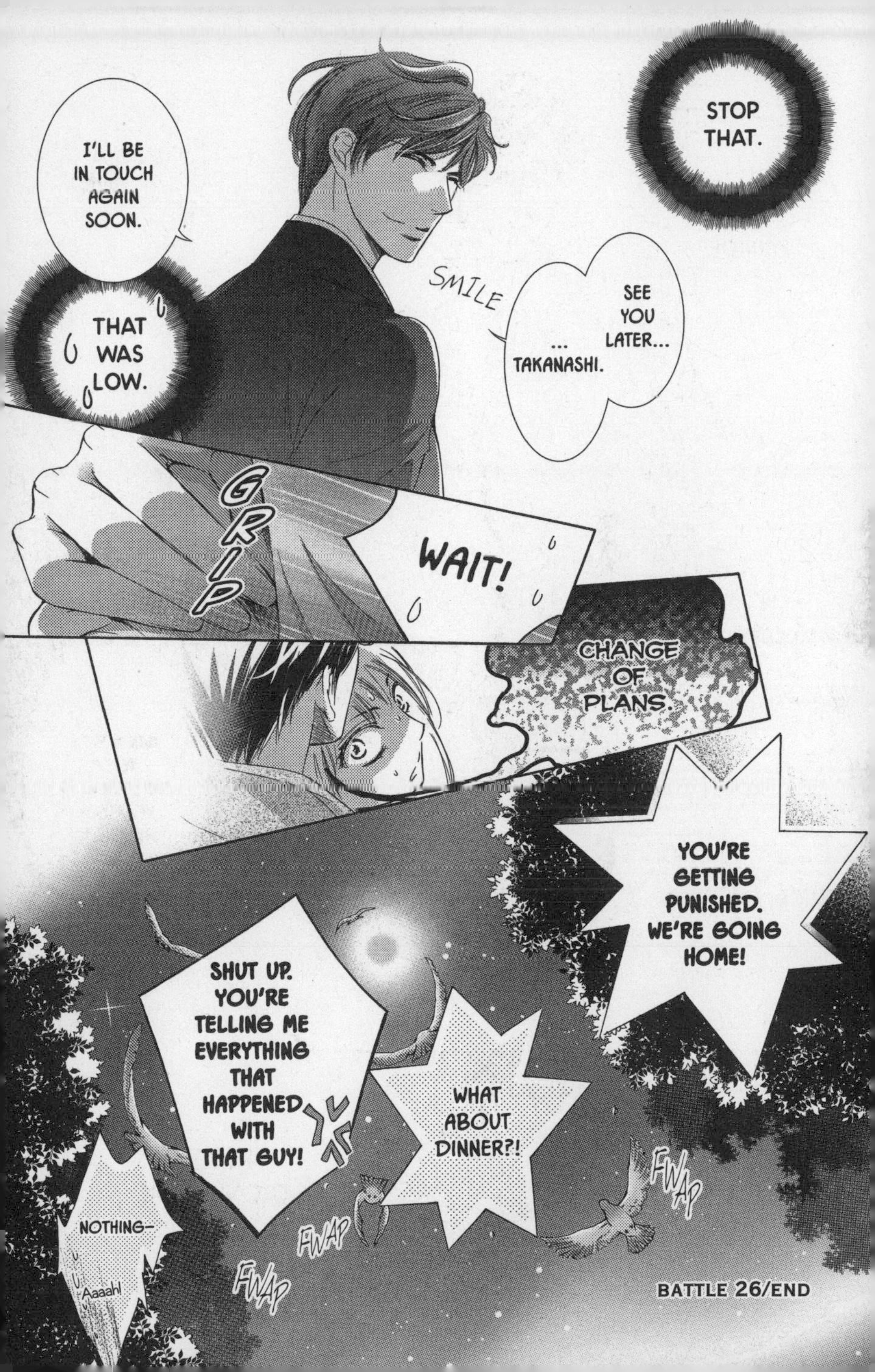
STOP THAT.
SMILE
SEE YOU LATER... ...TAKANASHI.
I'LL BE IN TOUCH AGAIN SOON.
THAT WAS LOW.
WAIT!
GRIP
CHANGE OF PLANS.
YOU'RE GETTING PUNISHED. WE'RE GOING HOME!
FWAP
WHAT ABOUT DINNER?!
SHUT UP. YOU'RE TELLING ME EVERYTHING THAT HAPPENED WITH THAT GUY!
FWAP
FWAP
NOTHING-
Aaaah!
BATTLE 26/END

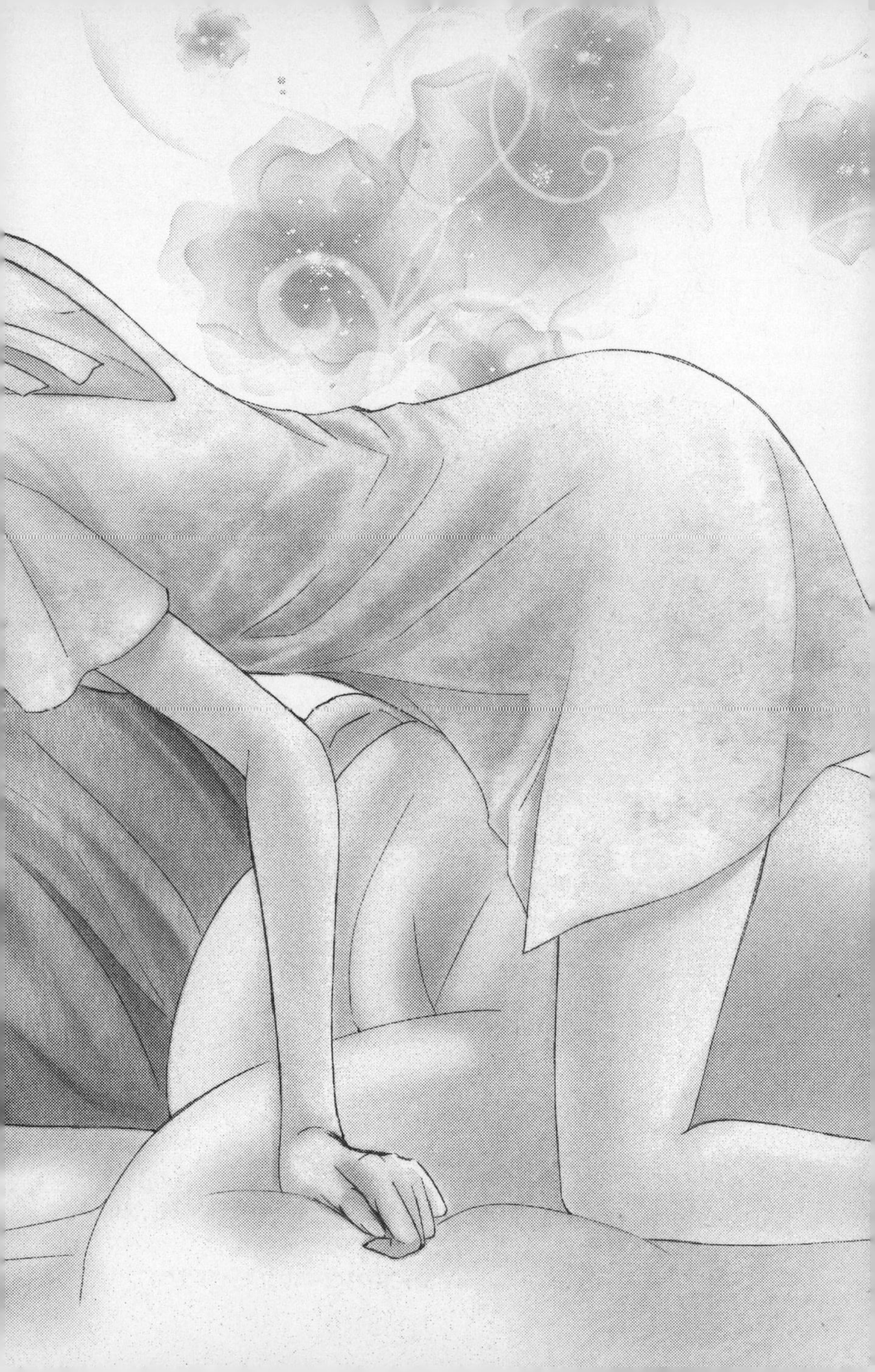

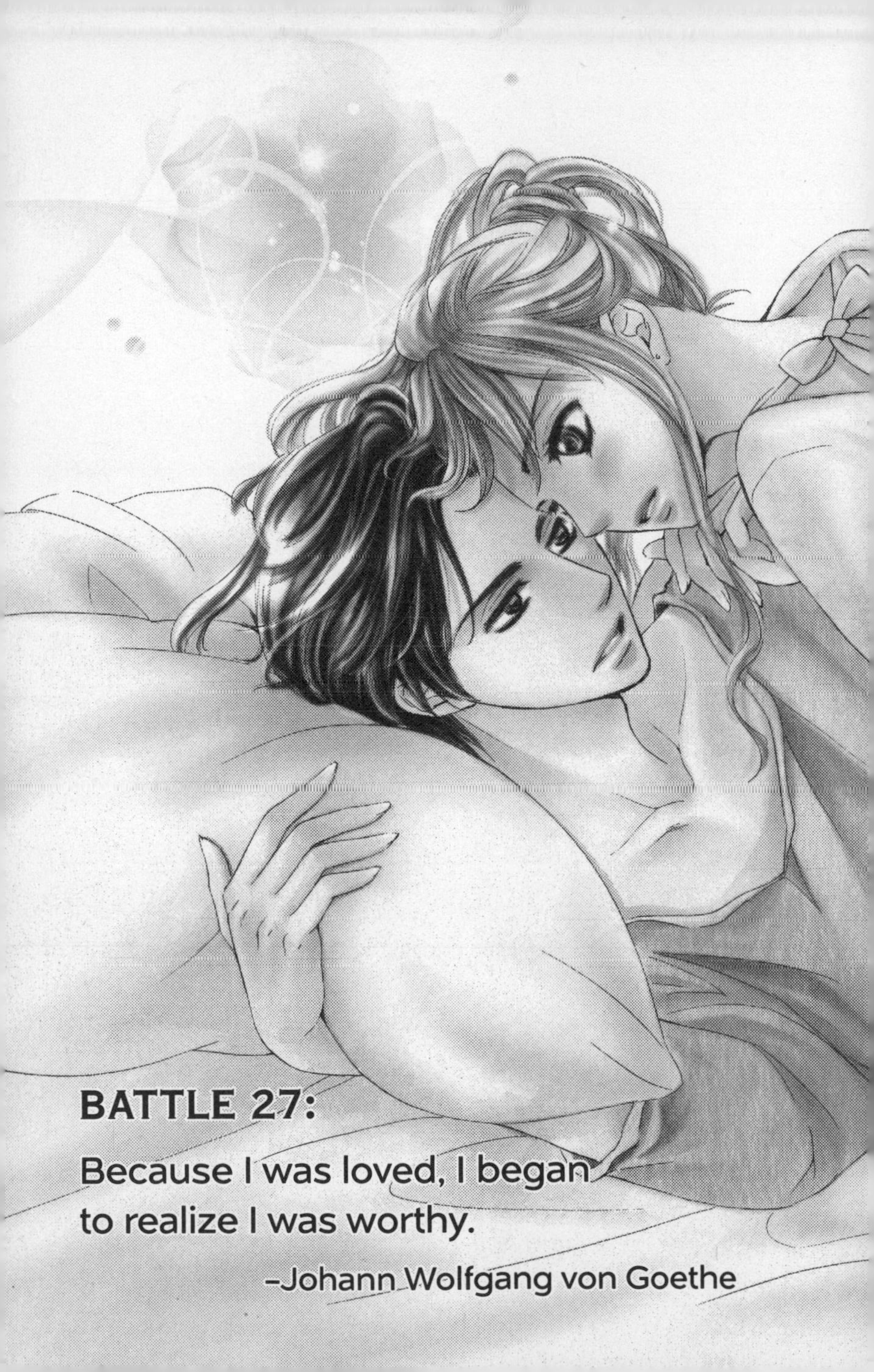
BATTLE 27:
Because I was loved, I began to realize I was worthy.
–Johann Wolfgang von Goethe

Everyone's
Getting
Married

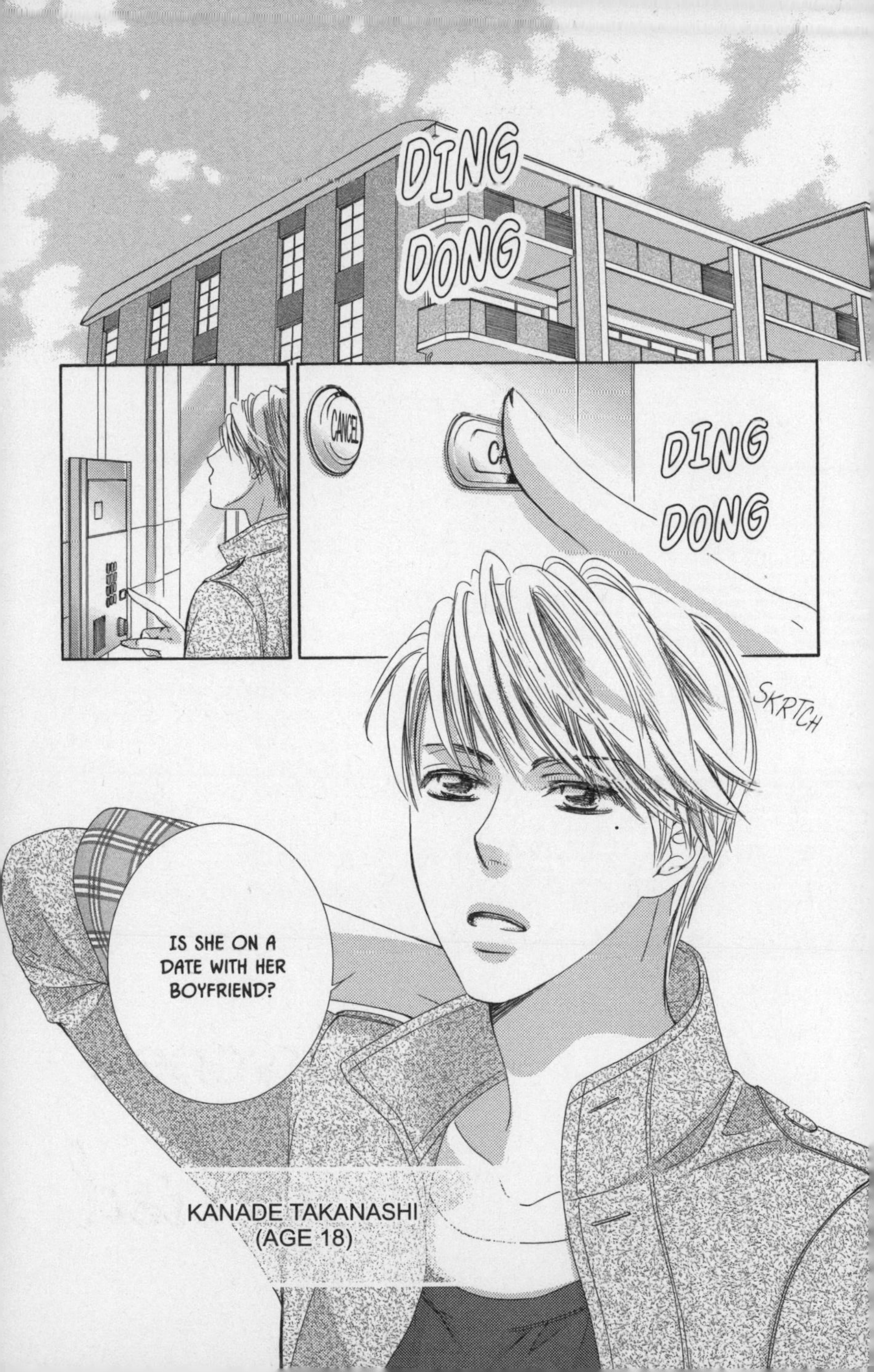
DING DONG
CANCEL
DING DONG
SKRTCH
IS SHE ON A DATE WITH HER BOYFRIEND?
KANADE TAKANASHI (AGE 18)

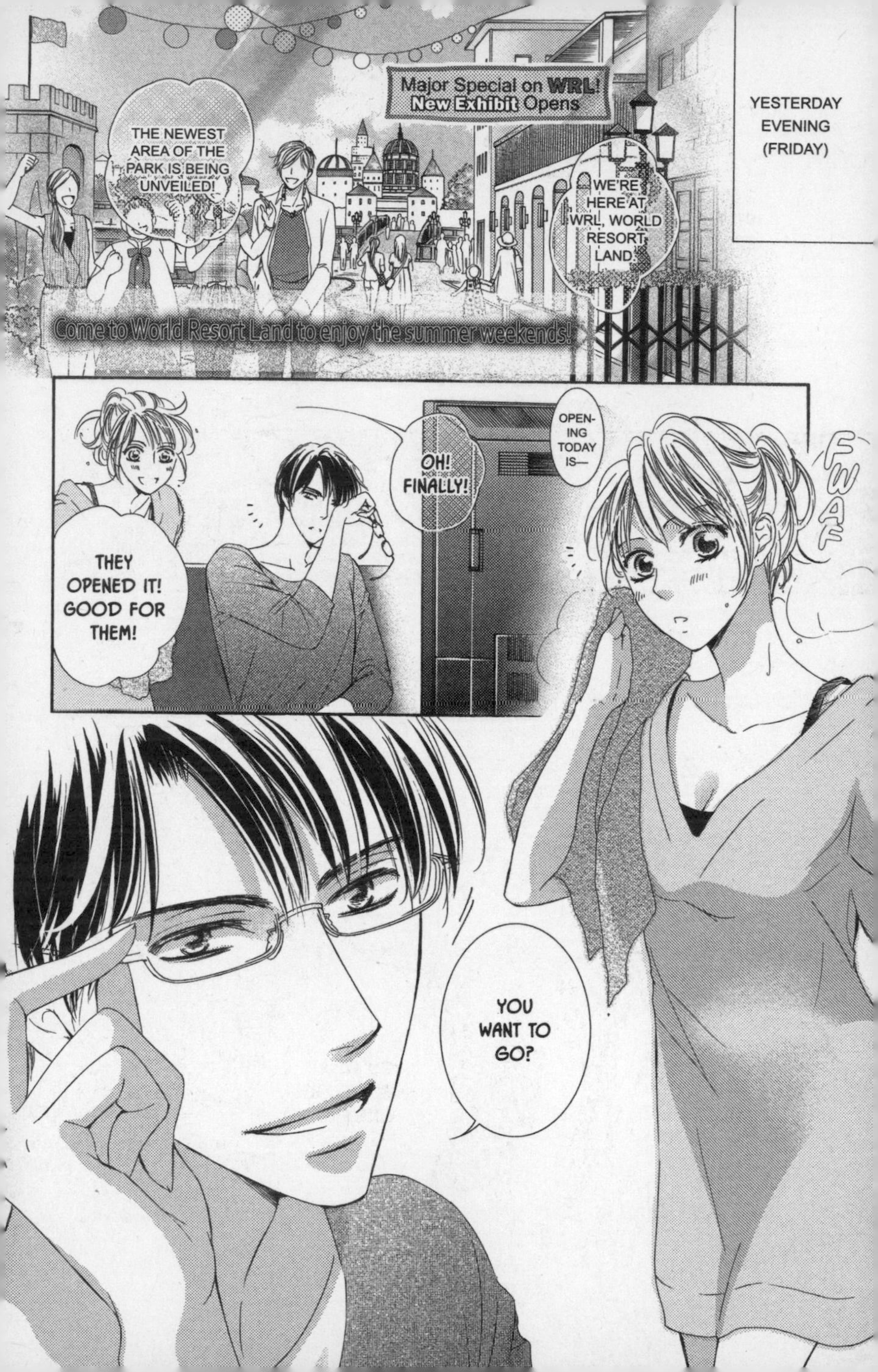
YESTERDAY EVENING (FRIDAY)
Major Special on WRL! New Exhibit Opens
WE'RE HERE AT WRL, WORLD RESORT LAND.
THE NEWEST AREA OF THE PARK IS BEING UNVEILED!
Come to World Resort Land to enjoy the summer weekends!
FWAF
OPEN-ING TODAY IS—
OH! FINALLY!
THEY OPENED IT! GOOD FOR THEM!
YOU WANT TO GO?

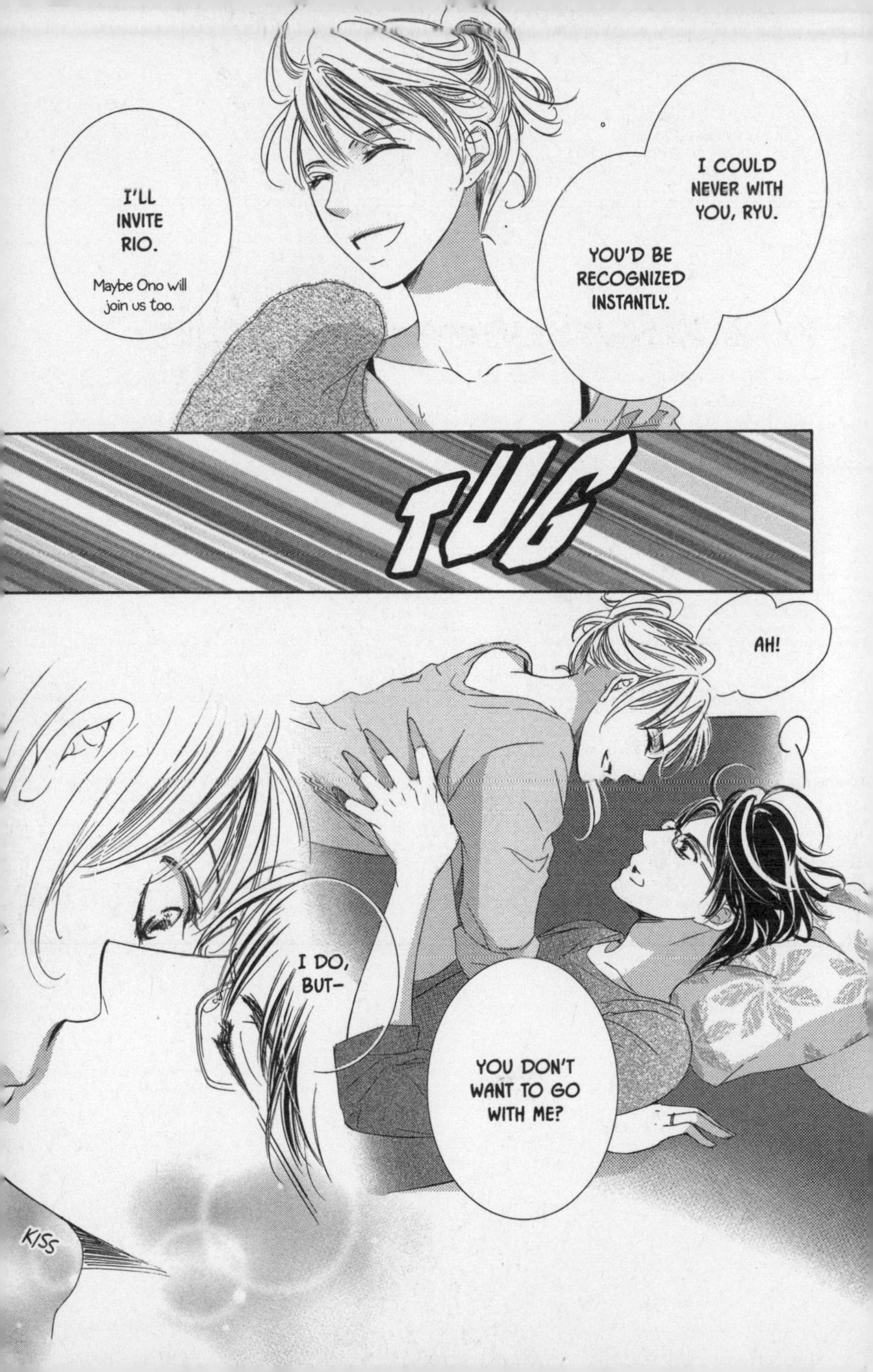
I COULD NEVER WITH YOU, RYU.
YOU'D BE RECOGNIZED INSTANTLY.
I'LL INVITE RIO.
Maybe Ono will join us too.
TUG
AH!
YOU DON'T WANT TO GO WITH ME?
I DO, BUT-
KISS

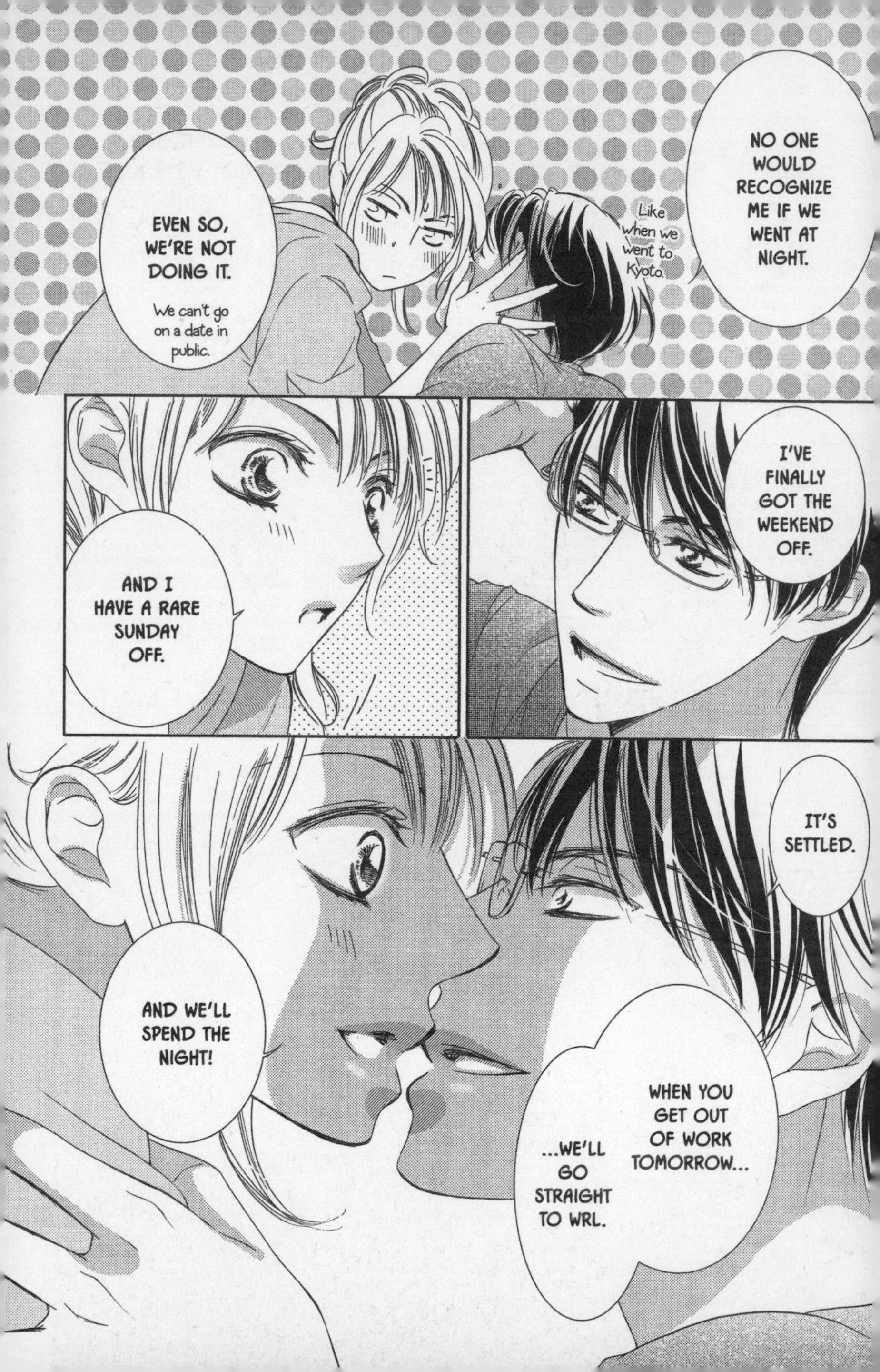
NO ONE WOULD RECOGNIZE ME IF WE WENT AT NIGHT.
Like when we went to Kyoto.
EVEN SO, WE'RE NOT DOING IT.
We can't go on a date in public.
I'VE FINALLY GOT THE WEEKEND OFF.
AND I HAVE A RARE SUNDAY OFF.
IT'S SETTLED.
WHEN YOU GET OUT OF WORK TOMORROW...
...WE'LL GO STRAIGHT TO WRL.
AND WE'LL SPEND THE NIGHT!

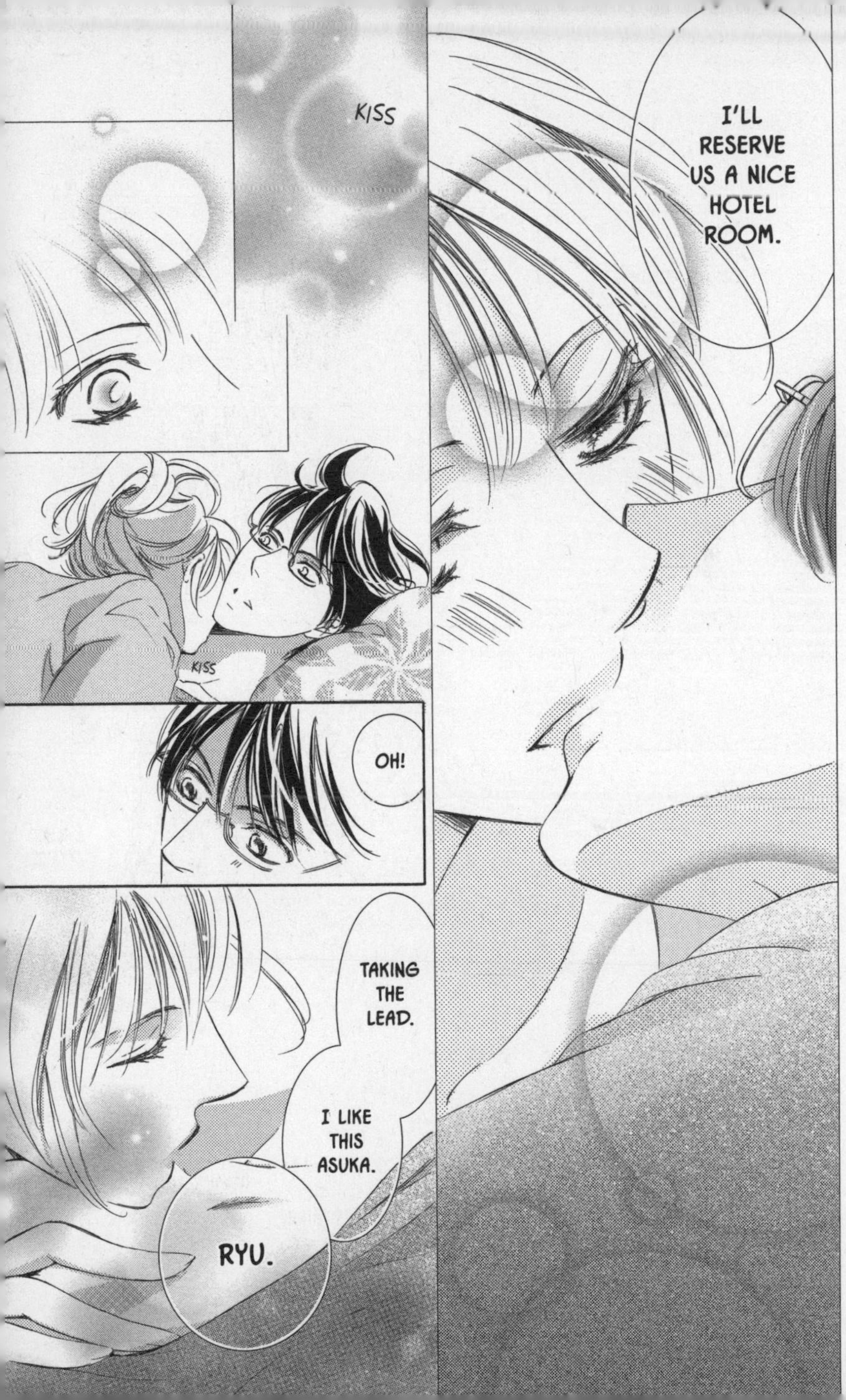
I'LL RESERVE US A NICE HOTEL ROOM.
KISS
KISS
OH!
TAKING THE LEAD.
I LIKE THIS ASUKA.
RYU.

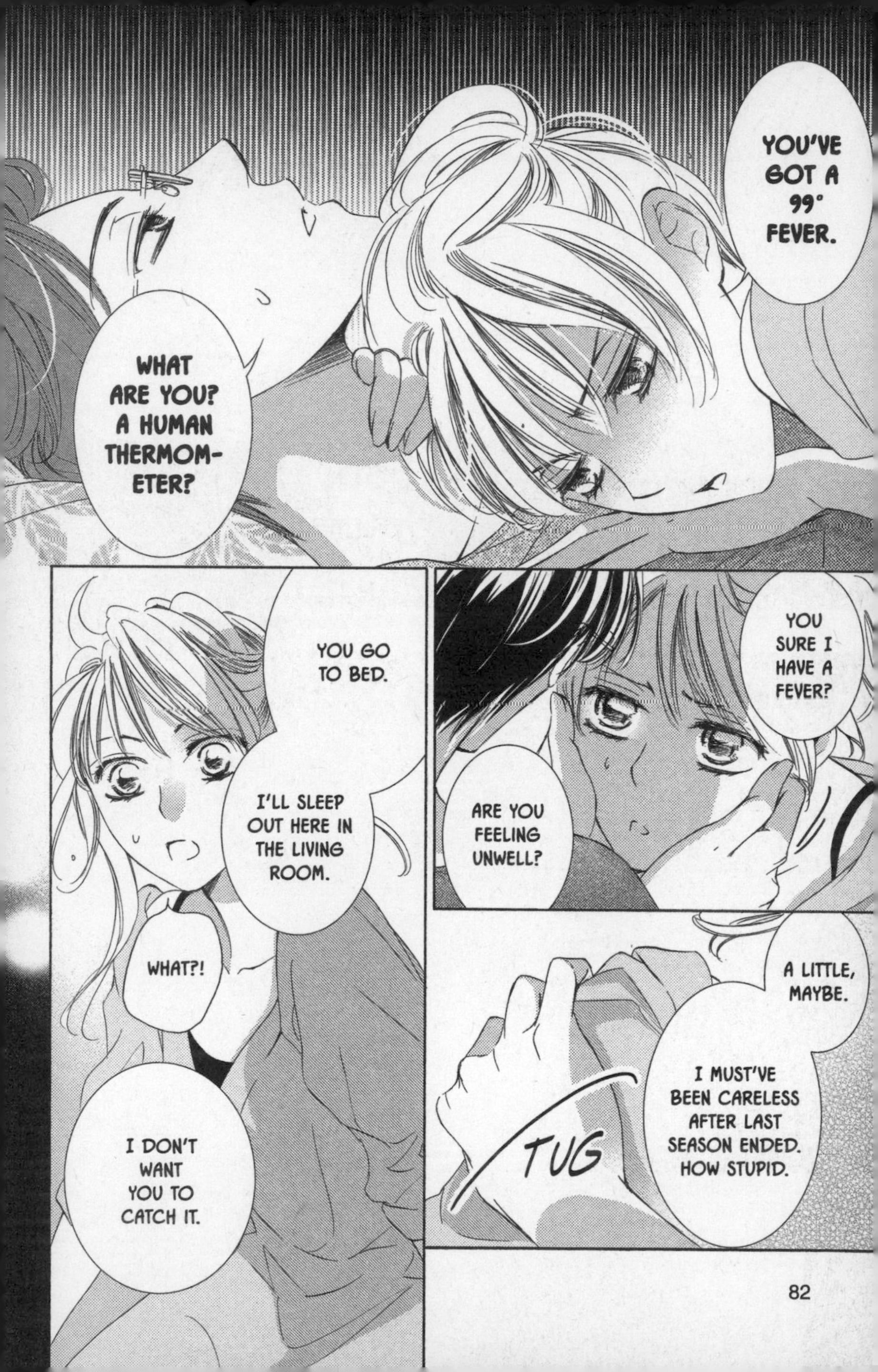
YOU'VE GOT A 99° FEVER.
WHAT ARE YOU? A HUMAN THERMOM-ETER?
YOU SURE I HAVE A FEVER?
ARE YOU FEELING UNWELL?
A LITTLE, MAYBE.
I MUST'VE BEEN CARELESS AFTER LAST SEASON ENDED. HOW STUPID.
TUG
YOU GO TO BED.
I'LL SLEEP OUT HERE IN THE LIVING ROOM.
WHAT?!
I DON'T WANT YOU TO CATCH IT.

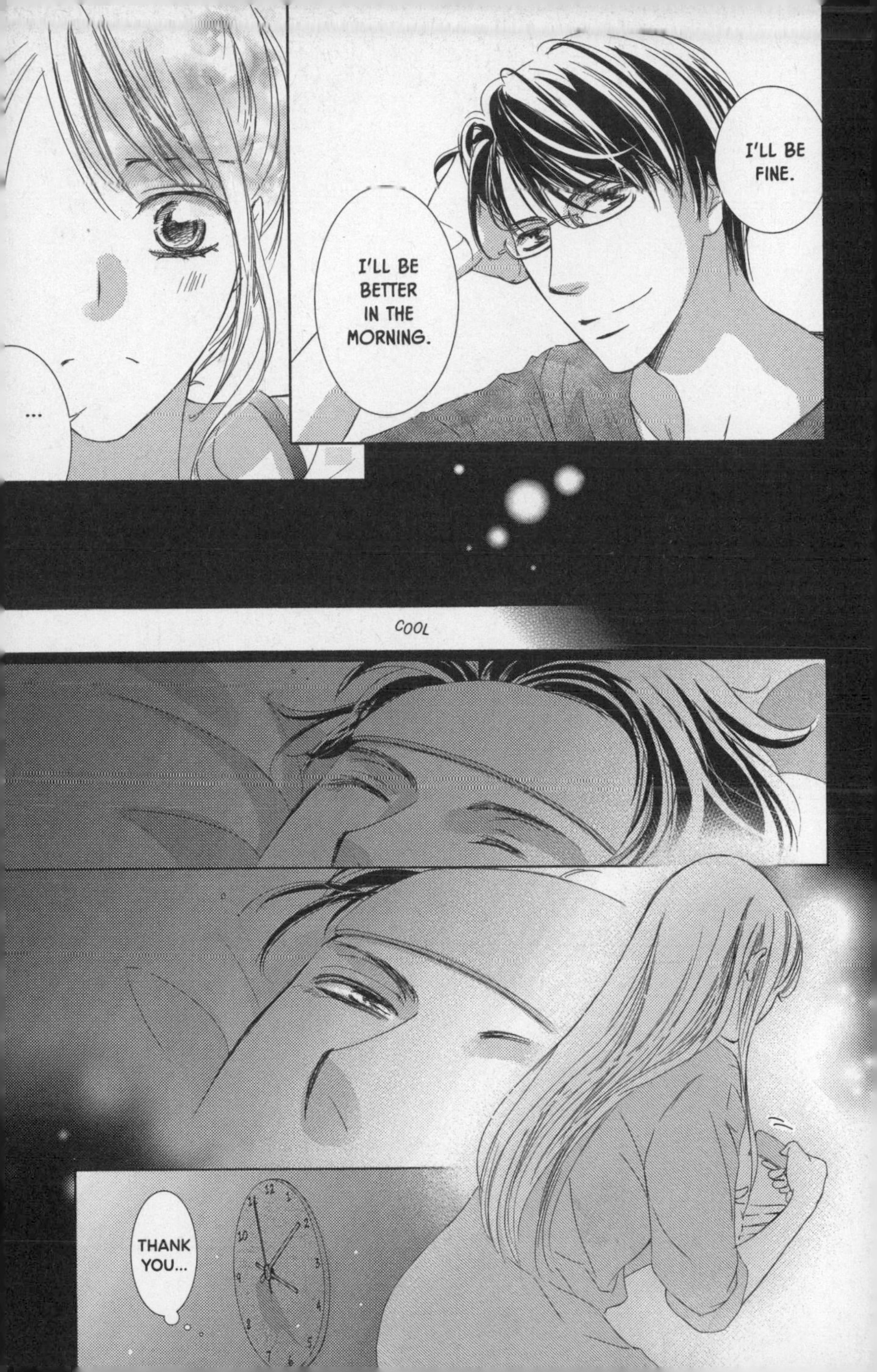
I'LL BE FINE.
I'LL BE BETTER IN THE MORNING.
...
COOL
THANK YOU...

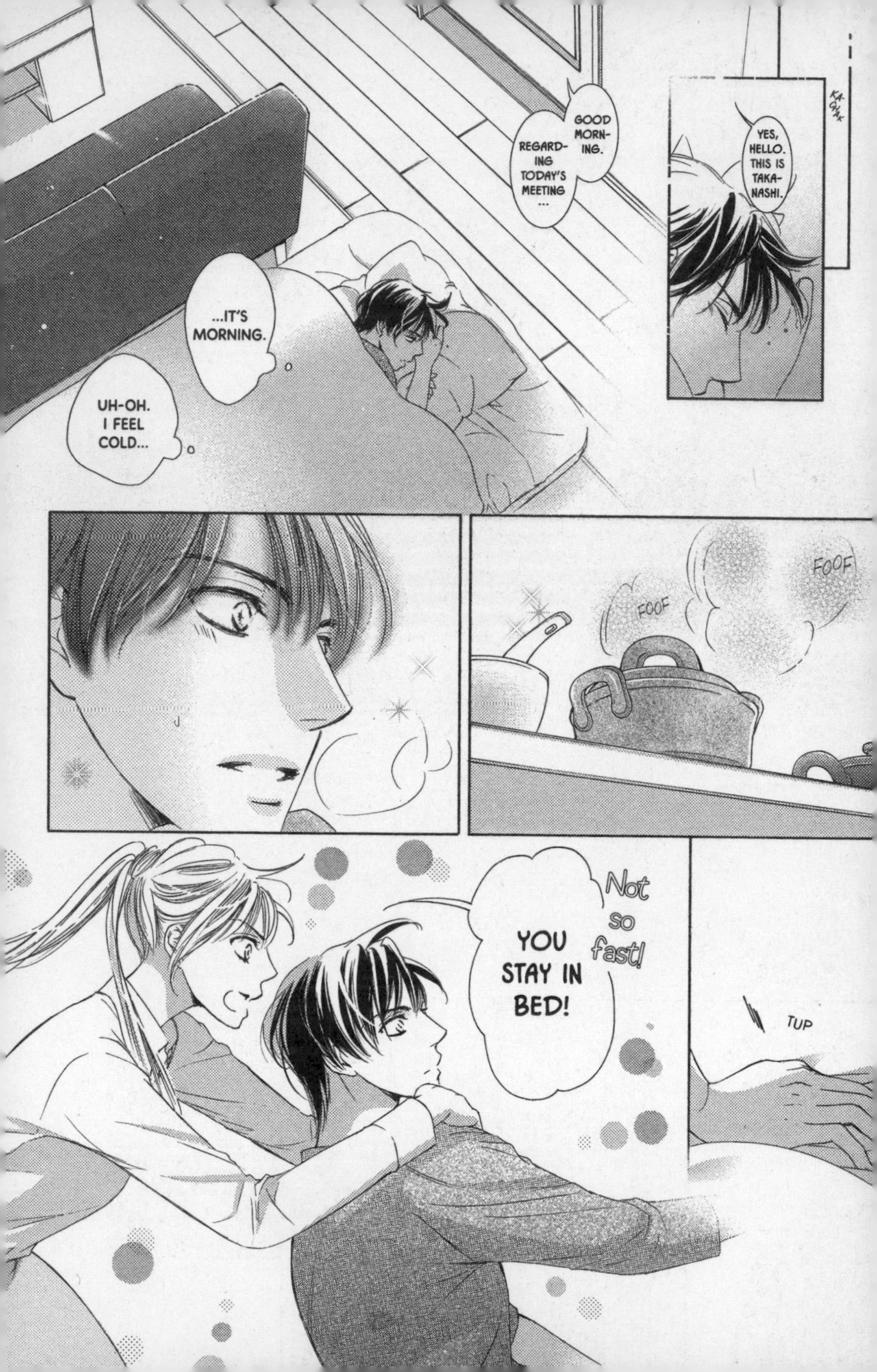
KA-CHAK
YES, HELLO. THIS IS TAKA-NASHI.
GOOD MORN-ING.
REGARD-ING TODAY'S MEETING ...
...IT'S MORNING.
UH-OH. I FEEL COLD...
FOOF
FOOF
TUP
Not so fast!
YOU STAY IN BED!

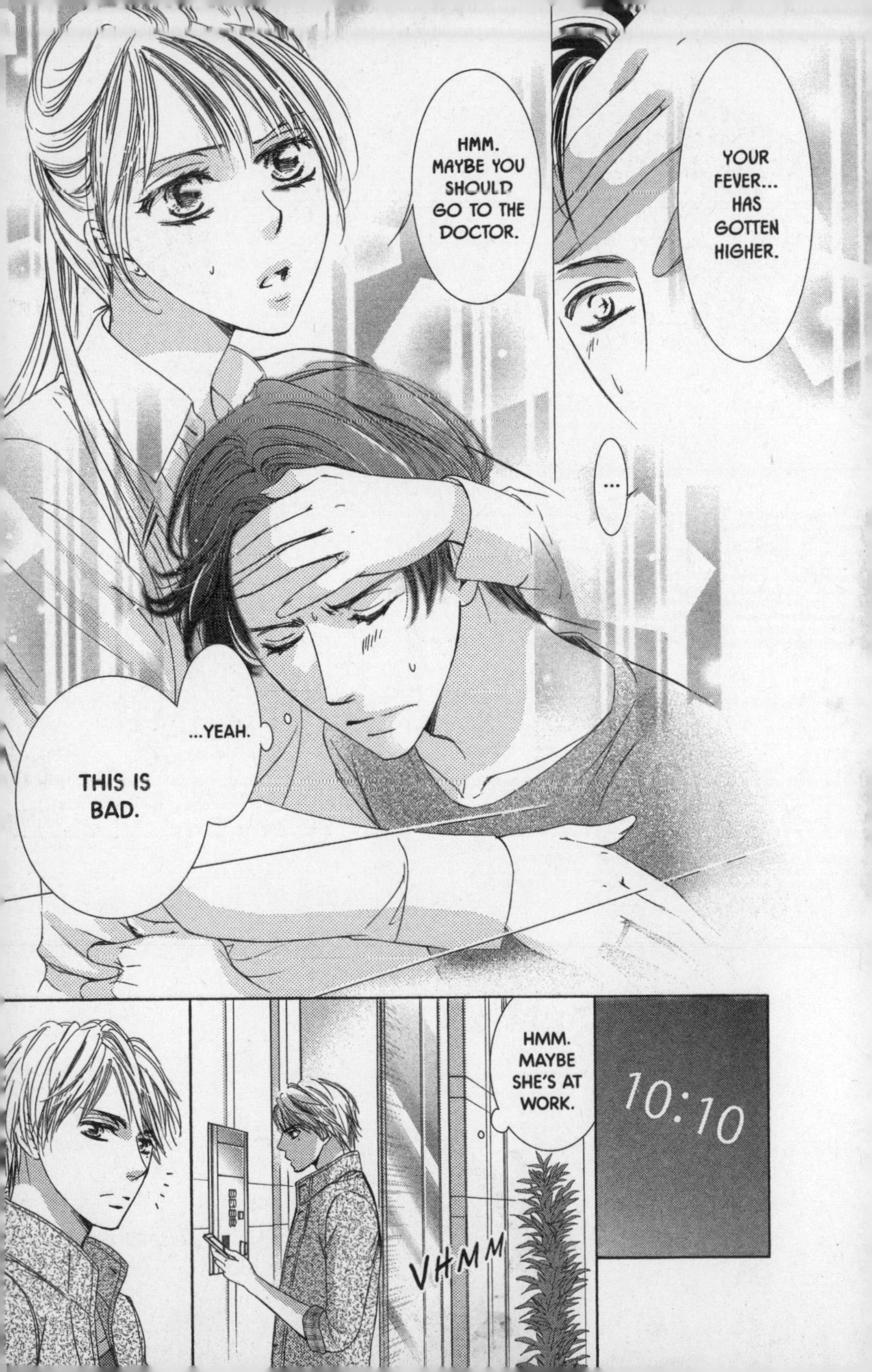
YOUR FEVER... HAS GOTTEN HIGHER.
HMM. MAYBE YOU SHOULD GO TO THE DOCTOR.
...
...YEAH.
THIS IS BAD.
10:10
HMM. MAYBE SHE'S AT WORK.
VHMM

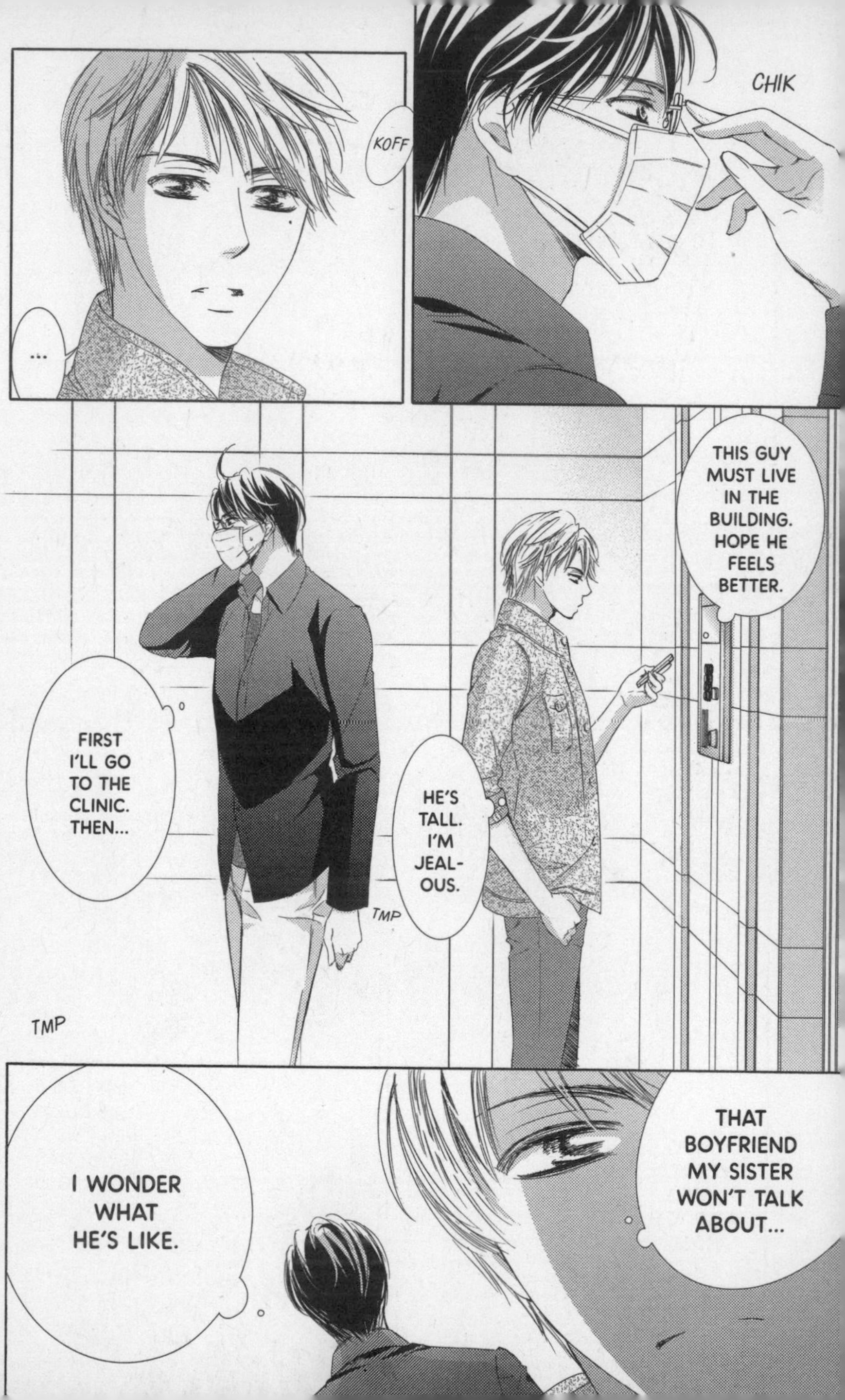
CHIK
KOFF
...
THIS GUY MUST LIVE IN THE BUILDING. HOPE HE FEELS BETTER.
HE'S TALL. I'M JEAL-OUS.
TMP
FIRST I'LL GO TO THE CLINIC. THEN...
TMP
THAT BOYFRIEND MY SISTER WON'T TALK ABOUT...
I WONDER WHAT HE'S LIKE.

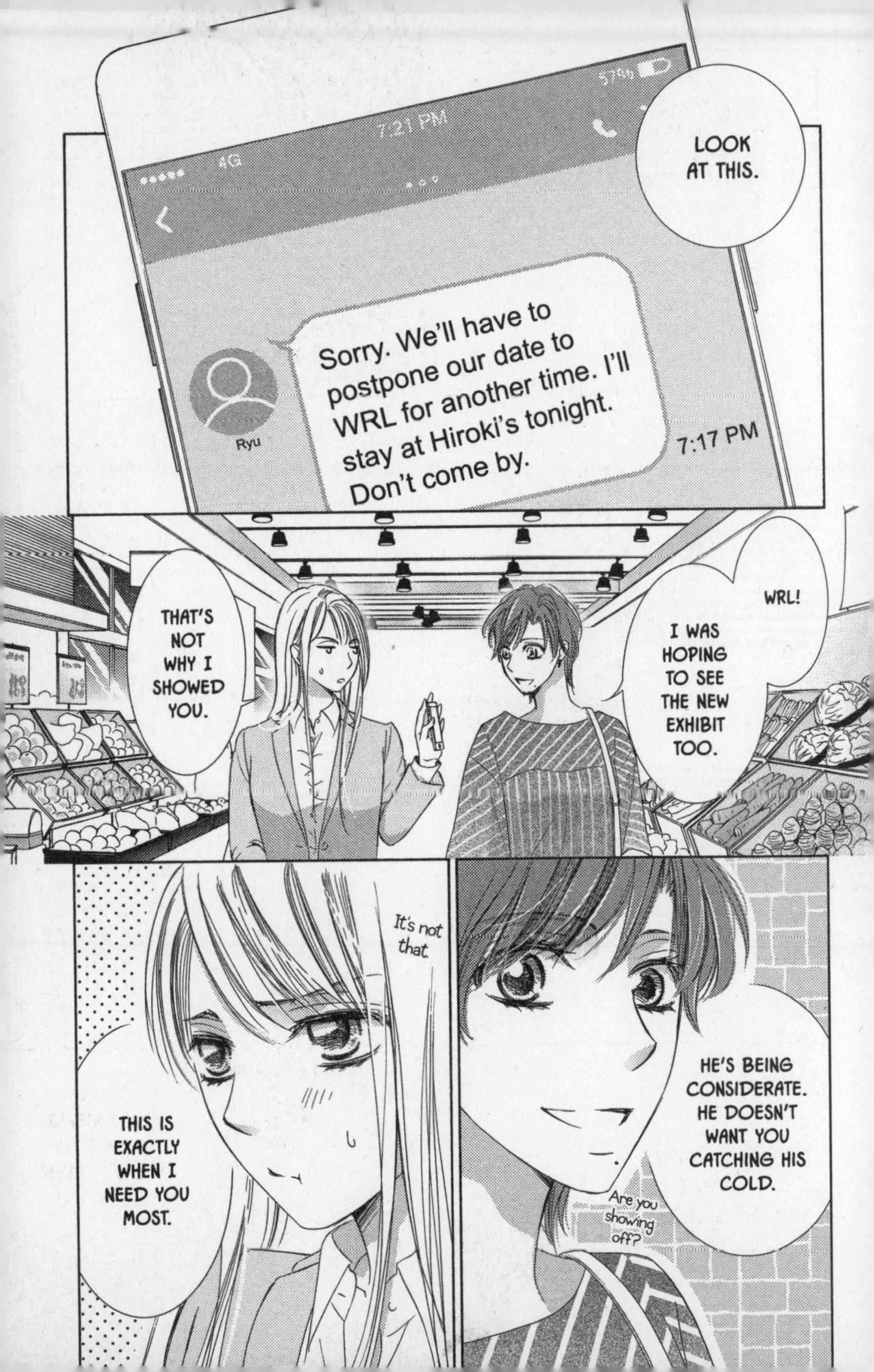
LOOK AT THIS.
4G
7:21 PM
Sorry. We'll have to postpone our date to WRL for another time. I'll stay at Hiroki's tonight. Don't come by.
Ryu
7:17 PM
WRL! I WAS HOPING TO SEE THE NEW EXHIBIT TOO.
THAT'S NOT WHY I SHOWED YOU.
HE'S BEING CONSIDERATE. HE DOESN'T WANT YOU CATCHING HIS COLD.
Are you showing off?
It's not that.
THIS IS EXACTLY WHEN I NEED YOU MOST.

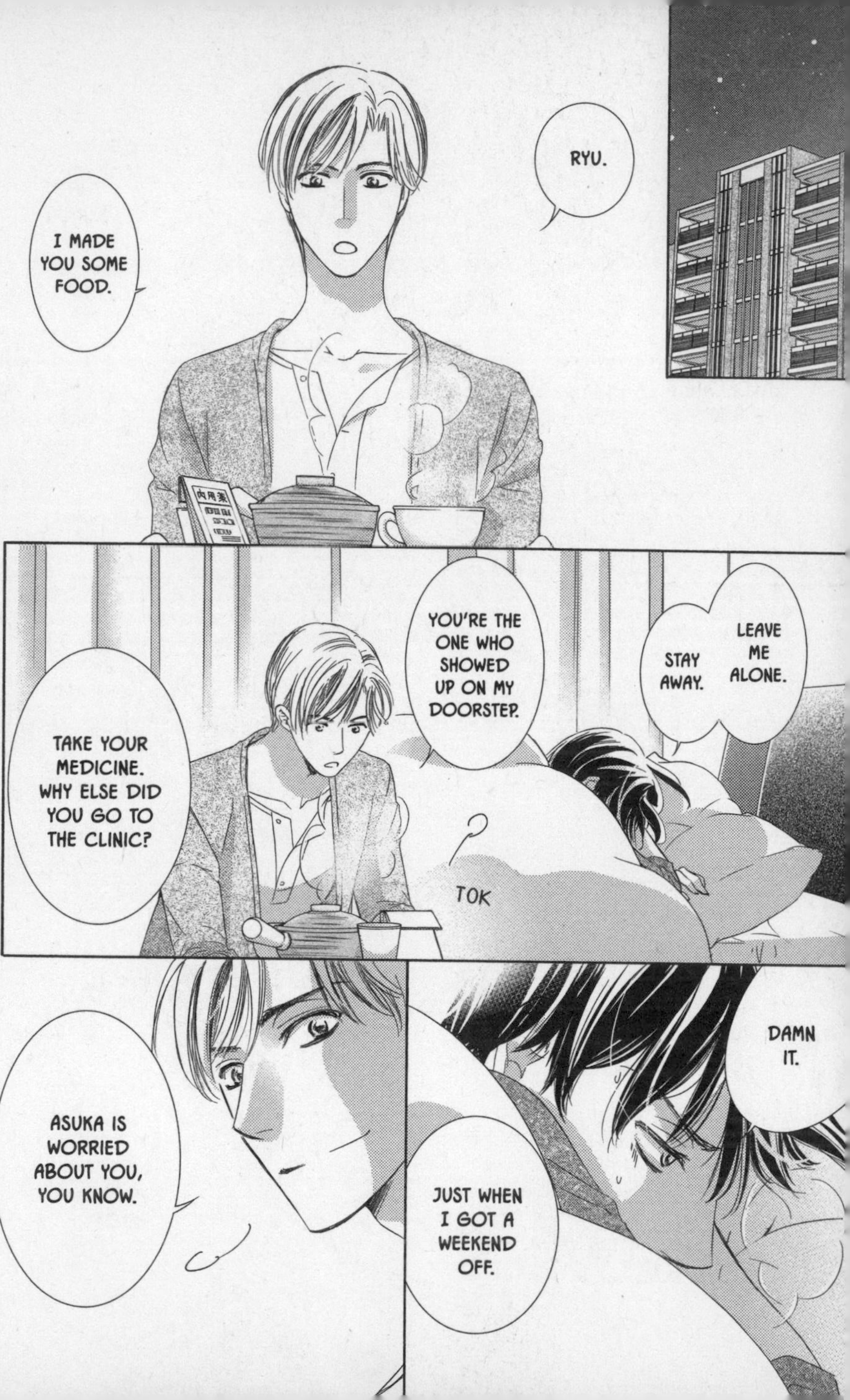
RYU.
I MADE YOU SOME FOOD.
内用薬
LEAVE ME ALONE.
STAY AWAY.
YOU'RE THE ONE WHO SHOWED UP ON MY DOORSTEP.
TOK
TAKE YOUR MEDICINE. WHY ELSE DID YOU GO TO THE CLINIC?
DAMN IT.
JUST WHEN I GOT A WEEKEND OFF.
ASUKA IS WORRIED ABOUT YOU, YOU KNOW.

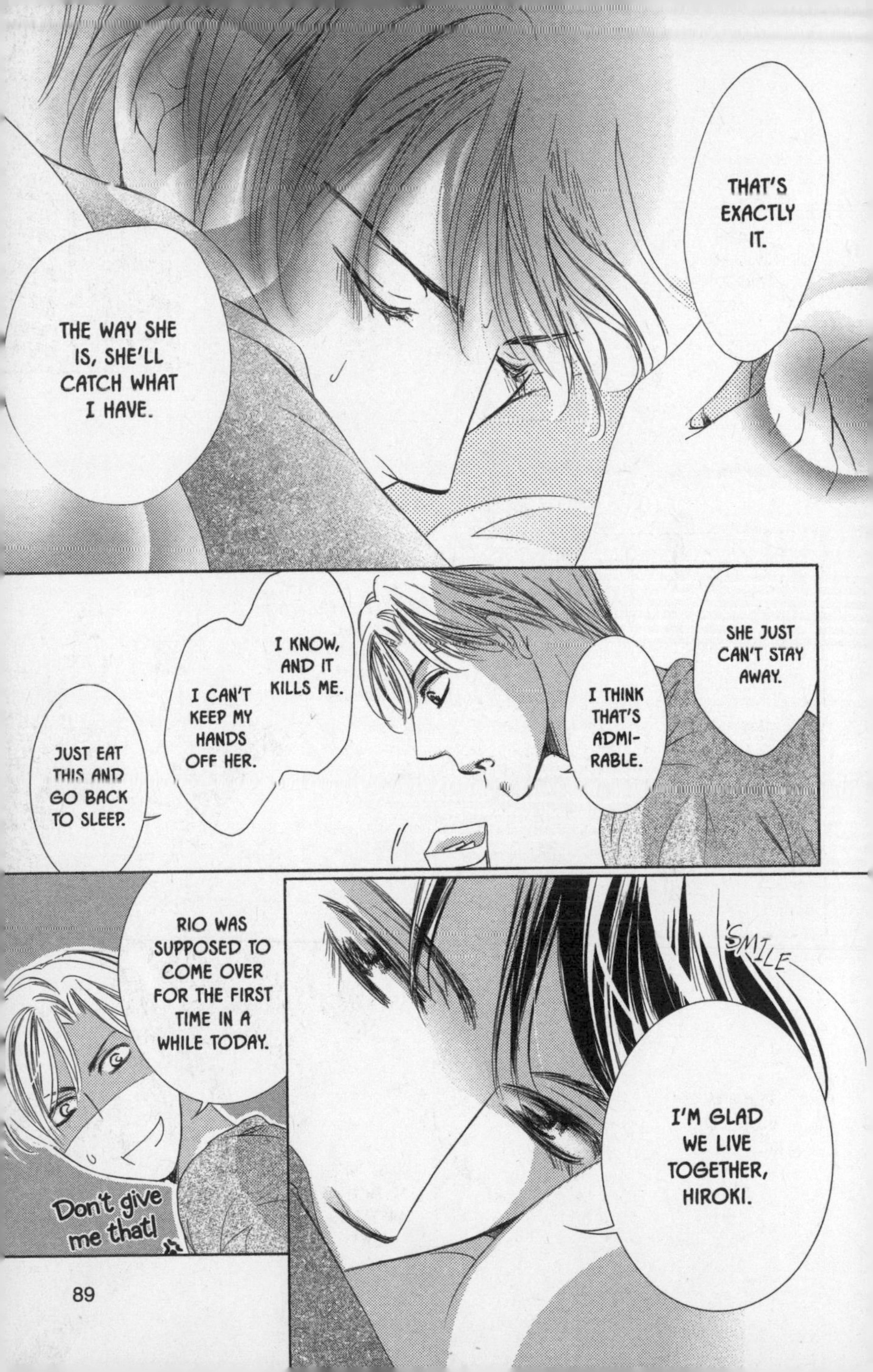
THAT'S EXACTLY IT.
THE WAY SHE IS, SHE'LL CATCH WHAT I HAVE.
SHE JUST CAN'T STAY AWAY.
I THINK THAT'S ADMI-RABLE.
I KNOW, AND IT KILLS ME.
I CAN'T KEEP MY HANDS OFF HER.
JUST EAT THIS AND GO BACK TO SLEEP.
SMILE
I'M GLAD WE LIVE TOGETHER, HIROKI.
RIO WAS SUPPOSED TO COME OVER FOR THE FIRST TIME IN A WHILE TODAY.
Don't give me that!

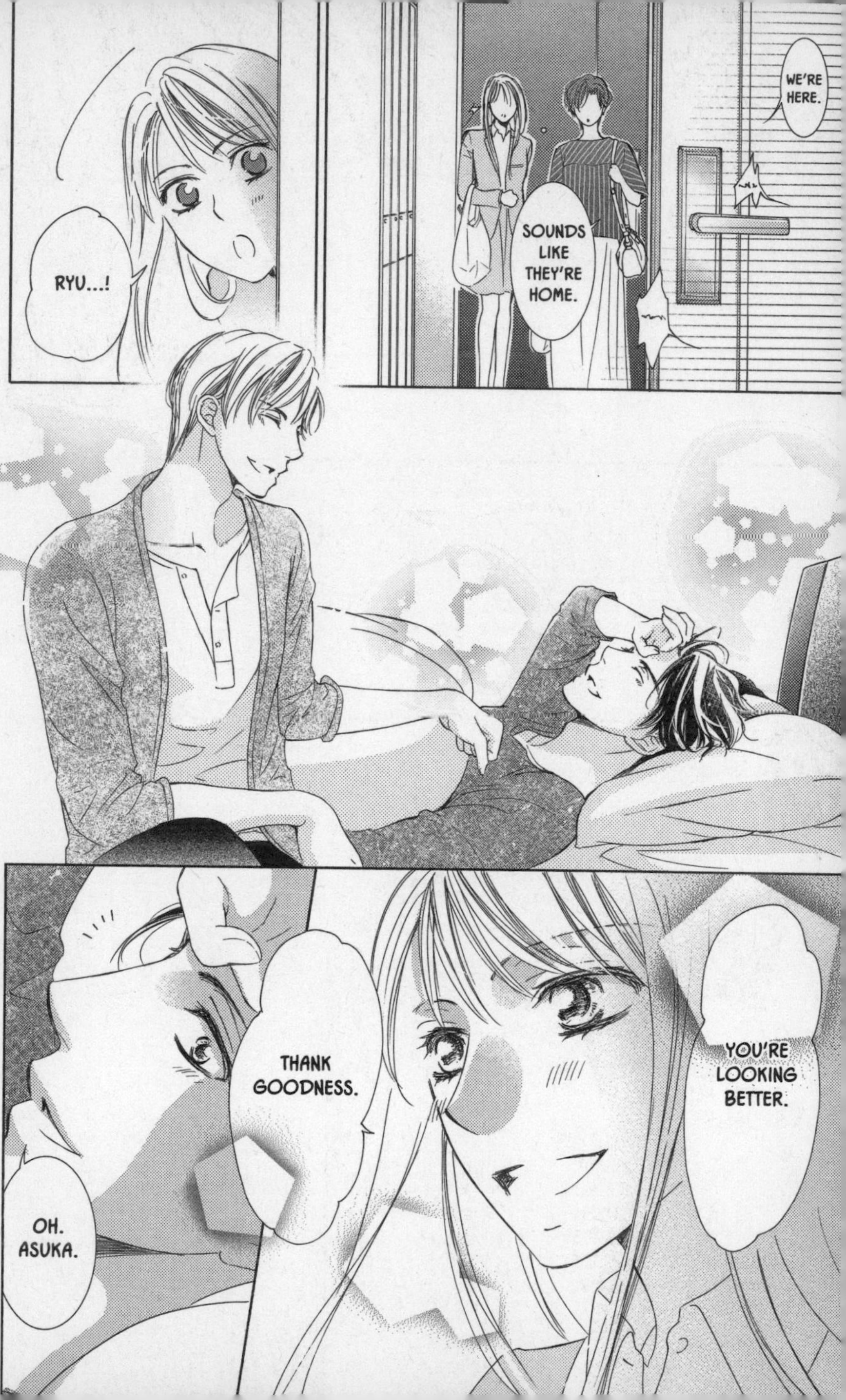
WE'RE HERE.
SOUNDS LIKE THEY'RE HOME.
RYU...!
YOU'RE LOOKING BETTER.
THANK GOODNESS.
OH. ASUKA.

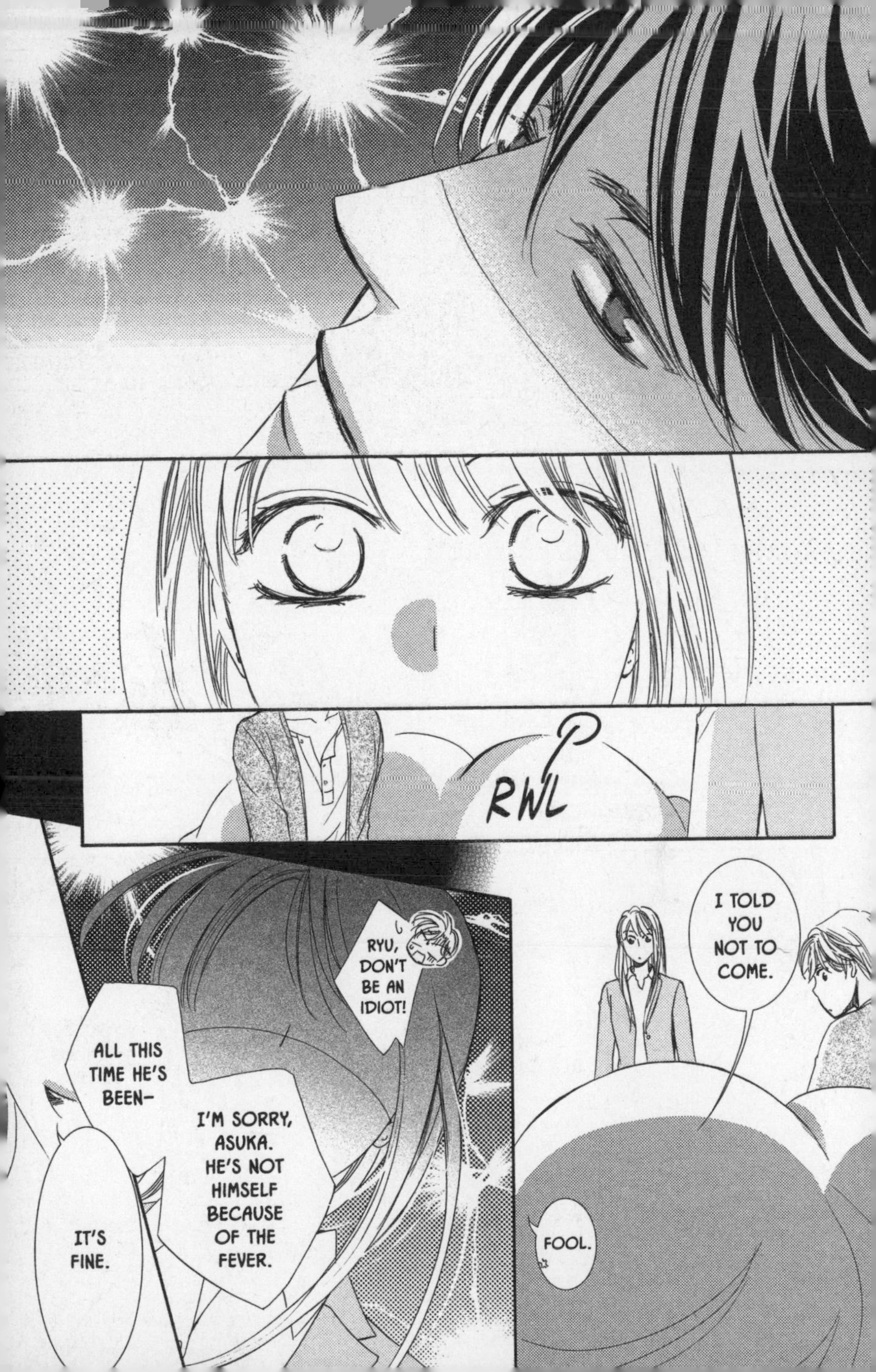
RWL
I TOLD YOU NOT TO COME.
FOOL.
RYU, DON'T BE AN IDIOT!
ALL THIS TIME HE'S BEEN—
I'M SORRY, ASUKA. HE'S NOT HIMSELF BECAUSE OF THE FEVER.
IT'S FINE.

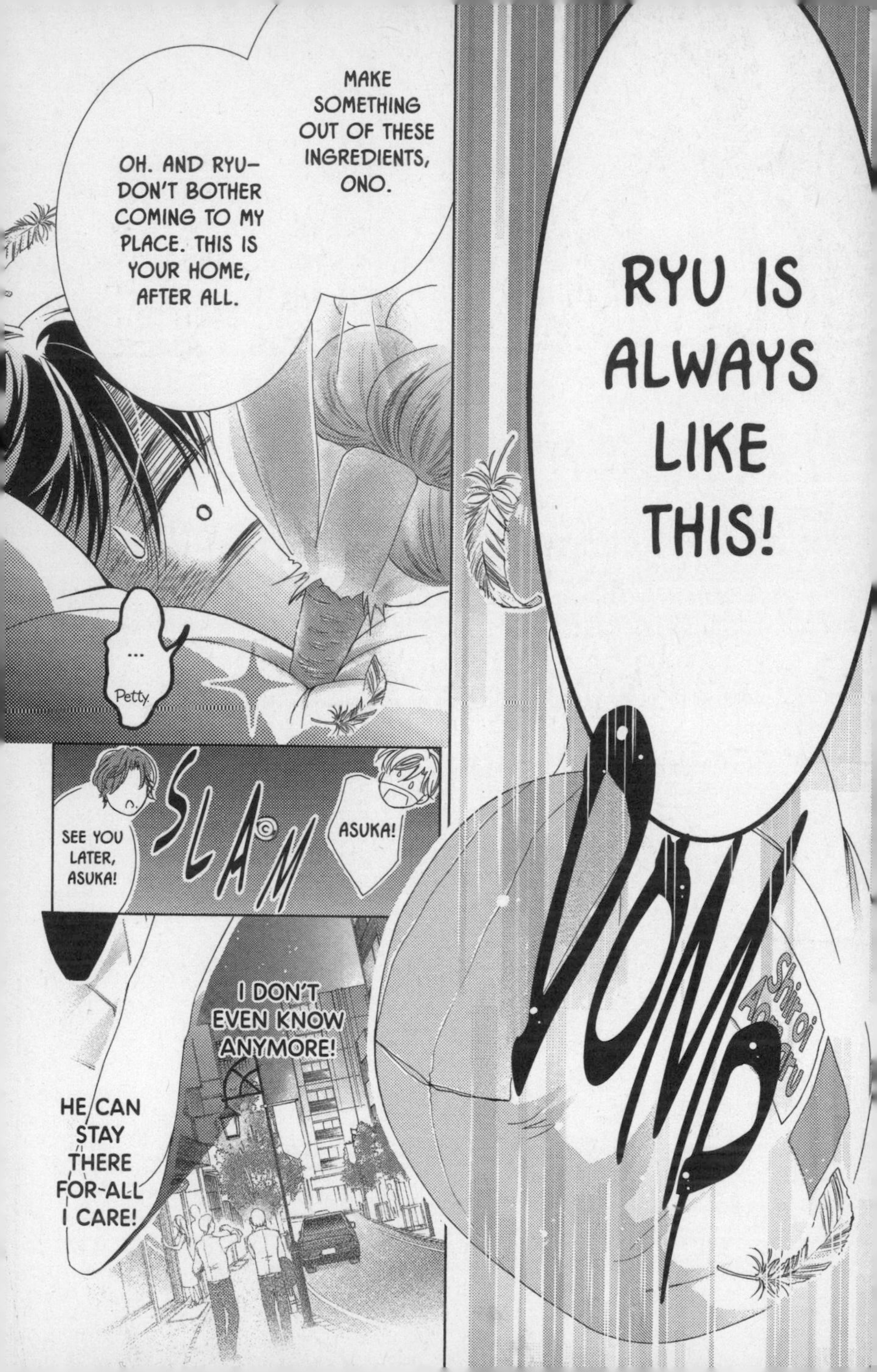
RYU IS ALWAYS LIKE THIS!
DOMP
Shiroi
MAKE SOMETHING OUT OF THESE INGREDIENTS, ONO.
OH. AND RYU—DON'T BOTHER COMING TO MY PLACE. THIS IS YOUR HOME, AFTER ALL.
...
Petty.
ASUKA!
SLAM
SEE YOU LATER, ASUKA!
I DON'T EVEN KNOW ANYMORE!
HE CAN STAY THERE FOR ALL I CARE!

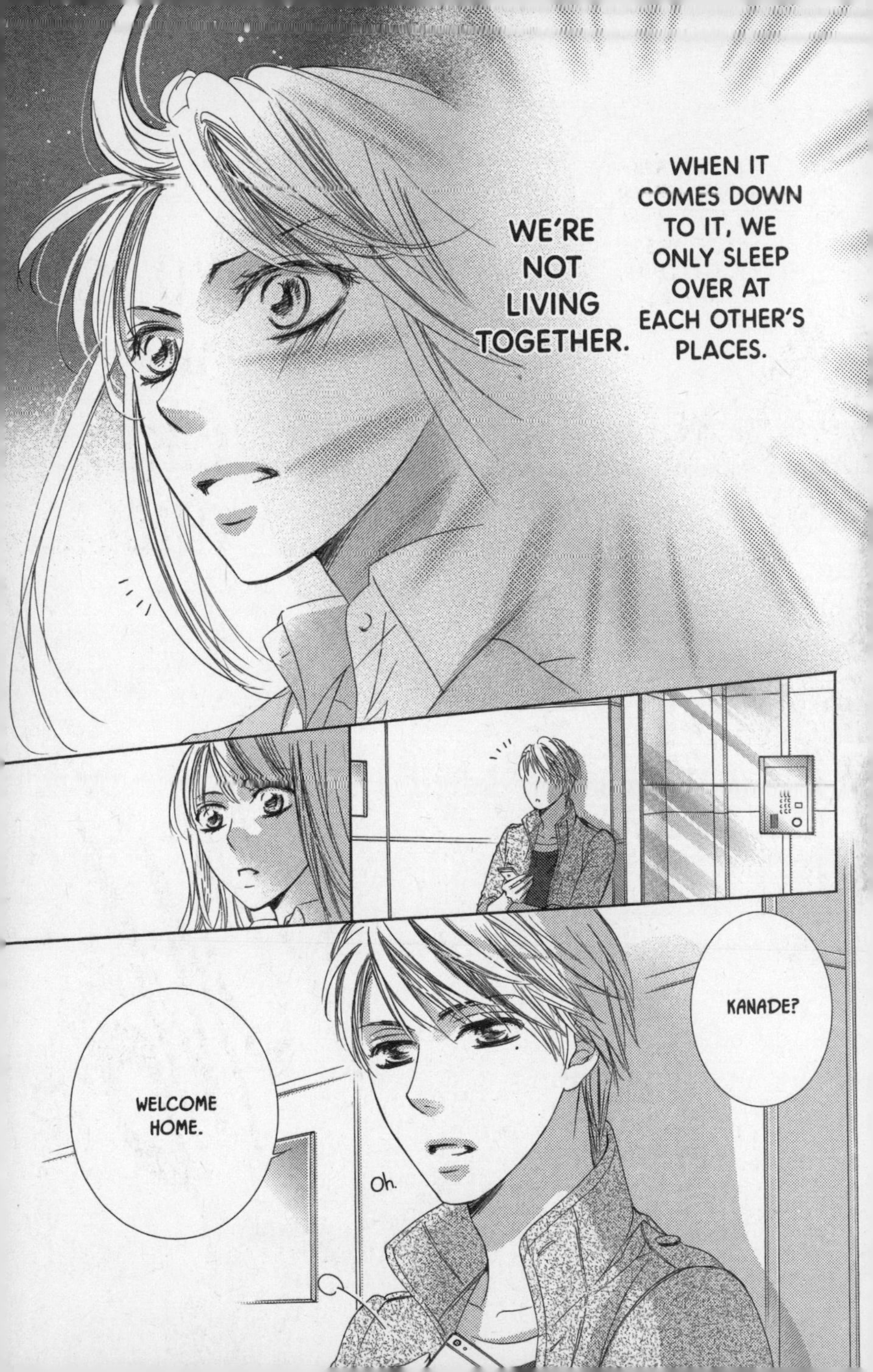
WHEN IT COMES DOWN TO IT, WE ONLY SLEEP OVER AT EACH OTHER'S PLACES.
WE'RE NOT LIVING TOGETHER.
KANADE?
Oh.
WELCOME HOME.

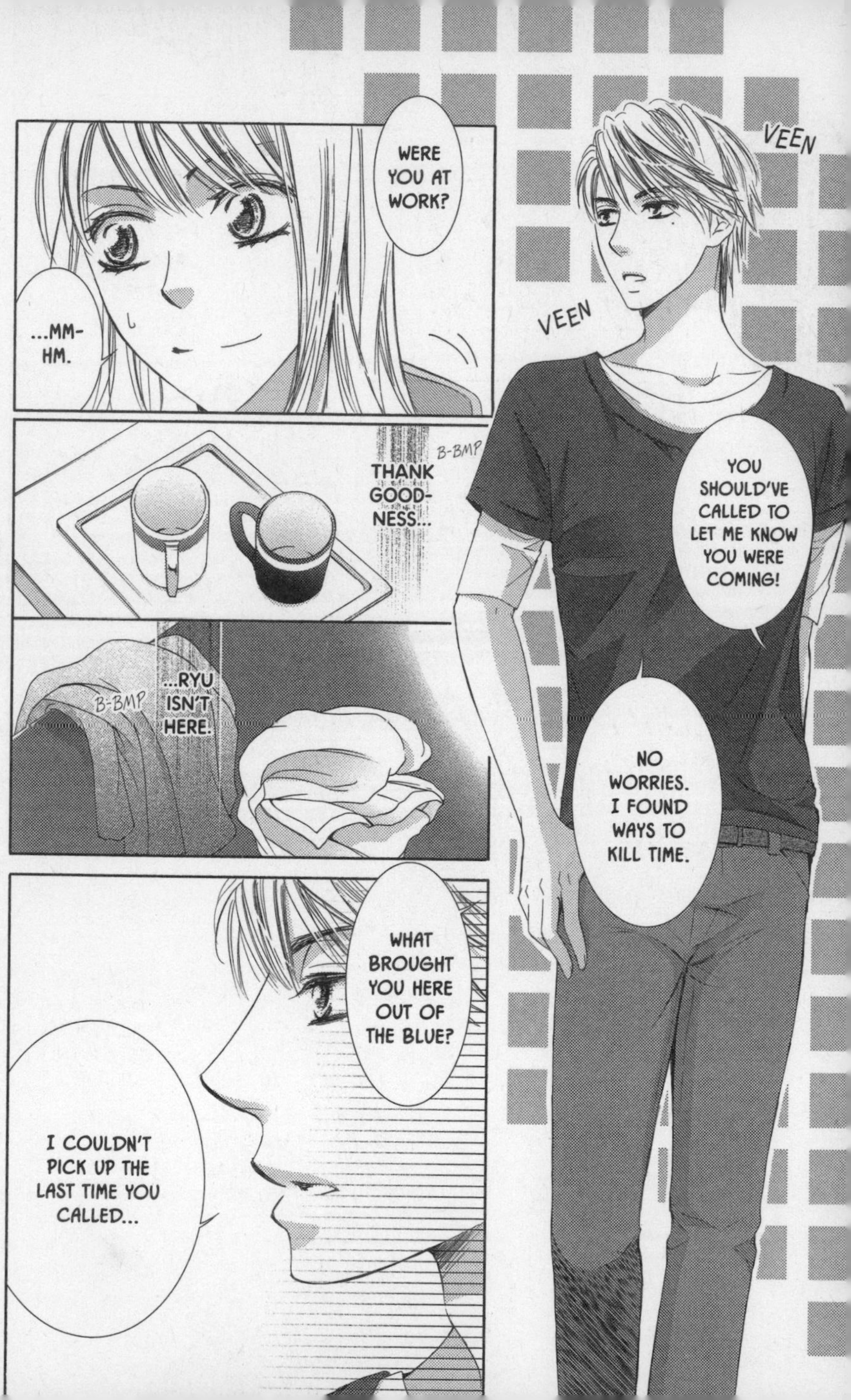
VEEN
VEEN
YOU SHOULD'VE CALLED TO LET ME KNOW YOU WERE COMING!
NO WORRIES. I FOUND WAYS TO KILL TIME.
WERE YOU AT WORK?
...MM-HM.
B-BMP
THANK GOODNESS...
...RYU ISN'T HERE.
B-BMP
WHAT BROUGHT YOU HERE OUT OF THE BLUE?
I COULDN'T PICK UP THE LAST TIME YOU CALLED...

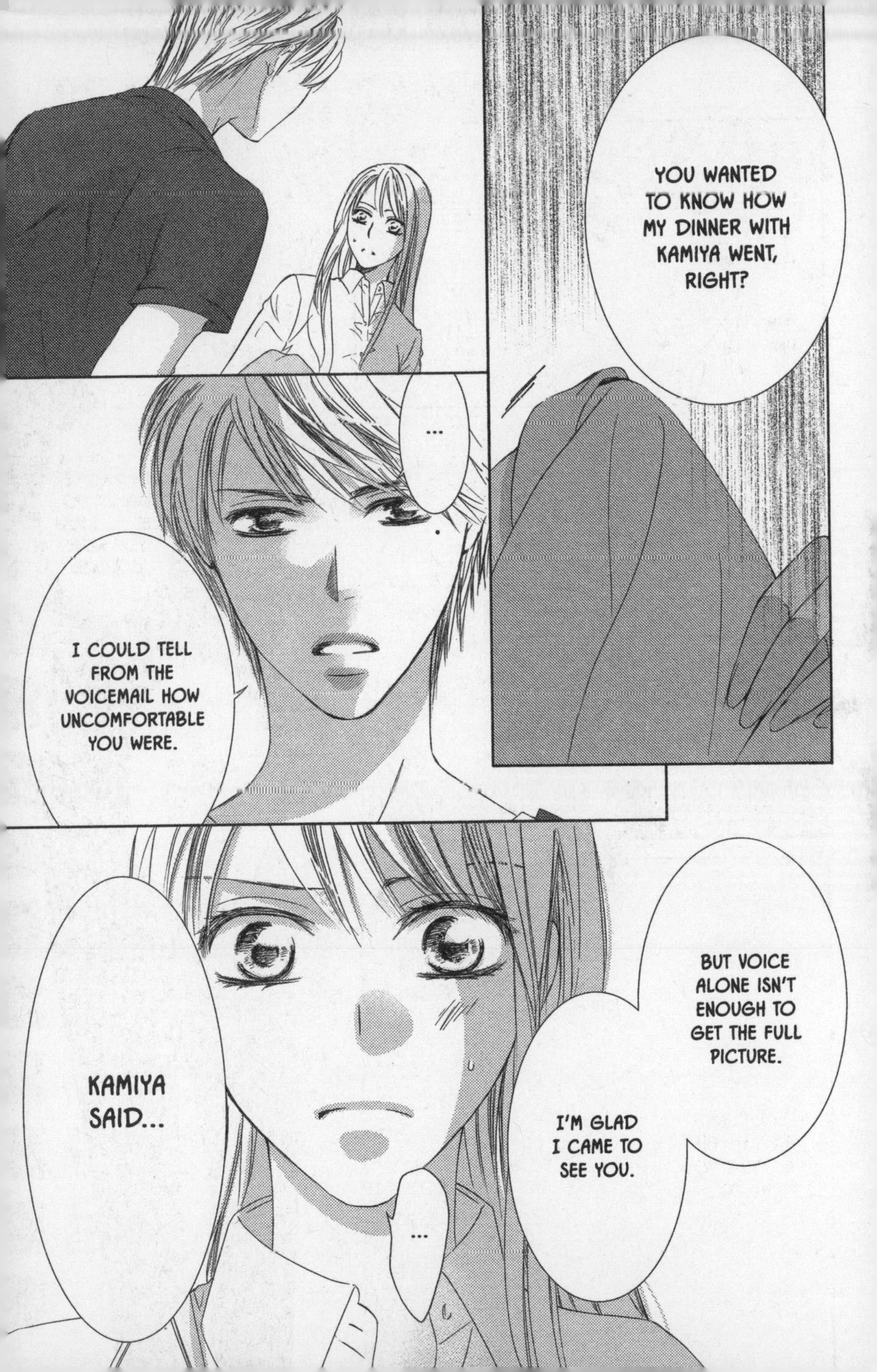
YOU WANTED TO KNOW HOW MY DINNER WITH KAMIYA WENT, RIGHT?
...
I COULD TELL FROM THE VOICEMAIL HOW UNCOMFORTABLE YOU WERE.
BUT VOICE ALONE ISN'T ENOUGH TO GET THE FULL PICTURE.
I'M GLAD I CAME TO SEE YOU.
...
KAMIYA SAID...

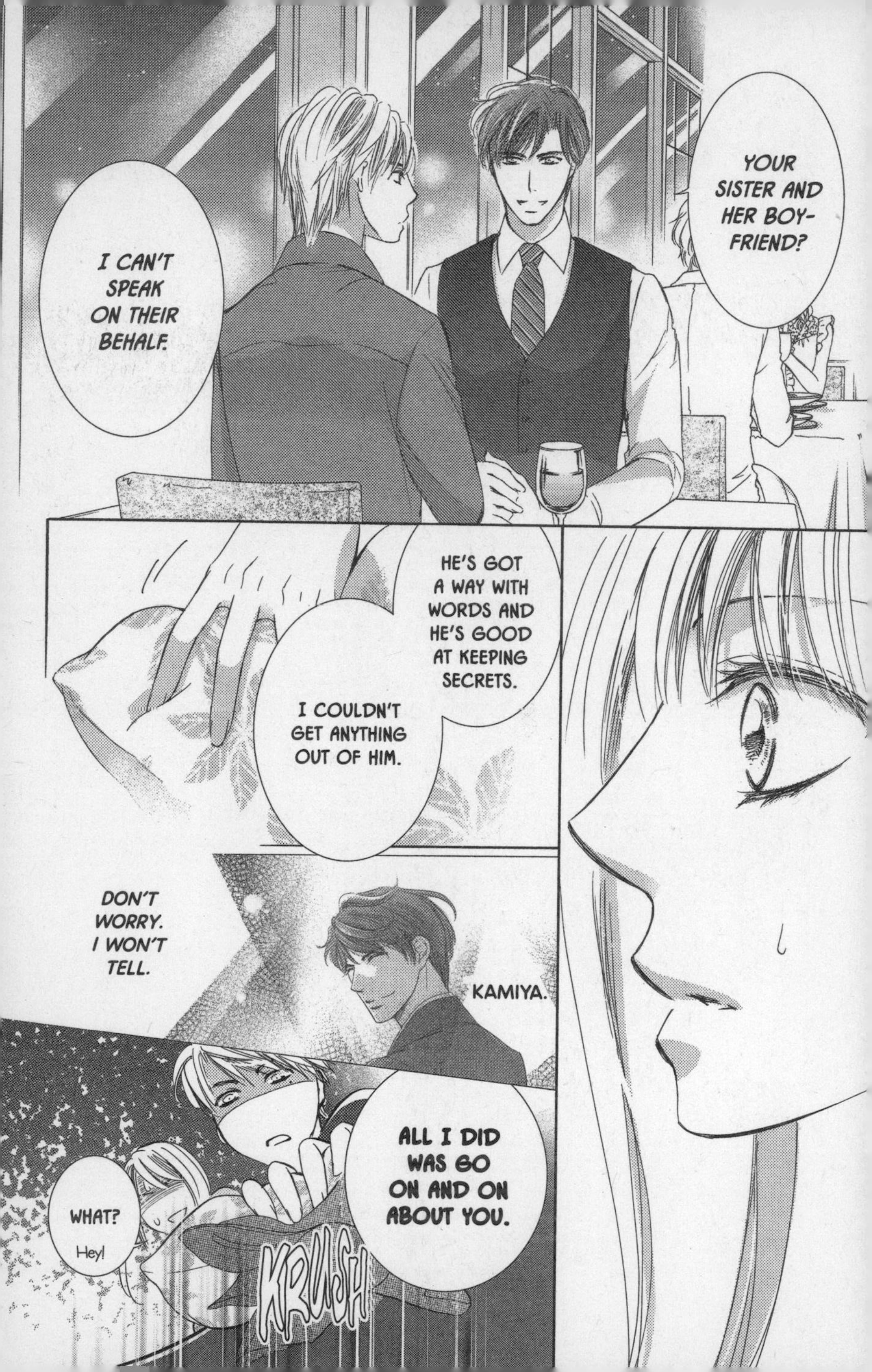
YOUR SISTER AND HER BOY-FRIEND?
I CAN'T SPEAK ON THEIR BEHALF.
HE'S GOT A WAY WITH WORDS AND HE'S GOOD AT KEEPING SECRETS.
I COULDN'T GET ANYTHING OUT OF HIM.
KAMIYA.
DON'T WORRY. I WON'T TELL.
ALL I DID WAS GO ON AND ON ABOUT YOU.
KRUSH
WHAT?
Hey!

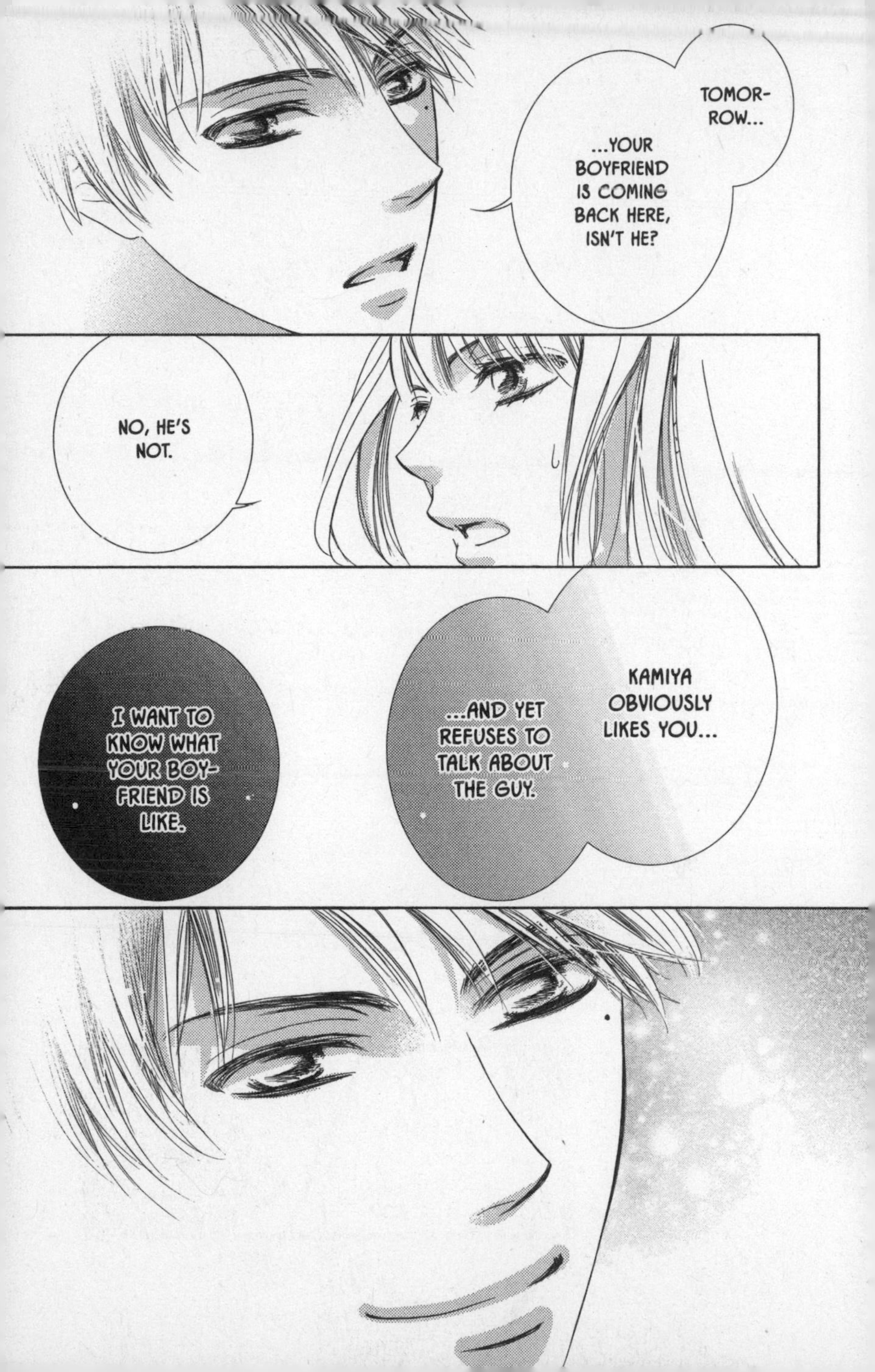
TOMOR-ROW...
...YOUR BOYFRIEND IS COMING BACK HERE, ISN'T HE?
NO, HE'S NOT.
KAMIYA OBVIOUSLY LIKES YOU...
...AND YET REFUSES TO TALK ABOUT THE GUY.
I WANT TO KNOW WHAT YOUR BOY-FRIEND IS LIKE.

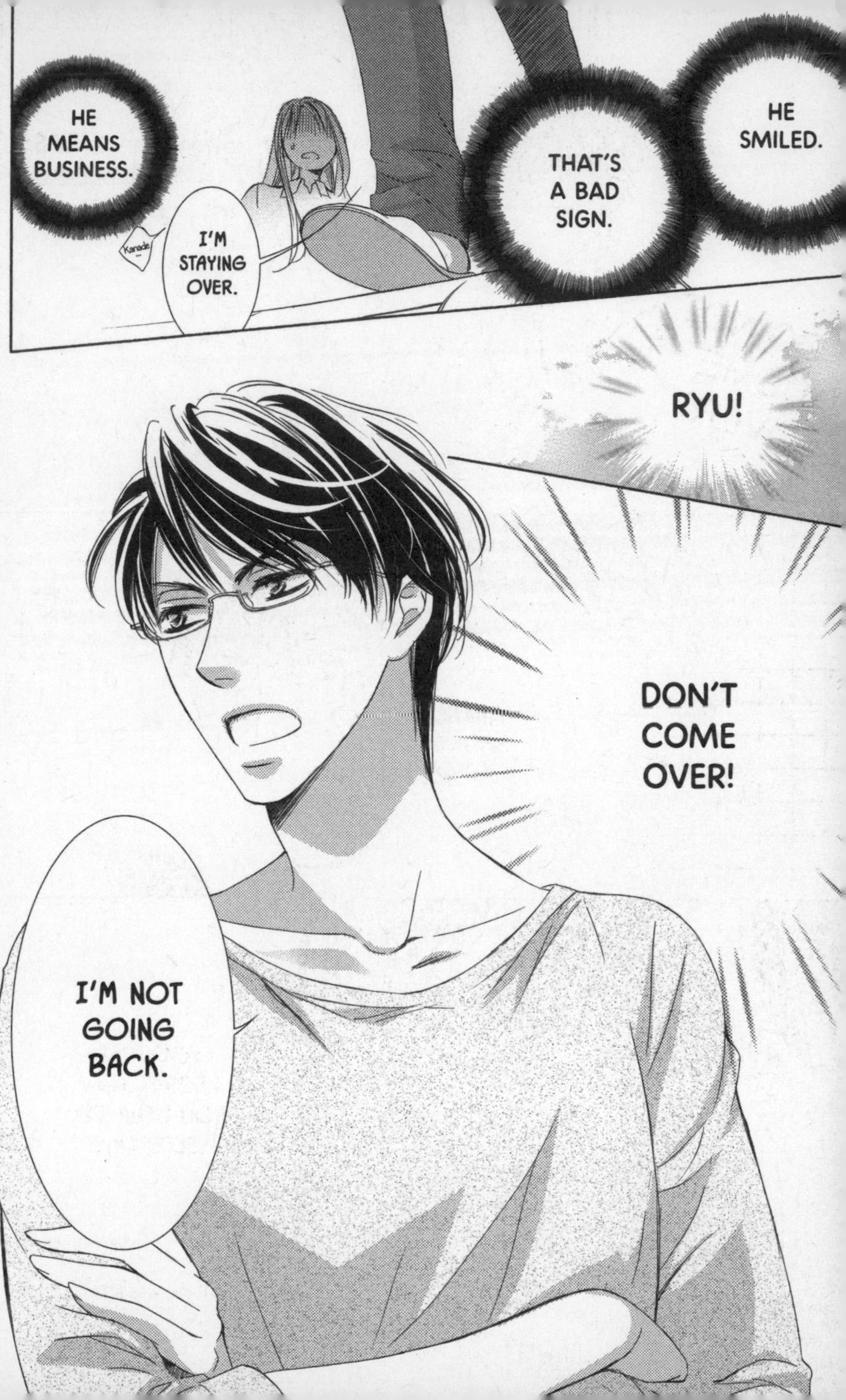
HE SMILED.
THAT'S A BAD SIGN.
HE MEANS BUSINESS.
Kanade
I'M STAYING OVER.
RYU!
DON'T COME OVER!
I'M NOT GOING BACK.

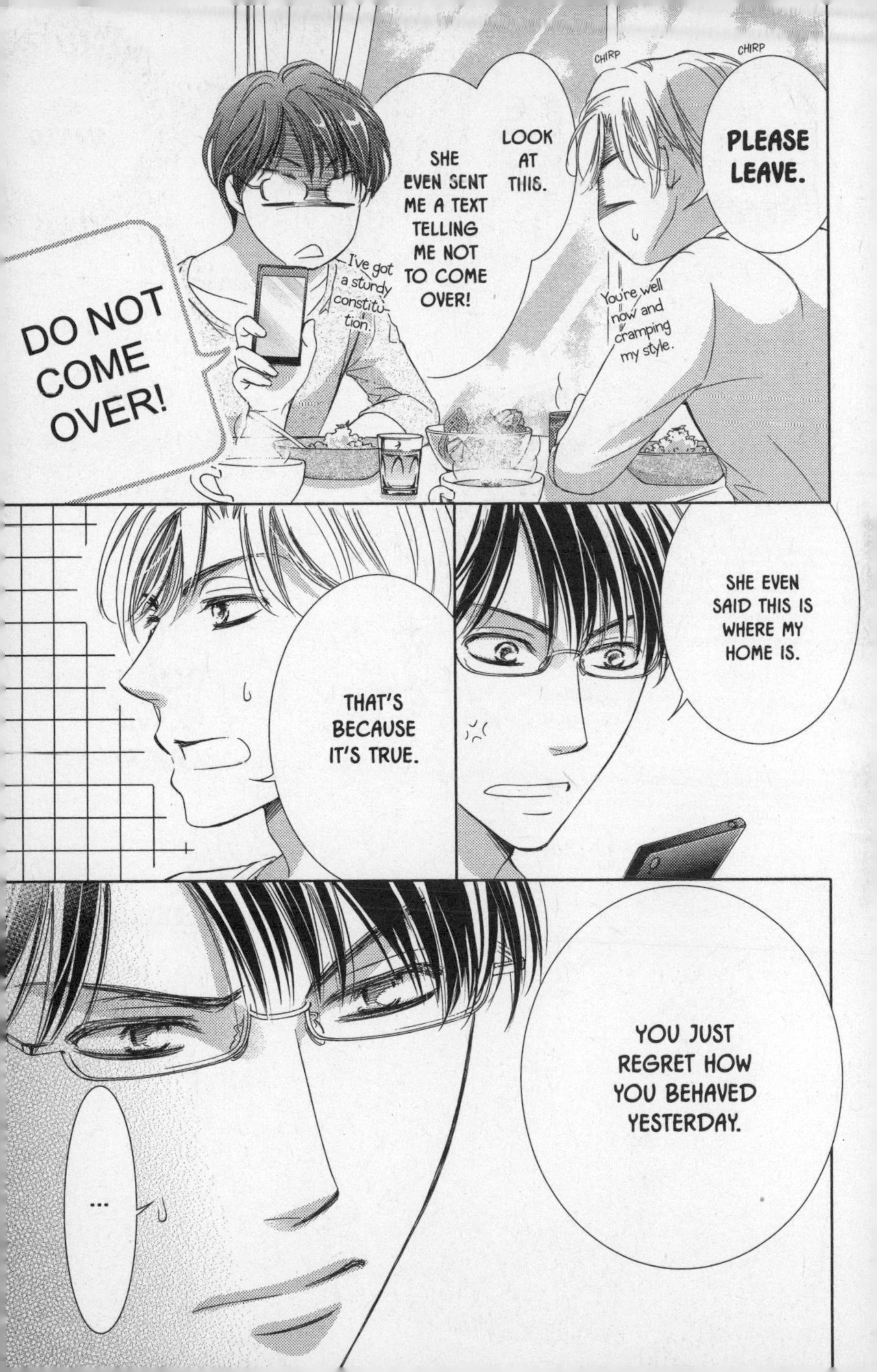
CHIRP
CHIRP
PLEASE LEAVE.
You're well now and cramping my style.
LOOK AT THIS.
SHE EVEN SENT ME A TEXT TELLING ME NOT TO COME OVER!
I've got a sturdy constitution.
DO NOT COME OVER!
SHE EVEN SAID THIS IS WHERE MY HOME IS.
THAT'S BECAUSE IT'S TRUE.
YOU JUST REGRET HOW YOU BEHAVED YESTERDAY.
...

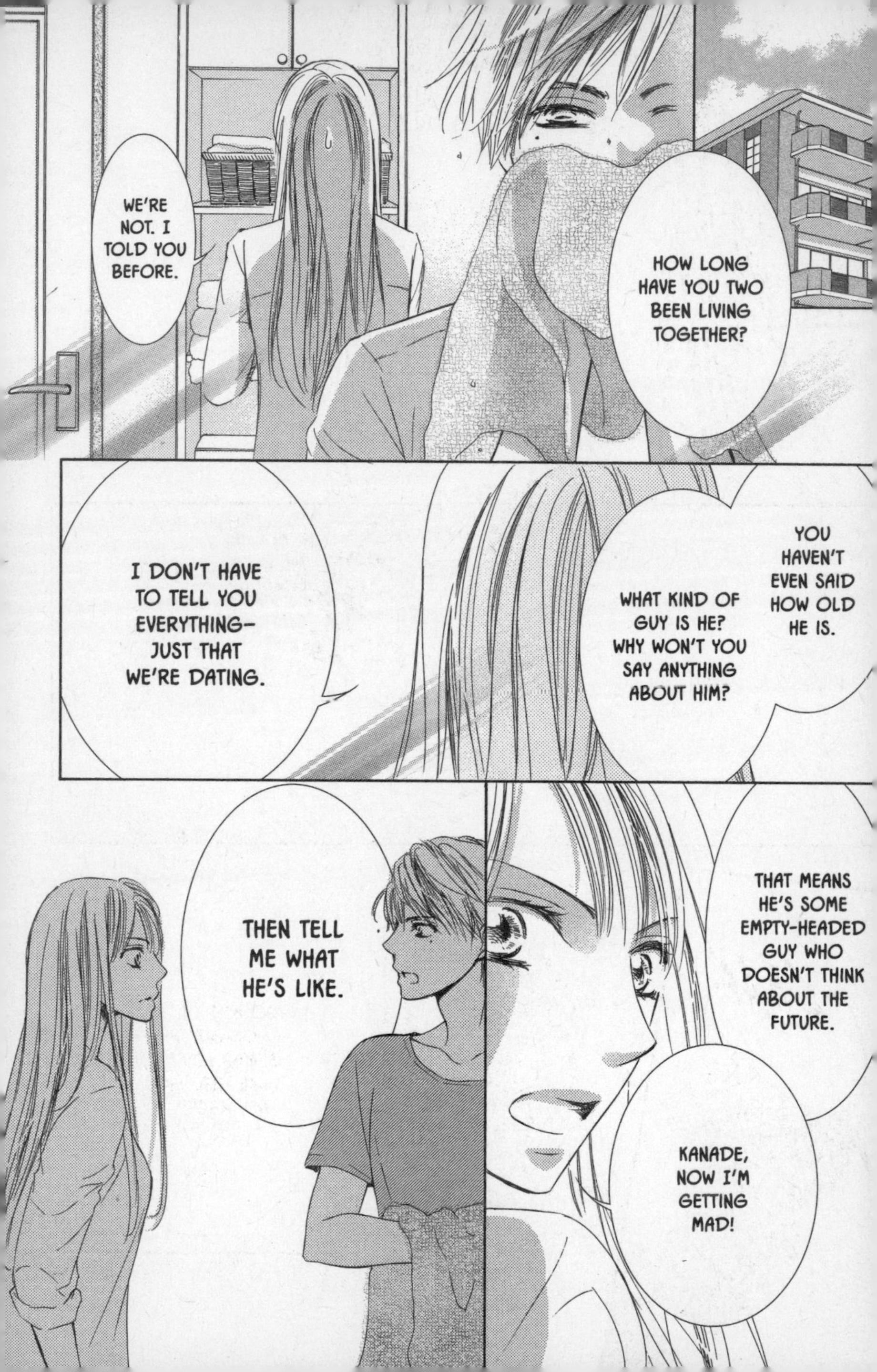
HOW LONG HAVE YOU TWO BEEN LIVING TOGETHER?
WE'RE NOT. I TOLD YOU BEFORE.
YOU HAVEN'T EVEN SAID HOW OLD HE IS.
WHAT KIND OF GUY IS HE? WHY WON'T YOU SAY ANYTHING ABOUT HIM?
I DON'T HAVE TO TELL YOU EVERYTHING—JUST THAT WE'RE DATING.
THAT MEANS HE'S SOME EMPTY-HEADED GUY WHO DOESN'T THINK ABOUT THE FUTURE.
KANADE, NOW I'M GETTING MAD!
THEN TELL ME WHAT HE'S LIKE.

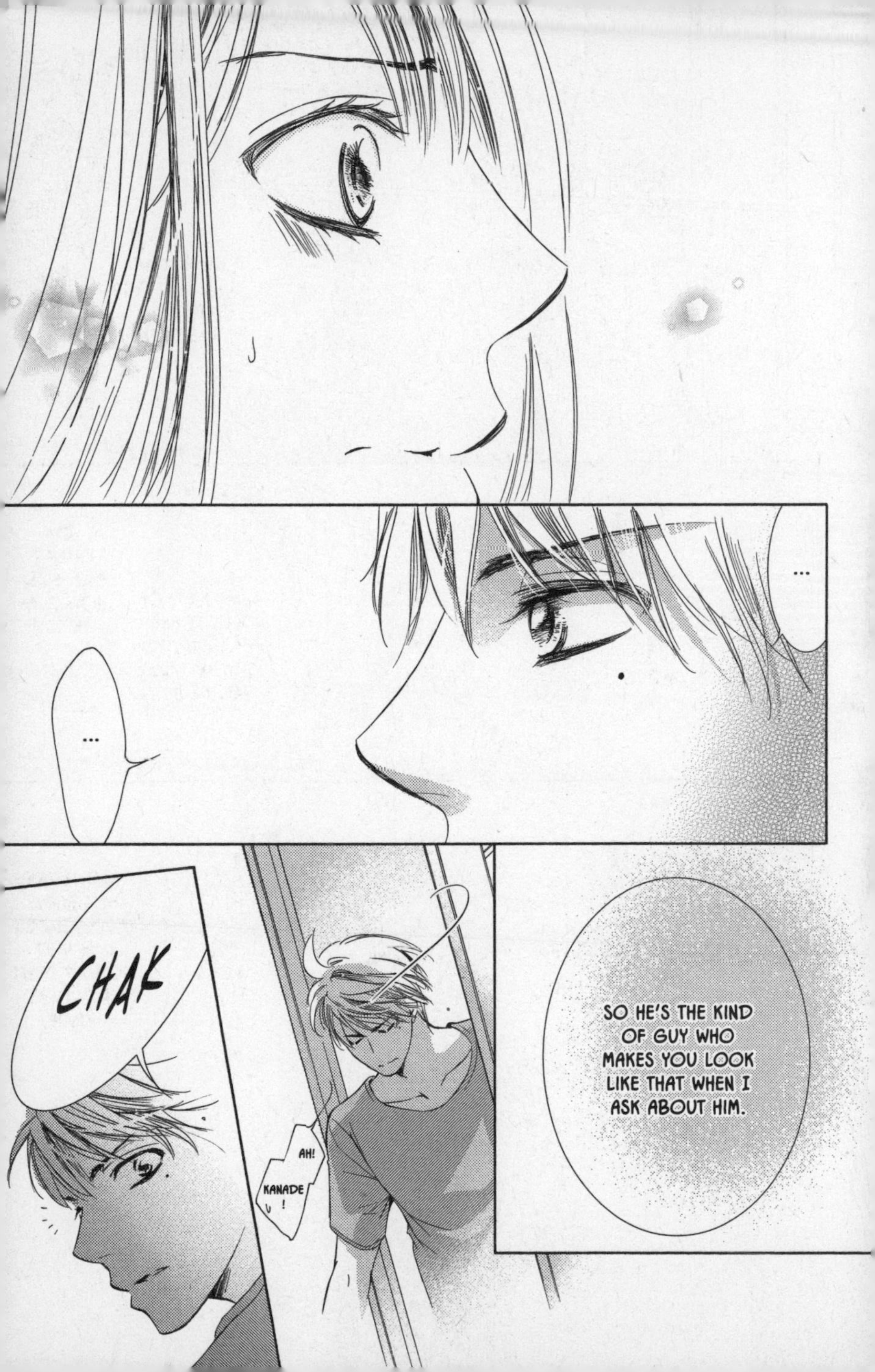
...
...
SO HE'S THE KIND OF GUY WHO MAKES YOU LOOK LIKE THAT WHEN I ASK ABOUT HIM.
AH!
KANADE!
CHAK

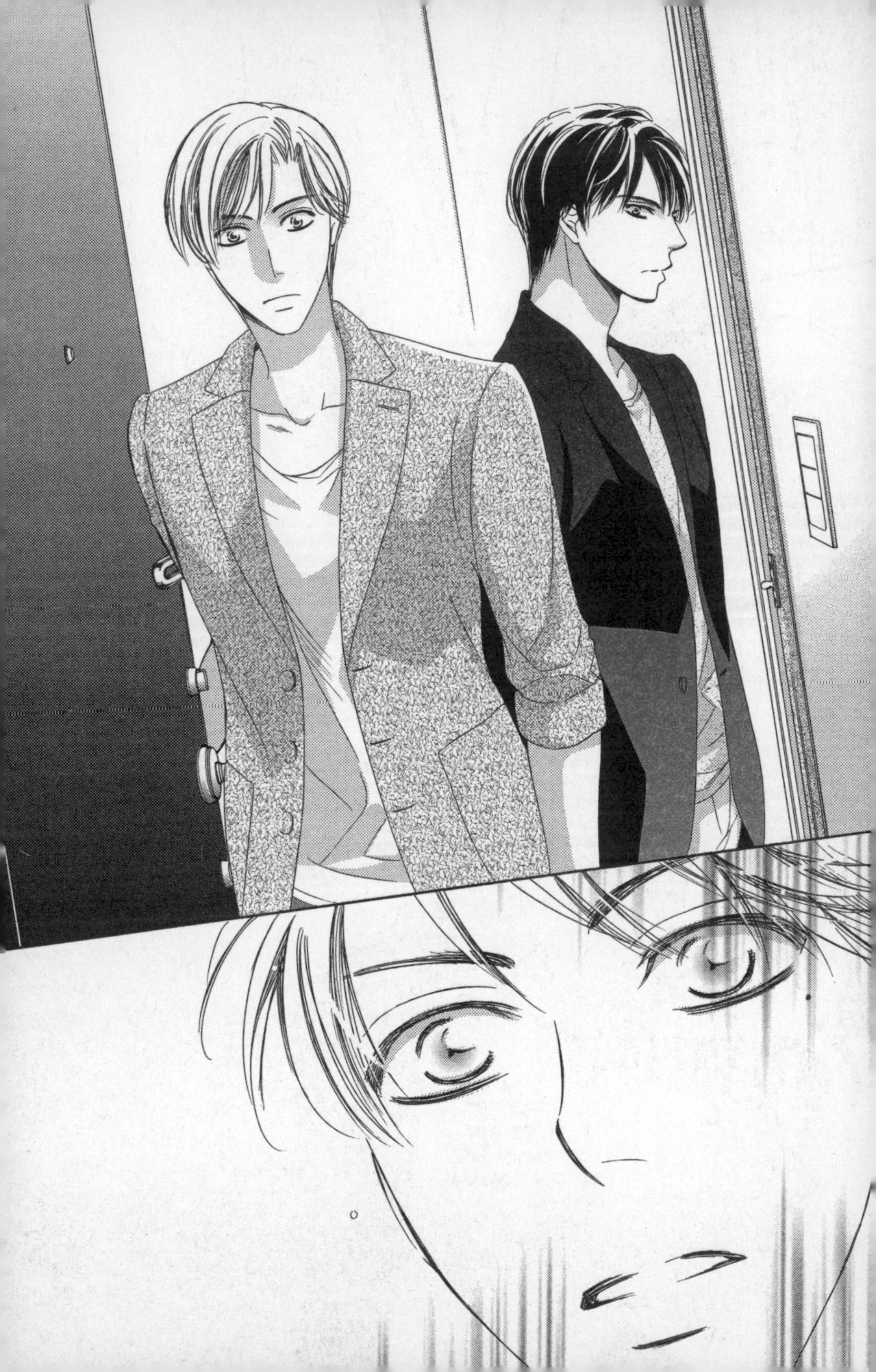

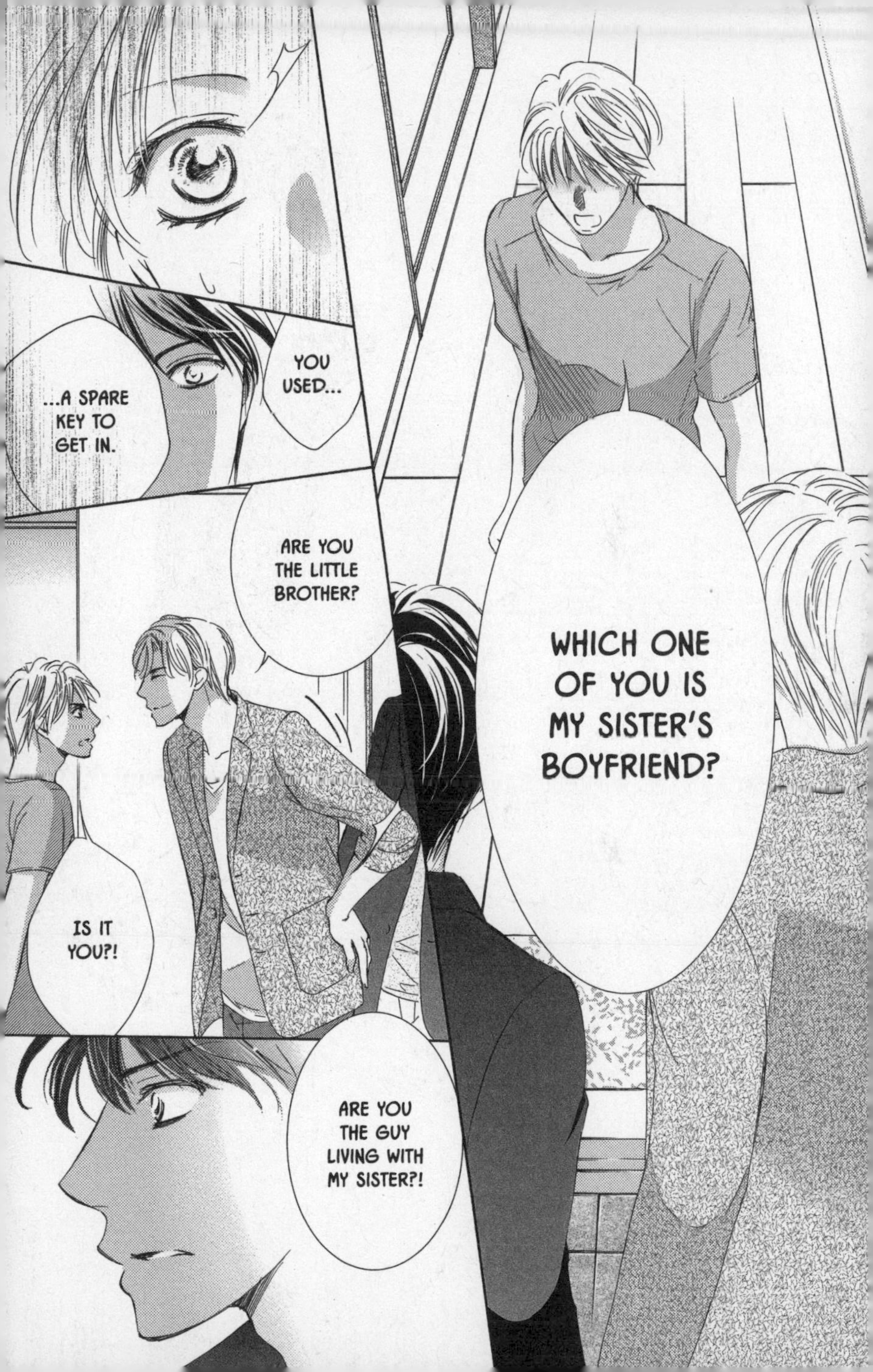
WHICH ONE OF YOU IS MY SISTER'S BOYFRIEND?
YOU USED...
...A SPARE KEY TO GET IN.
ARE YOU THE LITTLE BROTHER?
IS IT YOU?!
ARE YOU THE GUY LIVING WITH MY SISTER?!

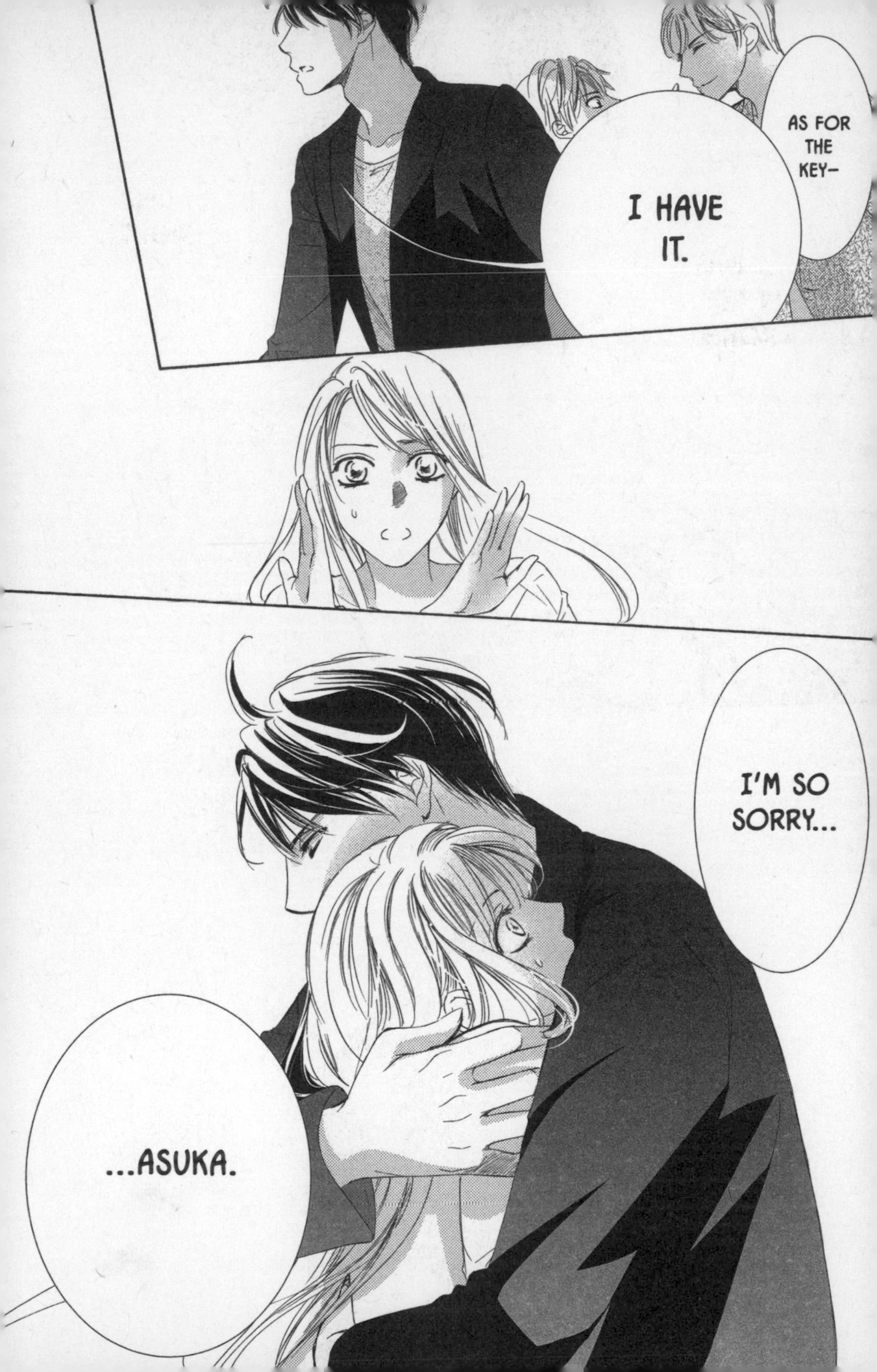
AS FOR THE KEY—
I HAVE IT.
I'M SO SORRY...
...ASUKA.

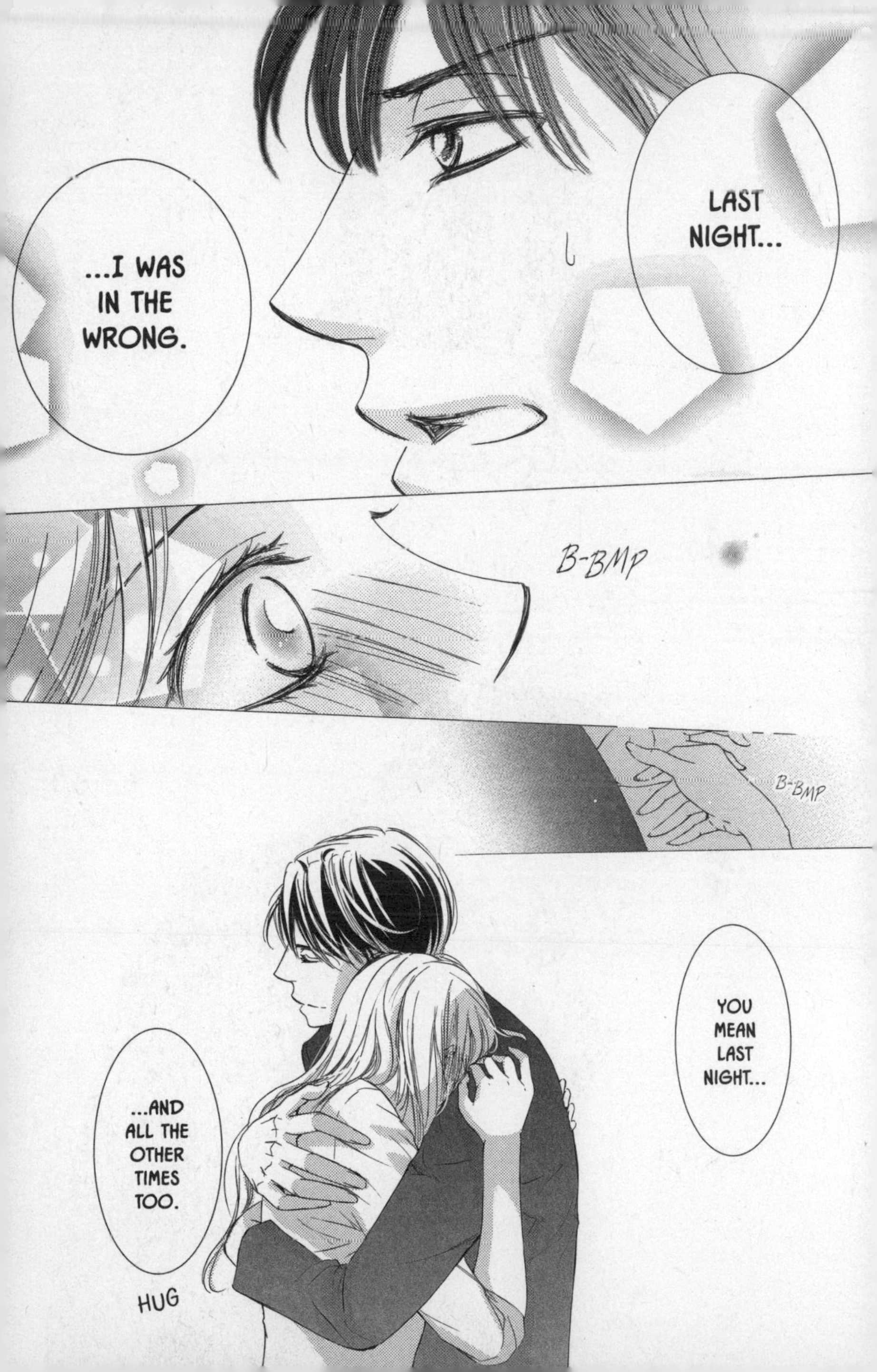
LAST NIGHT...
...I WAS IN THE WRONG.
B-BMP
B-BMP
YOU MEAN LAST NIGHT...
...AND ALL THE OTHER TIMES TOO.
HUG

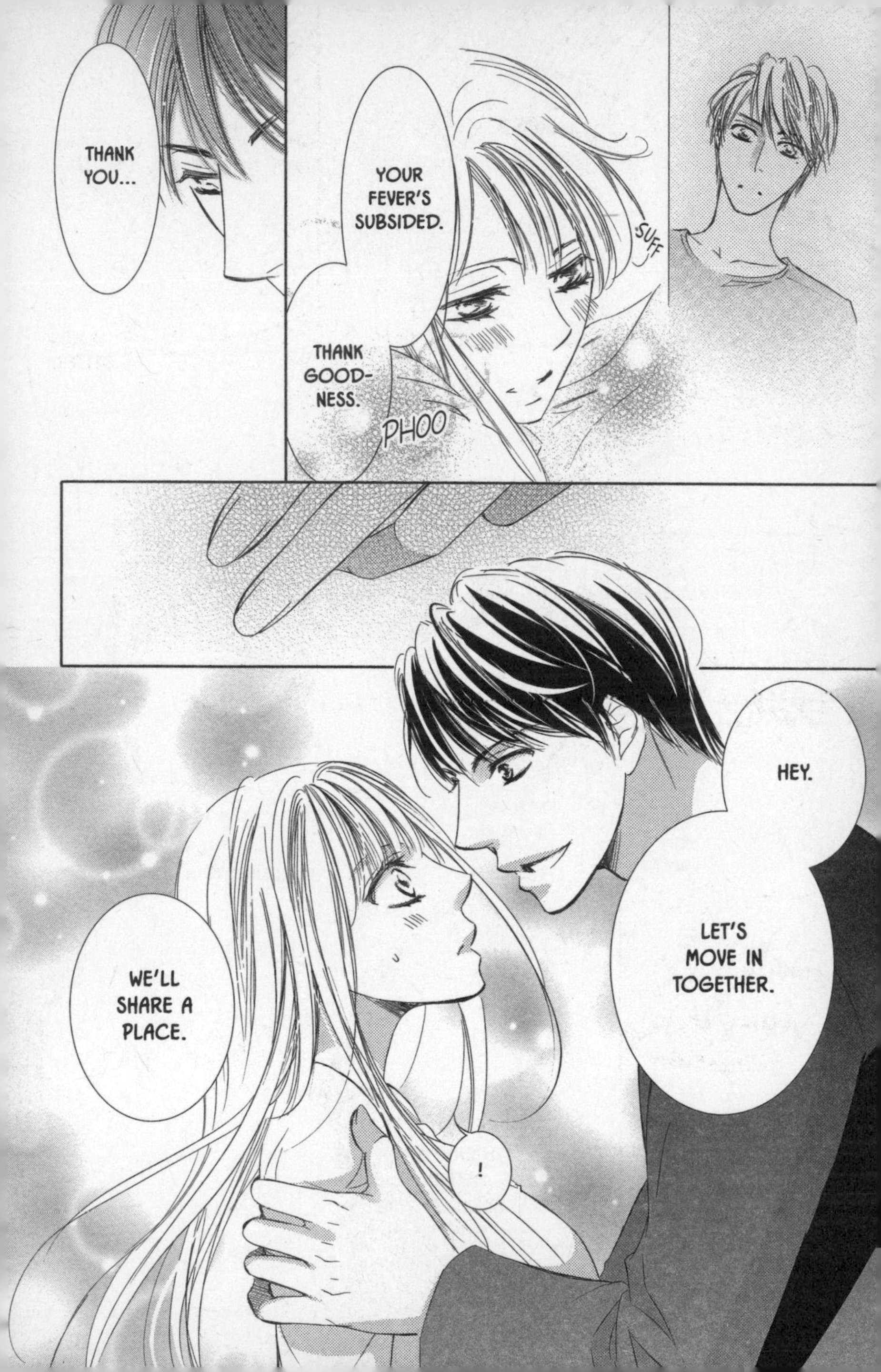
YOUR FEVER'S SUBSIDED.
SUFF
THANK GOODNESS.
PHOO
THANK YOU...
HEY.
LET'S MOVE IN TOGETHER.
WE'LL SHARE A PLACE.
!

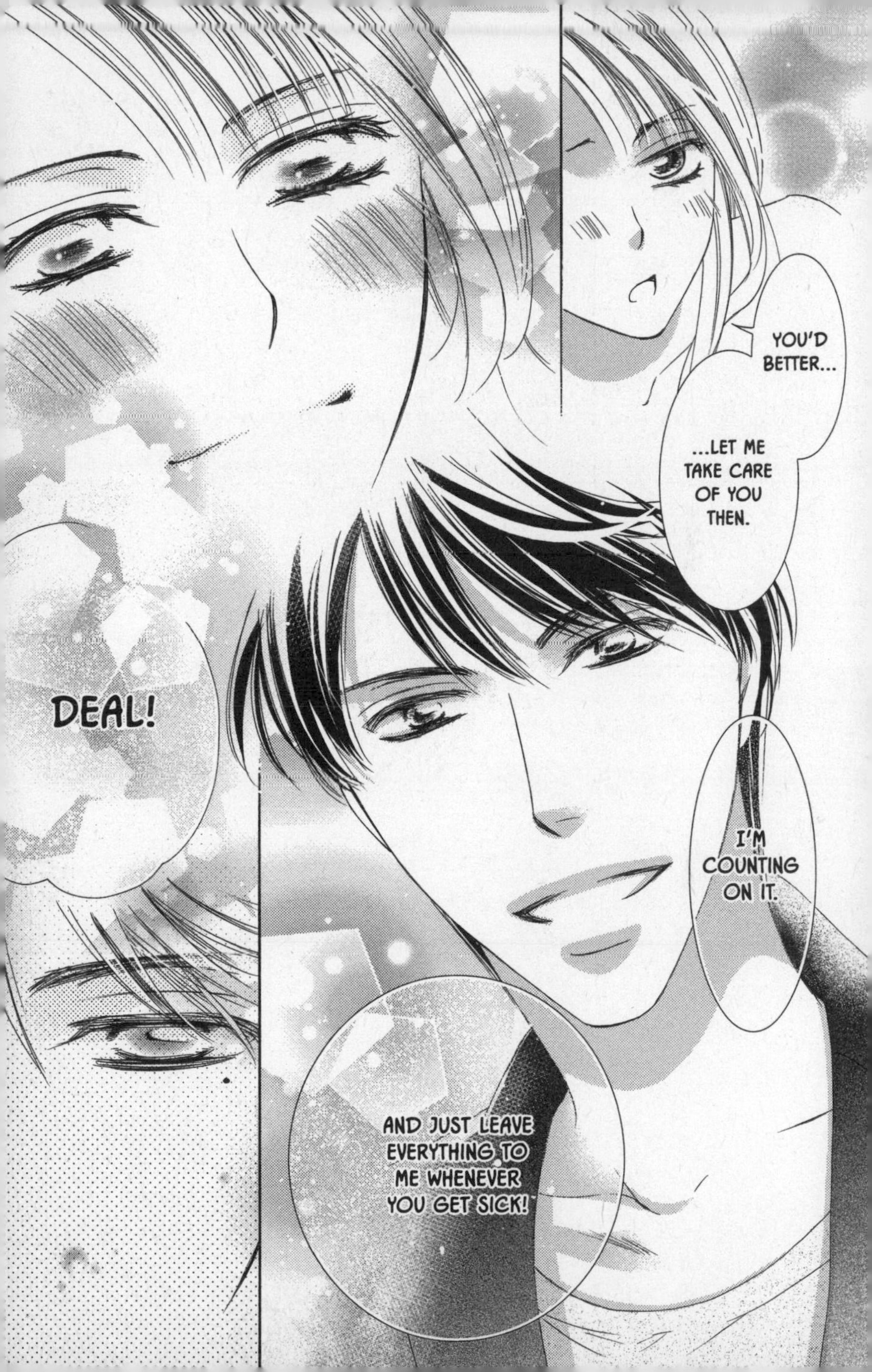
YOU'D BETTER...
...LET ME TAKE CARE OF YOU THEN.
I'M COUNTING ON IT.
AND JUST LEAVE EVERYTHING TO ME WHENEVER YOU GET SICK!
DEAL!

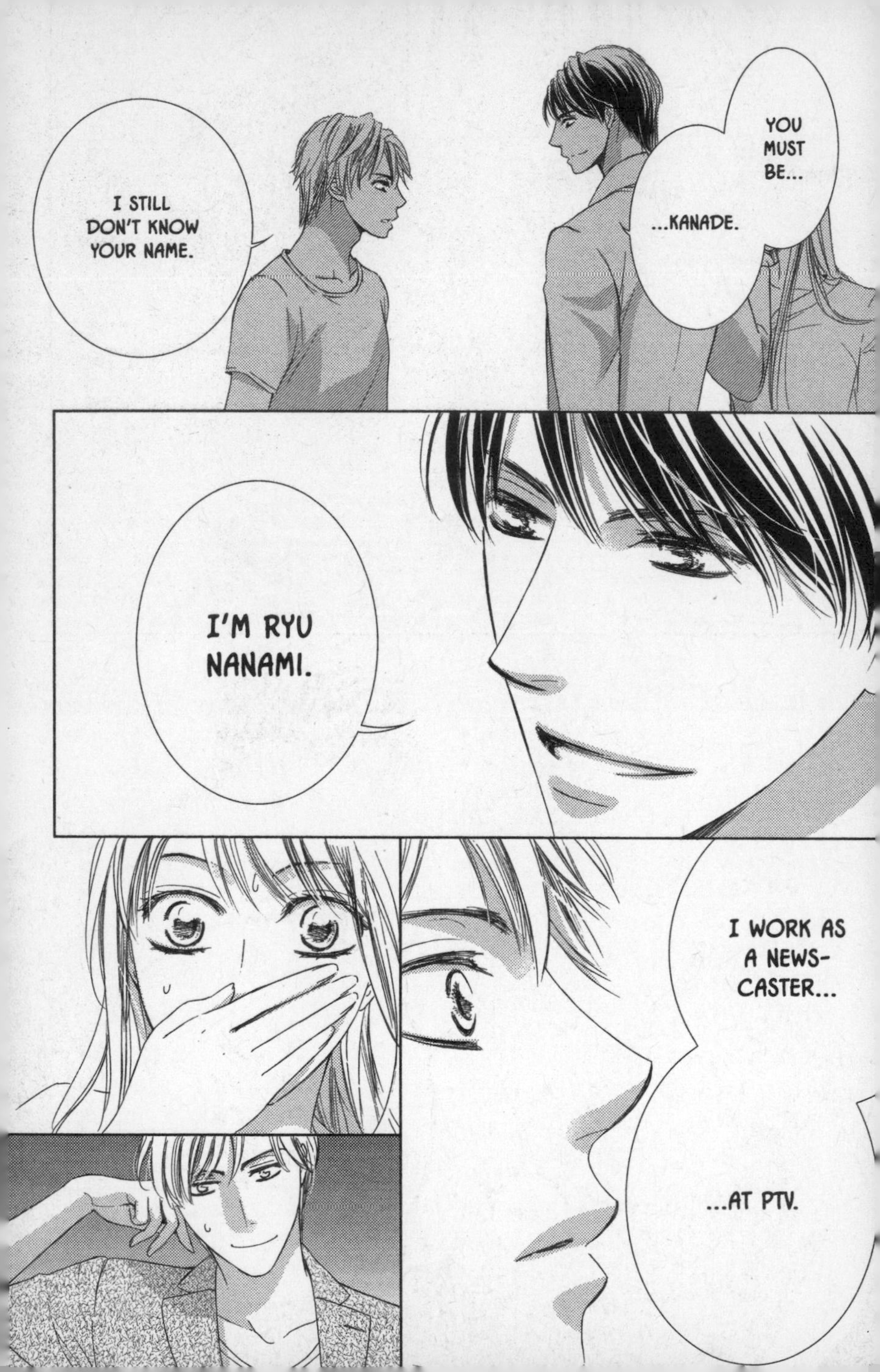
YOU MUST BE...
...KANADE.
I STILL DON'T KNOW YOUR NAME.
I'M RYU NANAMI.
I WORK AS A NEWS-CASTER...
...AT PTV.

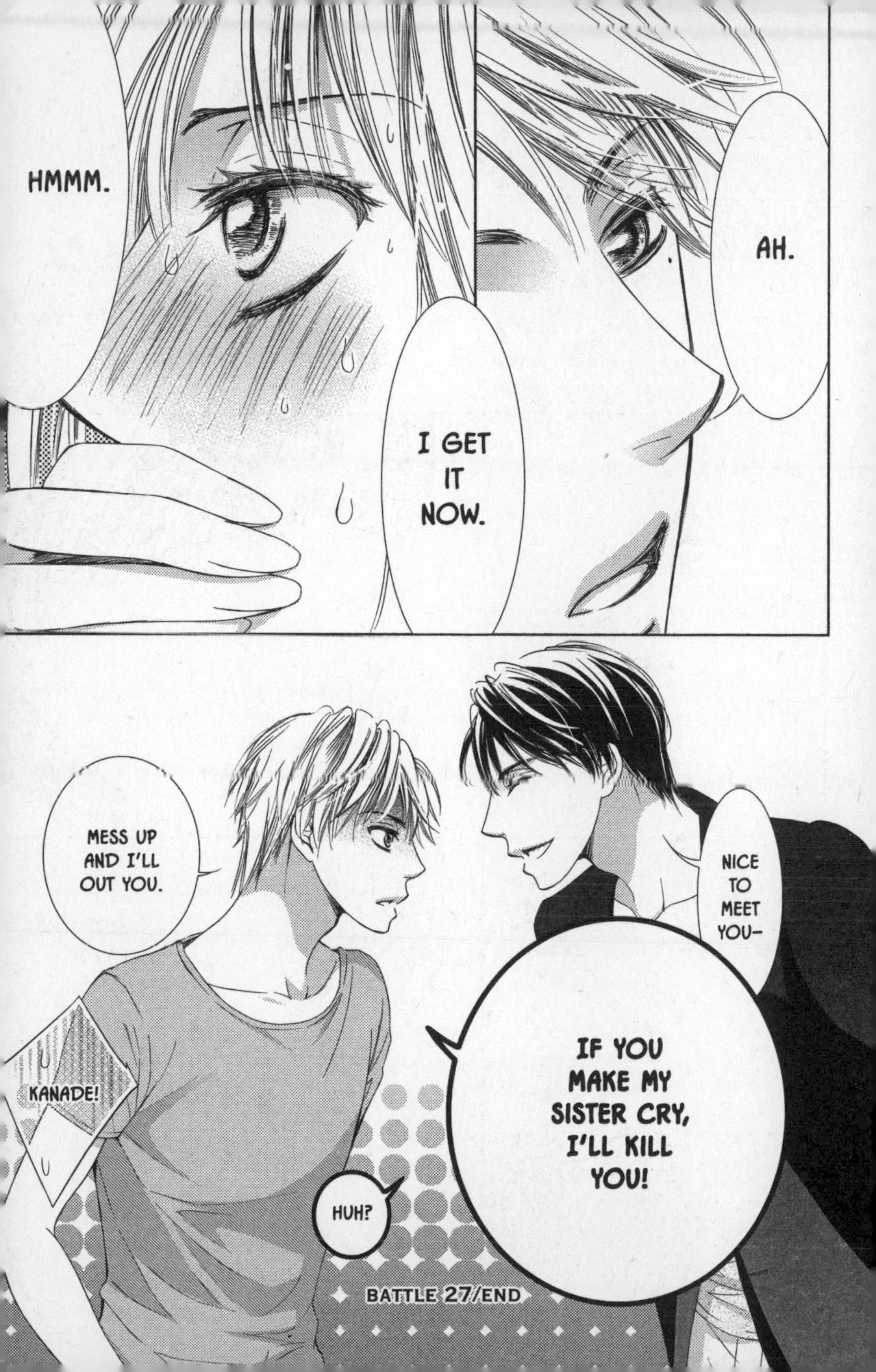
AH.
I GET IT NOW.
HMMM.
NICE TO MEET YOU—
IF YOU MAKE MY SISTER CRY, I'LL KILL YOU!
MESS UP AND I'LL OUT YOU.
HUH?
KANADE!
BATTLE 27/END

Promise me?

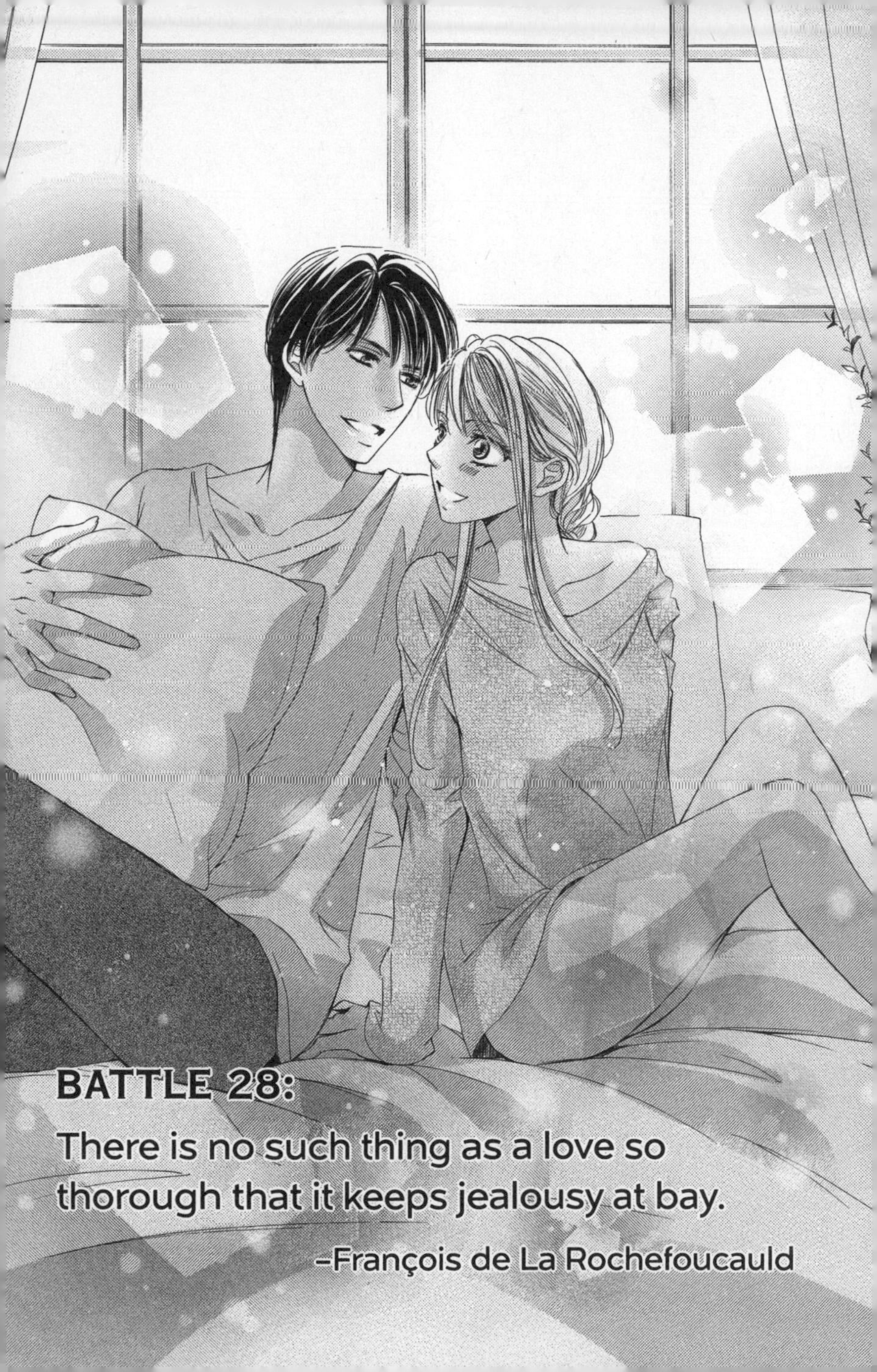
BATTLE 28:
There is no such thing as a love so thorough that it keeps jealousy at bay.
–François de La Rochefoucauld

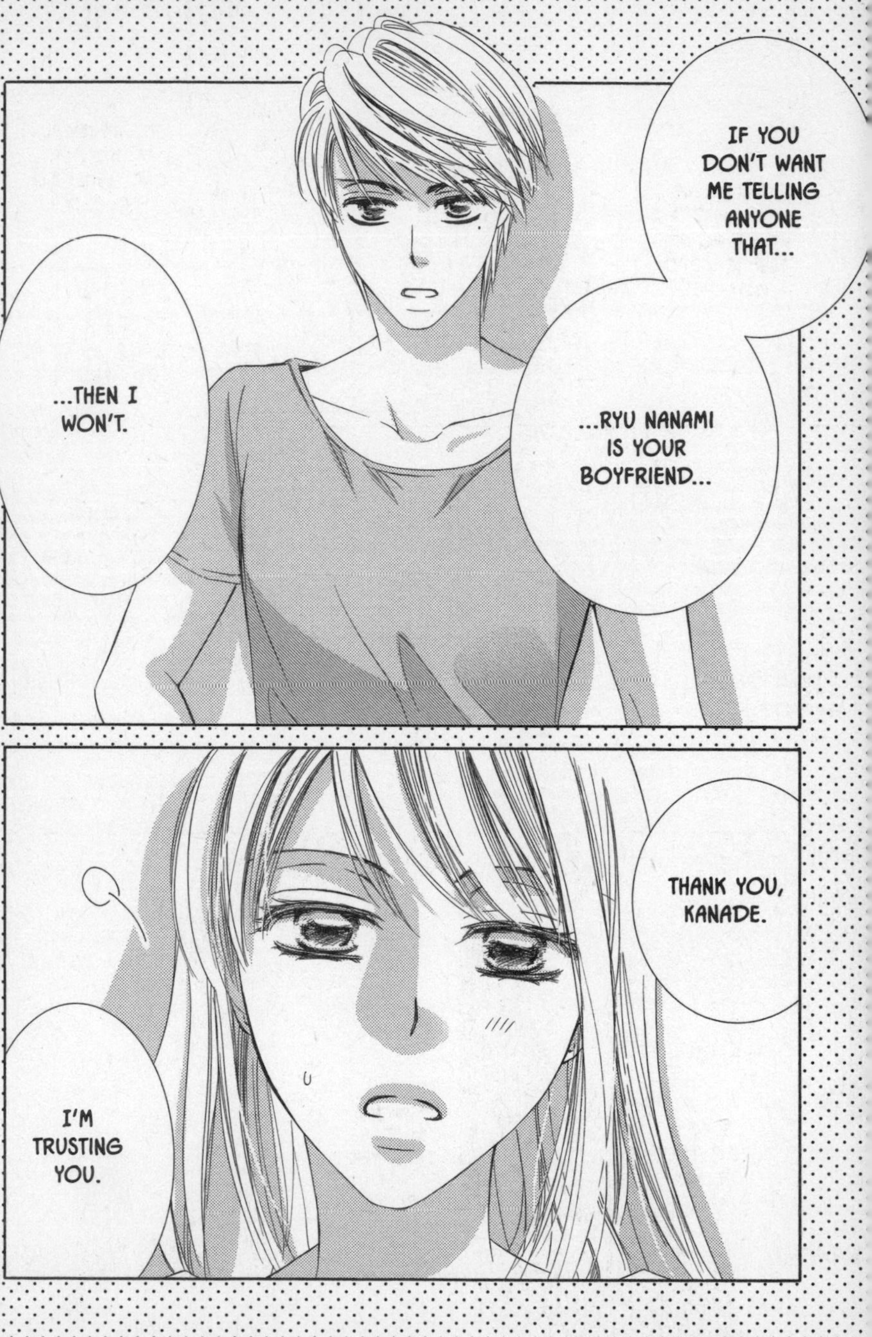
IF YOU DON'T WANT ME TELLING ANYONE THAT...
...RYU NANAMI IS YOUR BOYFRIEND...
...THEN I WON'T.
THANK YOU, KANADE.
I'M TRUSTING YOU.

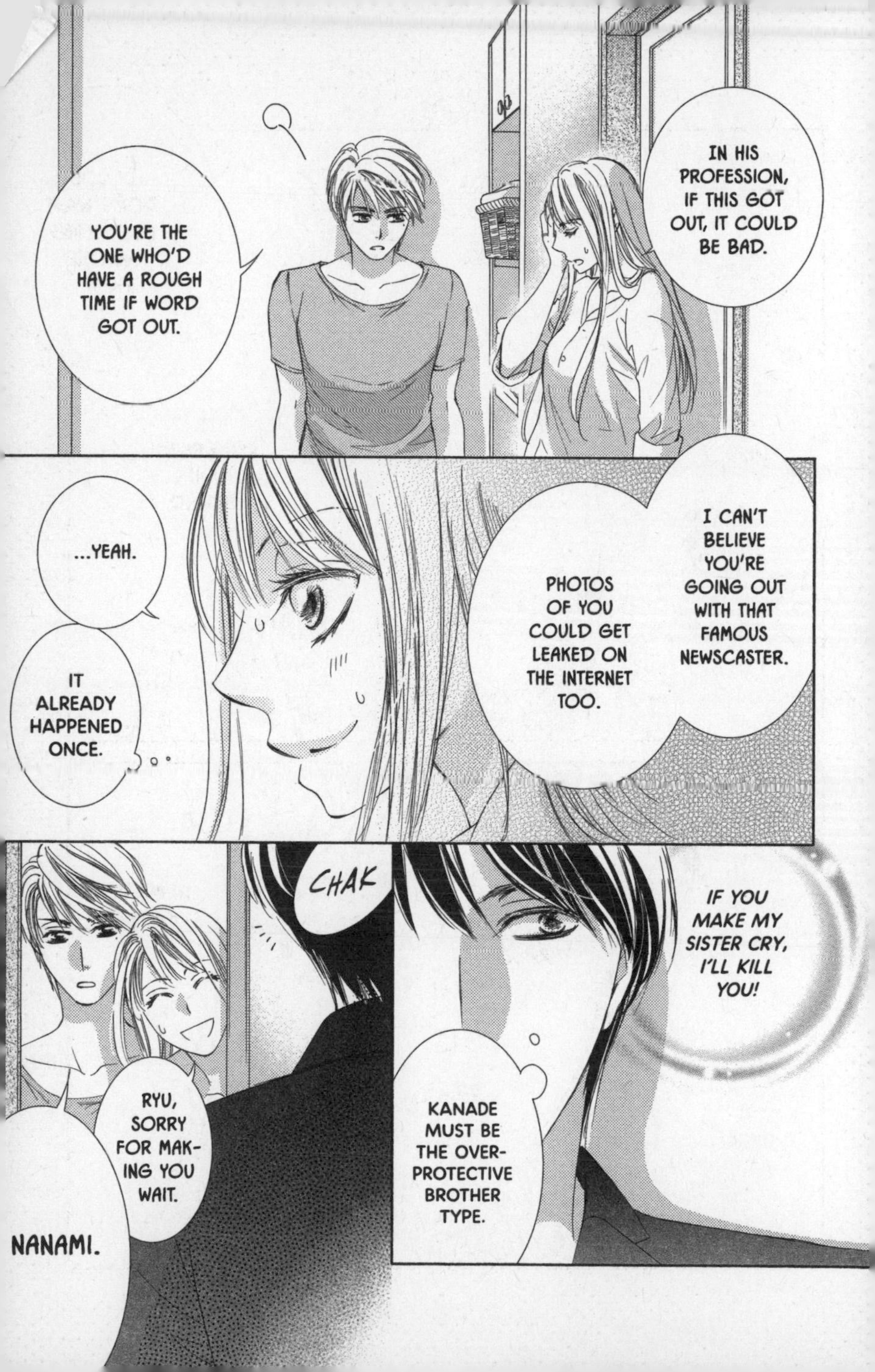
IN HIS PROFESSION, IF THIS GOT OUT, IT COULD BE BAD.
YOU'RE THE ONE WHO'D HAVE A ROUGH TIME IF WORD GOT OUT.
I CAN'T BELIEVE YOU'RE GOING OUT WITH THAT FAMOUS NEWSCASTER.
PHOTOS OF YOU COULD GET LEAKED ON THE INTERNET TOO.
...YEAH.
IT ALREADY HAPPENED ONCE.
IF YOU MAKE MY SISTER CRY, I'LL KILL YOU!
KANADE MUST BE THE OVER-PROTECTIVE BROTHER TYPE.
CHAK
RYU, SORRY FOR MAK-ING YOU WAIT.
NANAMI.

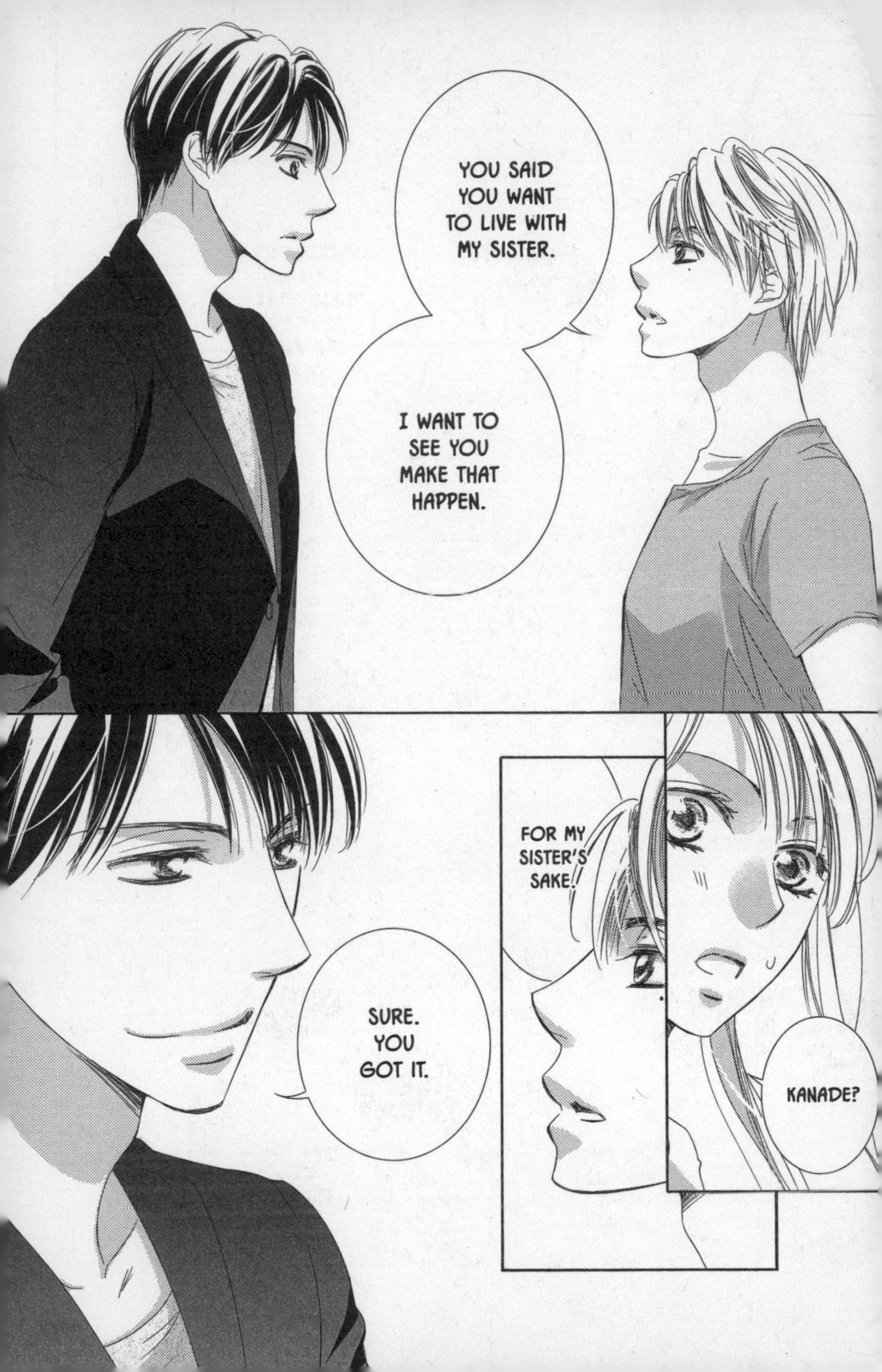
YOU SAID YOU WANT TO LIVE WITH MY SISTER.
I WANT TO SEE YOU MAKE THAT HAPPEN.
KANADE?
FOR MY SISTER'S SAKE.
SURE. YOU GOT IT.

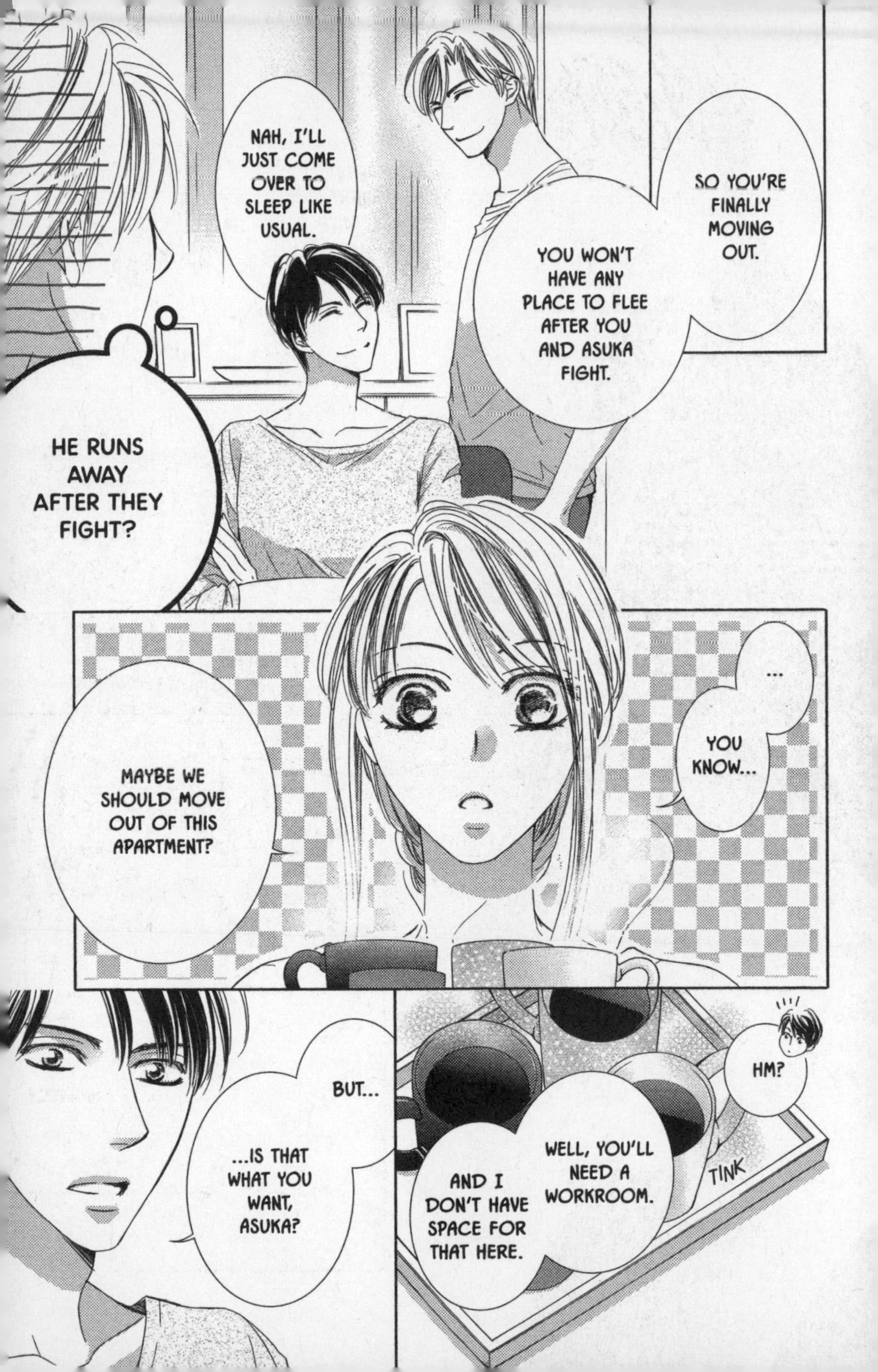
SO YOU'RE FINALLY MOVING OUT.
YOU WON'T HAVE ANY PLACE TO FLEE AFTER YOU AND ASUKA FIGHT.
NAH, I'LL JUST COME OVER TO SLEEP LIKE USUAL.
HE RUNS AWAY AFTER THEY FIGHT?
... YOU KNOW...
MAYBE WE SHOULD MOVE OUT OF THIS APARTMENT?
HM?
WELL, YOU'LL NEED A WORKROOM.
AND I DON'T HAVE SPACE FOR THAT HERE.
TINK
BUT...
...IS THAT WHAT YOU WANT, ASUKA?

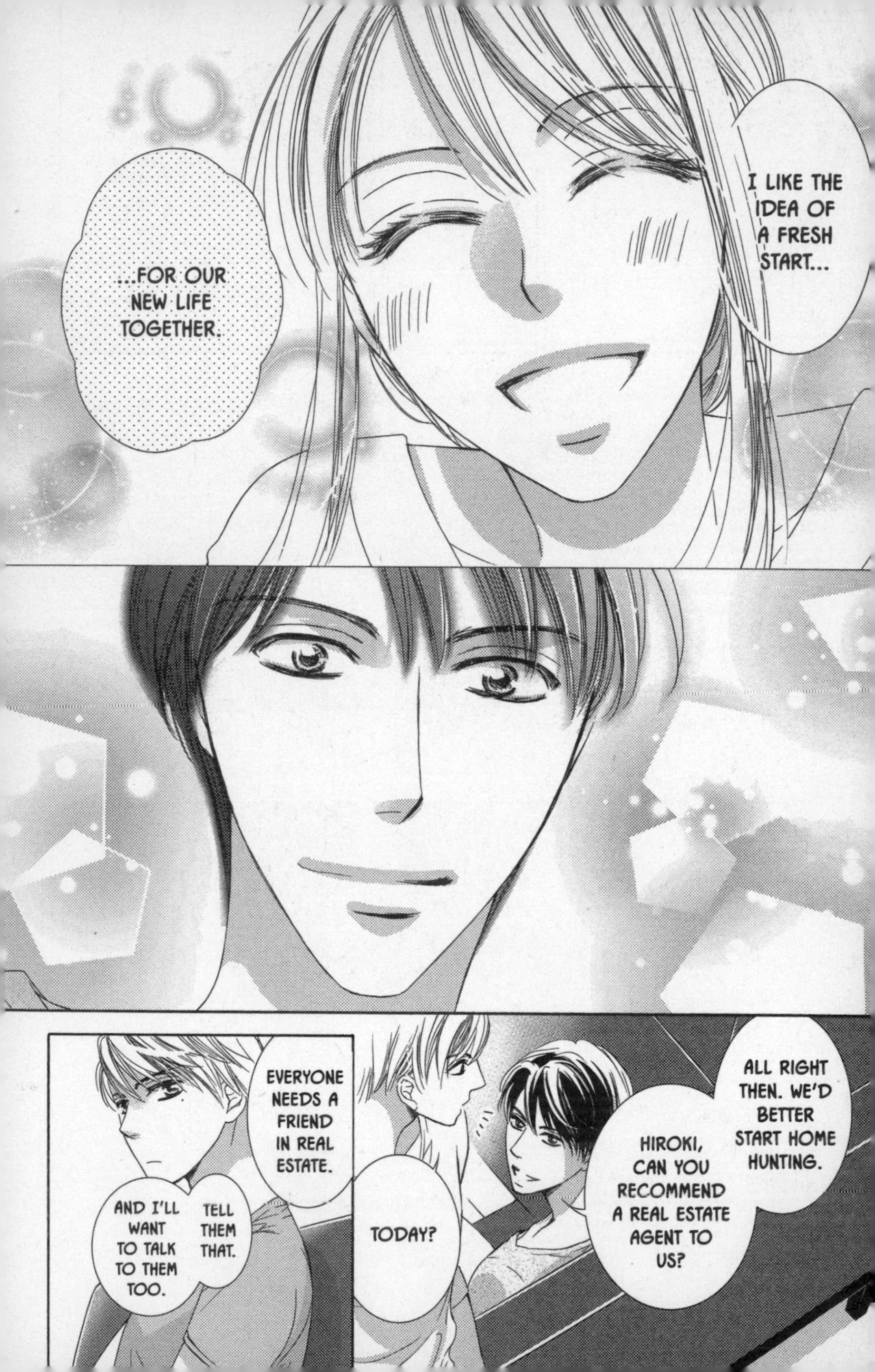
I LIKE THE IDEA OF A FRESH START...
...FOR OUR NEW LIFE TOGETHER.
ALL RIGHT THEN. WE'D BETTER START HOME HUNTING.
HIROKI, CAN YOU RECOMMEND A REAL ESTATE AGENT TO US?
EVERYONE NEEDS A FRIEND IN REAL ESTATE.
TODAY?
TELL THEM THAT.
AND I'LL WANT TO TALK TO THEM TOO.

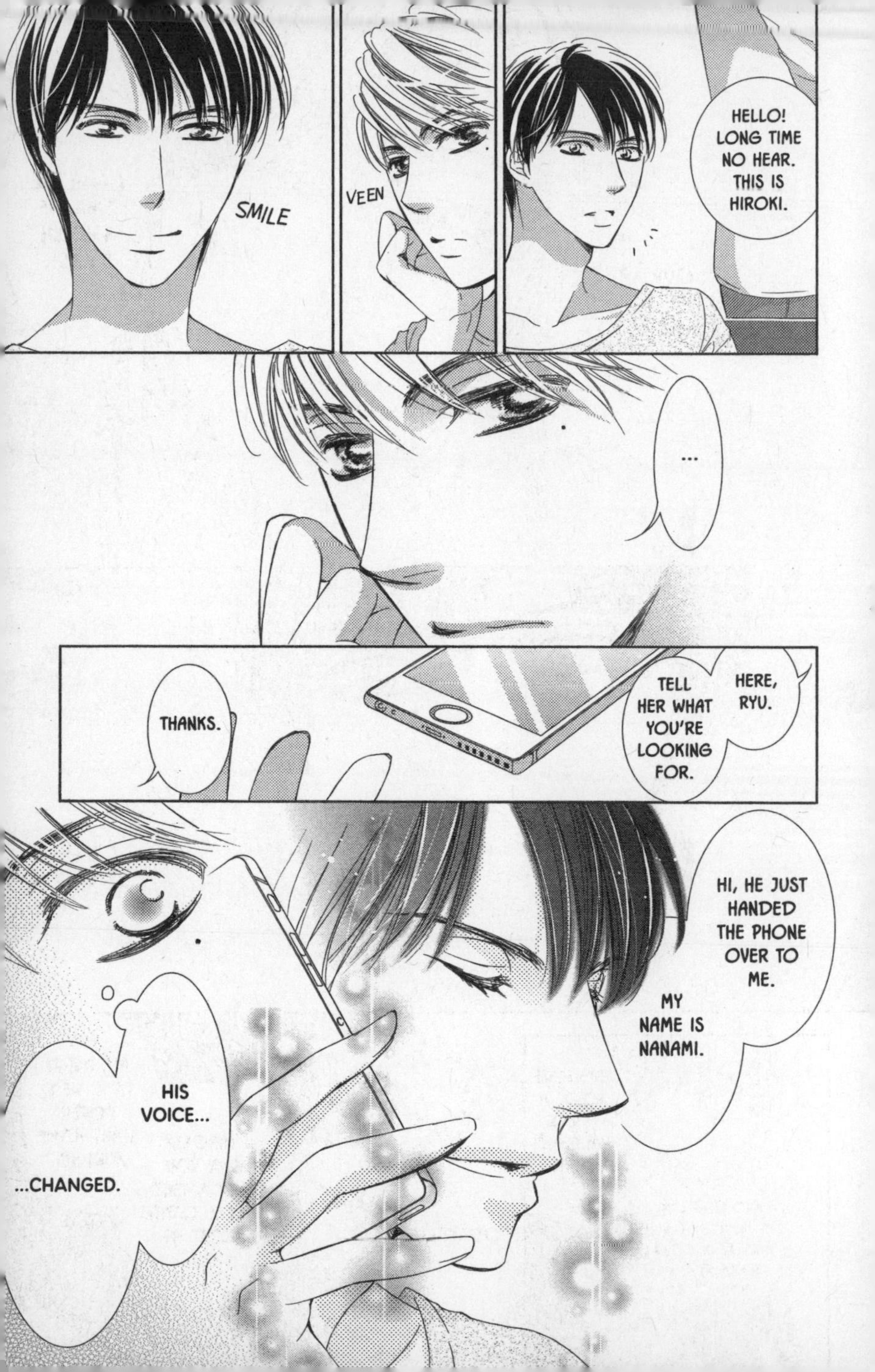
HELLO! LONG TIME NO HEAR. THIS IS HIROKI.
VEEN
SMILE
...
HERE, RYU.
TELL HER WHAT YOU'RE LOOKING FOR.
THANKS.
HI, HE JUST HANDED THE PHONE OVER TO ME.
MY NAME IS NANAMI.
HIS VOICE...
...CHANGED.

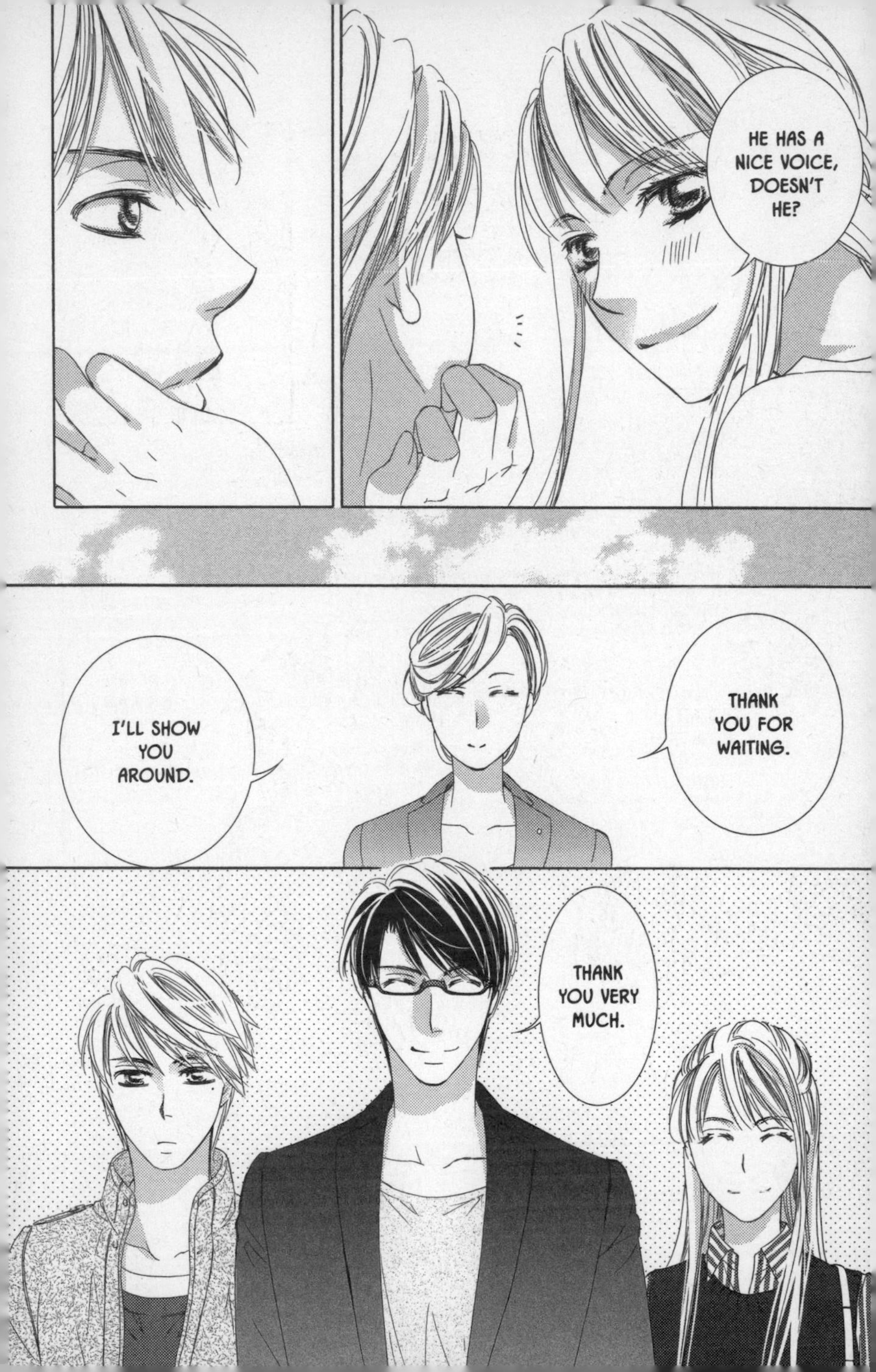
HE HAS A NICE VOICE, DOESN'T HE?
THANK YOU FOR WAITING.
I'LL SHOW YOU AROUND.
THANK YOU VERY MUCH.

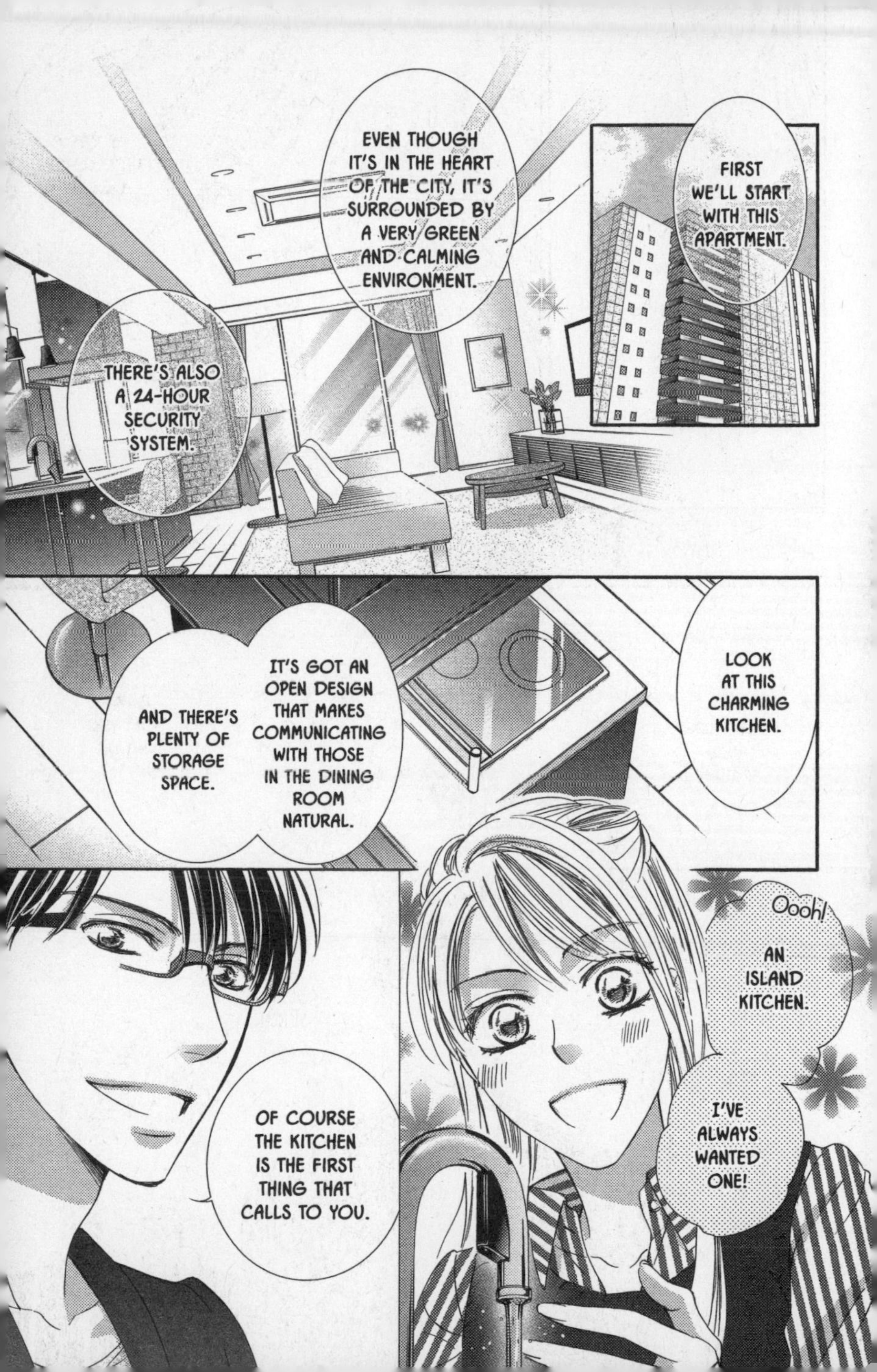
FIRST WE'LL START WITH THIS APARTMENT.
EVEN THOUGH IT'S IN THE HEART OF THE CITY, IT'S SURROUNDED BY A VERY GREEN AND CALMING ENVIRONMENT.
THERE'S ALSO A 24-HOUR SECURITY SYSTEM.
LOOK AT THIS CHARMING KITCHEN.
IT'S GOT AN OPEN DESIGN THAT MAKES COMMUNICATING WITH THOSE IN THE DINING ROOM NATURAL.
AND THERE'S PLENTY OF STORAGE SPACE.
Oooh!
AN ISLAND KITCHEN.
I'VE ALWAYS WANTED ONE!
OF COURSE THE KITCHEN IS THE FIRST THING THAT CALLS TO YOU.

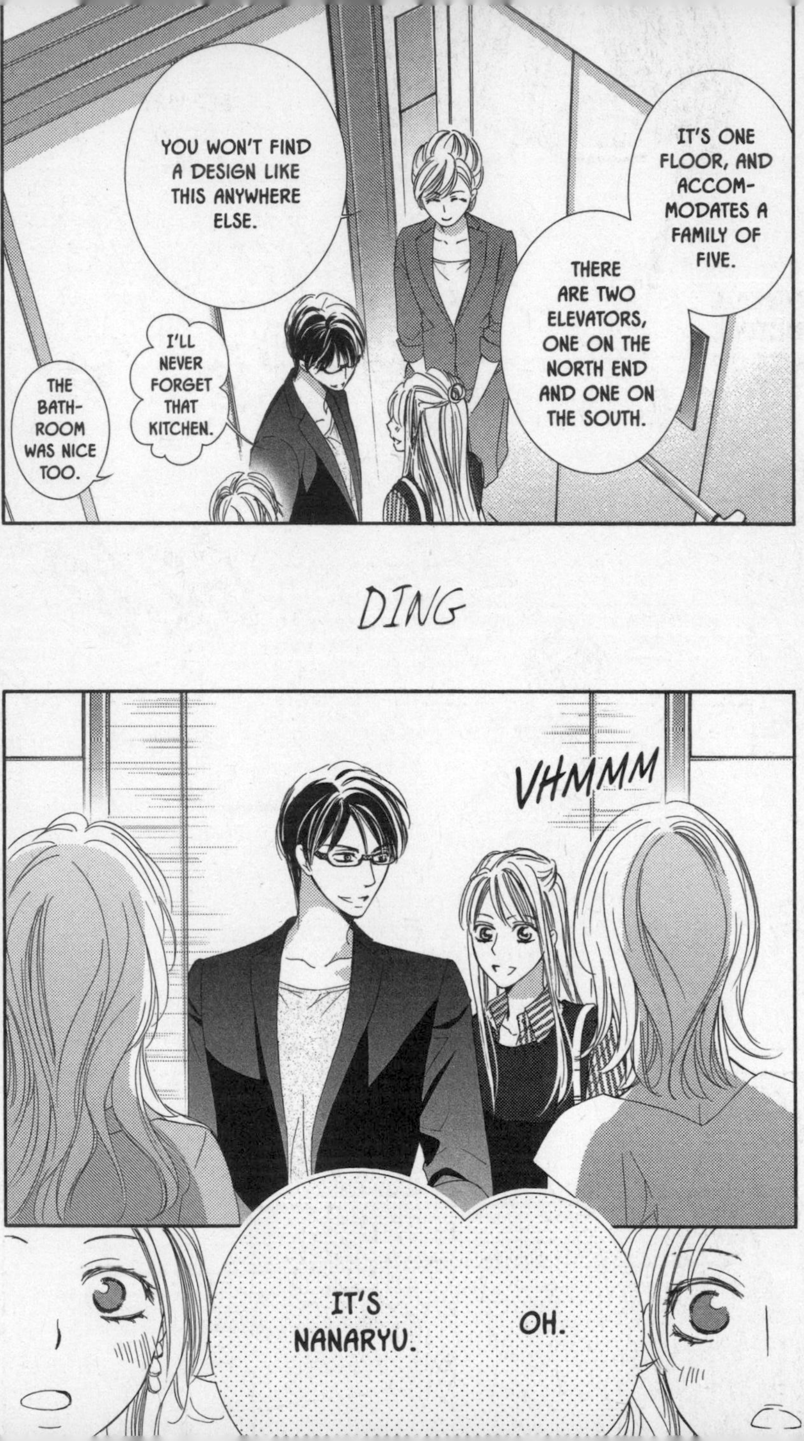
IT'S ONE FLOOR, AND ACCOM-MODATES A FAMILY OF FIVE.
THERE ARE TWO ELEVATORS, ONE ON THE NORTH END AND ONE ON THE SOUTH.
YOU WON'T FIND A DESIGN LIKE THIS ANYWHERE ELSE.
I'LL NEVER FORGET THAT KITCHEN.
THE BATH-ROOM WAS NICE TOO.
DING
VHMMM
OH.
IT'S NANARYU.

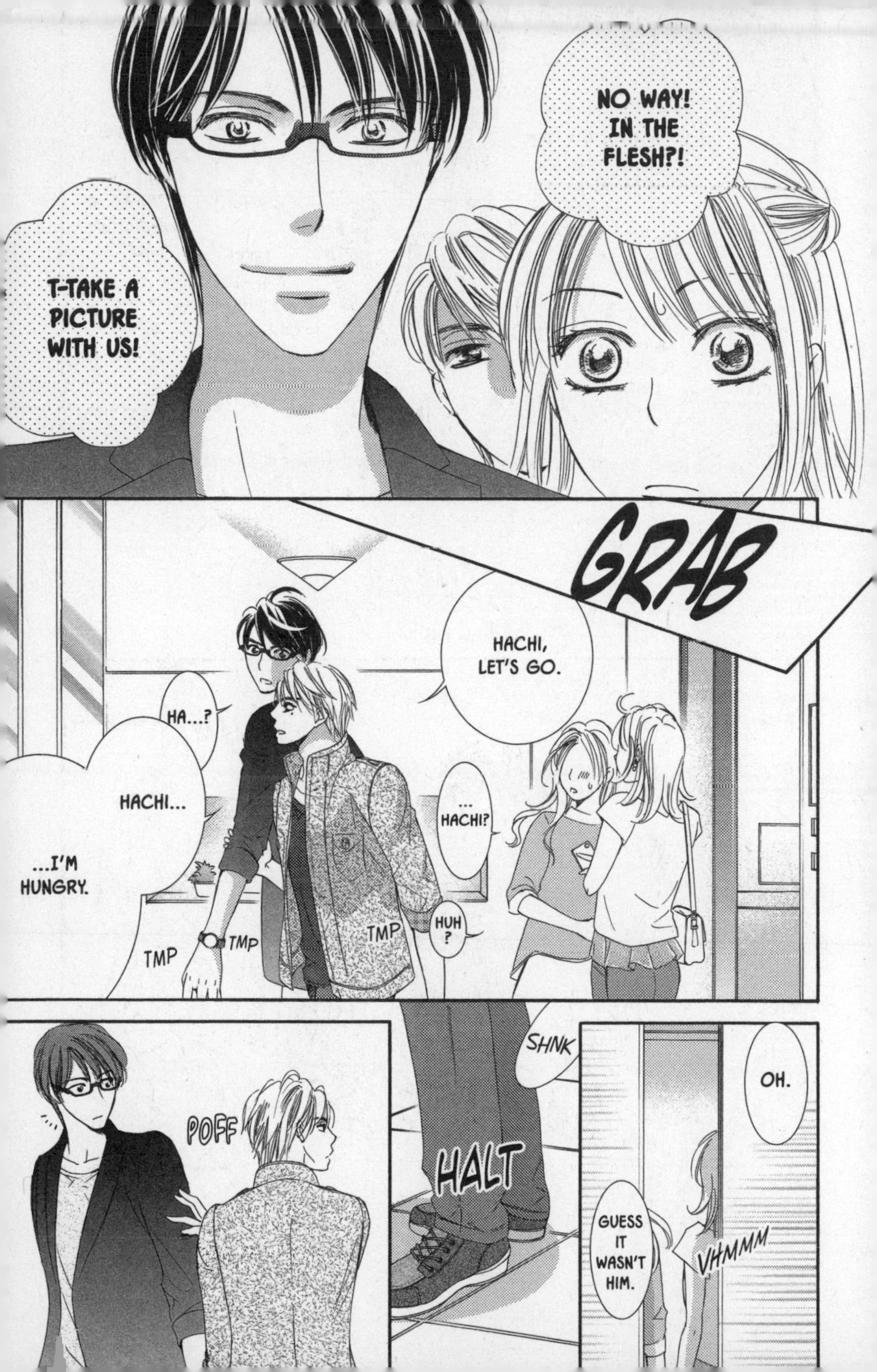
NO WAY! IN THE FLESH?!
T-TAKE A PICTURE WITH US!
GRAB
HACHI, LET'S GO.
...HACHI?
HUH?
TMP
HA...?
HACHI...
...I'M HUNGRY.
TMP
TMP
OH.
GUESS IT WASN'T HIM.
VHMMM
SHNK
HALT
POFF

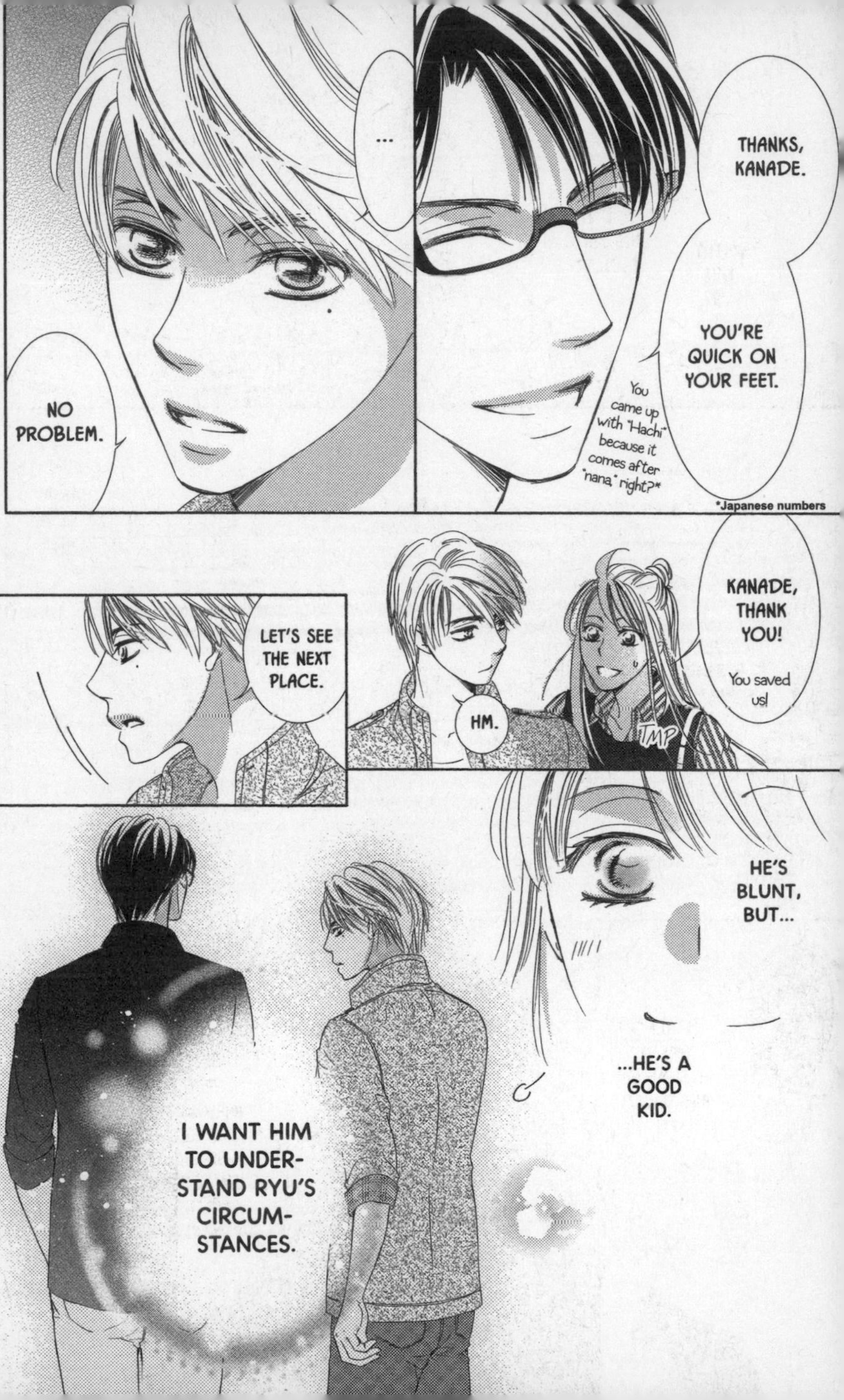
THANKS, KANADE.
YOU'RE QUICK ON YOUR FEET.
You came up with "Hachi" because it comes after "nana," right?*
*Japanese numbers
...
NO PROBLEM.
KANADE, THANK YOU!
You saved us!
TMP
HM.
LET'S SEE THE NEXT PLACE.
HE'S BLUNT, BUT...
...HE'S A GOOD KID.
I WANT HIM TO UNDER-STAND RYU'S CIRCUM-STANCES.

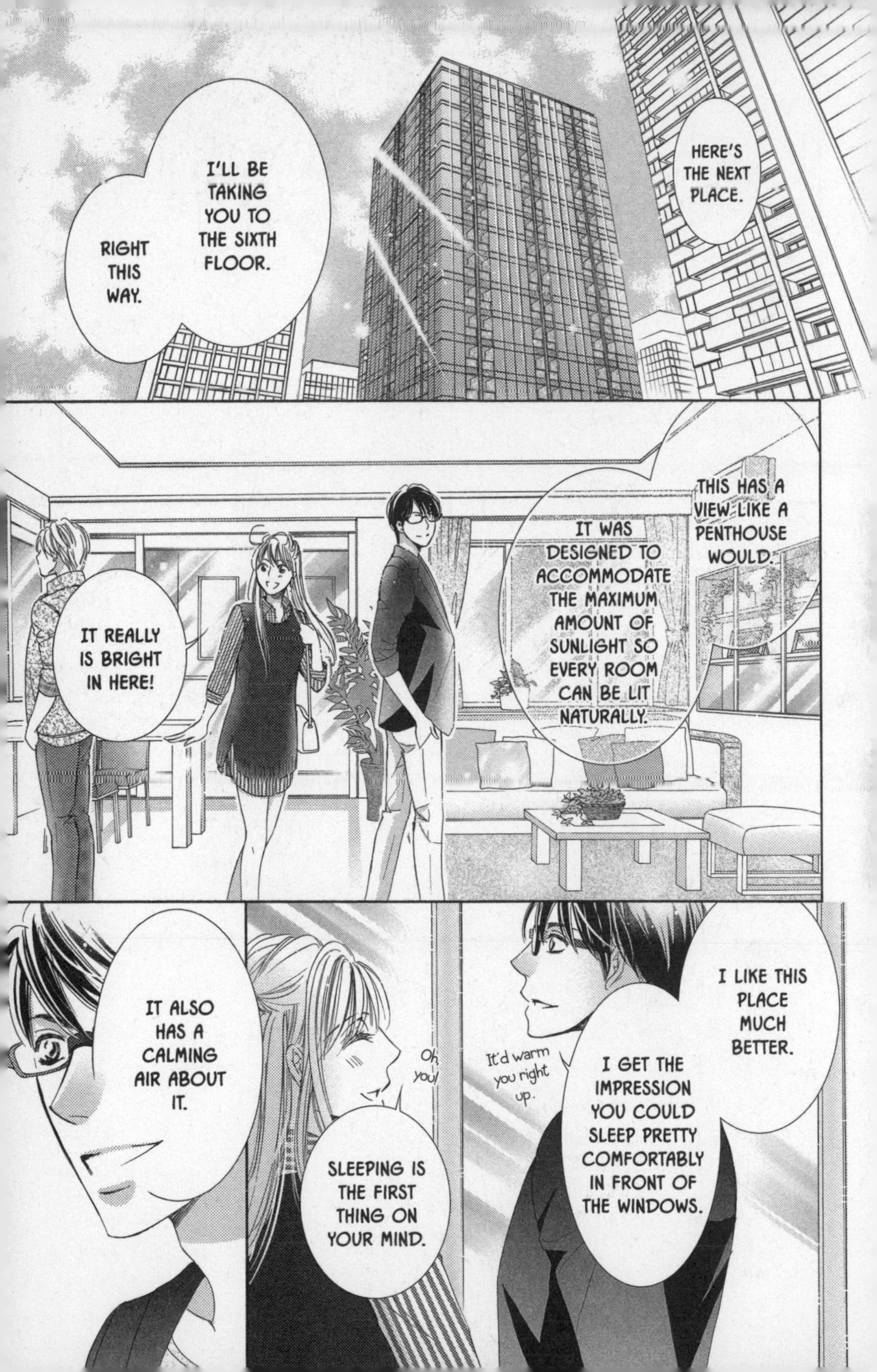
HERE'S THE NEXT PLACE.
I'LL BE TAKING YOU TO THE SIXTH FLOOR.
RIGHT THIS WAY.
THIS HAS A VIEW LIKE A PENTHOUSE WOULD.
IT WAS DESIGNED TO ACCOMMODATE THE MAXIMUM AMOUNT OF SUNLIGHT SO EVERY ROOM CAN BE LIT NATURALLY.
IT REALLY IS BRIGHT IN HERE!
I LIKE THIS PLACE MUCH BETTER.
I GET THE IMPRESSION YOU COULD SLEEP PRETTY COMFORTABLY IN FRONT OF THE WINDOWS.
It'd warm you right up.
Oh, you!
SLEEPING IS THE FIRST THING ON YOUR MIND.
IT ALSO HAS A CALMING AIR ABOUT IT.

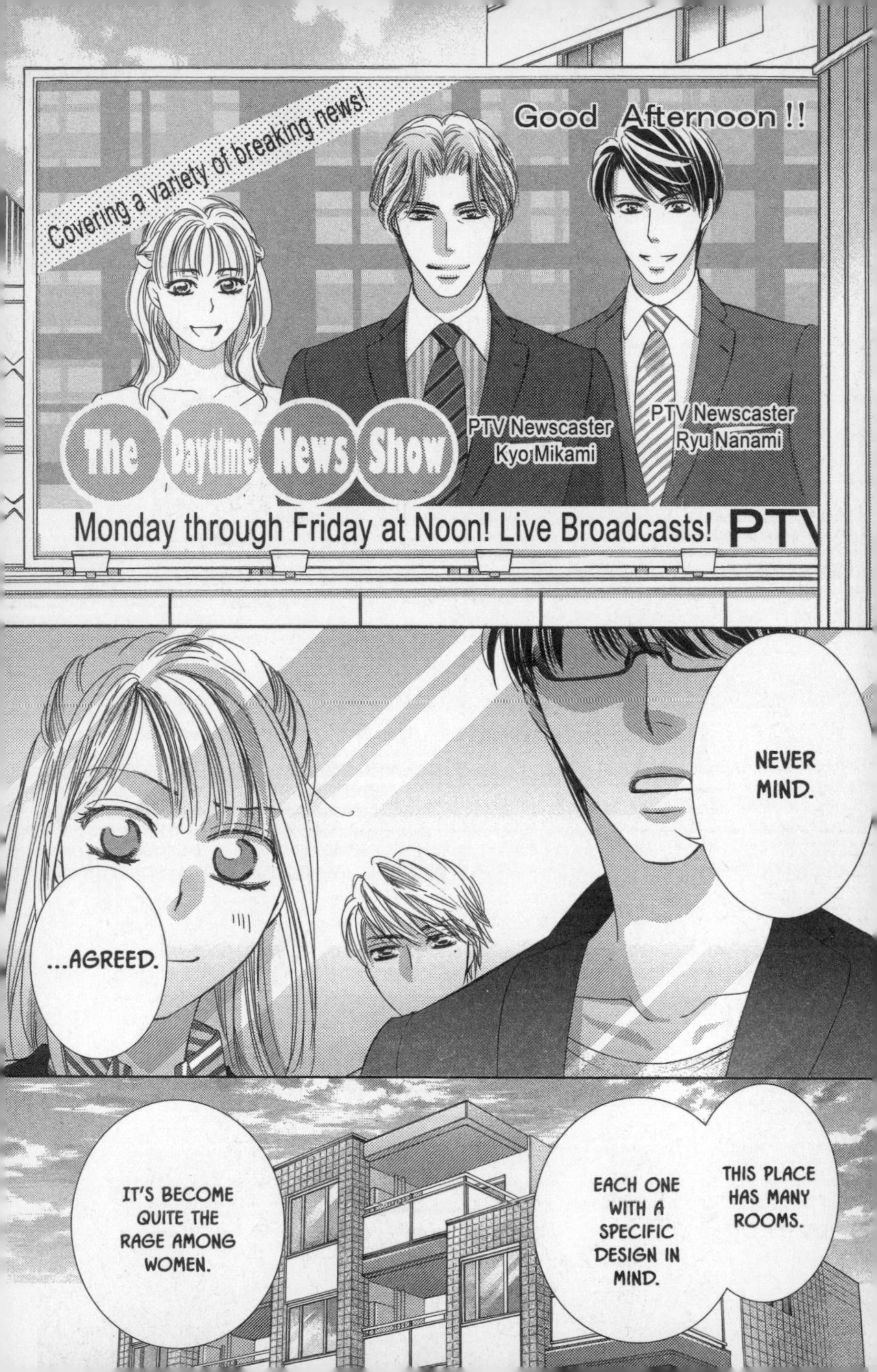
Covering a variety of breaking news!
Good Afternoon !!
The Daytime News Show
PTV Newscaster Kyo Mikami
PTV Newscaster Ryu Nanami
Monday through Friday at Noon! Live Broadcasts!
PTV
NEVER MIND.
...AGREED.
THIS PLACE HAS MANY ROOMS.
EACH ONE WITH A SPECIFIC DESIGN IN MIND.
IT'S BECOME QUITE THE RAGE AMONG WOMEN.

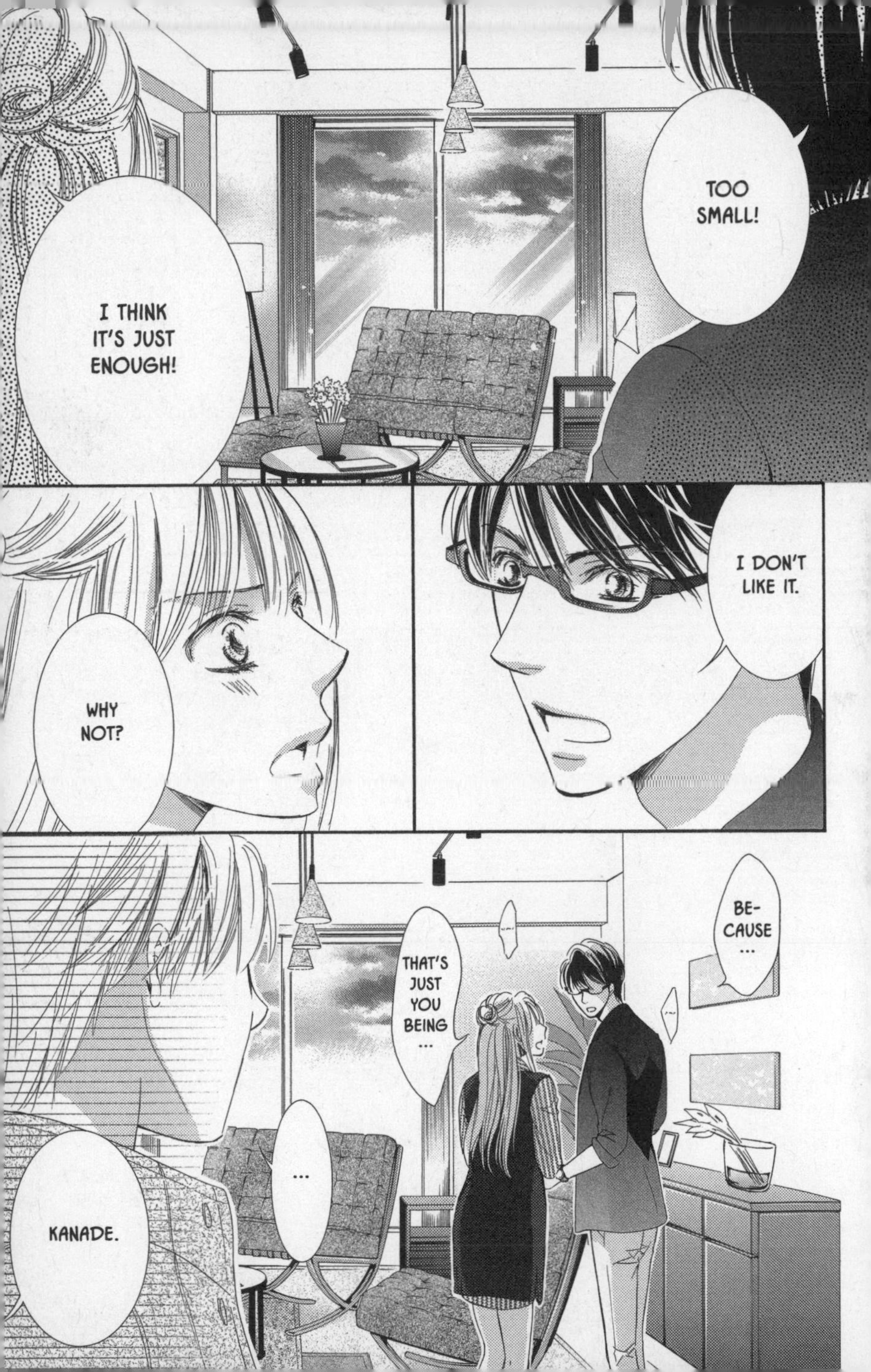
TOO SMALL!
I THINK IT'S JUST ENOUGH!
I DON'T LIKE IT.
WHY NOT?
BE-CAUSE ...
THAT'S JUST YOU BEING ...
...
KANADE.

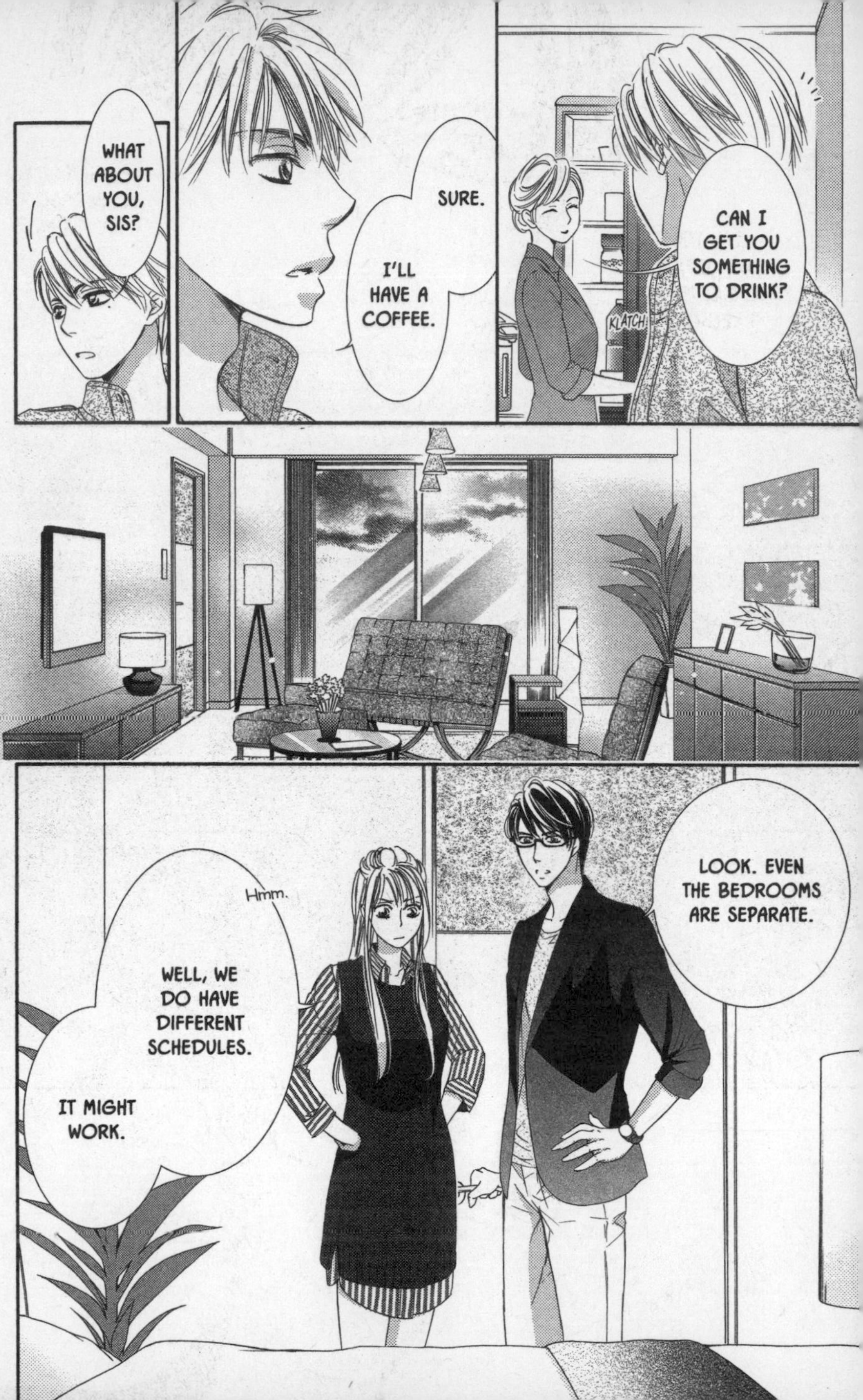
CAN I GET YOU SOMETHING TO DRINK?
KLATCH
SURE.
I'LL HAVE A COFFEE.
WHAT ABOUT YOU, SIS?
LOOK. EVEN THE BEDROOMS ARE SEPARATE.
Hmm.
WELL, WE DO HAVE DIFFERENT SCHEDULES.
IT MIGHT WORK.

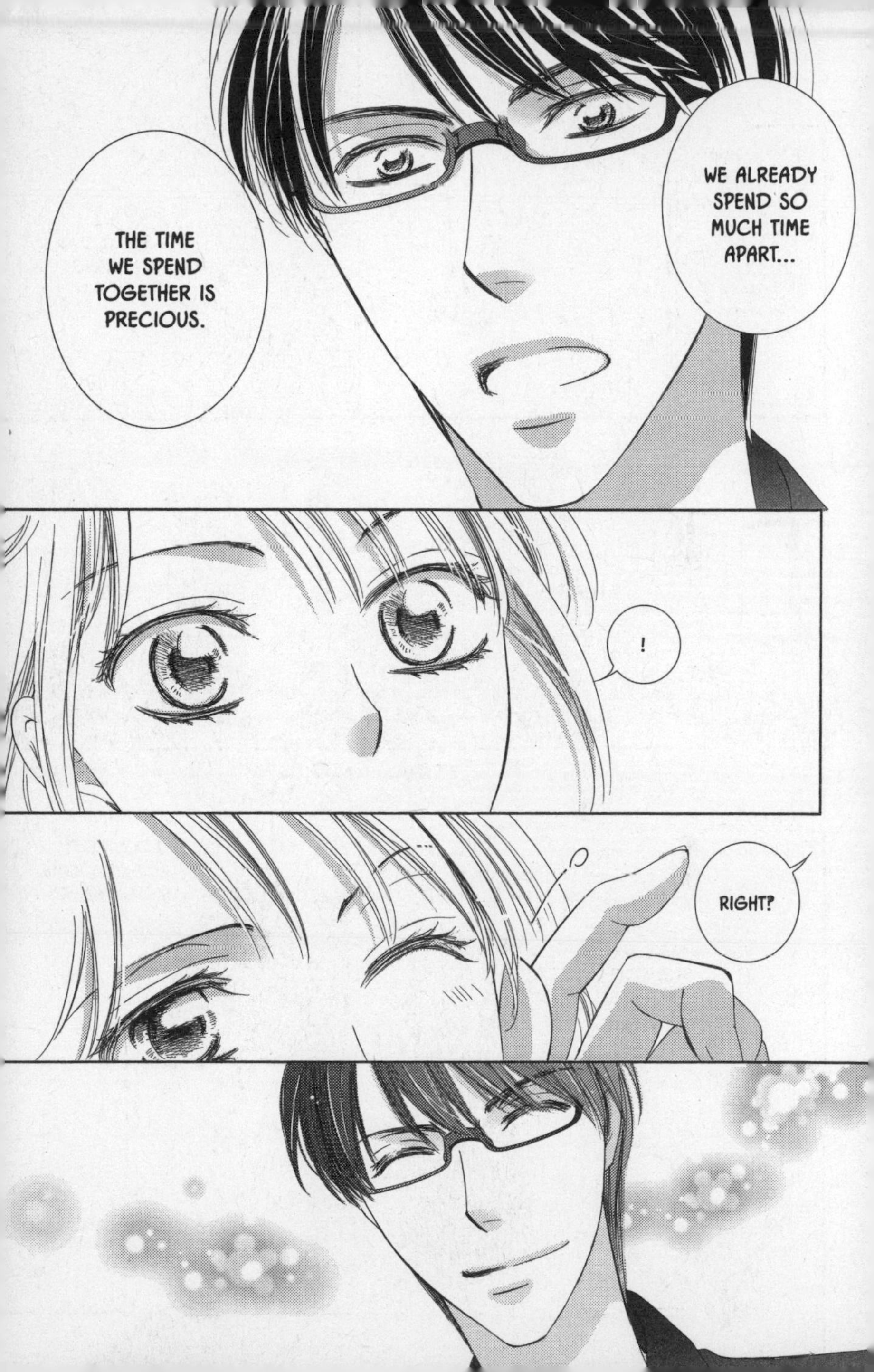
WE ALREADY SPEND SO MUCH TIME APART...
THE TIME WE SPEND TOGETHER IS PRECIOUS.
!
RIGHT?

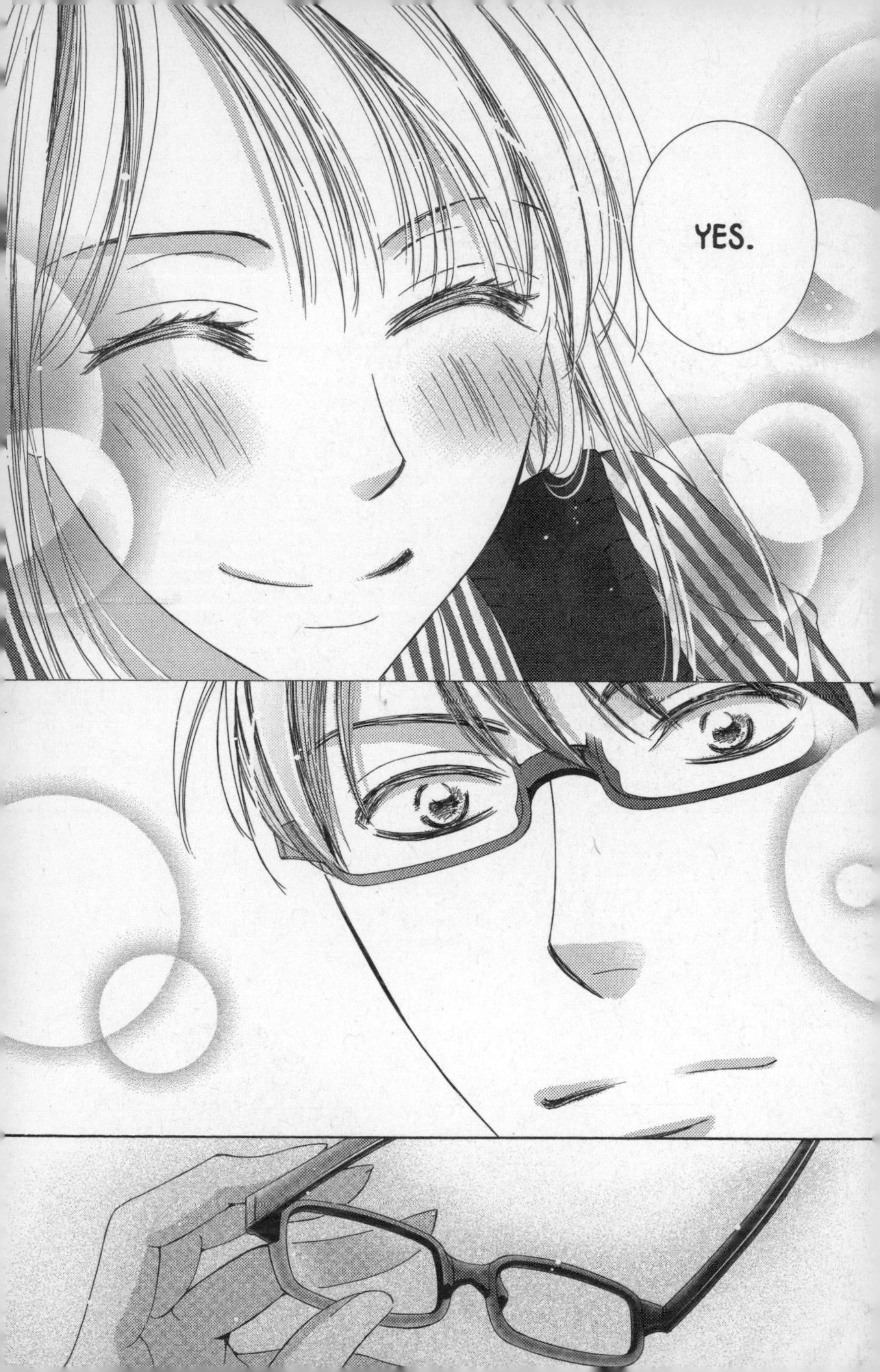
YES.

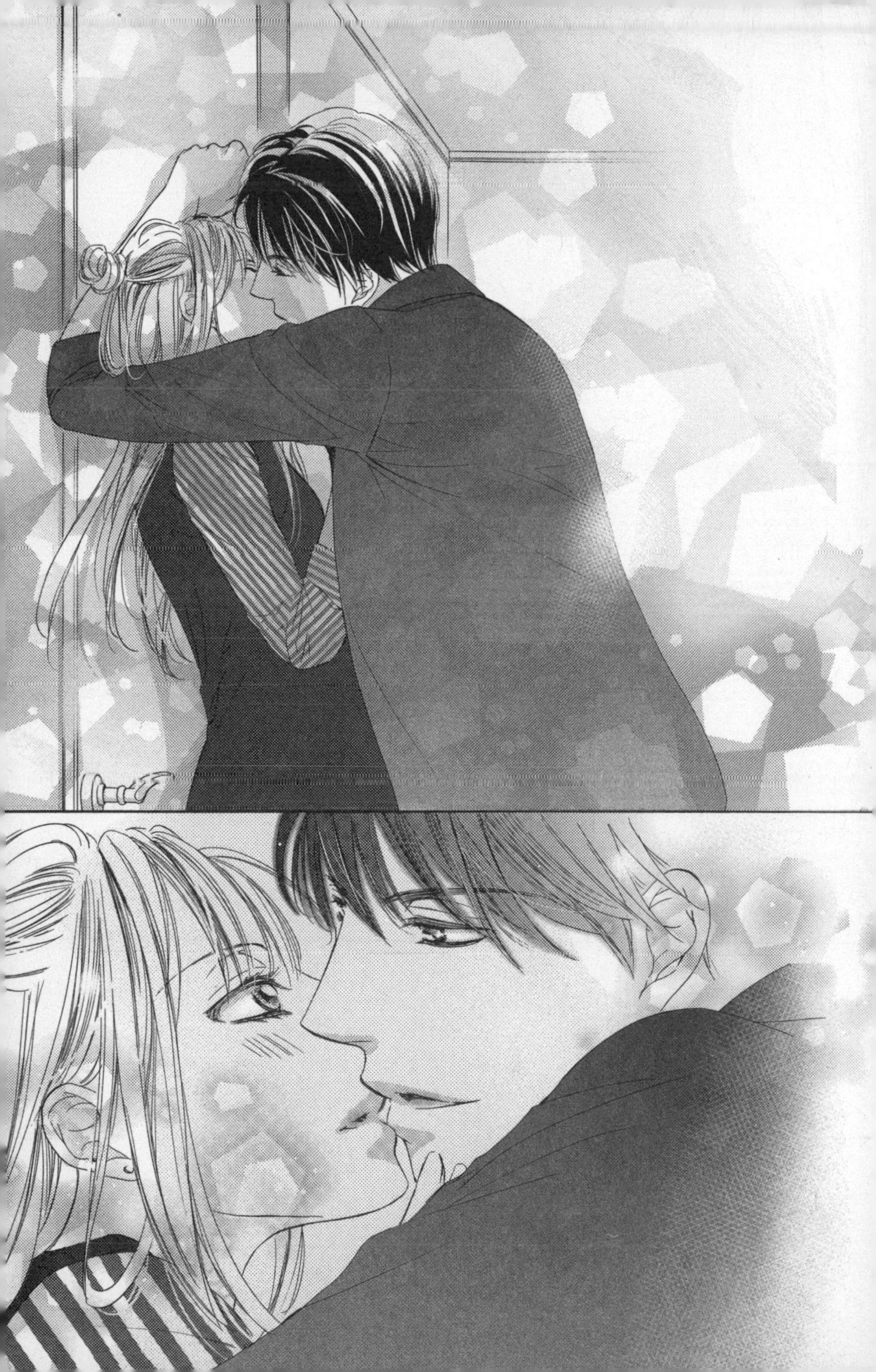

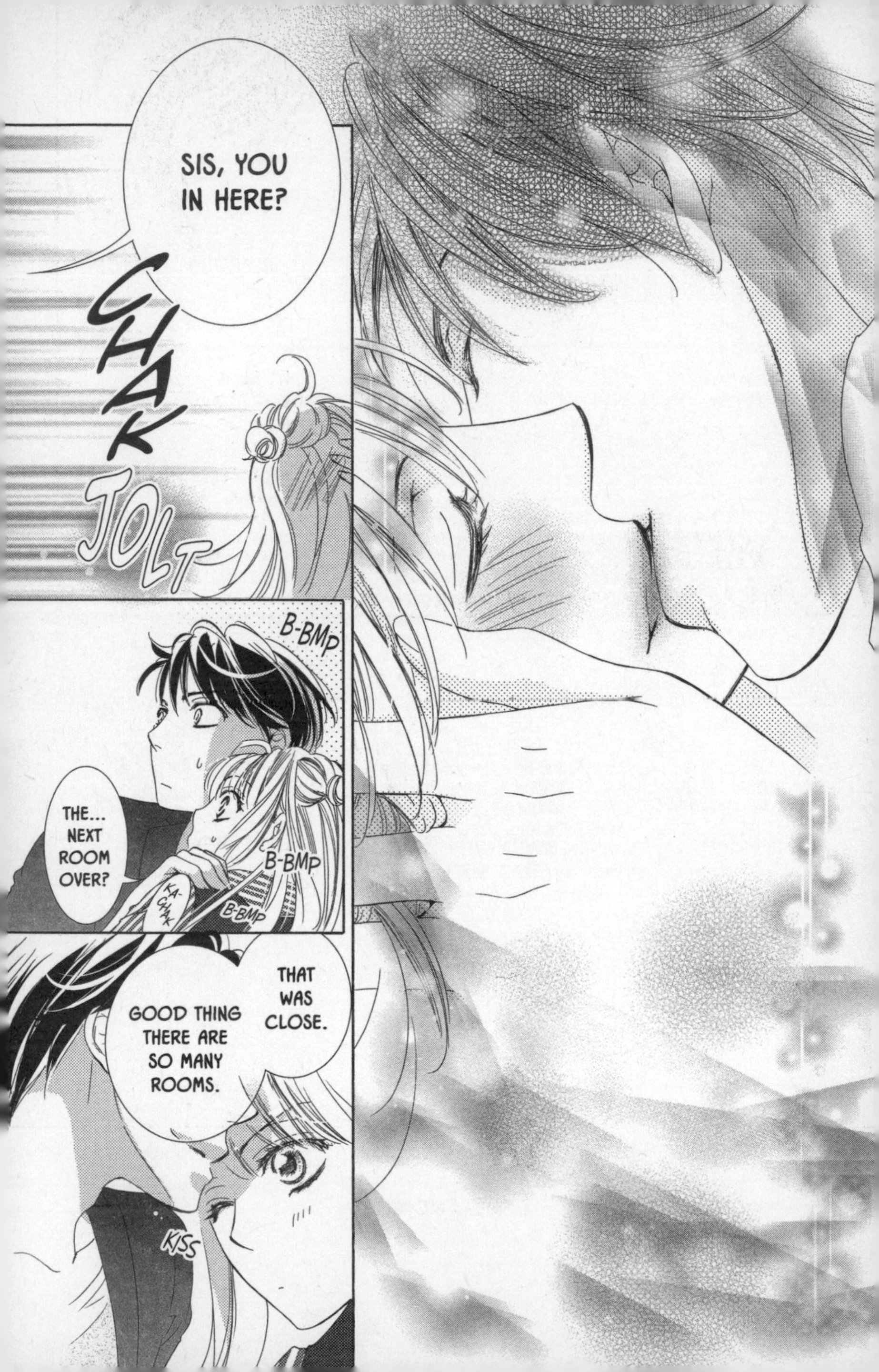
SIS, YOU IN HERE?
CHAK
JOLT
B-BMP
B-BMP
THE... NEXT ROOM OVER?
KA-CHAK
B-BMP
THAT WAS CLOSE.
GOOD THING THERE ARE SO MANY ROOMS.
KISS

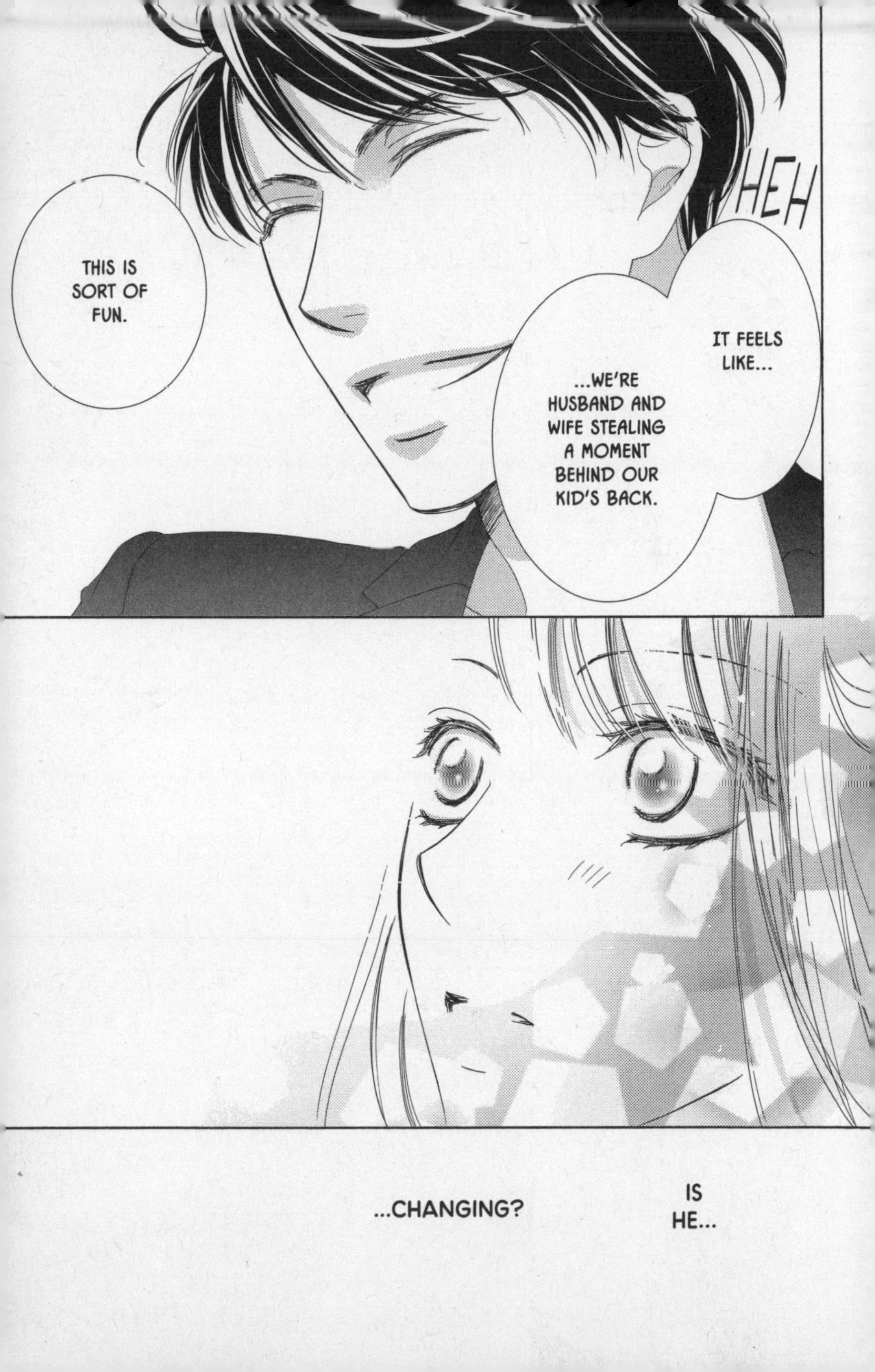
HEH
IT FEELS LIKE...
...WE'RE HUSBAND AND WIFE STEALING A MOMENT BEHIND OUR KID'S BACK.
THIS IS SORT OF FUN.
IS HE...
...CHANGING?

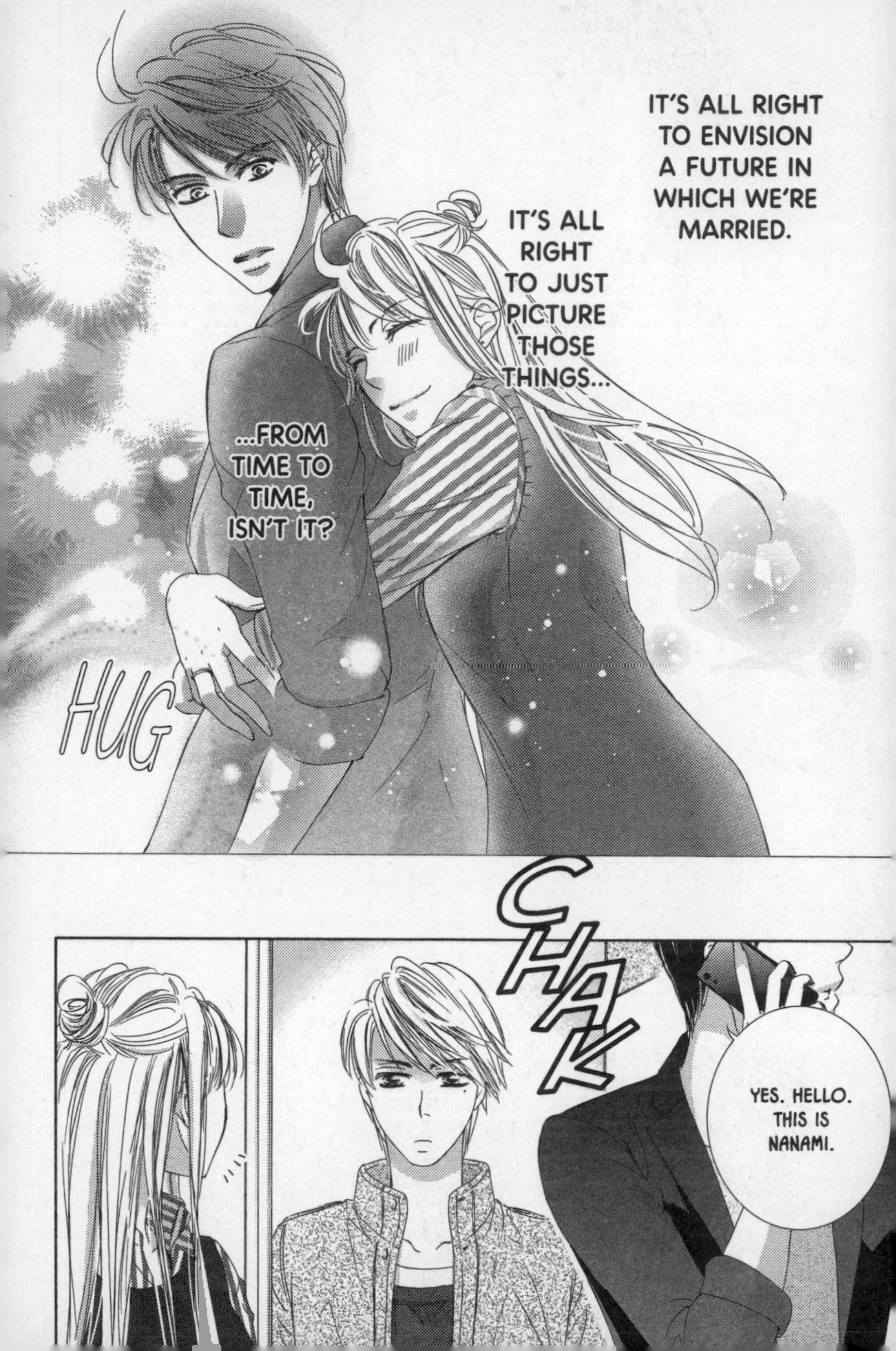
IT'S ALL RIGHT TO ENVISION A FUTURE IN WHICH WE'RE MARRIED.
IT'S ALL RIGHT TO JUST PICTURE THOSE THINGS...
...FROM TIME TO TIME, ISN'T IT?
HUG
CHAK
YES. HELLO. THIS IS NANAMI.

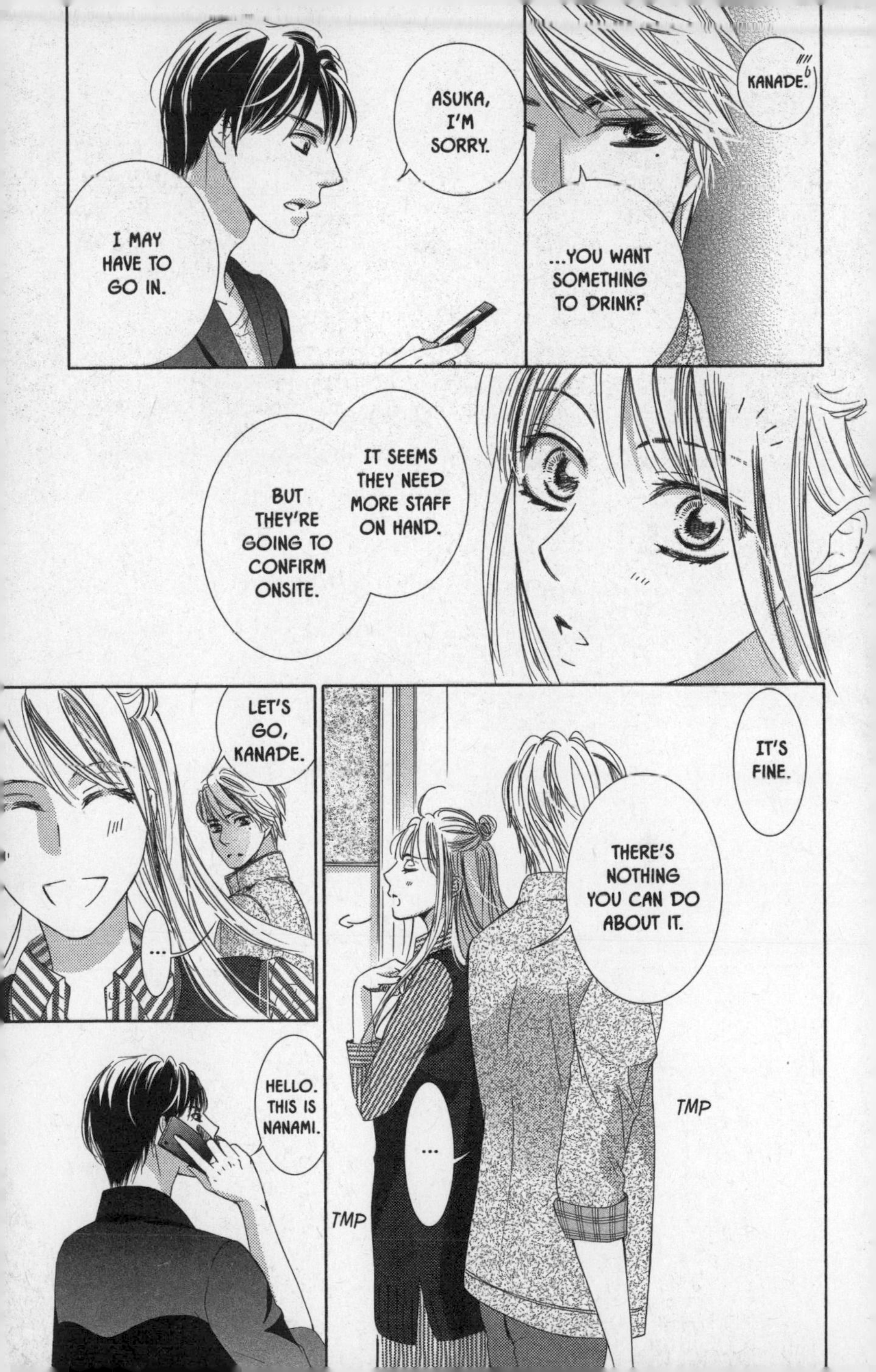
KANADE.
...YOU WANT SOMETHING TO DRINK?
ASUKA, I'M SORRY.
I MAY HAVE TO GO IN.
IT SEEMS THEY NEED MORE STAFF ON HAND.
BUT THEY'RE GOING TO CONFIRM ONSITE.
IT'S FINE.
THERE'S NOTHING YOU CAN DO ABOUT IT.
TMP
...
TMP
LET'S GO, KANADE.
...
HELLO. THIS IS NANAMI.

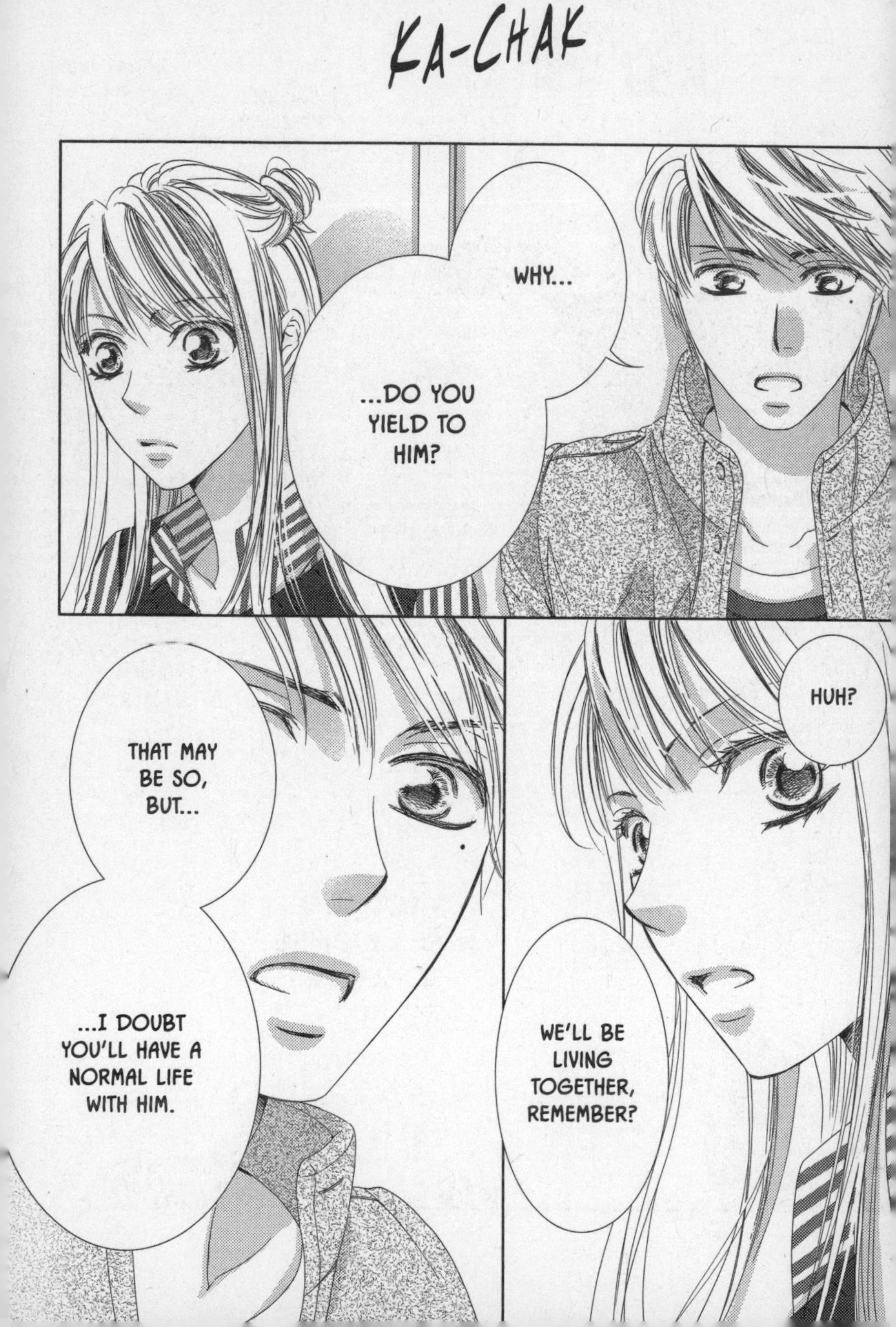
KA-CHAK
WHY...
...DO YOU YIELD TO HIM?
HUH?
WE'LL BE LIVING TOGETHER, REMEMBER?
THAT MAY BE SO, BUT...
...I DOUBT YOU'LL HAVE A NORMAL LIFE WITH HIM.

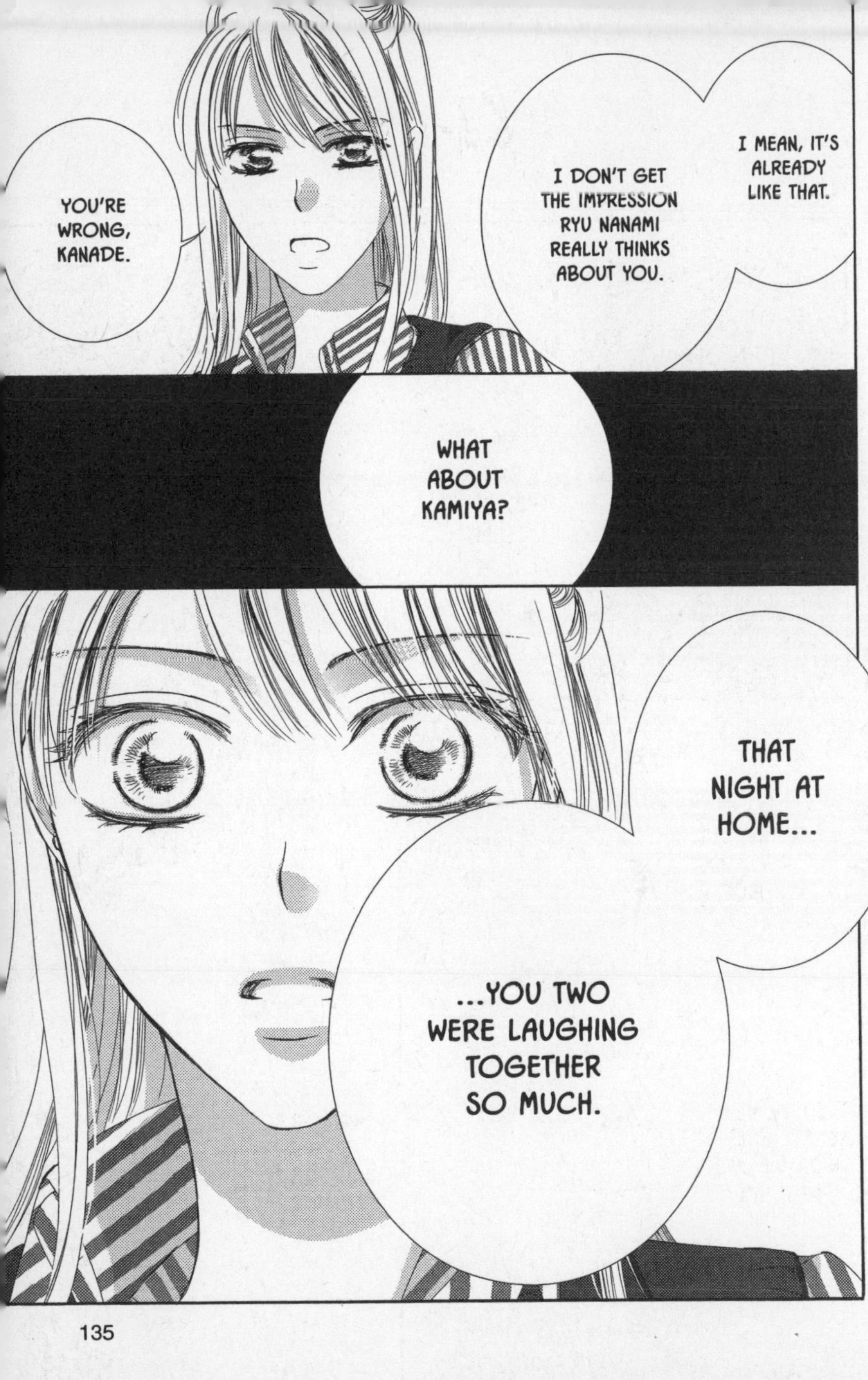
I MEAN, IT'S ALREADY LIKE THAT.
I DON'T GET THE IMPRESSION RYU NANAMI REALLY THINKS ABOUT YOU.
YOU'RE WRONG, KANADE.
WHAT ABOUT KAMIYA?
THAT NIGHT AT HOME...
...YOU TWO WERE LAUGHING TOGETHER SO MUCH.

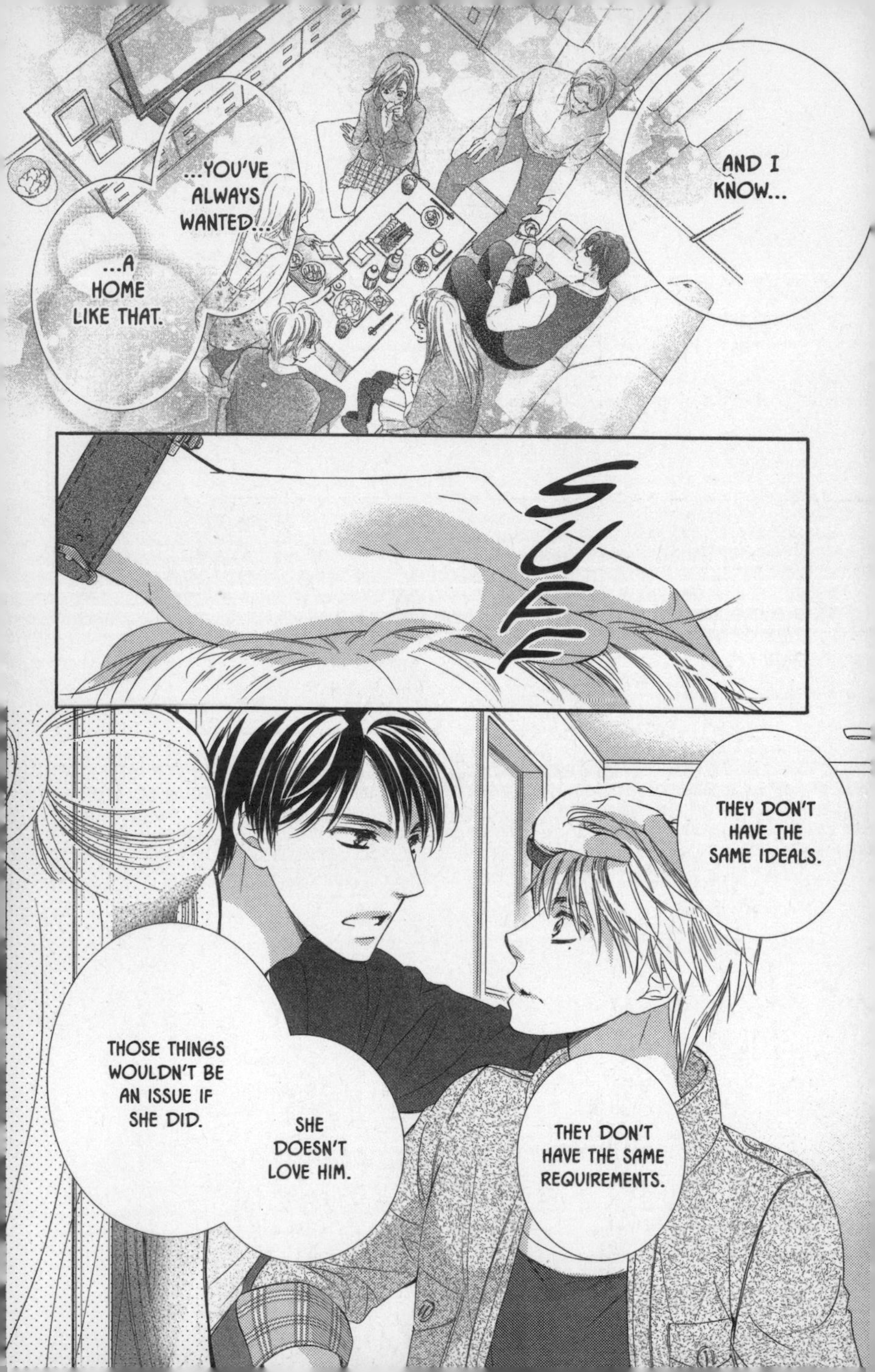
AND I KNOW...
...YOU'VE ALWAYS WANTED...
...A HOME LIKE THAT.
SUFF
THEY DON'T HAVE THE SAME IDEALS.
THEY DON'T HAVE THE SAME REQUIREMENTS.
SHE DOESN'T LOVE HIM.
THOSE THINGS WOULDN'T BE AN ISSUE IF SHE DID.

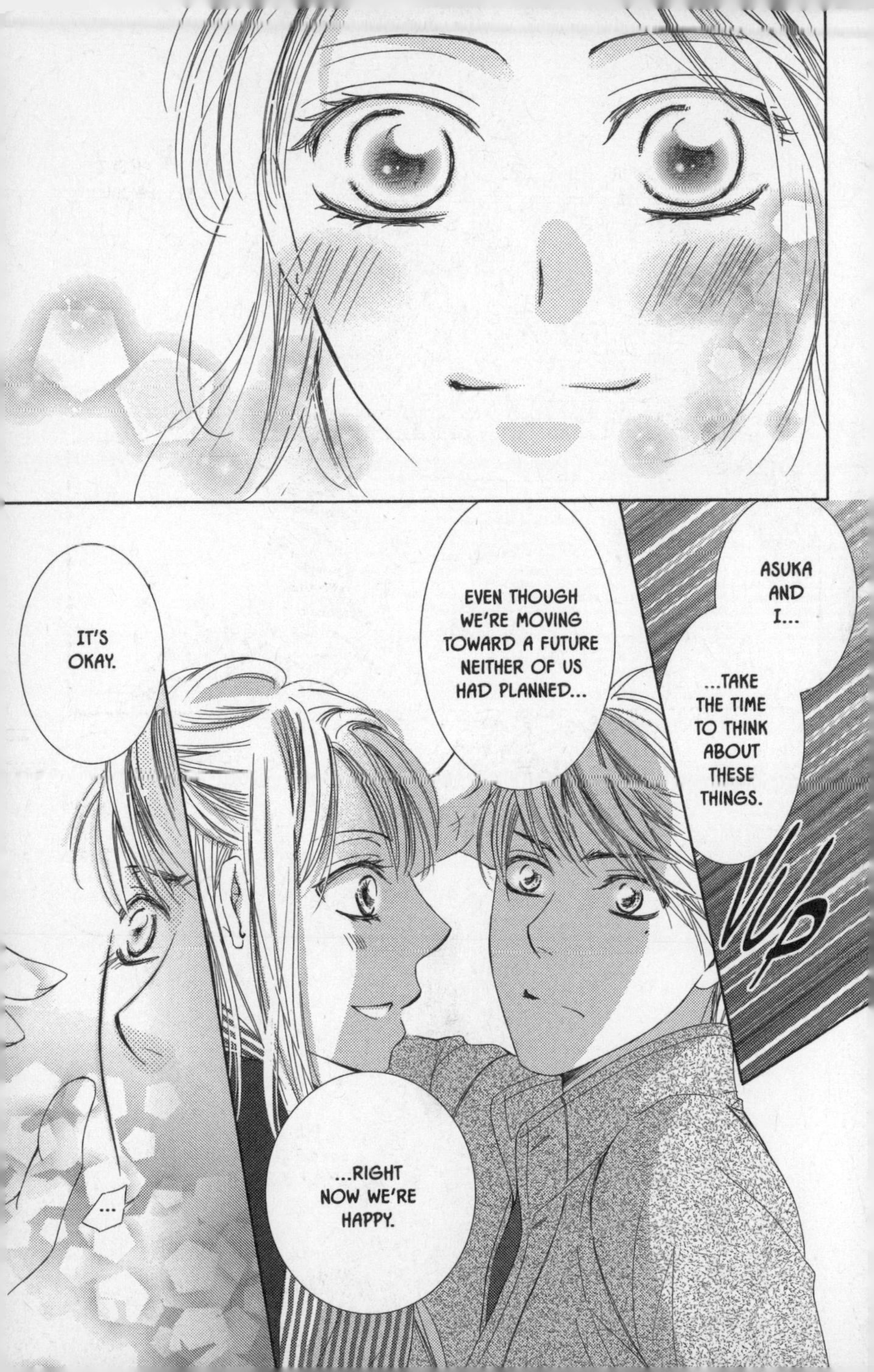
ASUKA AND I...
...TAKE THE TIME TO THINK ABOUT THESE THINGS.
EVEN THOUGH WE'RE MOVING TOWARD A FUTURE NEITHER OF US HAD PLANNED...
...RIGHT NOW WE'RE HAPPY.
IT'S OKAY.
...

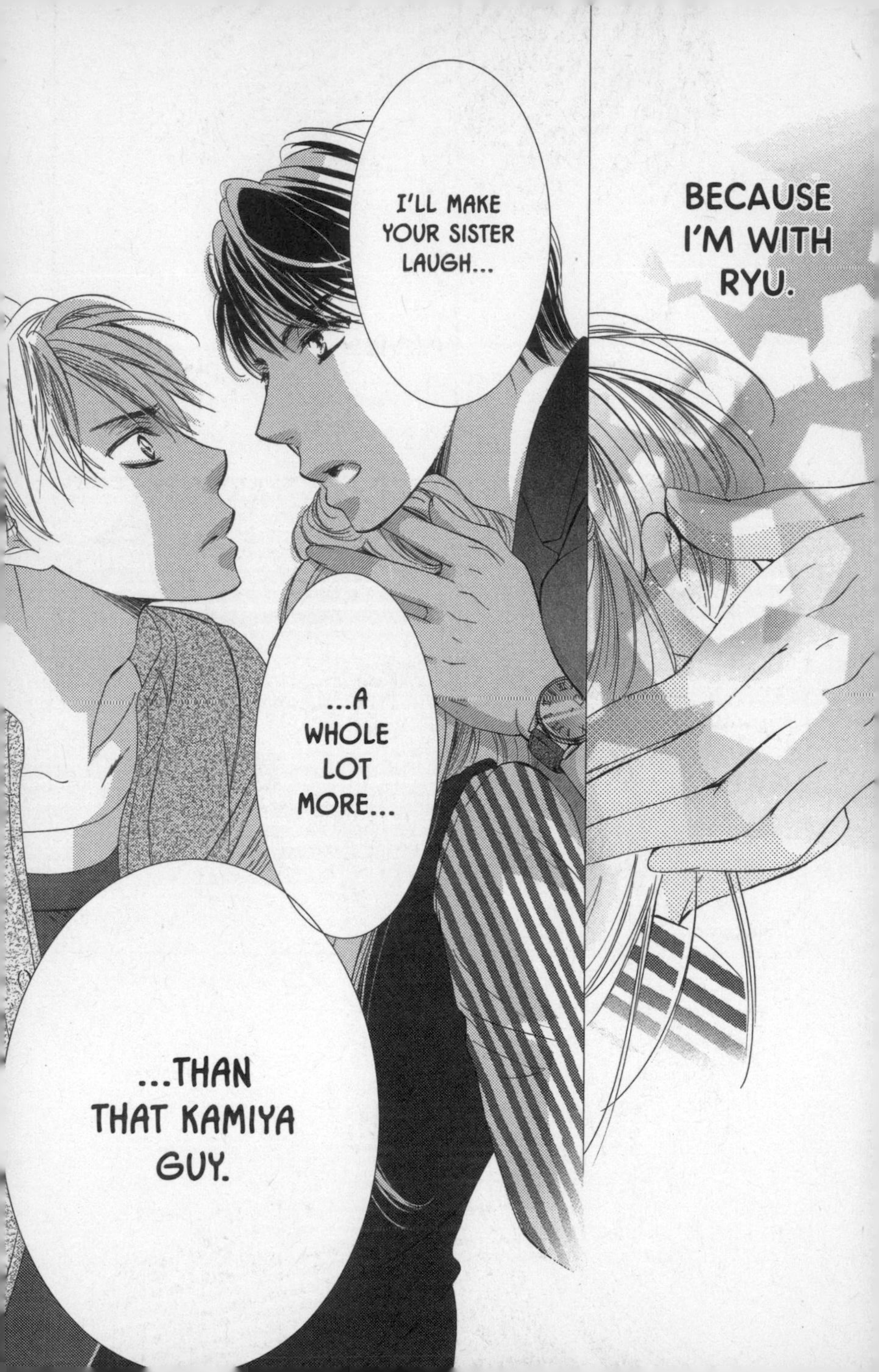
BECAUSE I'M WITH RYU.
I'LL MAKE YOUR SISTER LAUGH...
...A WHOLE LOT MORE...
...THAN THAT KAMIYA GUY.

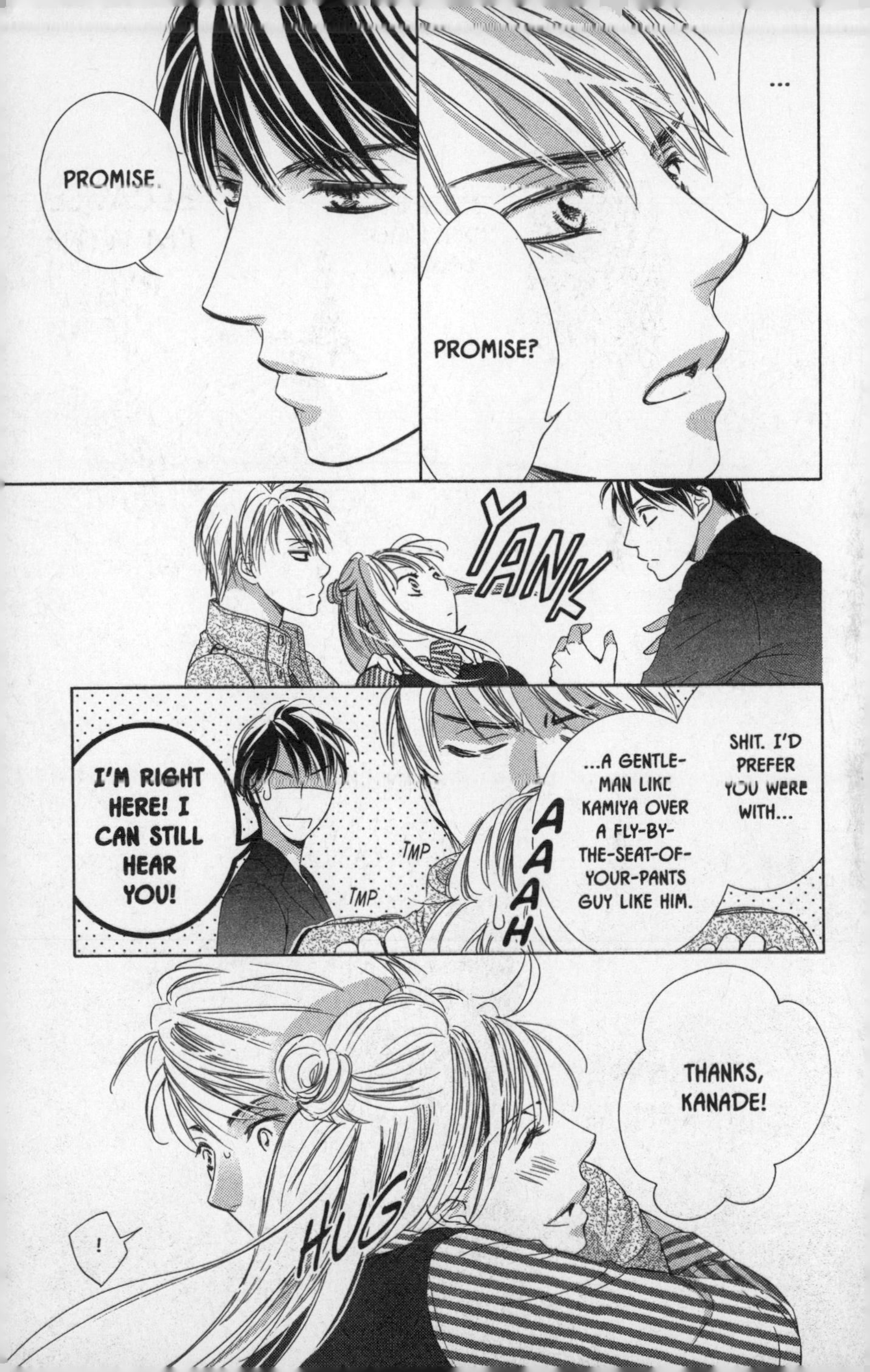
...
PROMISE?
PROMISE.
YANK
SHIT. I'D PREFER YOU WERE WITH...
...A GENTLE-MAN LIKE KAMIYA OVER A FLY-BY-THE-SEAT-OF-YOUR-PANTS GUY LIKE HIM.
AAAAH
TMP
TMP
I'M RIGHT HERE! I CAN STILL HEAR YOU!
THANKS, KANADE!
HUG
!

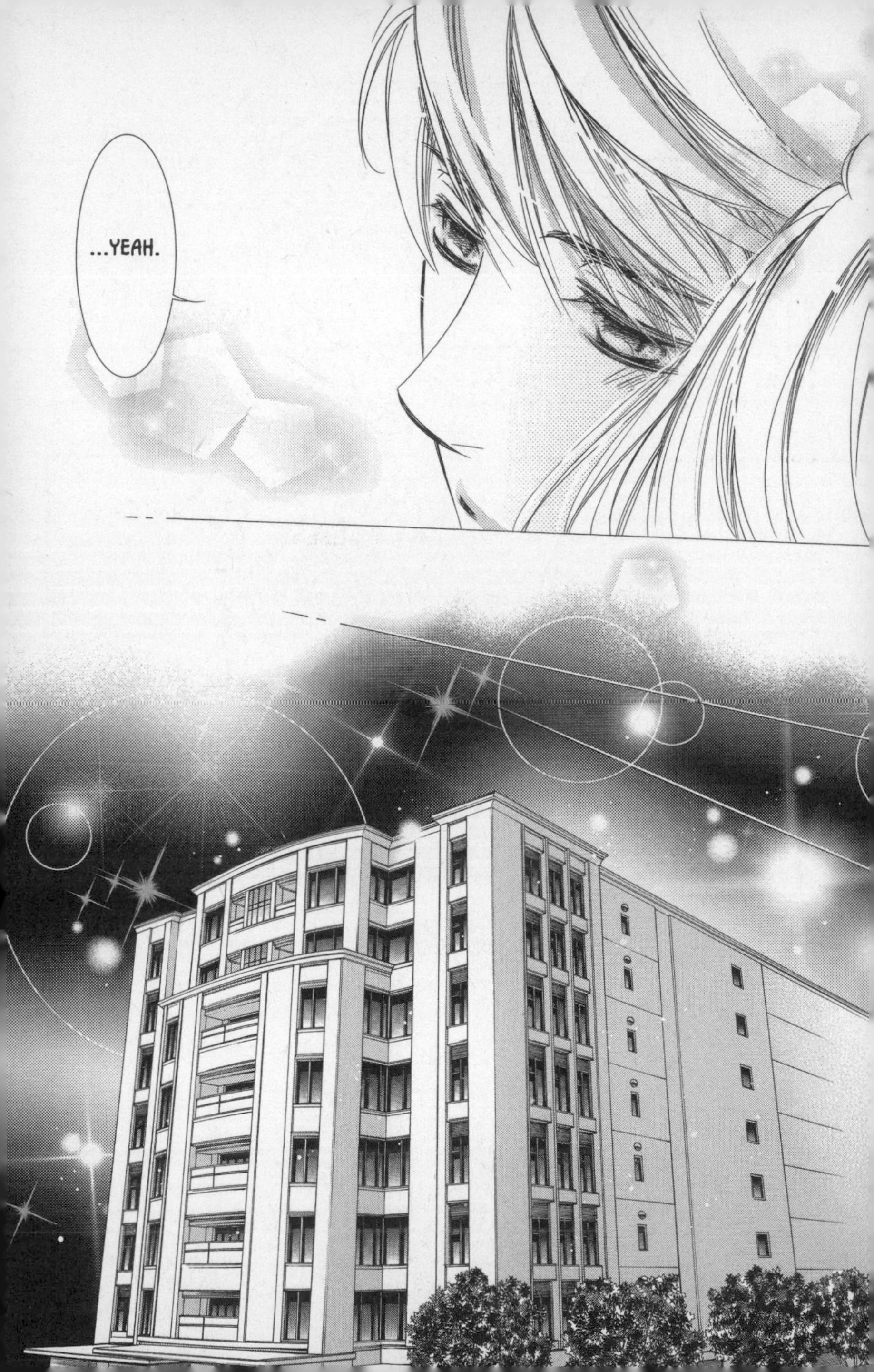
...YEAH.

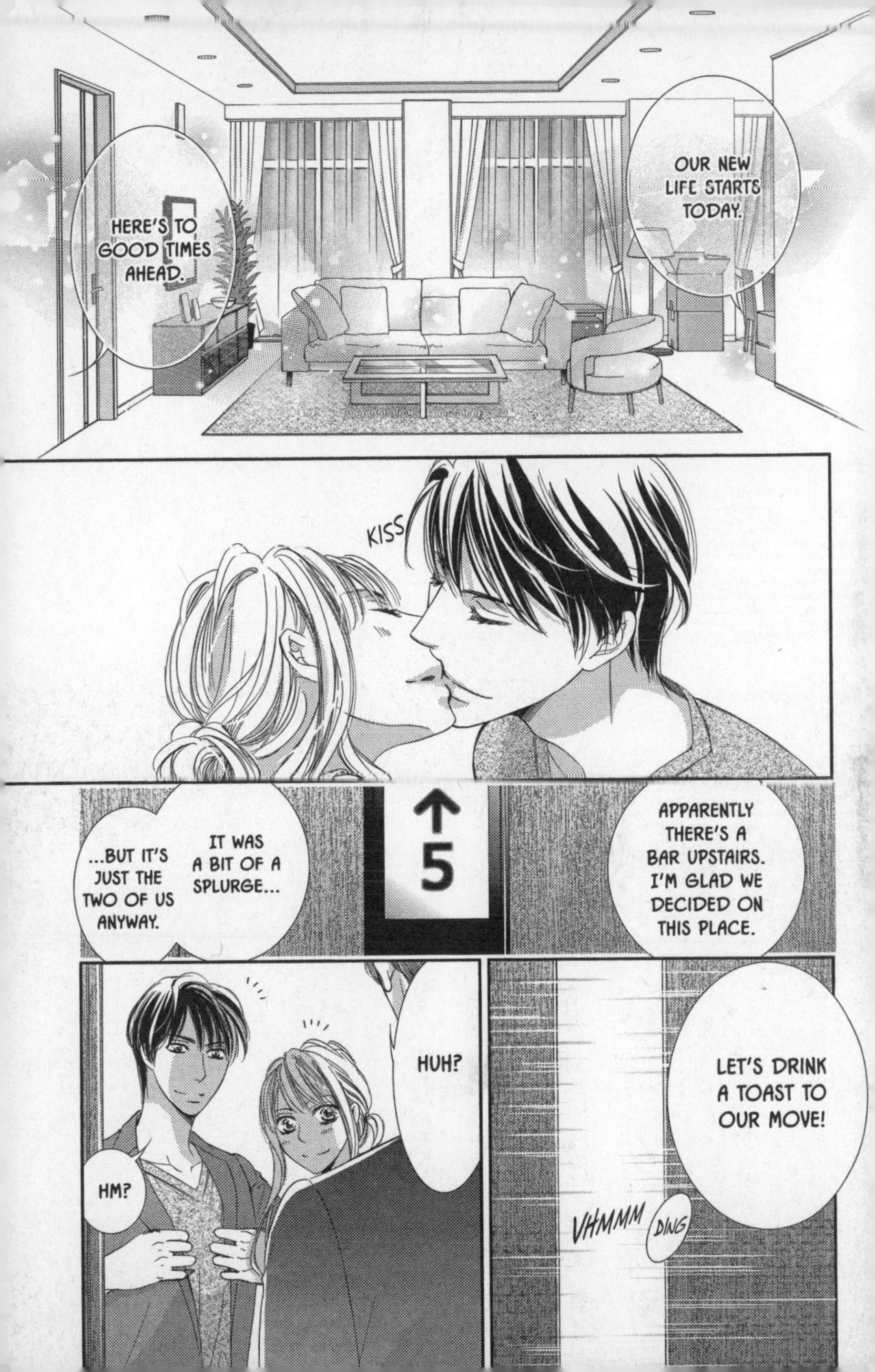
OUR NEW LIFE STARTS TODAY.
HERE'S TO GOOD TIMES AHEAD.
KISS
APPARENTLY THERE'S A BAR UPSTAIRS. I'M GLAD WE DECIDED ON THIS PLACE.
5
IT WAS A BIT OF A SPLURGE...
...BUT IT'S JUST THE TWO OF US ANYWAY.
LET'S DRINK A TOAST TO OUR MOVE!
DING
VHMMM
HUH?
HM?

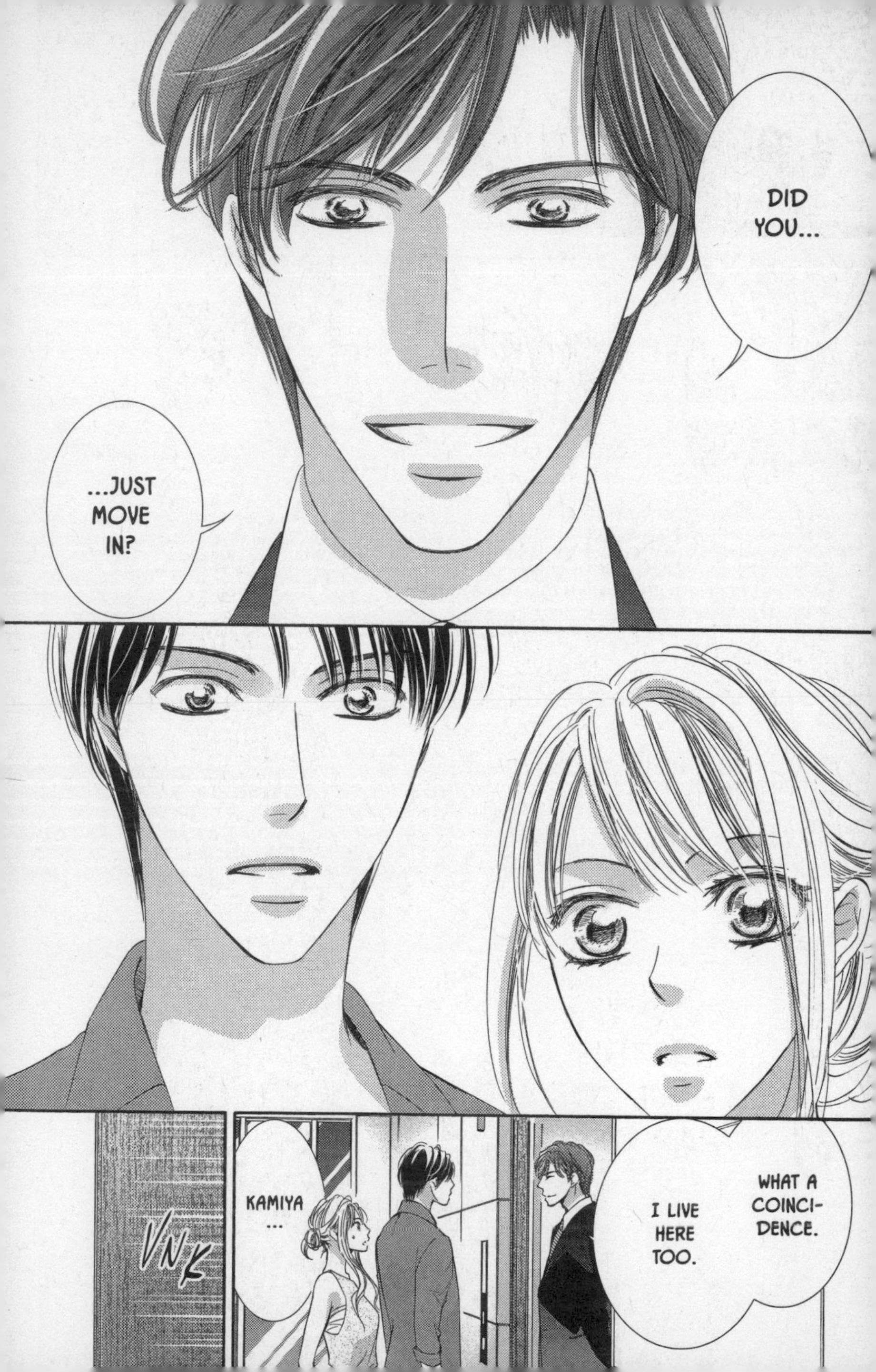
DID YOU...
...JUST MOVE IN?
WHAT A COINCI-DENCE.
I LIVE HERE TOO.
KAMIYA ...
VNK

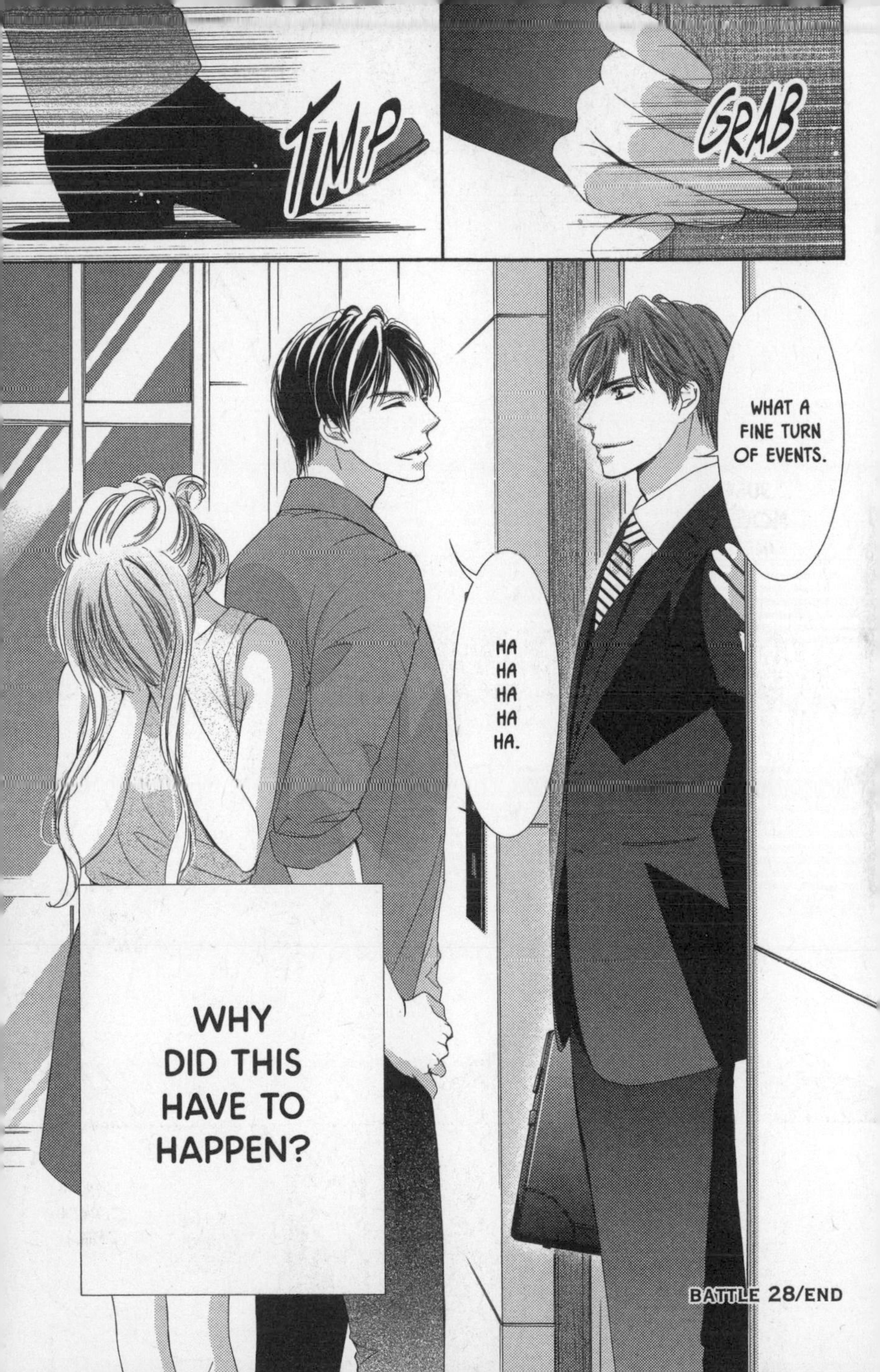
GRAB
TMP
WHAT A FINE TURN OF EVENTS.
HA HA HA HA HA.
WHY DID THIS HAVE TO HAPPEN?

BATTLE 28/END

I'll keep my word.

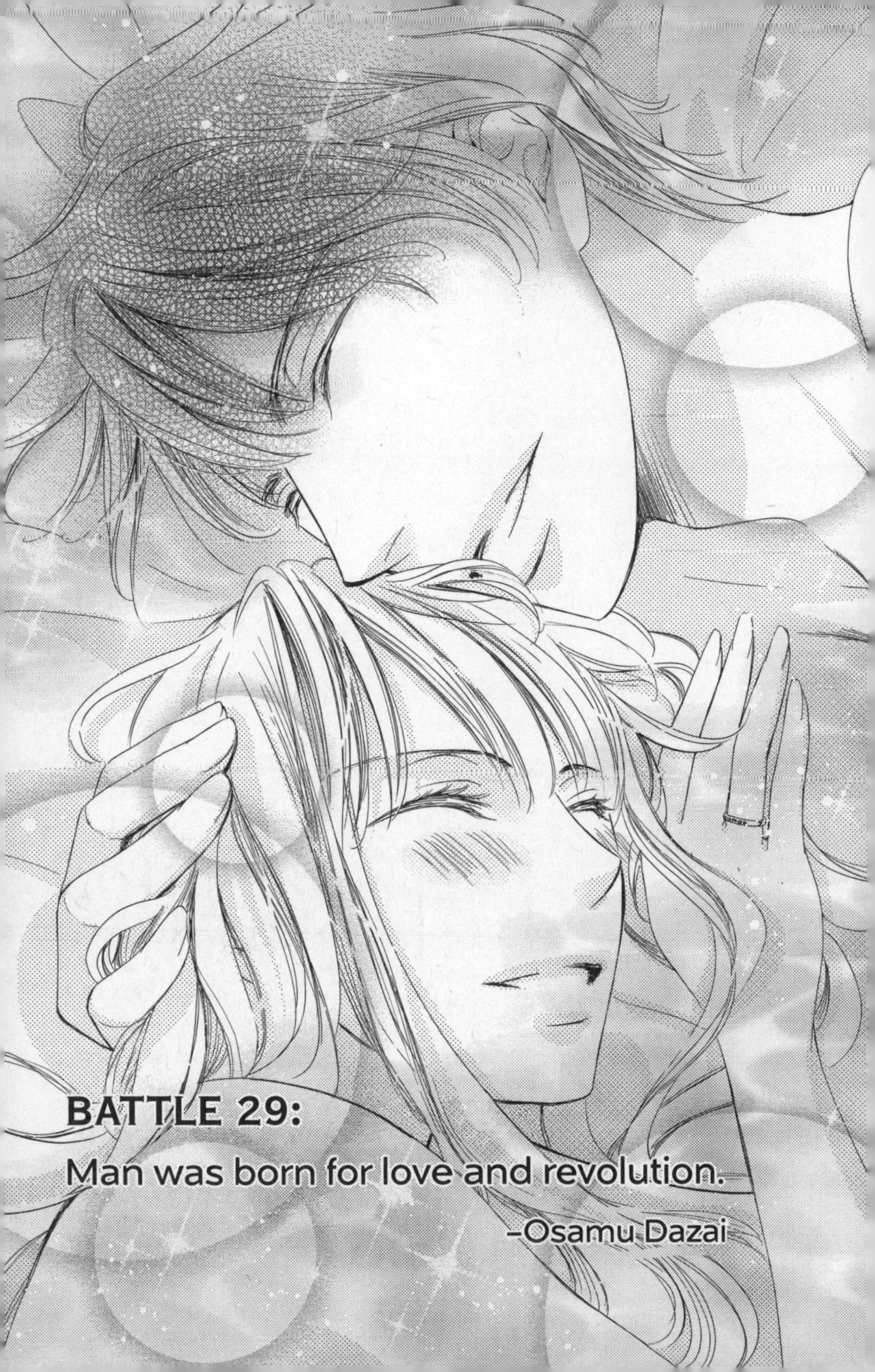
BATTLE 29:
Man was born for love and revolution.
–Osamu Dazai

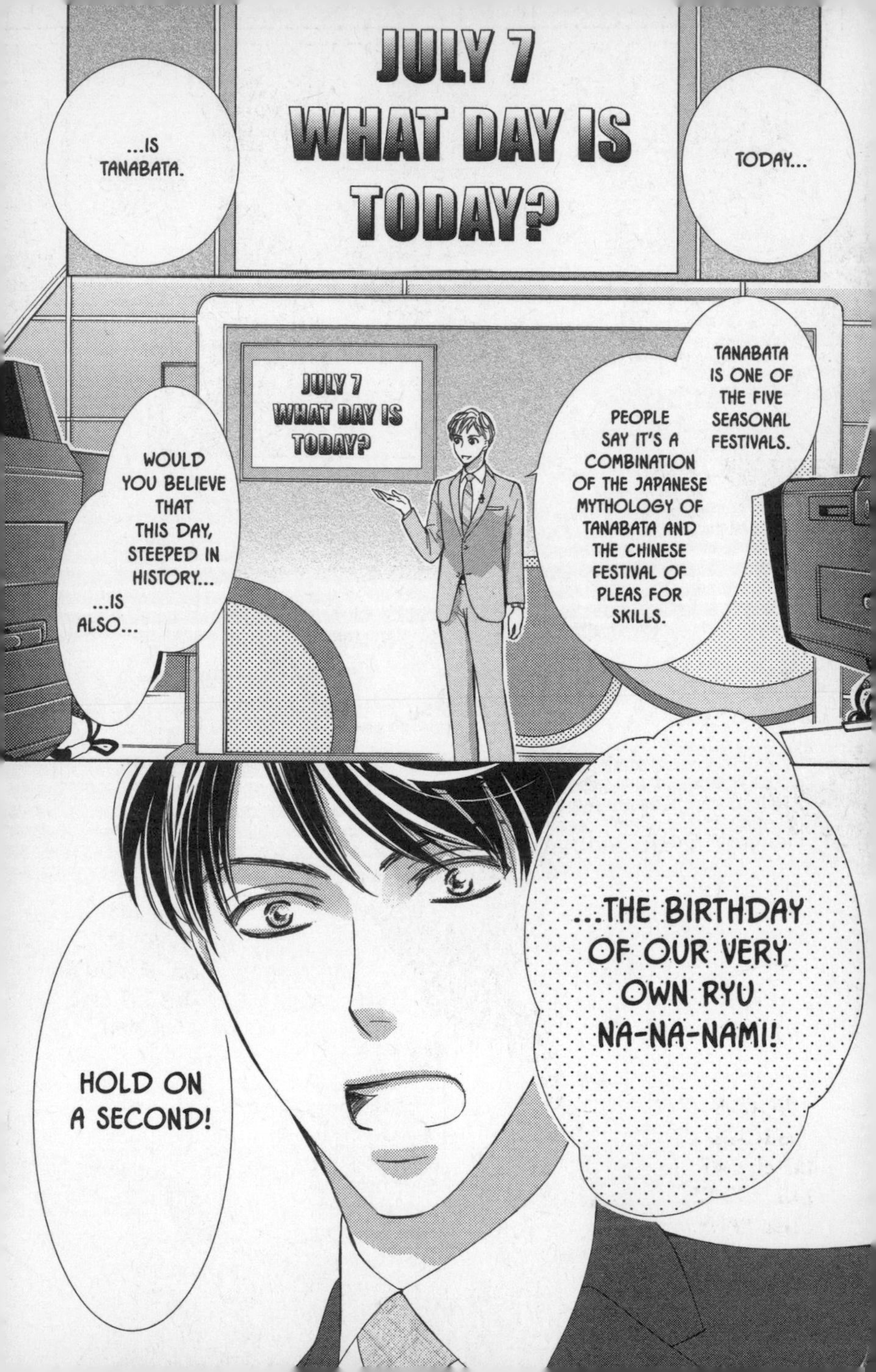
JULY 7 WHAT DAY IS TODAY?
TODAY...
...IS TANABATA.
JULY 7 WHAT DAY IS TODAY?
TANABATA IS ONE OF THE FIVE SEASONAL FESTIVALS.
PEOPLE SAY IT'S A COMBINATION OF THE JAPANESE MYTHOLOGY OF TANABATA AND THE CHINESE FESTIVAL OF PLEAS FOR SKILLS.
WOULD YOU BELIEVE THAT THIS DAY, STEEPED IN HISTORY...
...IS ALSO...
...THE BIRTHDAY OF OUR VERY OWN RYU NA-NA-NAMI!
HOLD ON A SECOND!

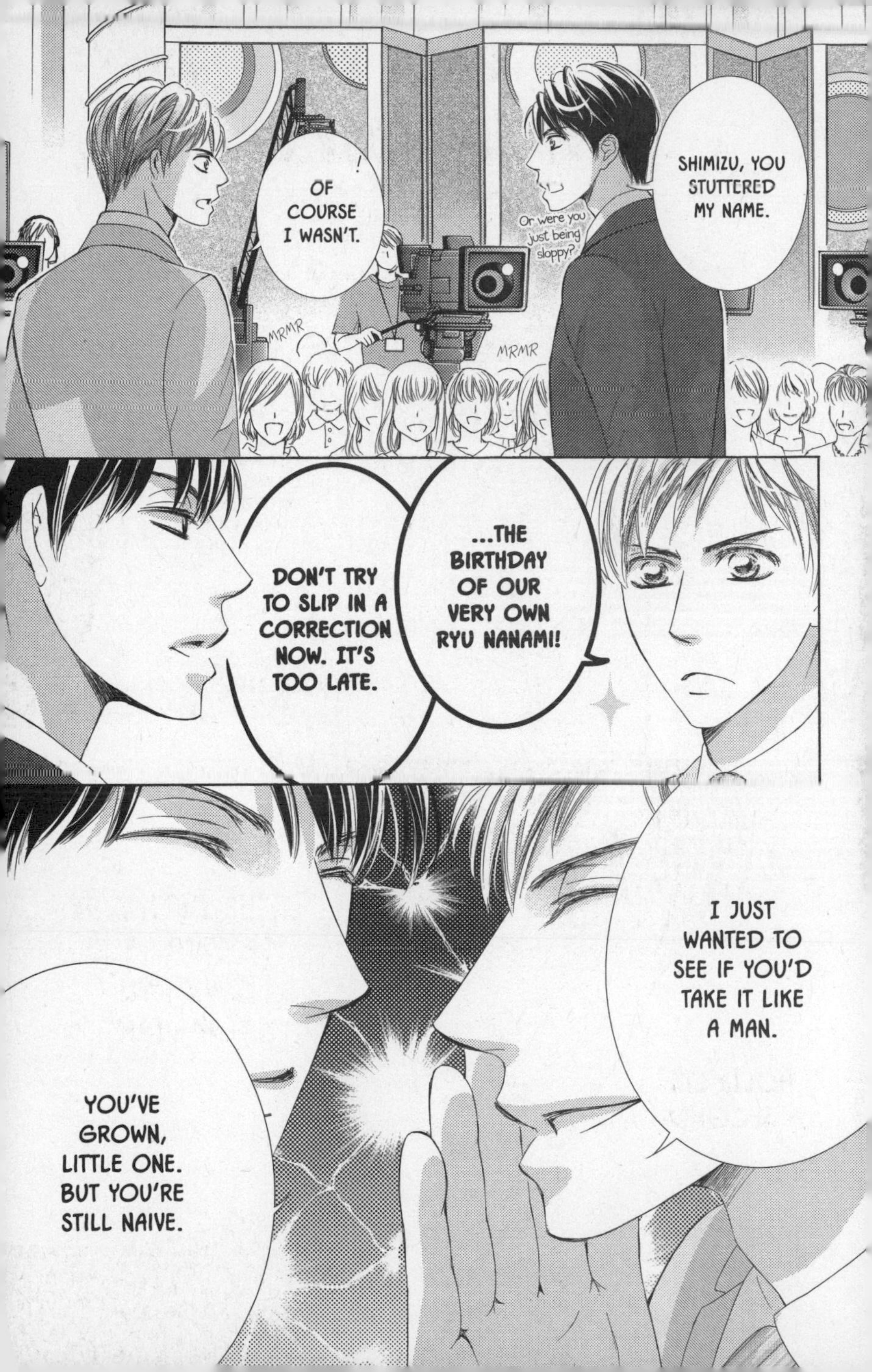
SHIMIZU, YOU STUTTERED MY NAME.
Or were you just being sloppy?
!
OF COURSE I WASN'T.
MRMR
MRMR
...THE BIRTHDAY OF OUR VERY OWN RYU NANAMI!
DON'T TRY TO SLIP IN A CORRECTION NOW. IT'S TOO LATE.
I JUST WANTED TO SEE IF YOU'D TAKE IT LIKE A MAN.
YOU'VE GROWN, LITTLE ONE. BUT YOU'RE STILL NAIVE.

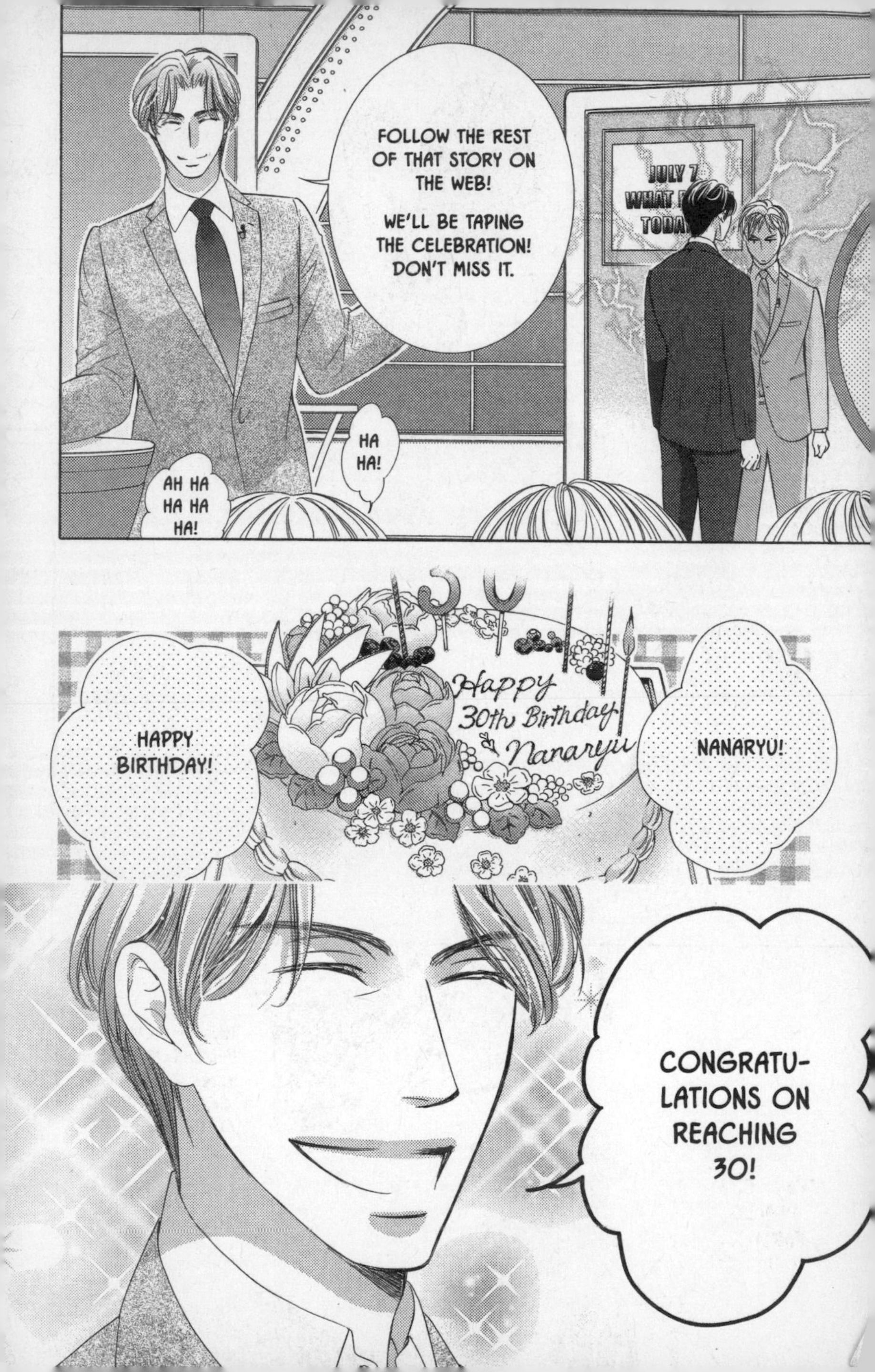
FOLLOW THE REST OF THAT STORY ON THE WEB!
WE'LL BE TAPING THE CELEBRATION! DON'T MISS IT.
JULY 7
HA HA!
AH HA HA HA HA!
NANARYU!
Happy 30th Birthday Nanaryu
HAPPY BIRTHDAY!
CONGRATU-LATIONS ON REACHING 30!

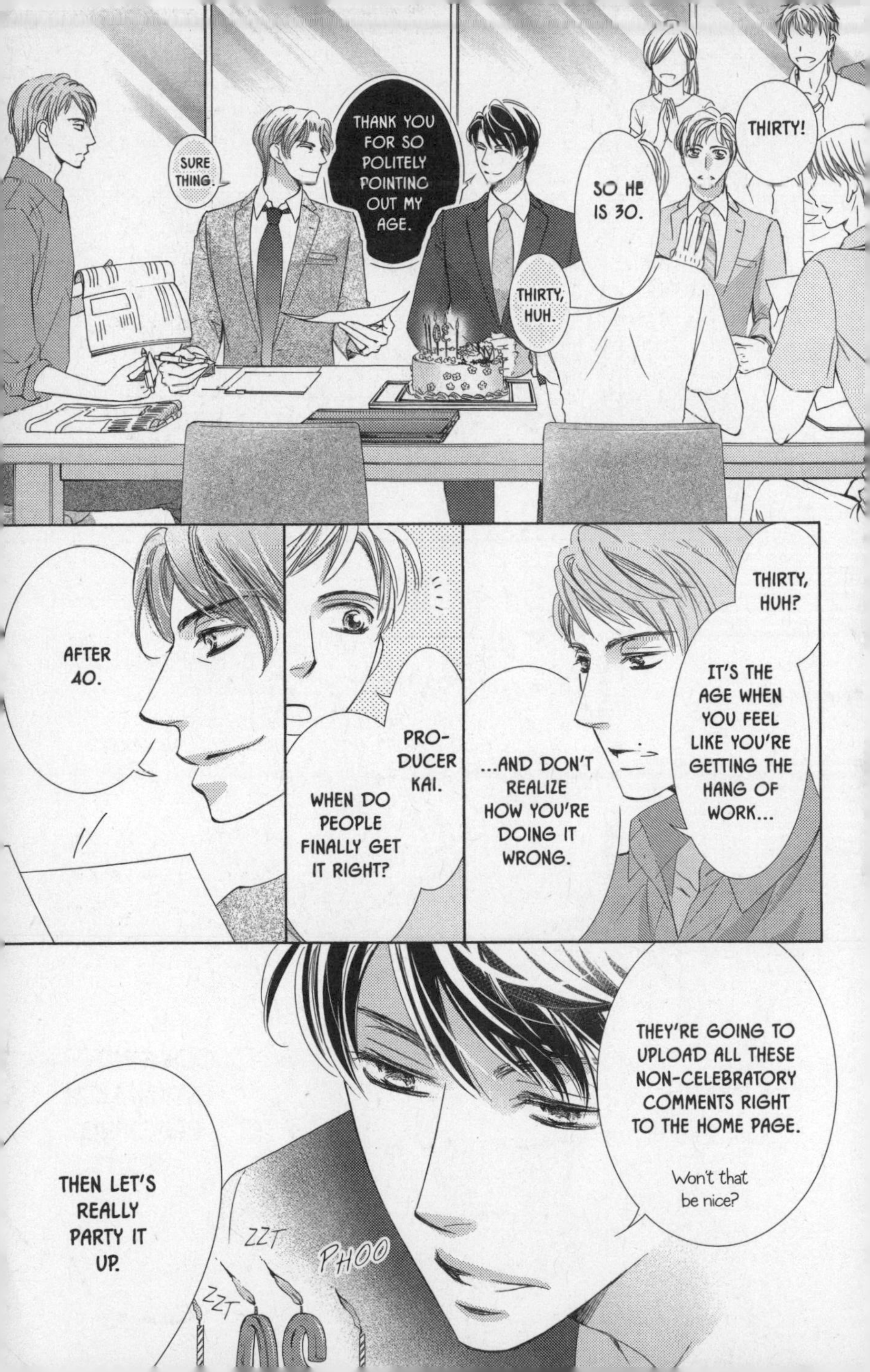
THIRTY!
SO HE IS 30.
THIRTY, HUH.
THANK YOU FOR SO POLITELY POINTING OUT MY AGE.
SURE THING.
THIRTY, HUH?
IT'S THE AGE WHEN YOU FEEL LIKE YOU'RE GETTING THE HANG OF WORK...
...AND DON'T REALIZE HOW YOU'RE DOING IT WRONG.
PRO-DUCER KAI.
WHEN DO PEOPLE FINALLY GET IT RIGHT?
AFTER 40.
THEY'RE GOING TO UPLOAD ALL THESE NON-CELEBRATORY COMMENTS RIGHT TO THE HOME PAGE.
Won't that be nice?
PHOO
ZZT
ZZT
THEN LET'S REALLY PARTY IT UP.

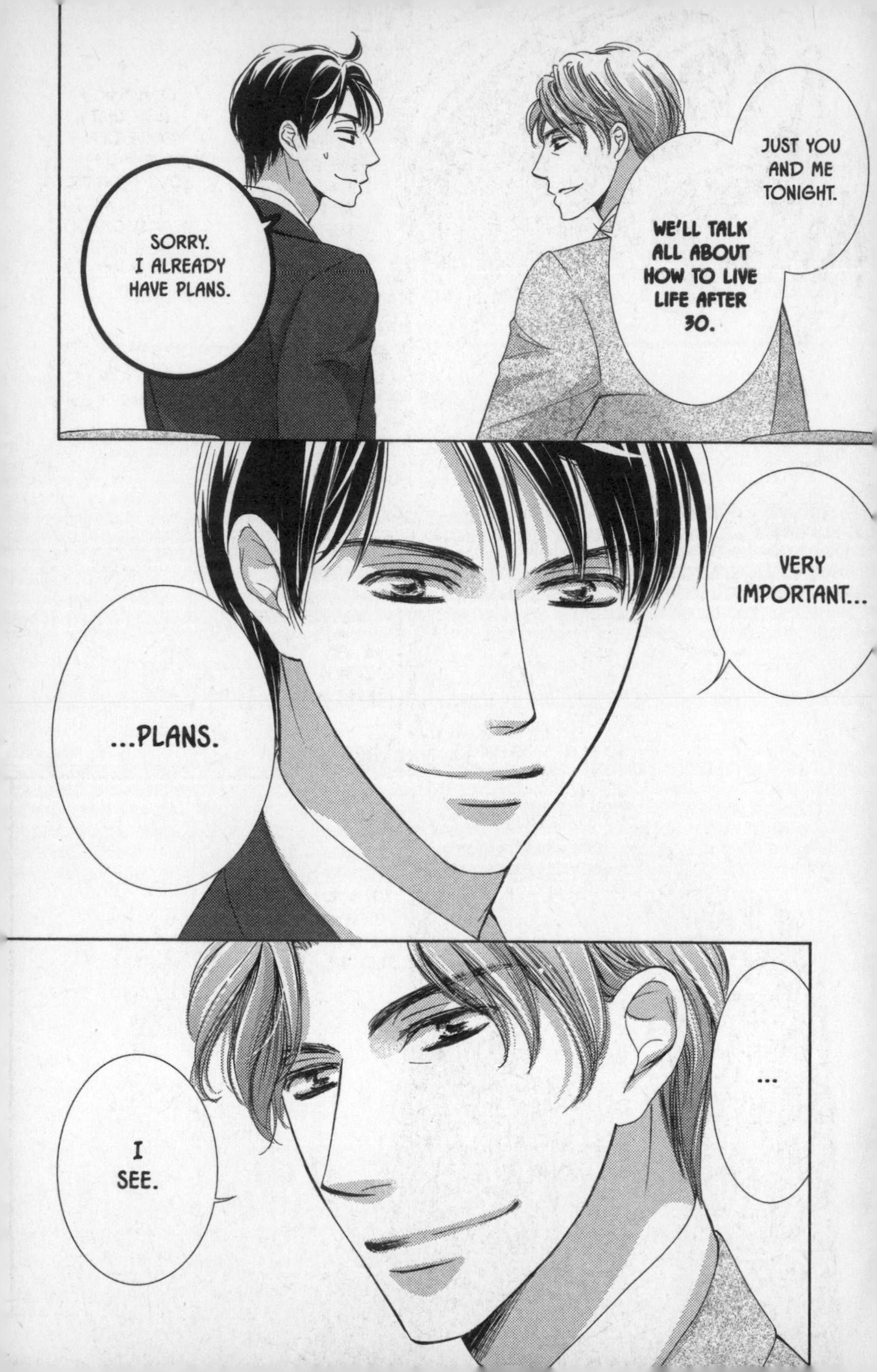
JUST YOU AND ME TONIGHT.
WE'LL TALK ALL ABOUT HOW TO LIVE LIFE AFTER 30.
SORRY. I ALREADY HAVE PLANS.
VERY IMPORTANT...
...PLANS.
...
I SEE.

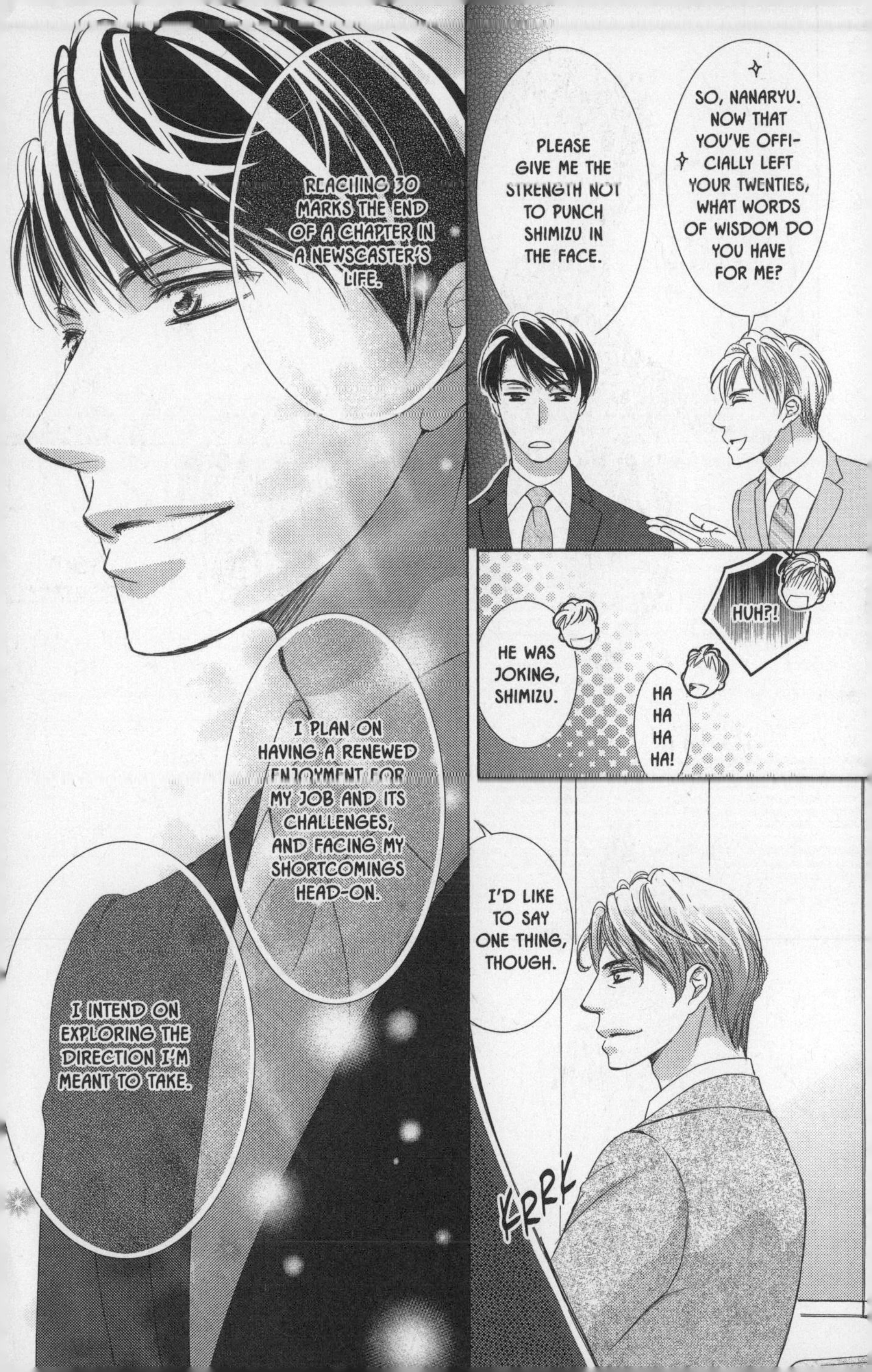
SO, NANARYU. NOW THAT YOU'VE OFFI-CIALLY LEFT YOUR TWENTIES, WHAT WORDS OF WISDOM DO YOU HAVE FOR ME?
PLEASE GIVE ME THE STRENGTH NOT TO PUNCH SHIMIZU IN THE FACE.
HUH?!
HA HA HA HA!
HE WAS JOKING, SHIMIZU.
I'D LIKE TO SAY ONE THING, THOUGH.
KRRK
REACHING 30 MARKS THE END OF A CHAPTER IN A NEWSCASTER'S LIFE.
I PLAN ON HAVING A RENEWED ENJOYMENT FOR MY JOB AND ITS CHALLENGES, AND FACING MY SHORTCOMINGS HEAD-ON.
I INTEND ON EXPLORING THE DIRECTION I'M MEANT TO TAKE.

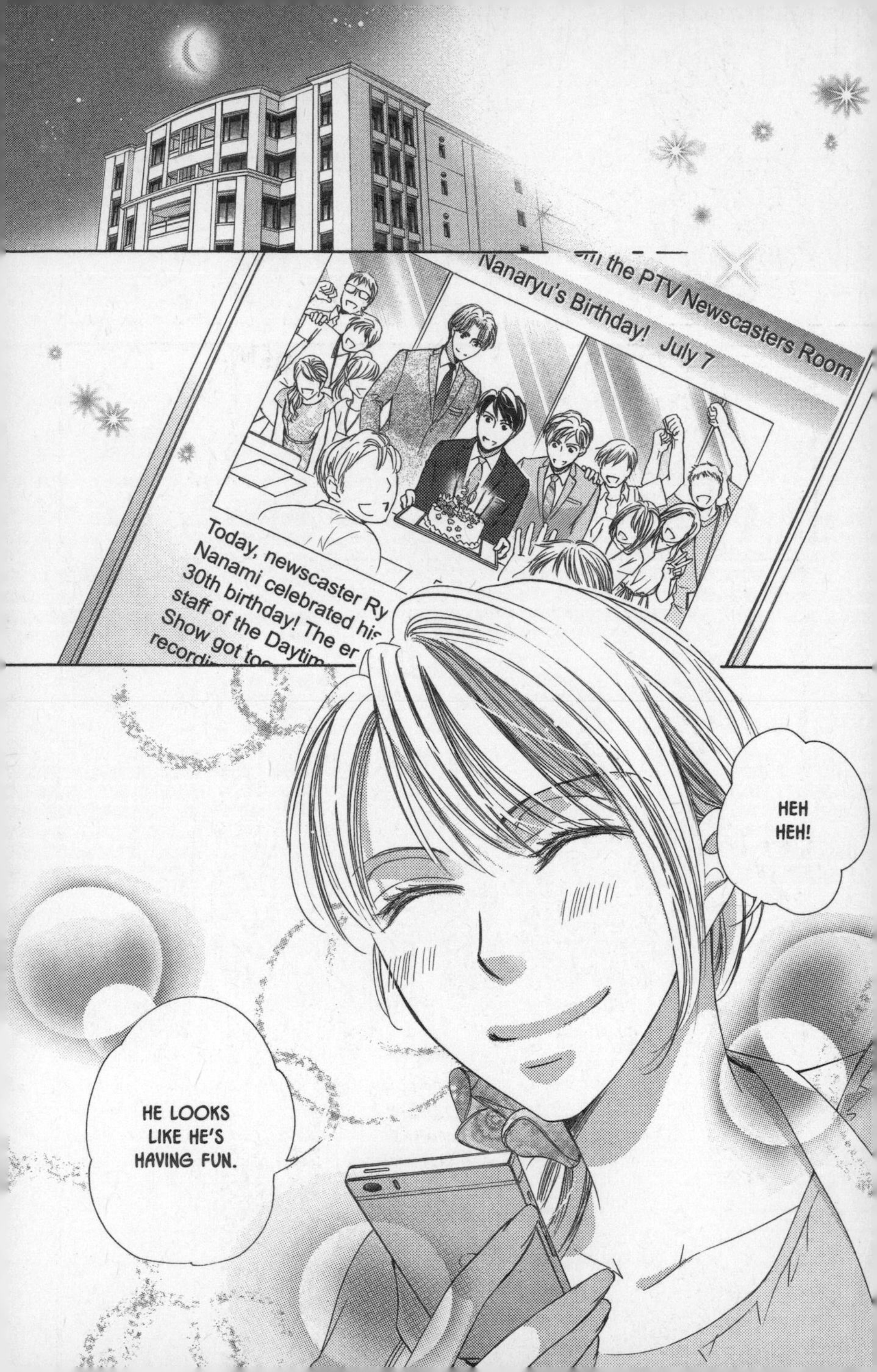
the PTV Newscasters Room
Nanaryu's Birthday! July 7
Today, newscaster Ry
Nanami celebrated his
30th birthday! The er
staff of the Daytim
Show got tog
HEH HEH!
HE LOOKS LIKE HE'S HAVING FUN.

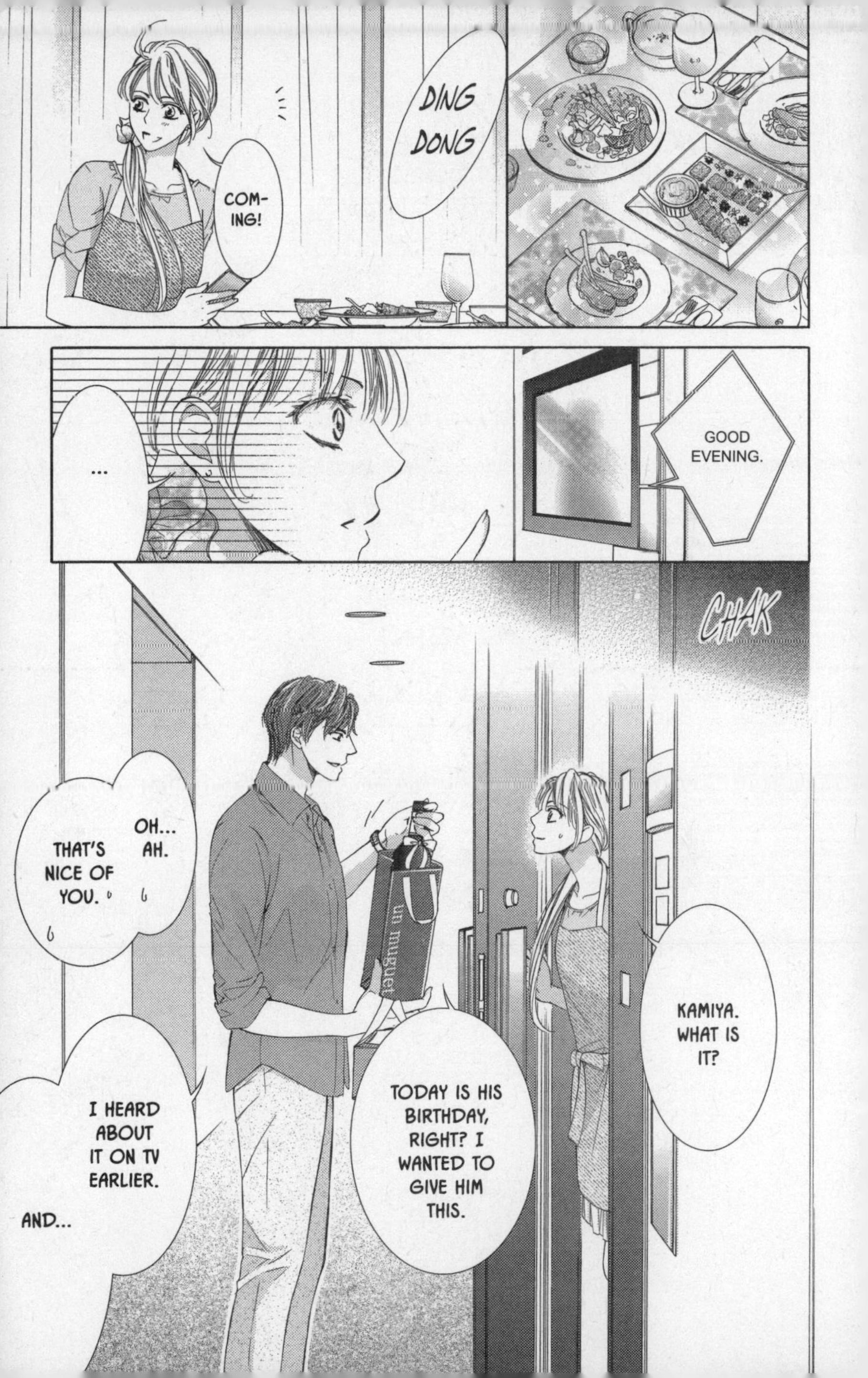
DING DONG
COM-ING!
GOOD EVENING.
...
CHAK
KAMIYA. WHAT IS IT?
TODAY IS HIS BIRTHDAY, RIGHT? I WANTED TO GIVE HIM THIS.
un muguet
OH... AH. THAT'S NICE OF YOU.
I HEARD ABOUT IT ON TV EARLIER.
AND...

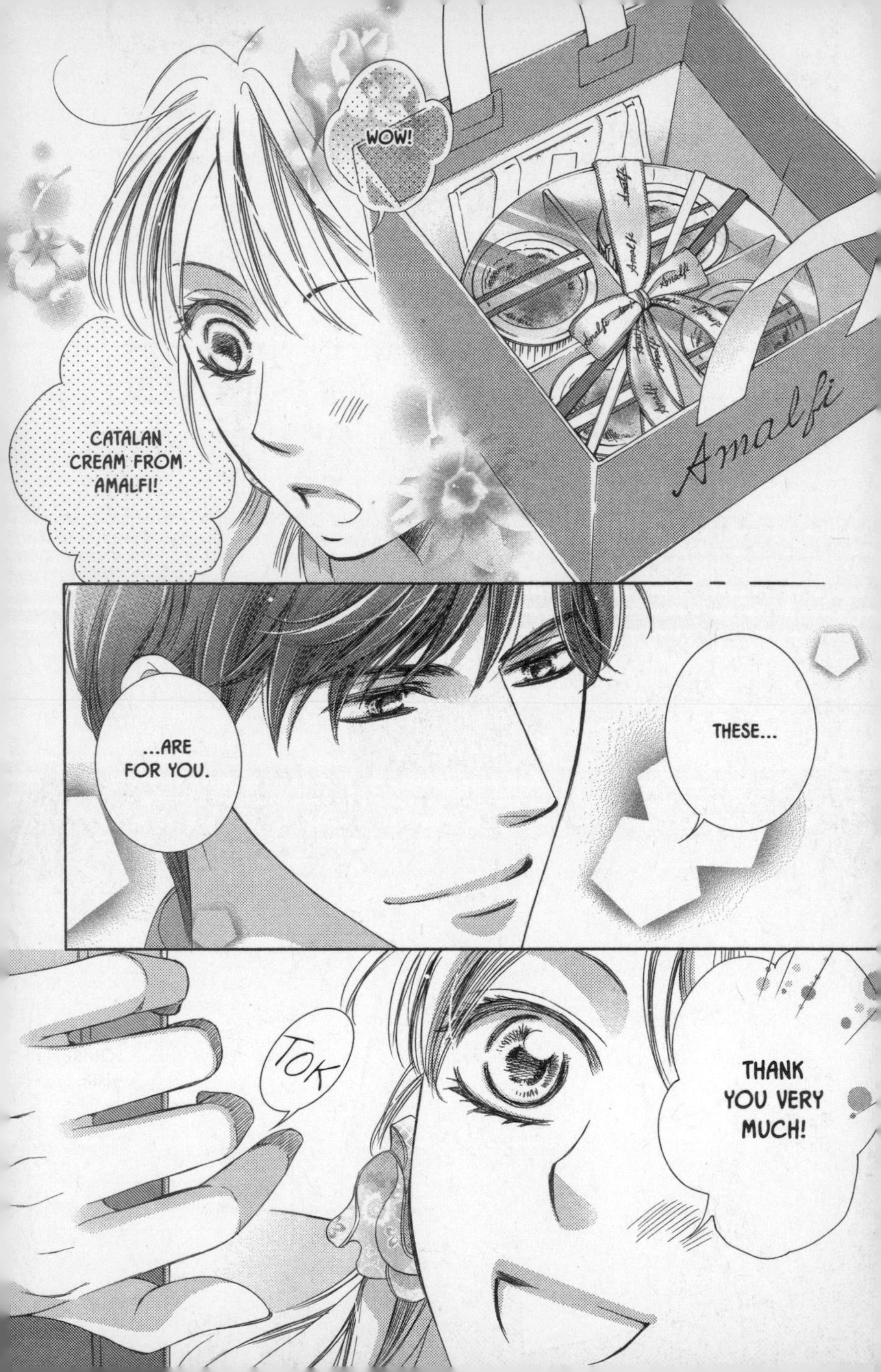
WOW!
Amalfi
CATALAN CREAM FROM AMALFI!
THESE...
...ARE FOR YOU.
THANK YOU VERY MUCH!
TOK

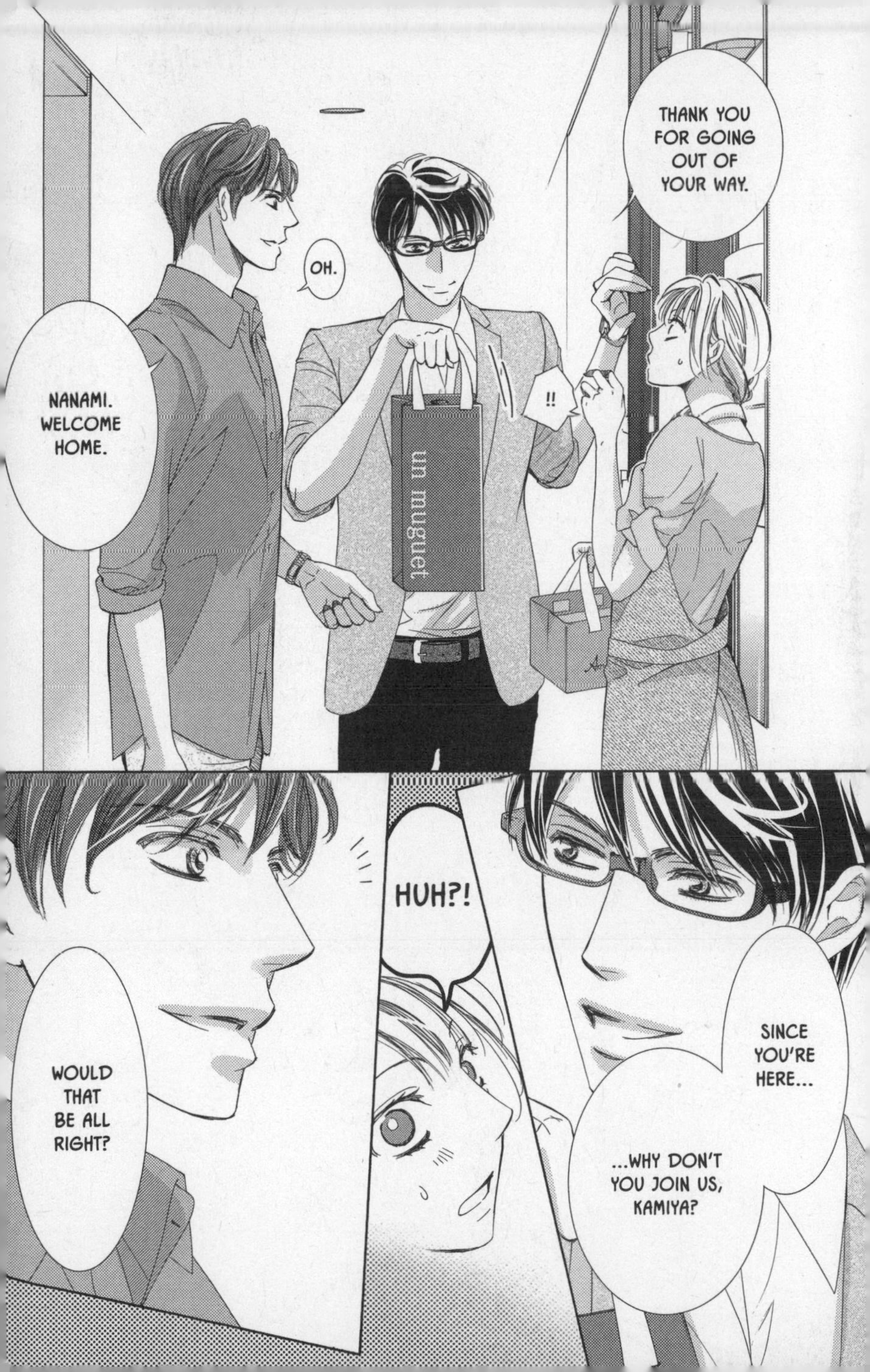
THANK YOU FOR GOING OUT OF YOUR WAY.
OH.
!!
un muguet
NANAMI. WELCOME HOME.
SINCE YOU'RE HERE...
...WHY DON'T YOU JOIN US, KAMIYA?
HUH?!
WOULD THAT BE ALL RIGHT?

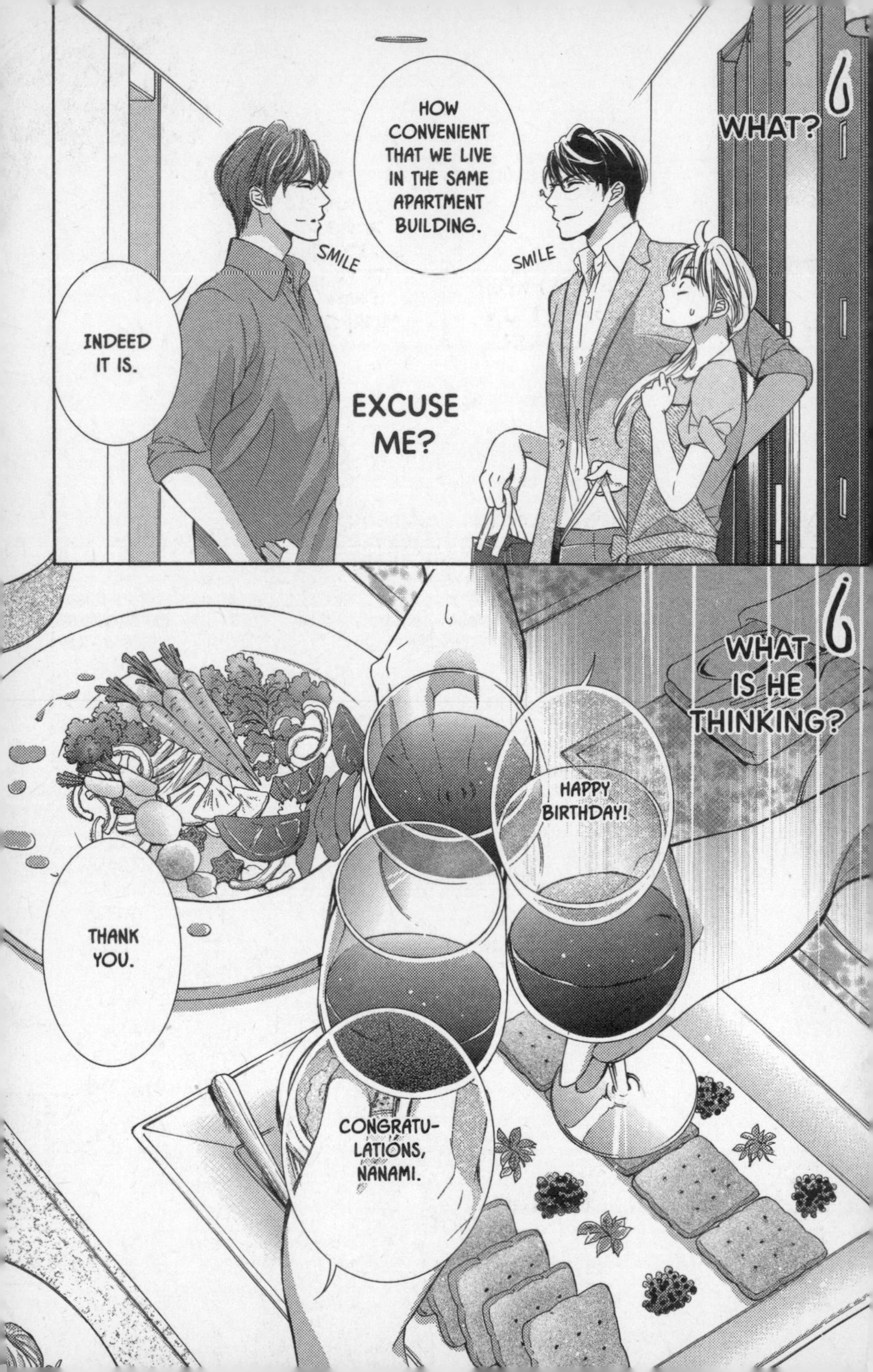
WHAT?
HOW CONVENIENT THAT WE LIVE IN THE SAME APARTMENT BUILDING.
SMILE
SMILE
INDEED IT IS.
EXCUSE ME?
WHAT IS HE THINKING?
HAPPY BIRTHDAY!
THANK YOU.
CONGRATU-LATIONS, NANAMI.

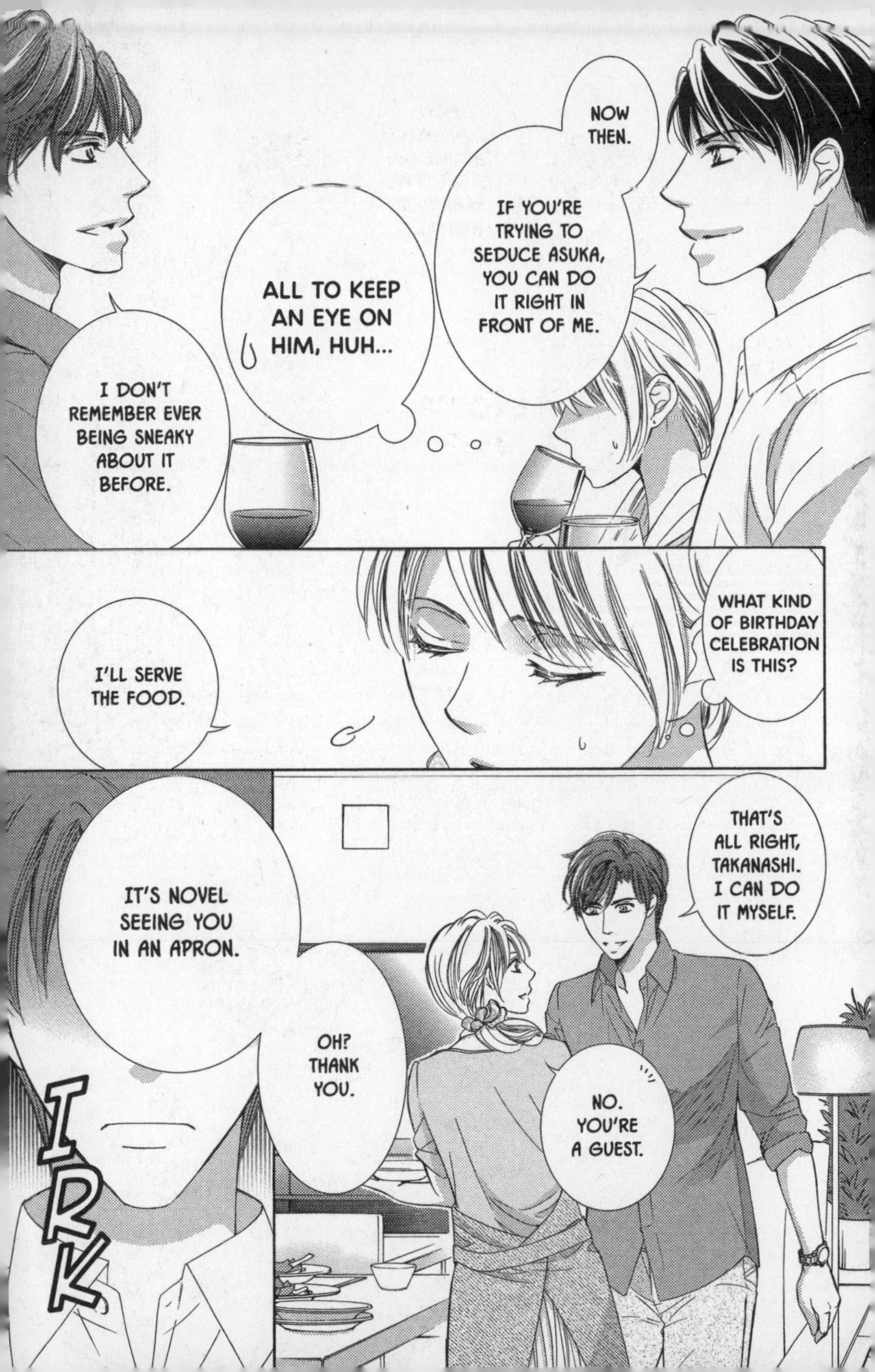
NOW THEN.
IF YOU'RE TRYING TO SEDUCE ASUKA, YOU CAN DO IT RIGHT IN FRONT OF ME.
ALL TO KEEP AN EYE ON HIM, HUH...
I DON'T REMEMBER EVER BEING SNEAKY ABOUT IT BEFORE.
WHAT KIND OF BIRTHDAY CELEBRATION IS THIS?
I'LL SERVE THE FOOD.
THAT'S ALL RIGHT, TAKANASHI. I CAN DO IT MYSELF.
NO. YOU'RE A GUEST.
IT'S NOVEL SEEING YOU IN AN APRON.
OH? THANK YOU.
IRK

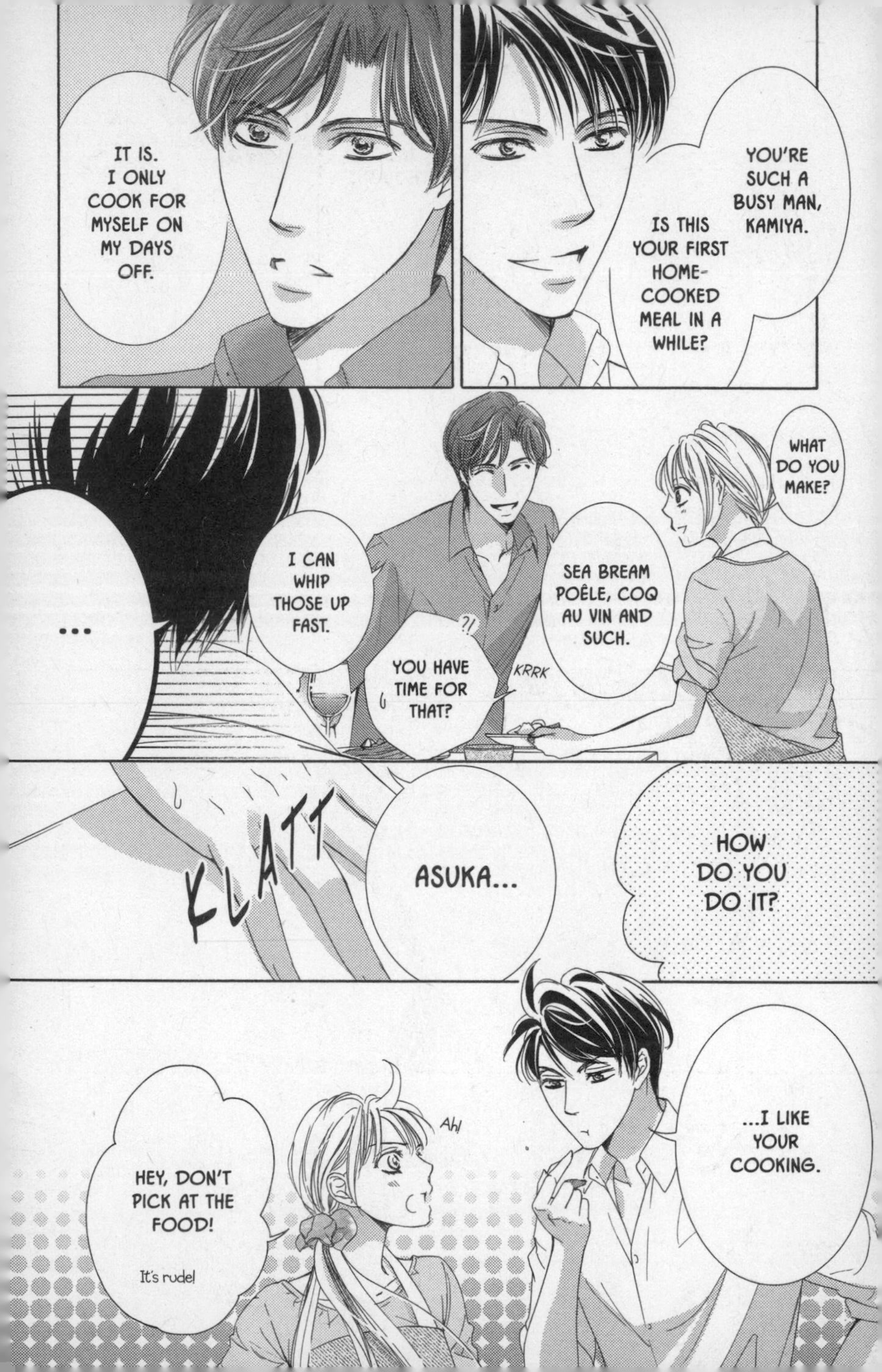
YOU'RE SUCH A BUSY MAN, KAMIYA.
IS THIS YOUR FIRST HOME-COOKED MEAL IN A WHILE?
IT IS. I ONLY COOK FOR MYSELF ON MY DAYS OFF.
WHAT DO YOU MAKE?
SEA BREAM POÊLE, COQ AU VIN AND SUCH.
I CAN WHIP THOSE UP FAST.
KRRK
?!
YOU HAVE TIME FOR THAT?
...
HOW DO YOU DO IT?
ASUKA...
KLATT
...I LIKE YOUR COOKING.
Ah!
HEY, DON'T PICK AT THE FOOD!
It's rude!

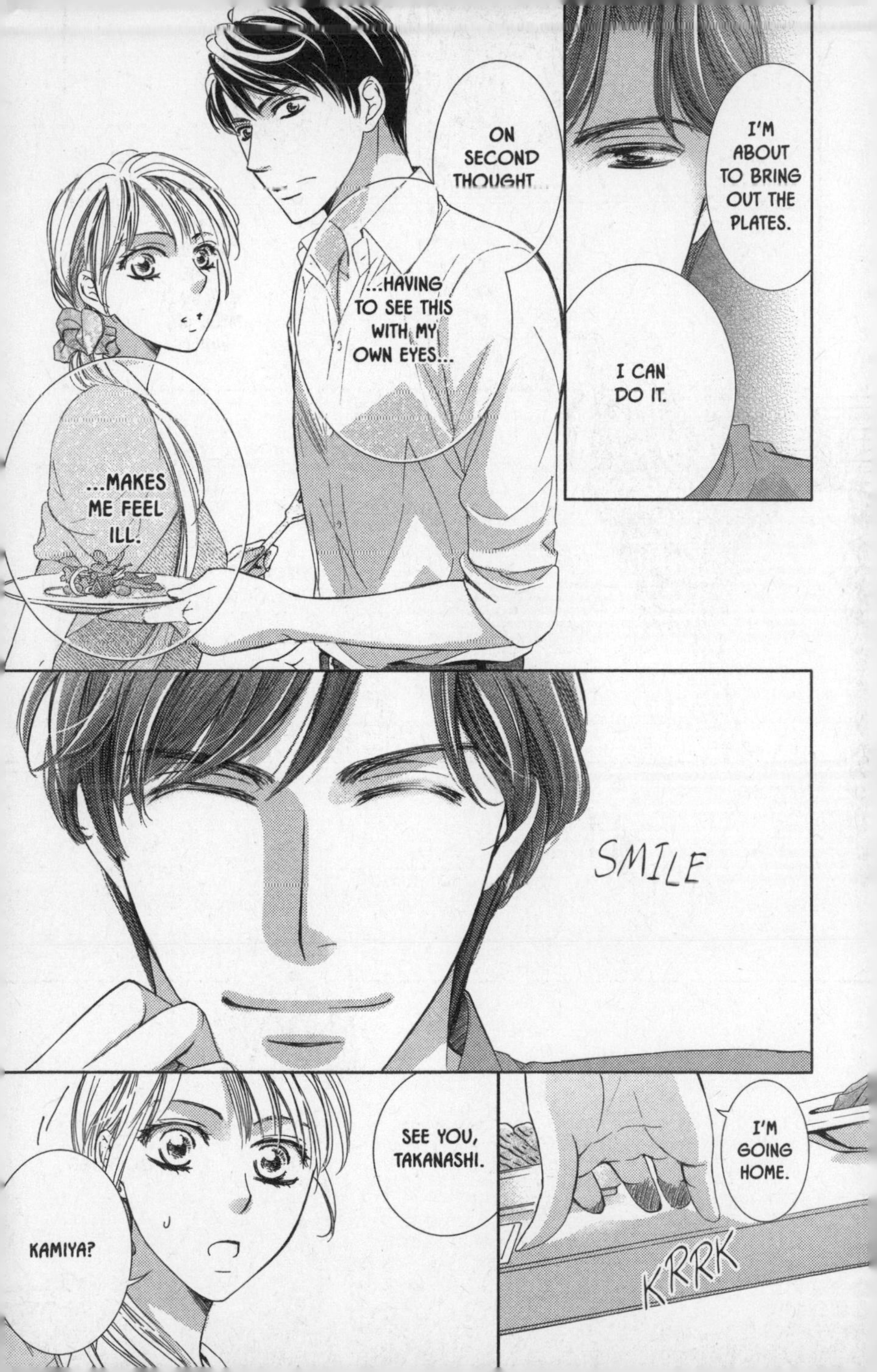
I'M ABOUT TO BRING OUT THE PLATES.
I CAN DO IT.
ON SECOND THOUGHT...
...HAVING TO SEE THIS WITH MY OWN EYES...
...MAKES ME FEEL ILL.
SMILE
I'M GOING HOME.
KRRK
SEE YOU, TAKANASHI.
KAMIYA?

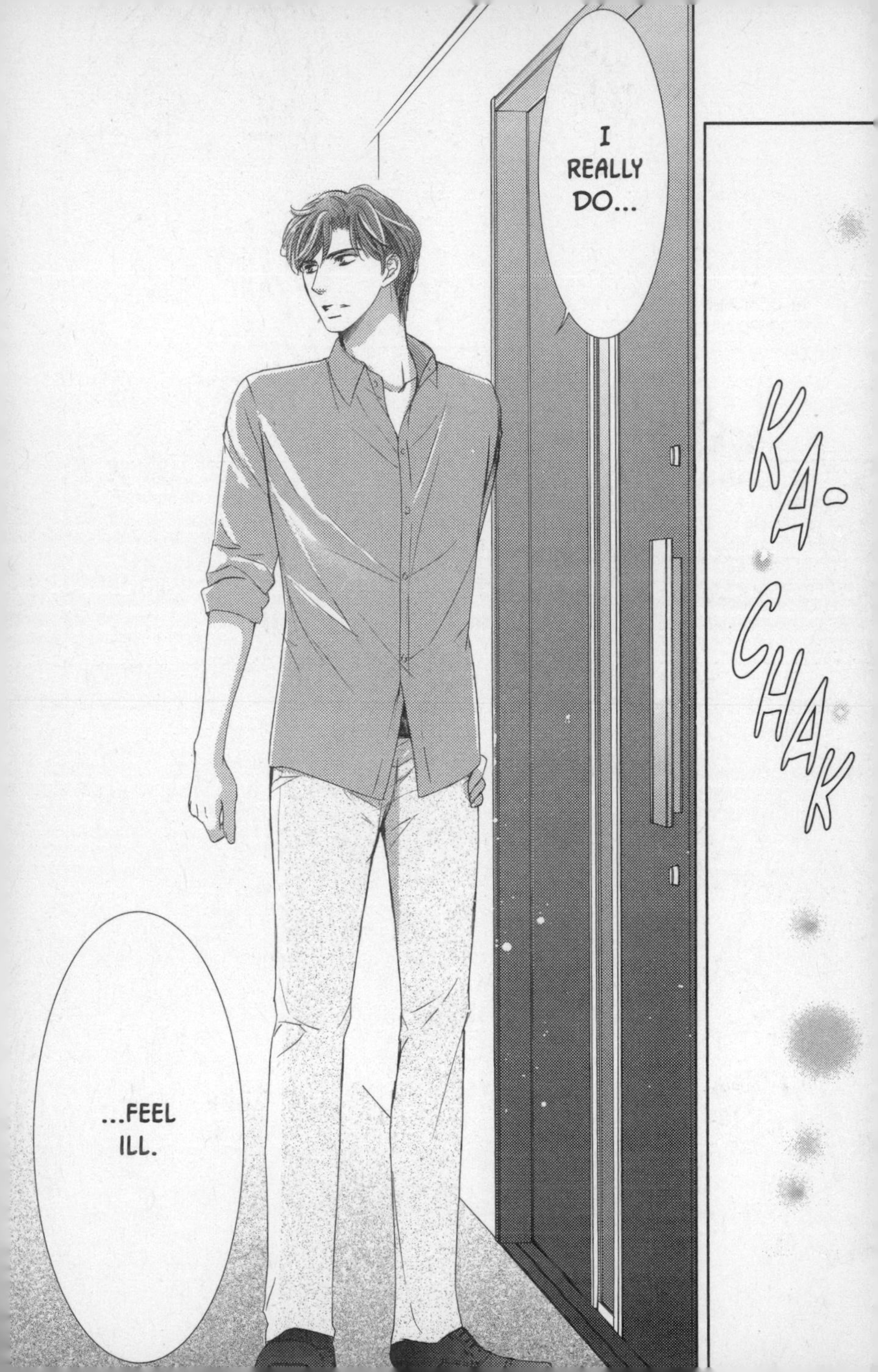
I REALLY DO...
KA-CHAK
...FEEL ILL.

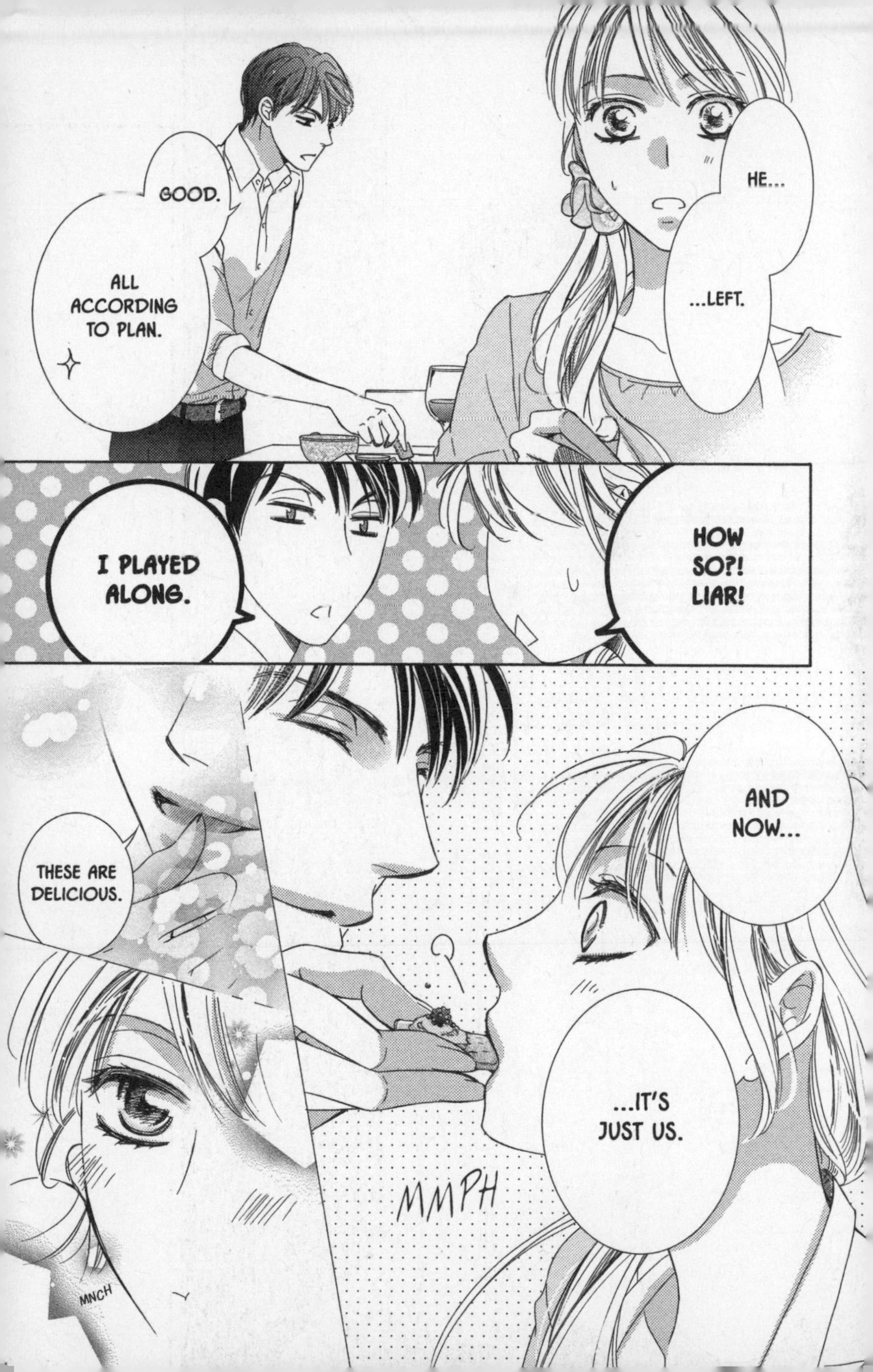
HE...
...LEFT.
GOOD.
ALL ACCORDING TO PLAN.
HOW SO?! LIAR!
I PLAYED ALONG.
AND NOW...
...IT'S JUST US.
MMPH
THESE ARE DELICIOUS.
MNCH

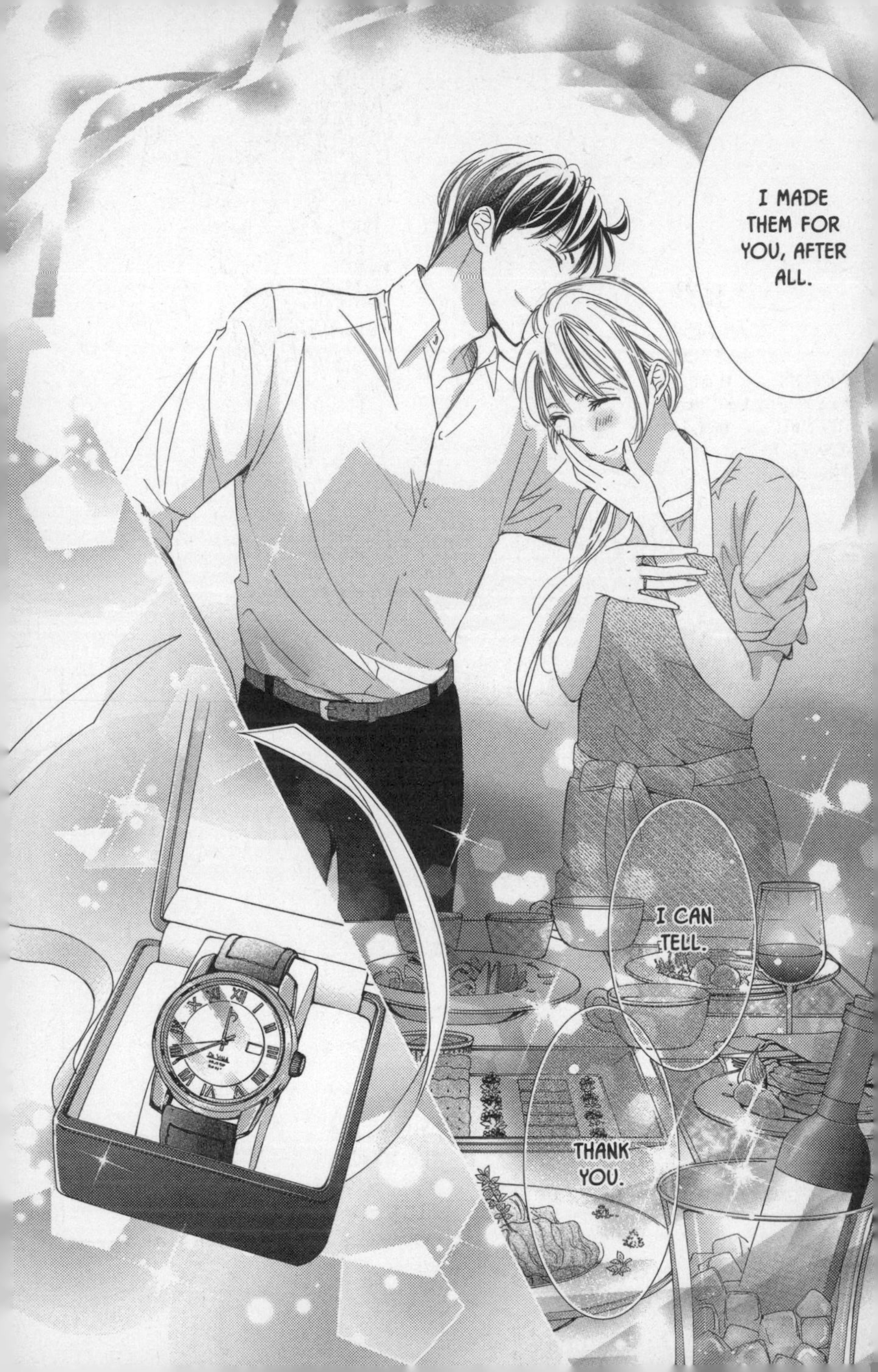
I MADE THEM FOR YOU, AFTER ALL.
I CAN TELL.
THANK YOU.

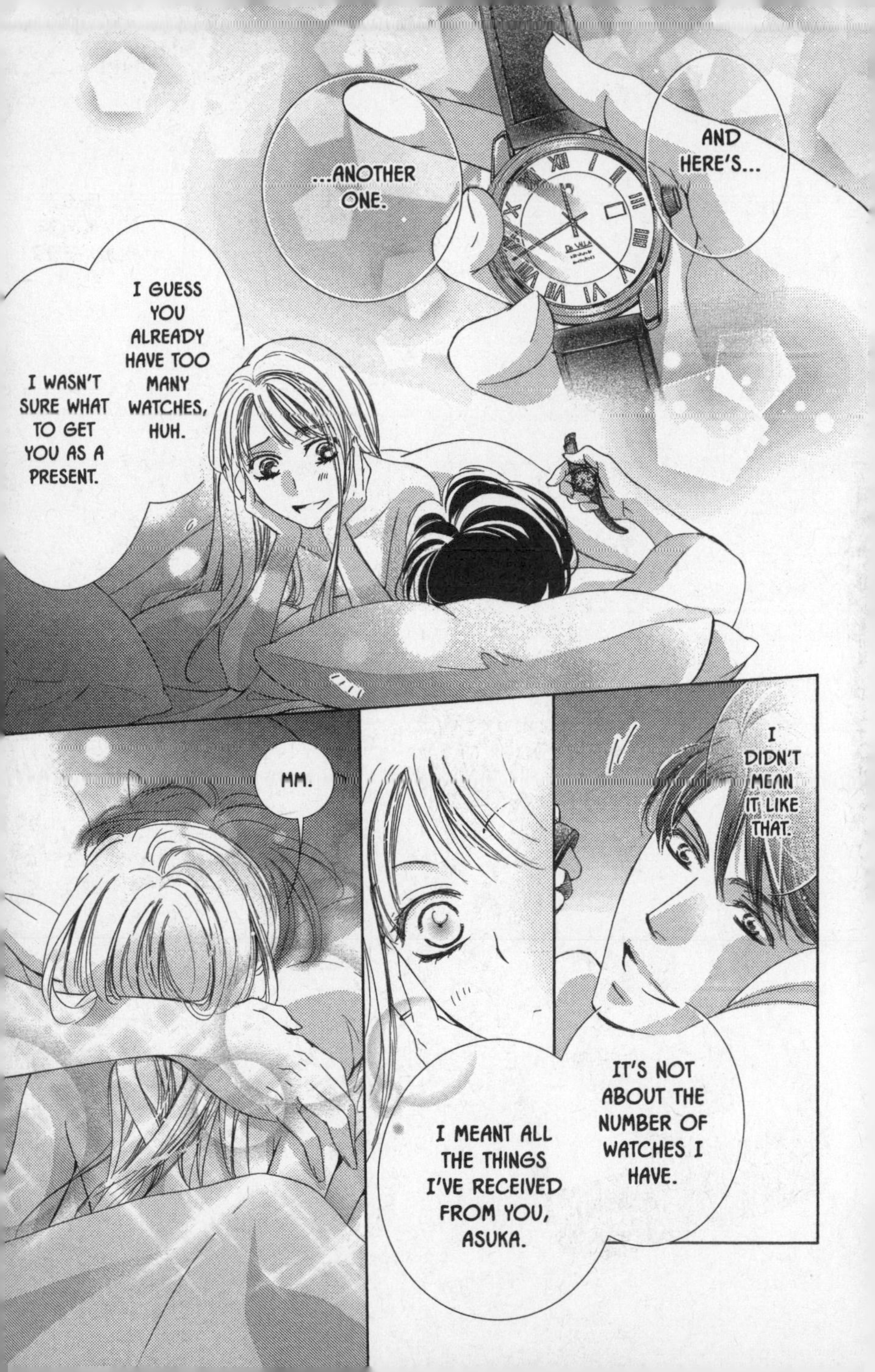
AND HERE'S...
...ANOTHER ONE.
I GUESS YOU ALREADY HAVE TOO MANY WATCHES, HUH.
I WASN'T SURE WHAT TO GET YOU AS A PRESENT.
I DIDN'T MEAN IT LIKE THAT.
IT'S NOT ABOUT THE NUMBER OF WATCHES I HAVE.
I MEANT ALL THE THINGS I'VE RECEIVED FROM YOU, ASUKA.
MM.

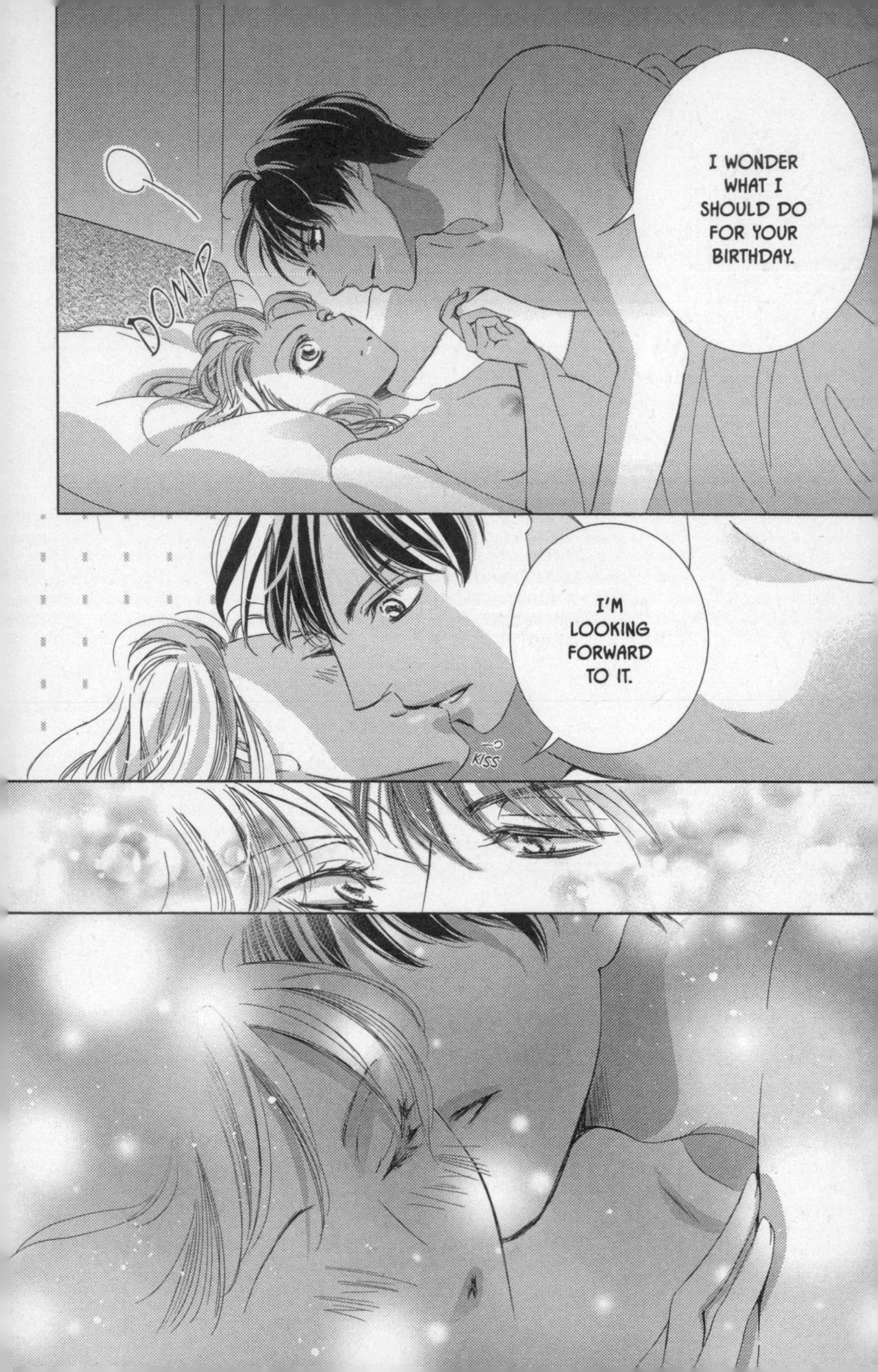
I WONDER WHAT I SHOULD DO FOR YOUR BIRTHDAY.
DOMP
I'M LOOKING FORWARD TO IT.
KISS

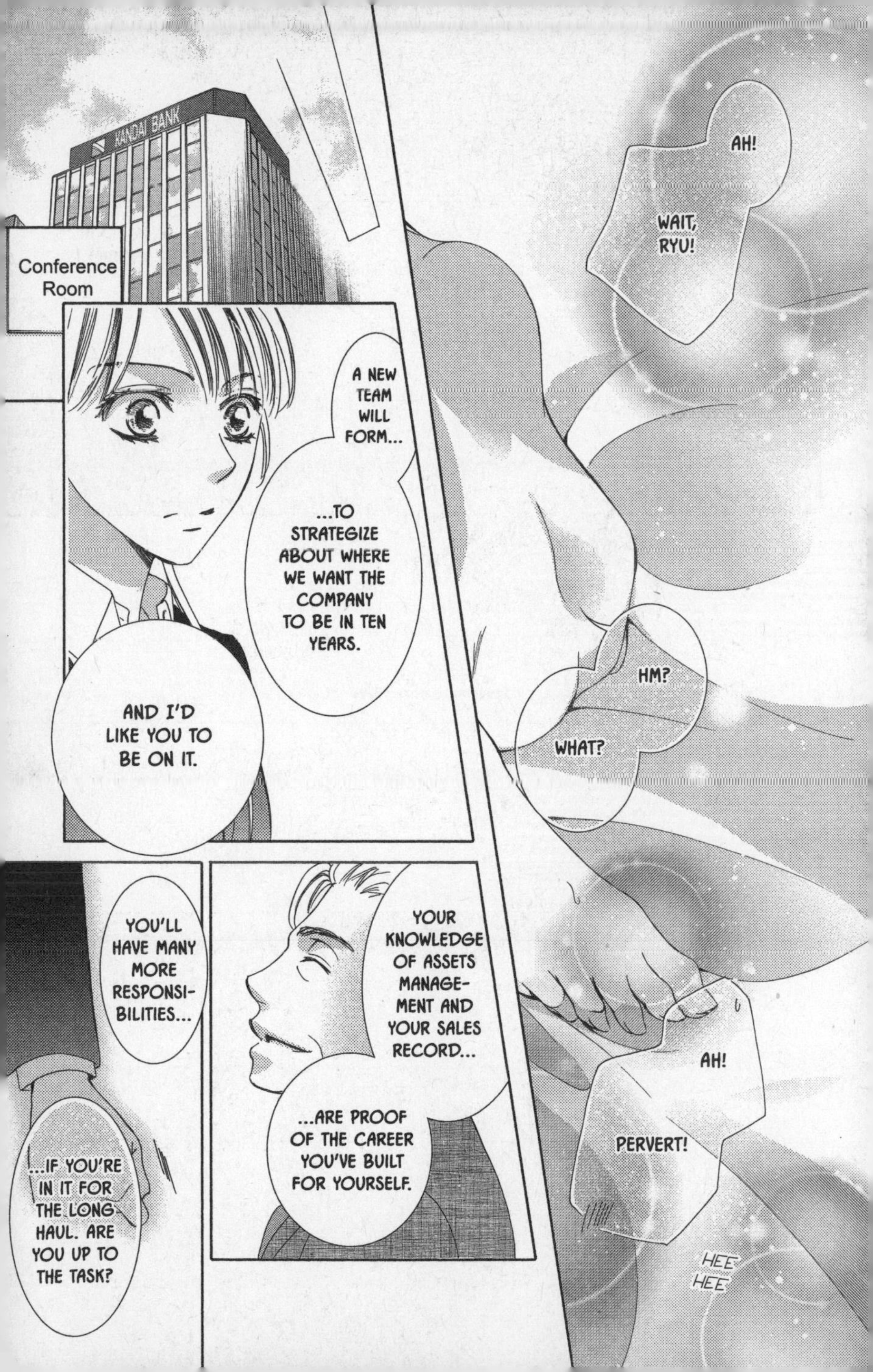
AH!
WAIT, RYU!
HM?
WHAT?
AH!
PERVERT!
HEE HEE
BANDAI BANK
Conference Room
A NEW TEAM WILL FORM...
...TO STRATEGIZE ABOUT WHERE WE WANT THE COMPANY TO BE IN TEN YEARS.
AND I'D LIKE YOU TO BE ON IT.
YOUR KNOWLEDGE OF ASSETS MANAGE-MENT AND YOUR SALES RECORD...
...ARE PROOF OF THE CAREER YOU'VE BUILT FOR YOURSELF.
YOU'LL HAVE MANY MORE RESPONSI-BILITIES...
...IF YOU'RE IN IT FOR THE LONG HAUL. ARE YOU UP TO THE TASK?

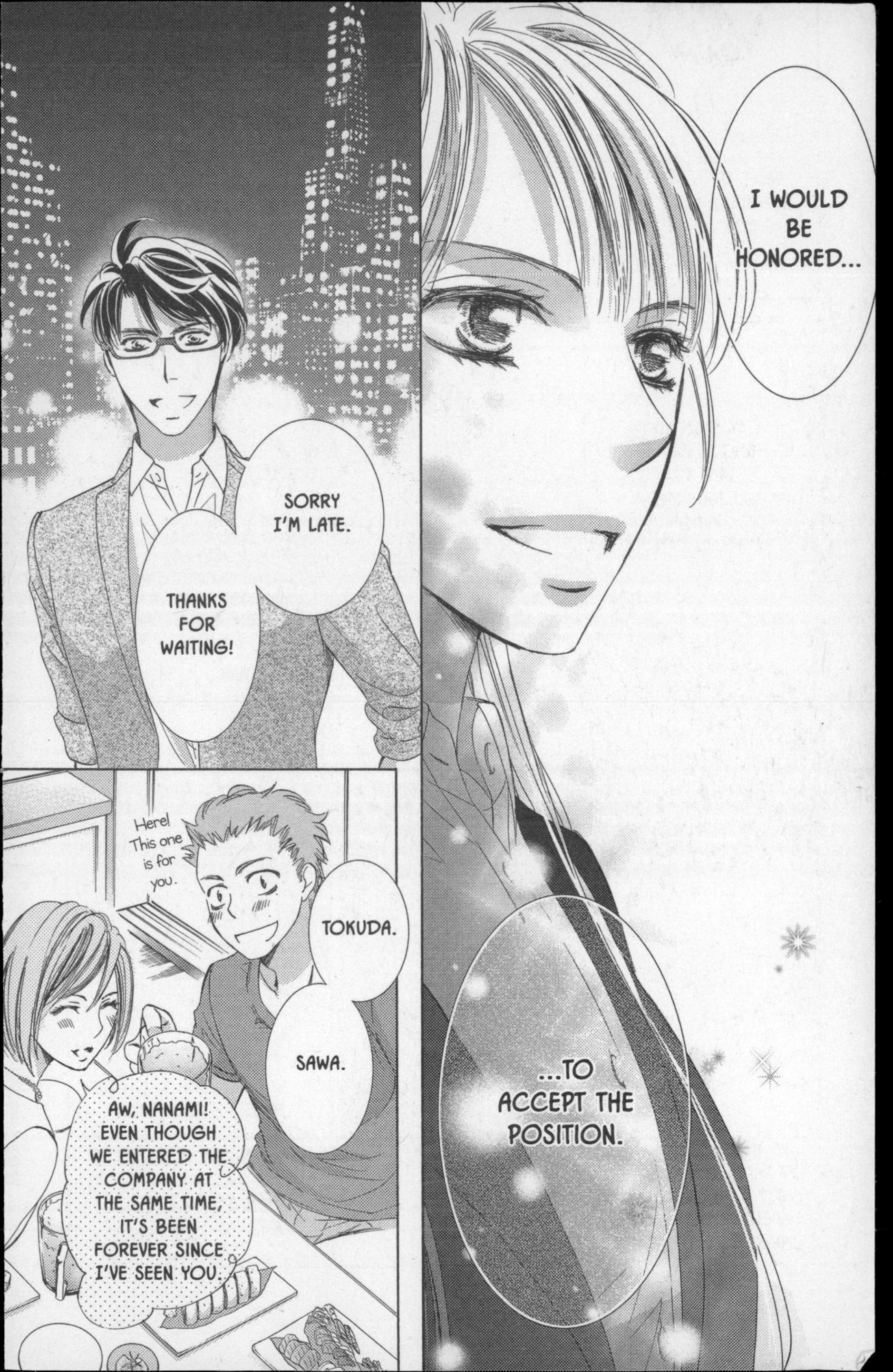
I WOULD BE HONORED...
...TO ACCEPT THE POSITION.
SORRY I'M LATE.
THANKS FOR WAITING!
TOKUDA.
SAWA.
Here! This one is for you.
AW, NANAMI! EVEN THOUGH WE ENTERED THE COMPANY AT THE SAME TIME, IT'S BEEN FOREVER SINCE I'VE SEEN YOU.

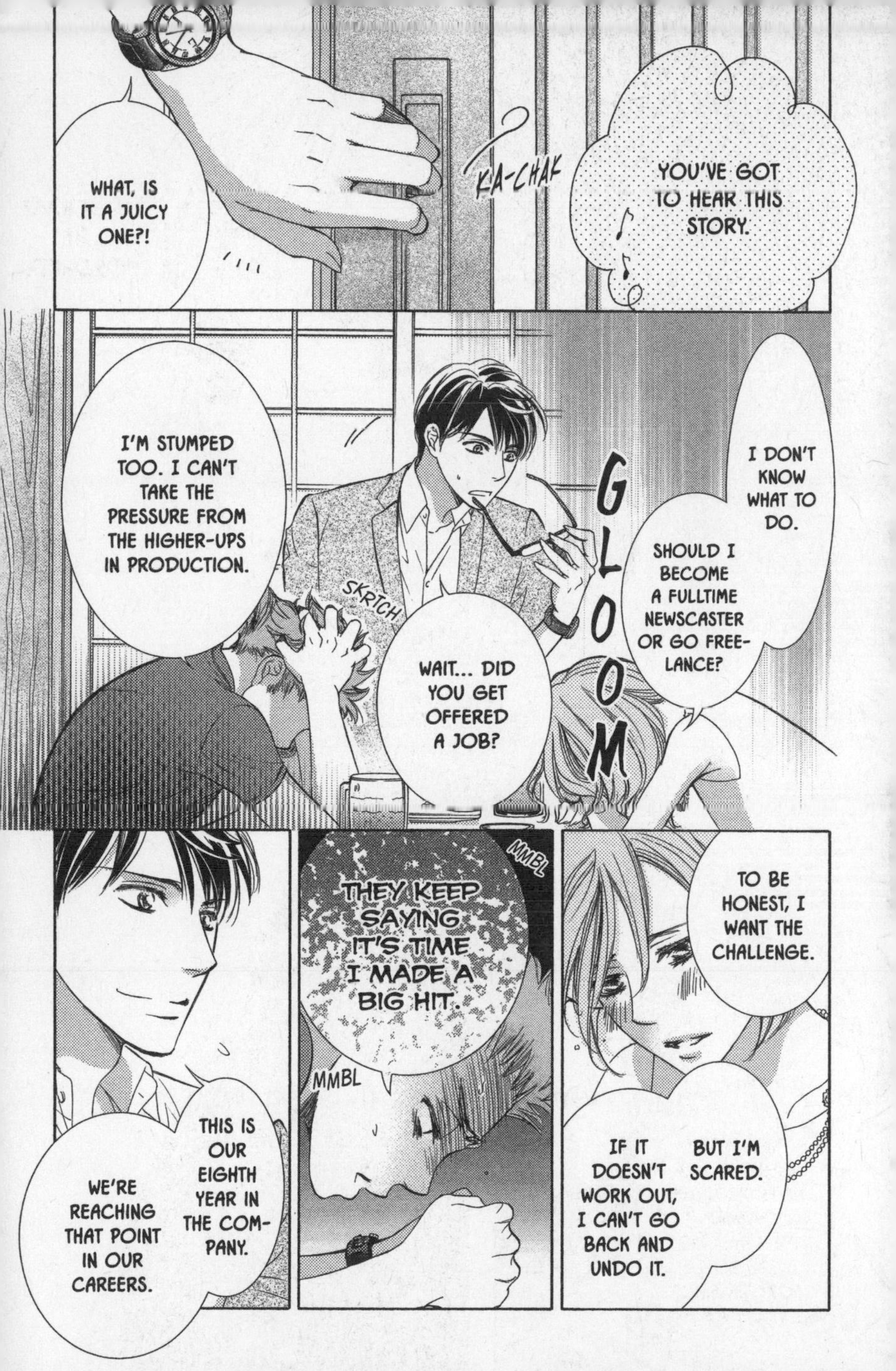
YOU'VE GOT TO HEAR THIS STORY.
KA-CHAK
WHAT, IS IT A JUICY ONE?!
I DON'T KNOW WHAT TO DO.
SHOULD I BECOME A FULLTIME NEWSCASTER OR GO FREE-LANCE?
GLOOM
WAIT... DID YOU GET OFFERED A JOB?
SKRTCH
I'M STUMPED TOO. I CAN'T TAKE THE PRESSURE FROM THE HIGHER-UPS IN PRODUCTION.
TO BE HONEST, I WANT THE CHALLENGE.
BUT I'M SCARED.
IF IT DOESN'T WORK OUT, I CAN'T GO BACK AND UNDO IT.
MMBL
THEY KEEP SAYING IT'S TIME I MADE A BIG HIT.
MMBL
THIS IS OUR EIGHTH YEAR IN THE COMPANY.
WE'RE REACHING THAT POINT IN OUR CAREERS.

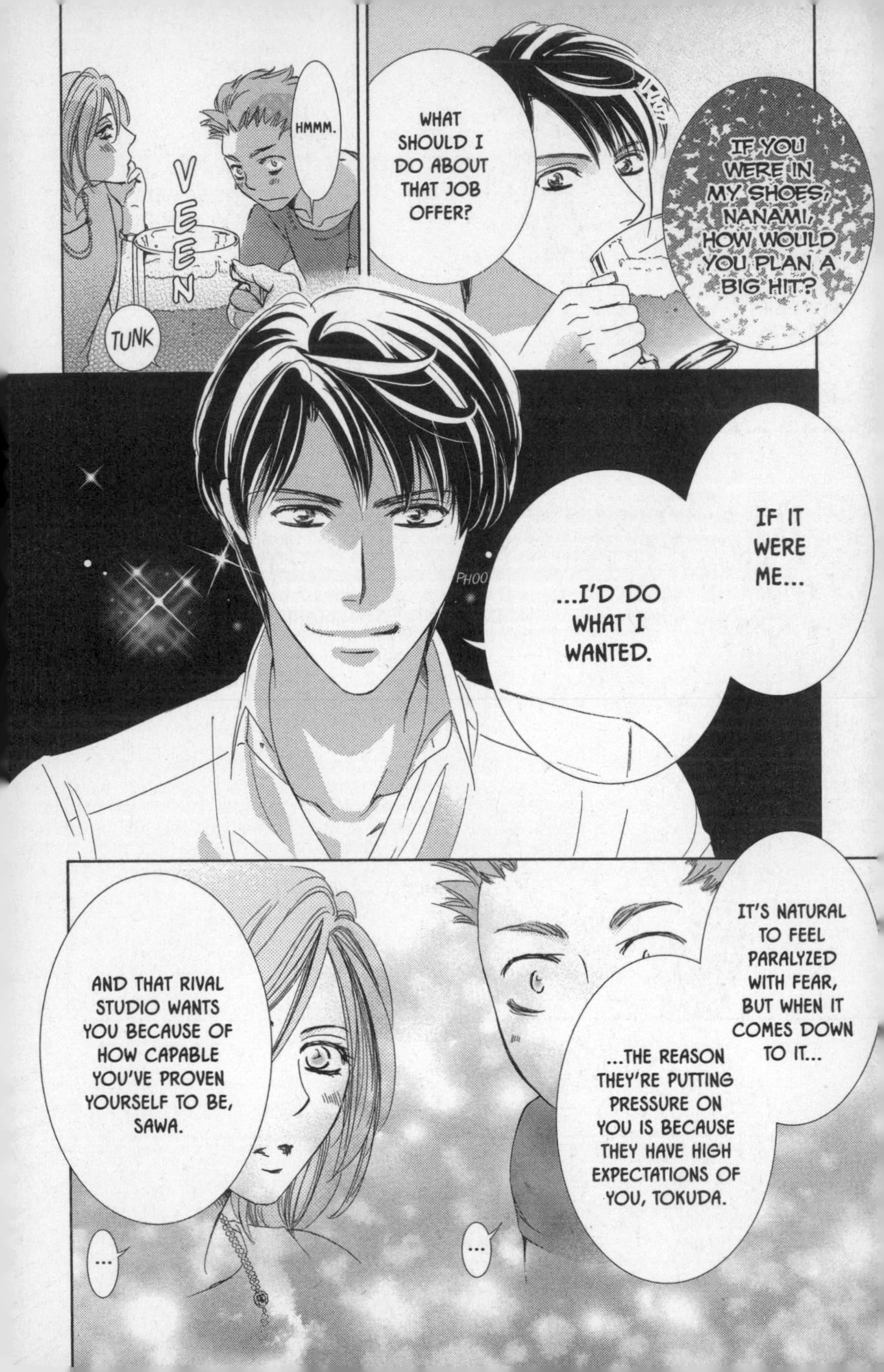
IF YOU WERE IN MY SHOES, NANAMI, HOW WOULD YOU PLAN A BIG HIT?
WHAT SHOULD I DO ABOUT THAT JOB OFFER?
HMMM.
VEEN
TUNK
IF IT WERE ME...
...I'D DO WHAT I WANTED.
PHOO
IT'S NATURAL TO FEEL PARALYZED WITH FEAR, BUT WHEN IT COMES DOWN TO IT...
...THE REASON THEY'RE PUTTING PRESSURE ON YOU IS BECAUSE THEY HAVE HIGH EXPECTATIONS OF YOU, TOKUDA.
AND THAT RIVAL STUDIO WANTS YOU BECAUSE OF HOW CAPABLE YOU'VE PROVEN YOURSELF TO BE, SAWA.
...
...

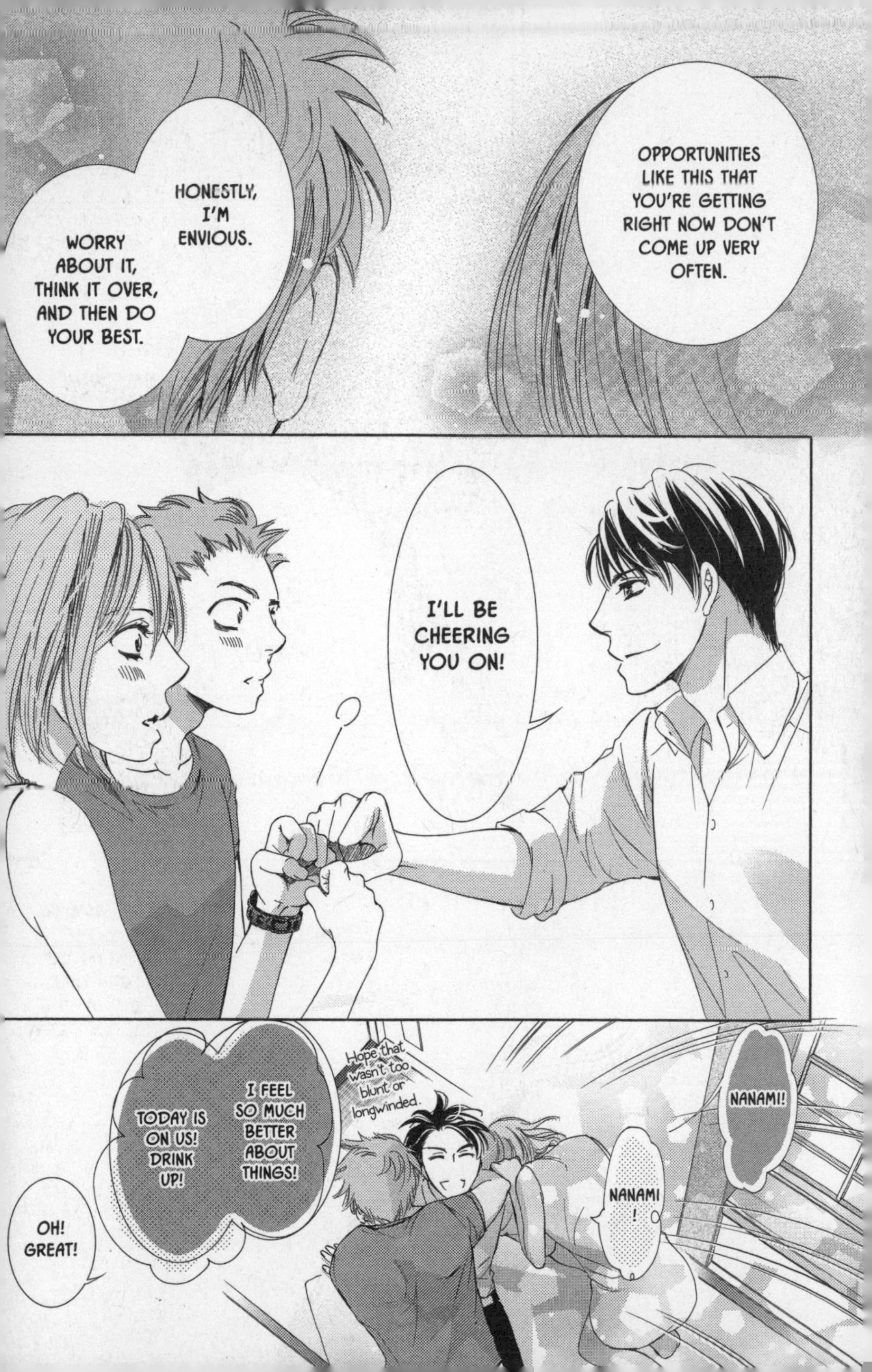
OPPORTUNITIES LIKE THIS THAT YOU'RE GETTING RIGHT NOW DON'T COME UP VERY OFTEN.
HONESTLY, I'M ENVIOUS.
WORRY ABOUT IT, THINK IT OVER, AND THEN DO YOUR BEST.
I'LL BE CHEERING YOU ON!
NANAMI!
NANAMI!
Hope that wasn't too blunt or longwinded.
I FEEL SO MUCH BETTER ABOUT THINGS!
TODAY IS ON US! DRINK UP!
OH! GREAT!

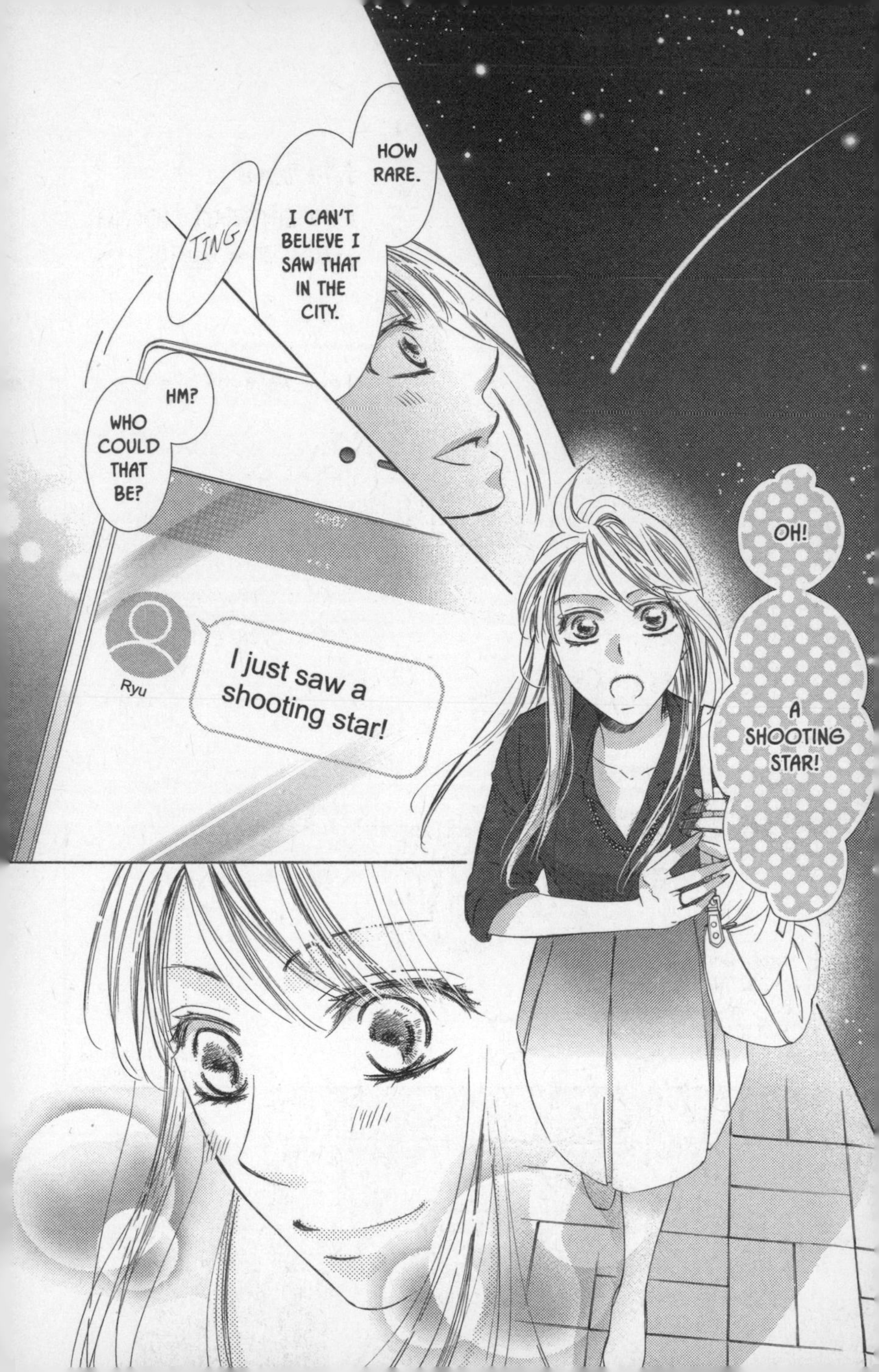
OH!
A SHOOTING STAR!
HOW RARE.
I CAN'T BELIEVE I SAW THAT IN THE CITY.
TING
HM?
WHO COULD THAT BE?
Ryu
I just saw a shooting star!

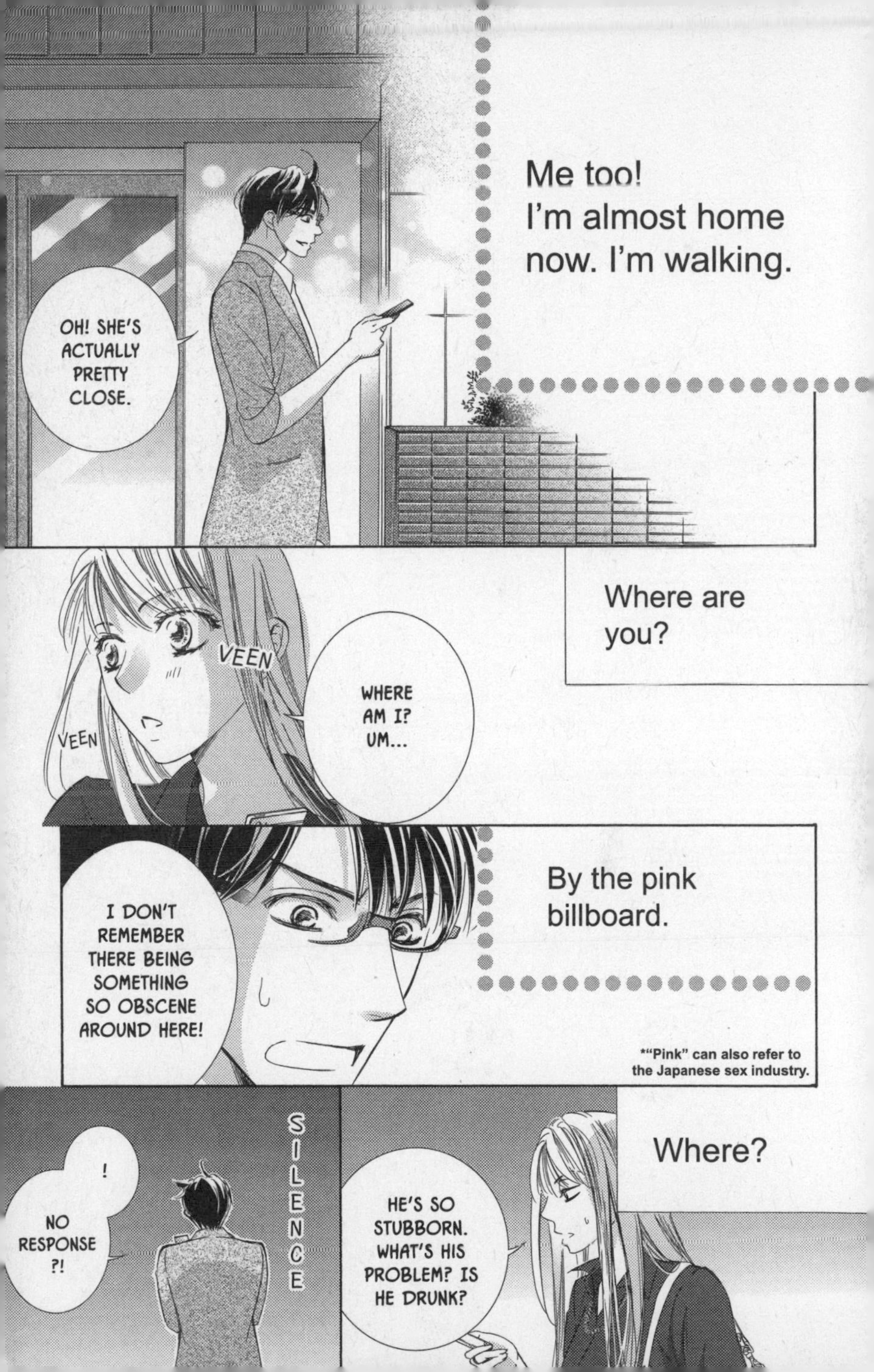
Me too!
I'm almost home now. I'm walking.
OH! SHE'S ACTUALLY PRETTY CLOSE.
Where are you?
VEEN
VEEN
WHERE AM I? UM...
By the pink billboard.
I DON'T REMEMBER THERE BEING SOMETHING SO OBSCENE AROUND HERE!
*"Pink" can also refer to the Japanese sex industry.
Where?
HE'S SO STUBBORN. WHAT'S HIS PROBLEM? IS HE DRUNK?
SILENCE
!
NO RESPONSE ?!

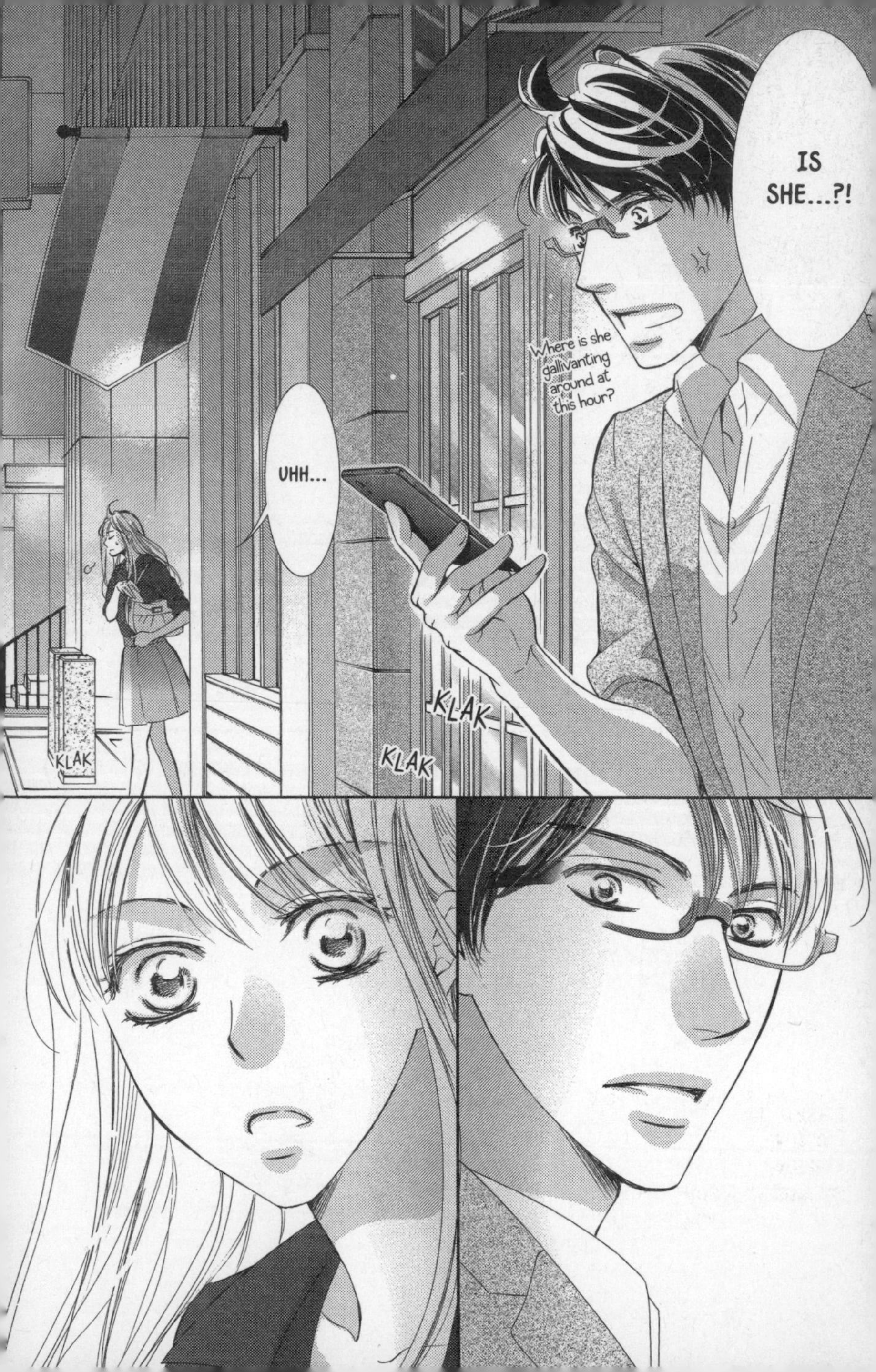
IS SHE...?!
Where is she gallivanting around at this hour?
UHH...
KLAK
KLAK
KLAK

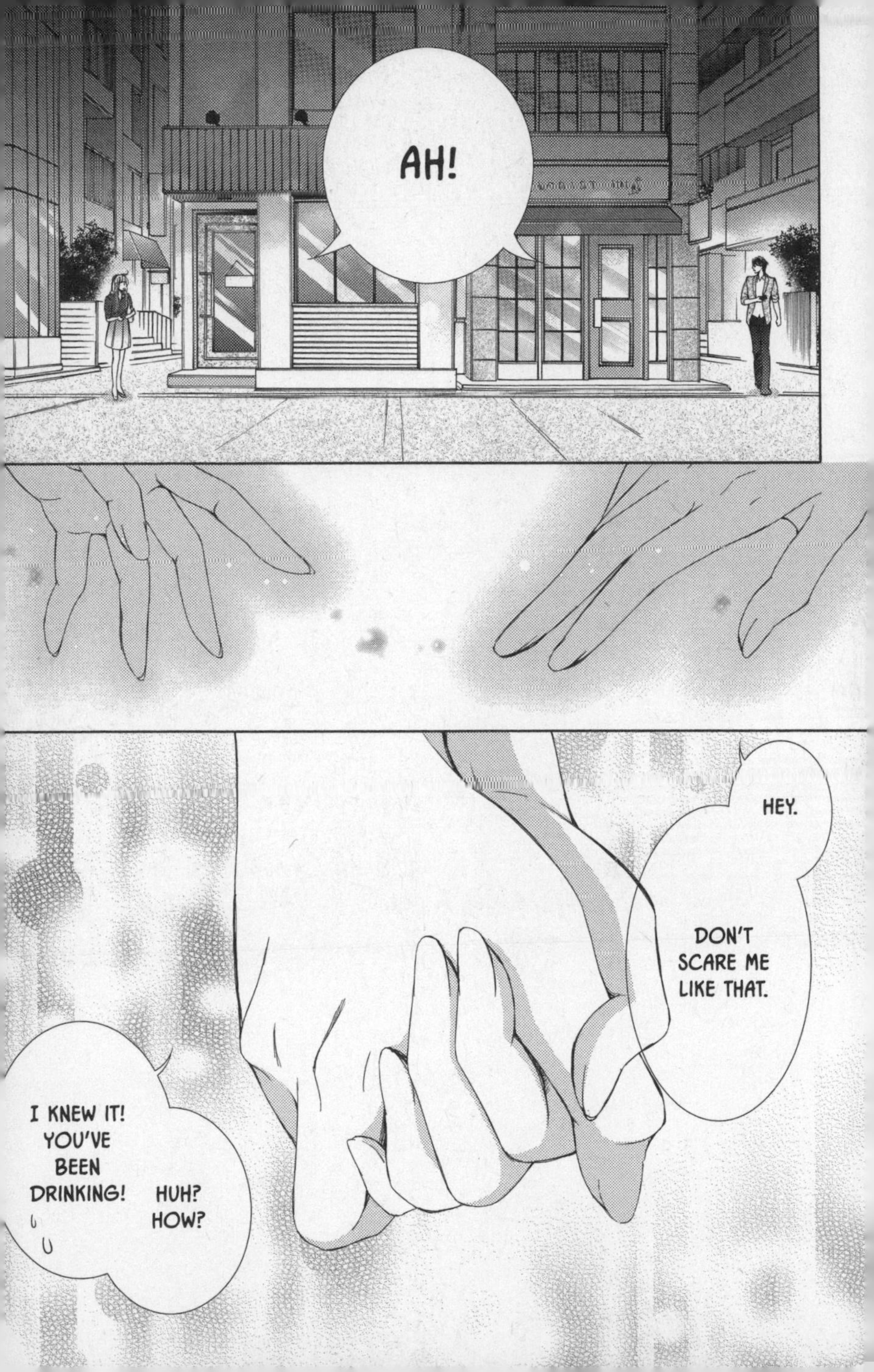
AH!
HEY.
DON'T SCARE ME LIKE THAT.
I KNEW IT! YOU'VE BEEN DRINKING!
HUH? HOW?

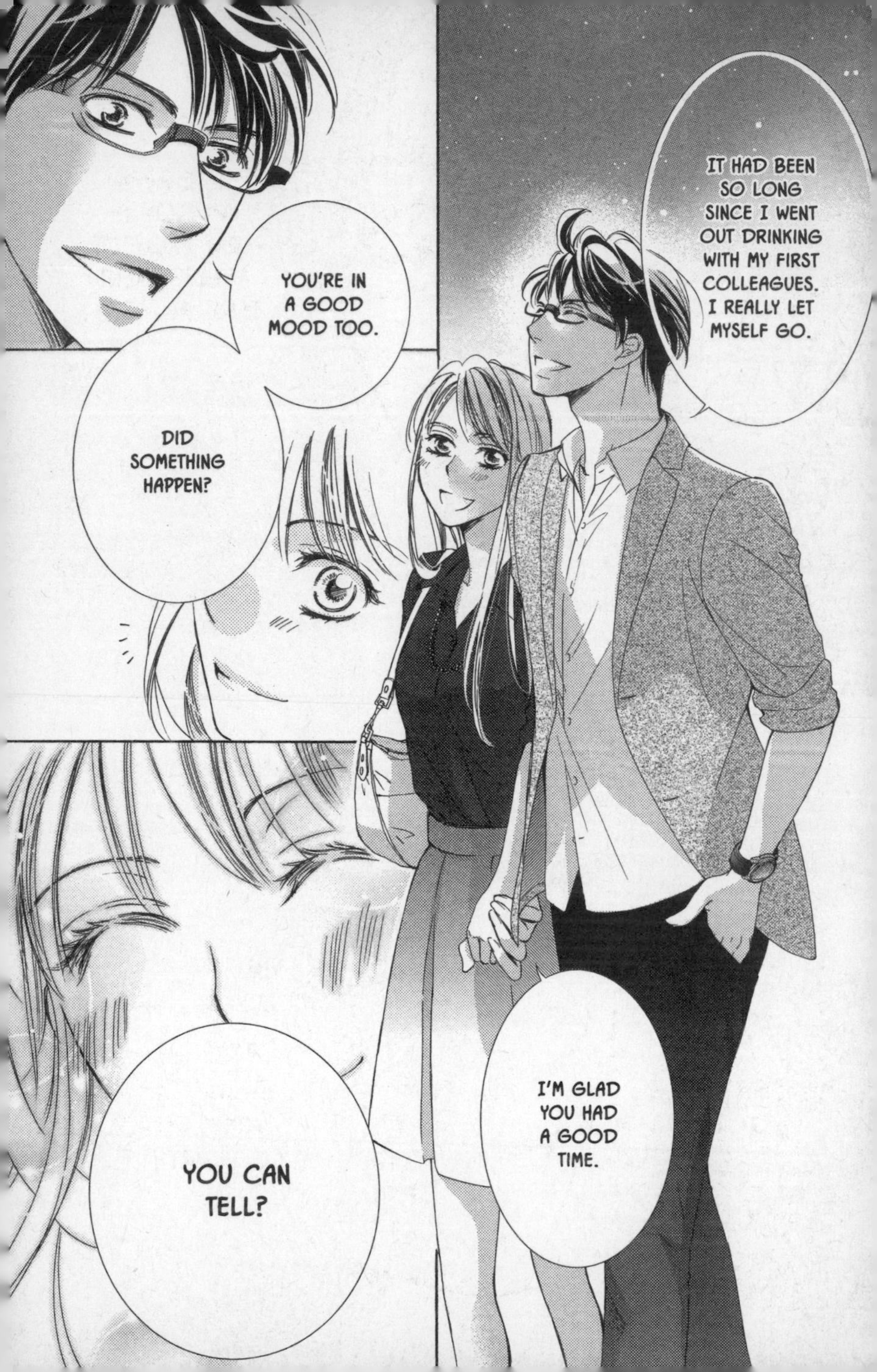
IT HAD BEEN SO LONG SINCE I WENT OUT DRINKING WITH MY FIRST COLLEAGUES. I REALLY LET MYSELF GO.
I'M GLAD YOU HAD A GOOD TIME.
YOU'RE IN A GOOD MOOD TOO.
DID SOMETHING HAPPEN?
YOU CAN TELL?

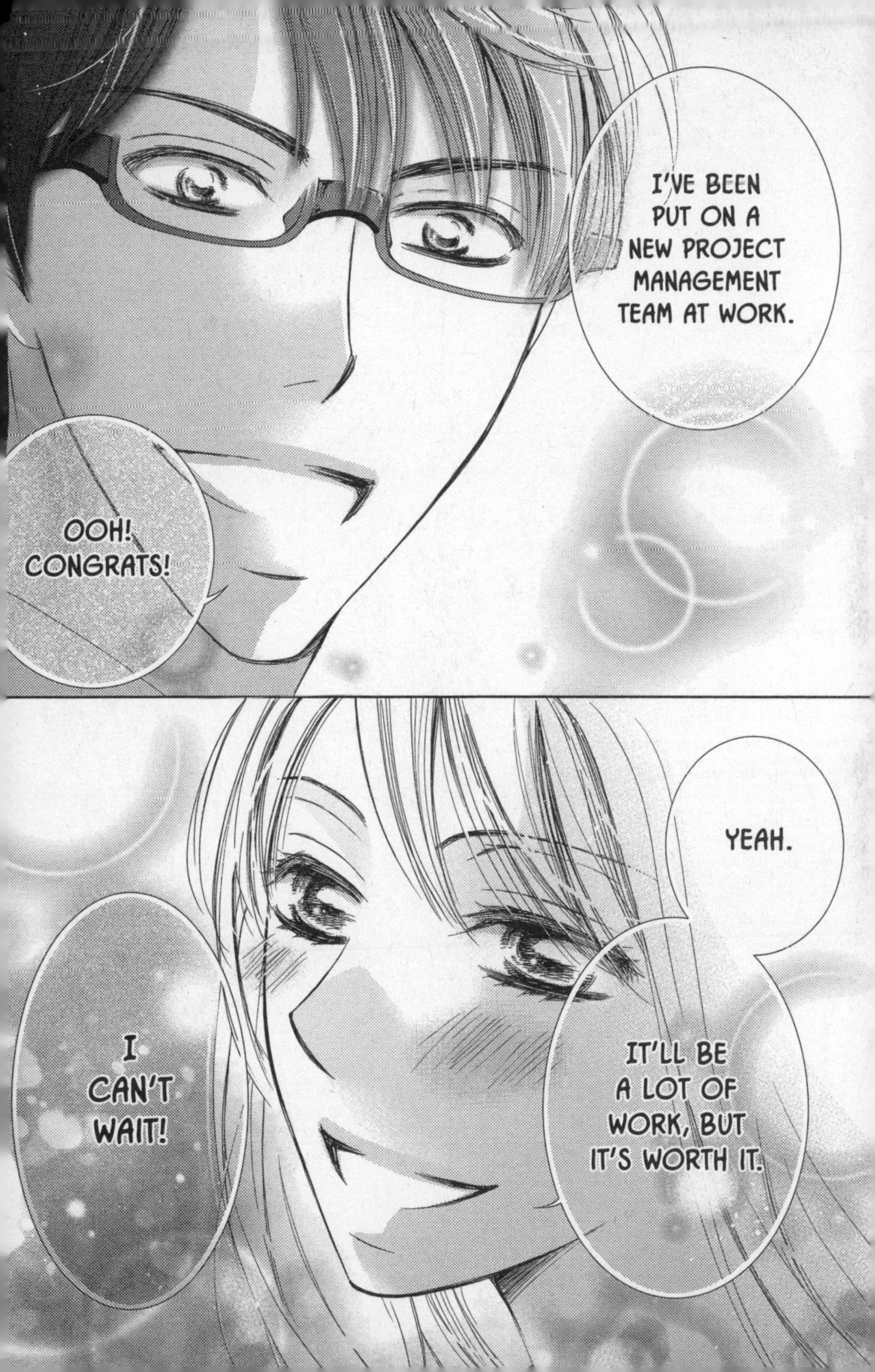
I'VE BEEN PUT ON A NEW PROJECT MANAGEMENT TEAM AT WORK.
OOH! CONGRATS!
YEAH.
IT'LL BE A LOT OF WORK, BUT IT'S WORTH IT.
I CAN'T WAIT!

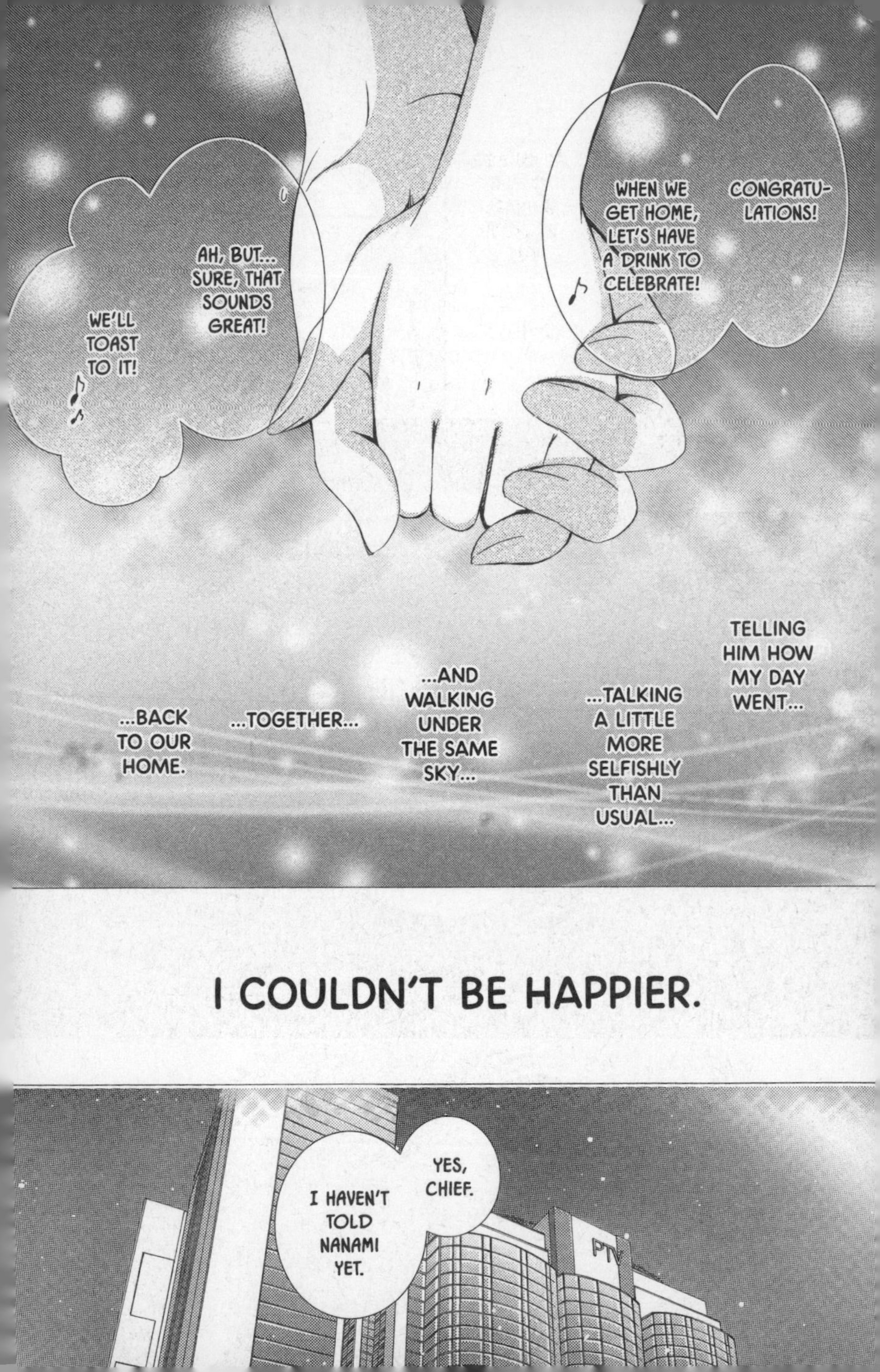
CONGRATU-LATIONS!
WHEN WE GET HOME, LET'S HAVE A DRINK TO CELEBRATE!
AH, BUT... SURE, THAT SOUNDS GREAT!
WE'LL TOAST TO IT!
TELLING HIM HOW MY DAY WENT...
...TALKING A LITTLE MORE SELFISHLY THAN USUAL...
...AND WALKING UNDER THE SAME SKY...
...TOGETHER...
...BACK TO OUR HOME.
I COULDN'T BE HAPPIER.
YES, CHIEF.
I HAVEN'T TOLD NANAMI YET.
PTV

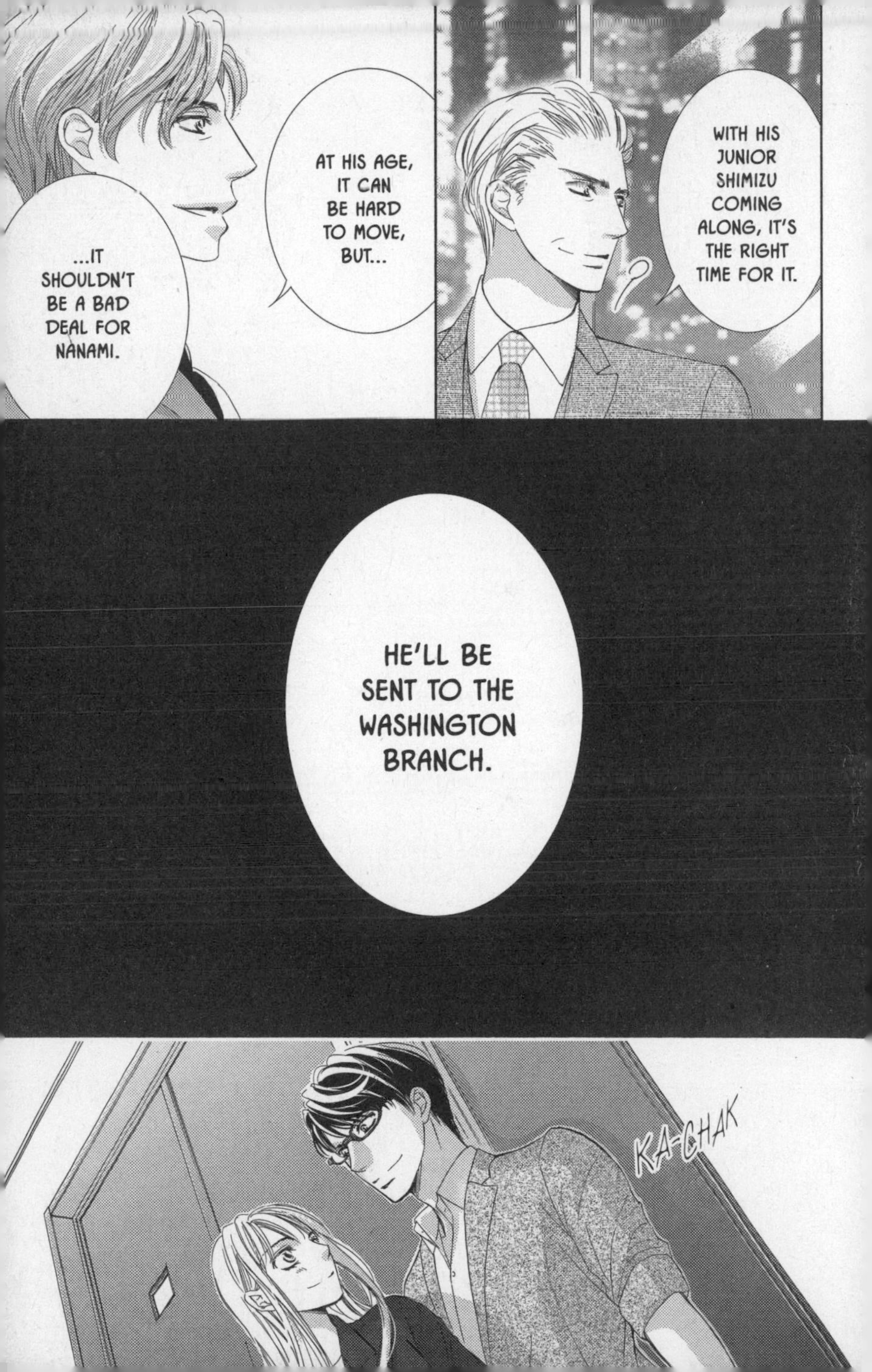
WITH HIS JUNIOR SHIMIZU COMING ALONG, IT'S THE RIGHT TIME FOR IT.
AT HIS AGE, IT CAN BE HARD TO MOVE, BUT...
...IT SHOULDN'T BE A BAD DEAL FOR NANAMI.
HE'LL BE SENT TO THE WASHINGTON BRANCH.
KA-CHAK

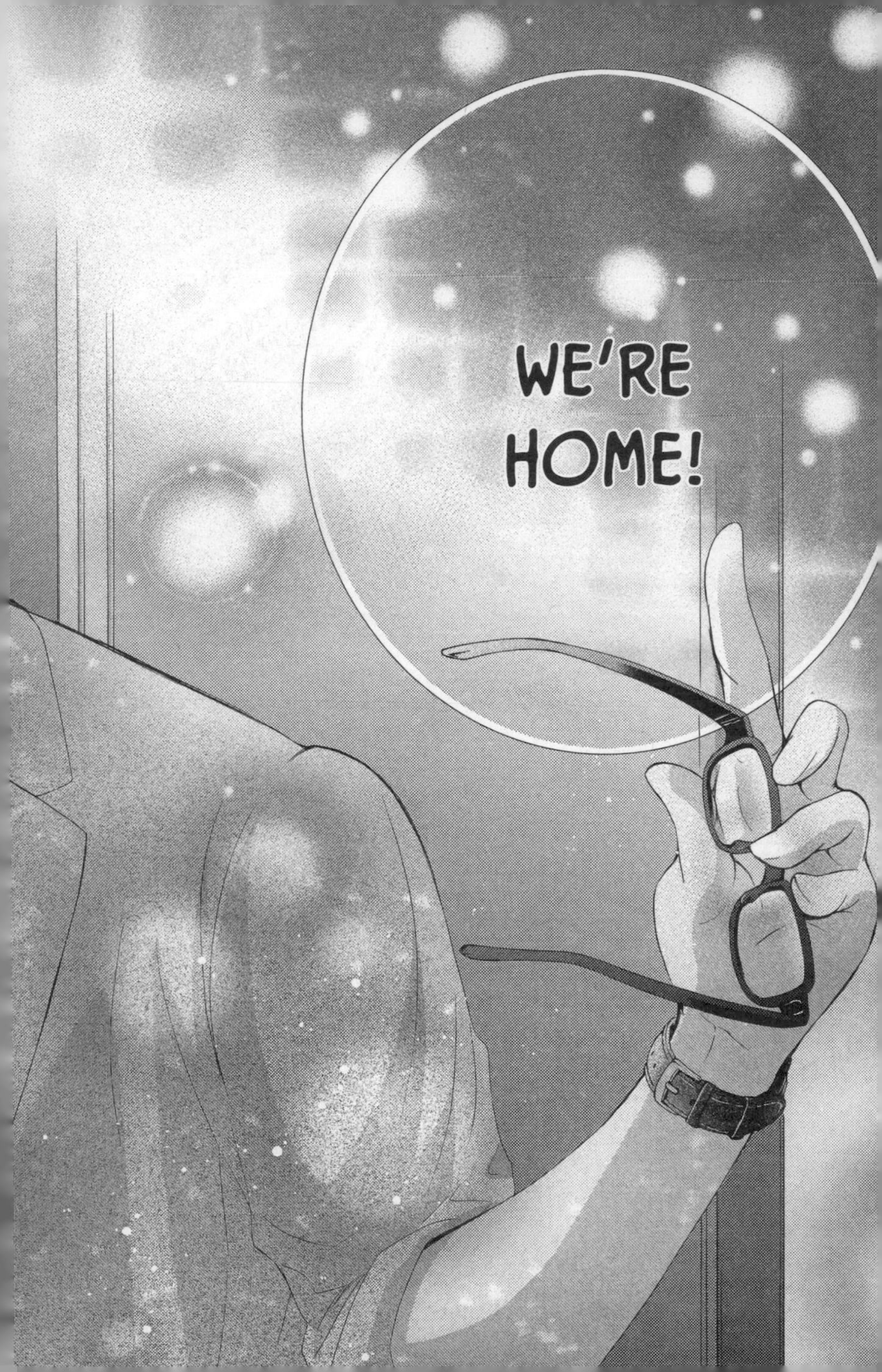
WE'RE HOME!

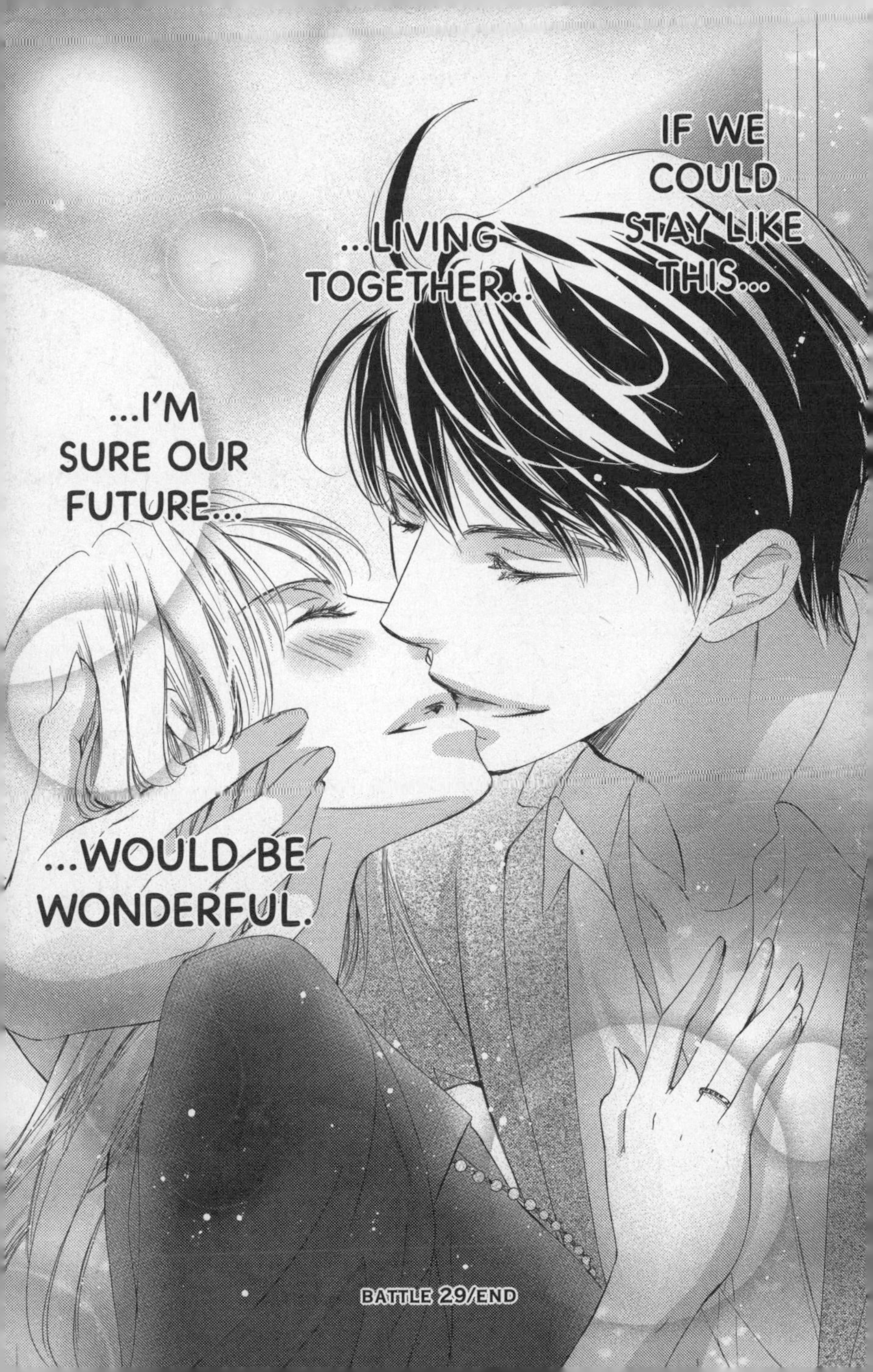
IF WE COULD STAY LIKE THIS...
...LIVING TOGETHER...
...I'M SURE OUR FUTURE...
...WOULD BE WONDERFUL.
BATTLE 29/END

GREETINGS

Hello, this is Izumi Miyazono.
Thank you for picking up volume 6 of *Everyone's Getting Married*.
The story continues. On to volume 7! Thank you to everyone who helped me out with putting this together, even when you're already so busy.

The bonus story in this volume is called "Nanaryu's Miscalculation." I had a lot of fun drawing all their muscles... *(laugh)* But I'd still like to draw Ryu and Kamiya spending an evening talking together. They'd probably cover a wide range of subjects. I wonder which would come out the victor. *(laugh)*

Along with this sixth volume, I was able to release *I Know This Is Sudden, but I'm Stealing You Tonight*. (Doesn't that title sound familiar?) It's a collection of older short stories of mine plus two "Nanaryu's ___" stories. Since it involves old works and a currently running story, does that make it a collaboration?! ...It certainly feels that way... I really hope you'll check it out! ^^

Since this is the first time I've ever had two books go on sale at the same time, I'm both excited and nervous. Maybe it'll be fun to look at them side by side? They're both about Asuka and Ryu.

I hope to see you in the next volume! Thank you very much! ✒

Special thanks ♥: Keiko S., Megumi M., Emi Y., my family, my editor and everyone involved.

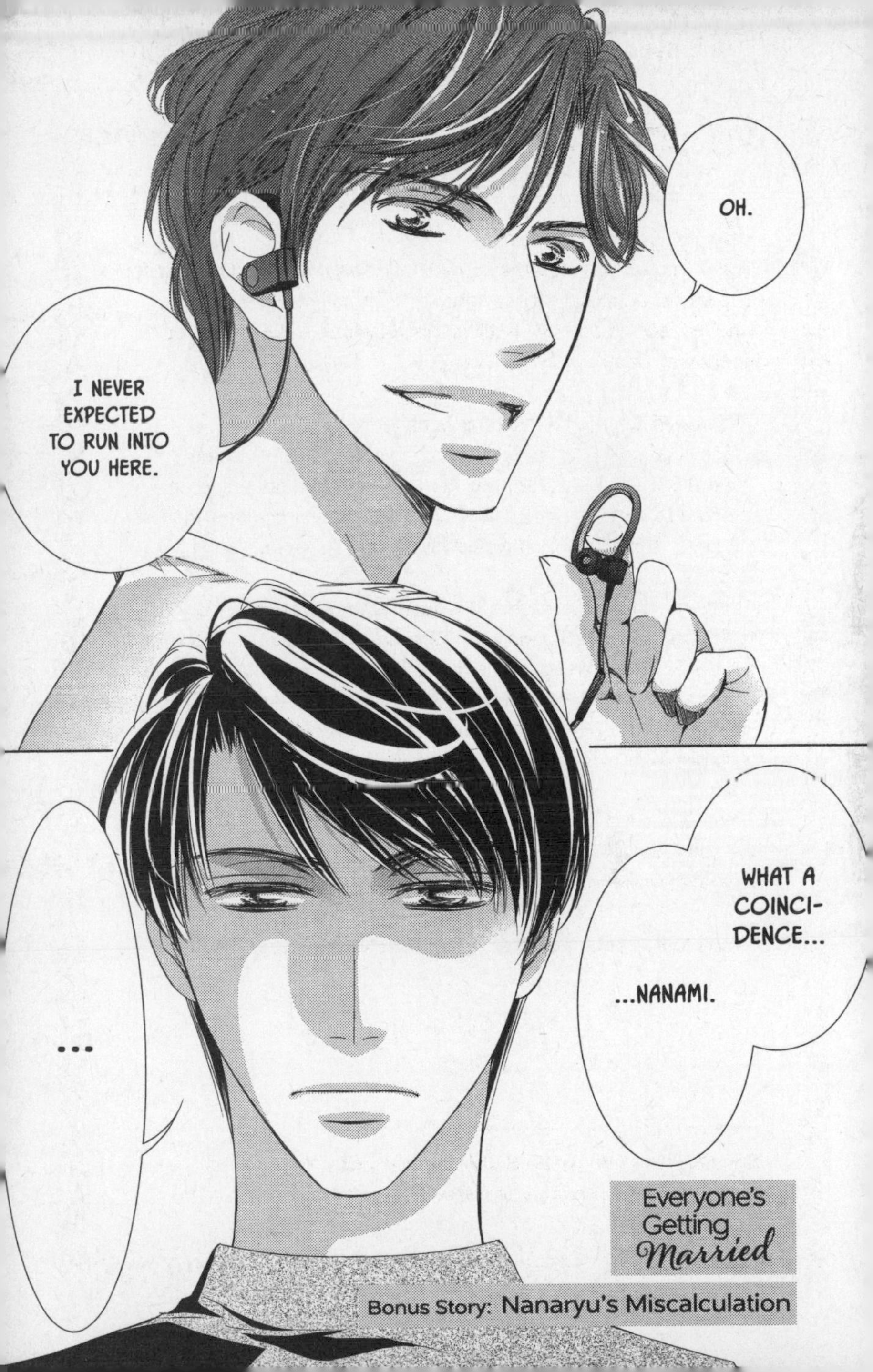
OH.
I NEVER EXPECTED TO RUN INTO YOU HERE.
WHAT A COINCIDENCE...
...NANAMI.
...
Everyone's Getting Married
Bonus Story: Nanaryu's Miscalculation

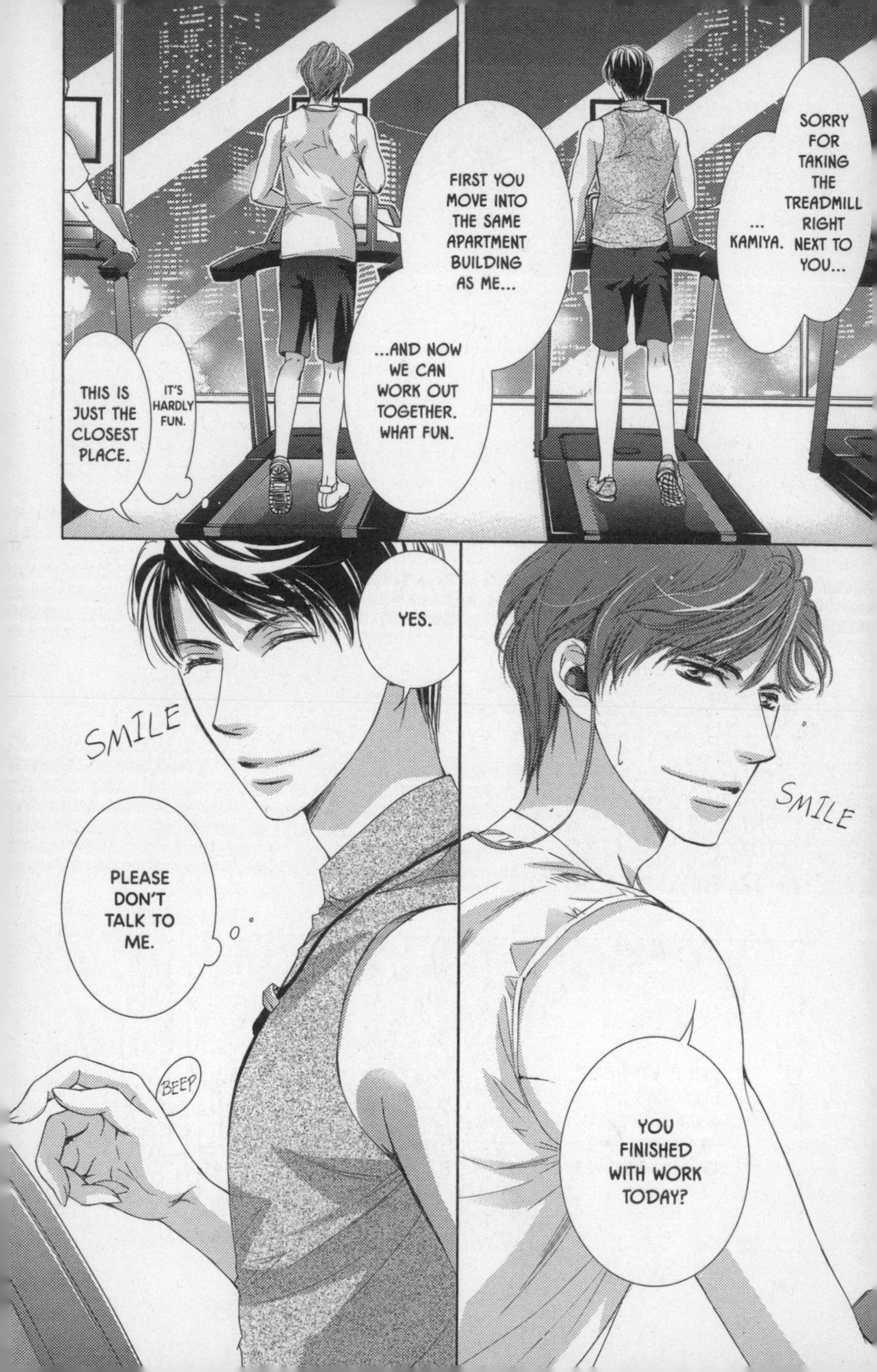
SORRY FOR TAKING THE TREADMILL RIGHT NEXT TO YOU...
... KAMIYA.
FIRST YOU MOVE INTO THE SAME APARTMENT BUILDING AS ME...
...AND NOW WE CAN WORK OUT TOGETHER. WHAT FUN.
IT'S HARDLY FUN.
THIS IS JUST THE CLOSEST PLACE.
SMILE
YOU FINISHED WITH WORK TODAY?
YES.
SMILE
PLEASE DON'T TALK TO ME.
BEEP

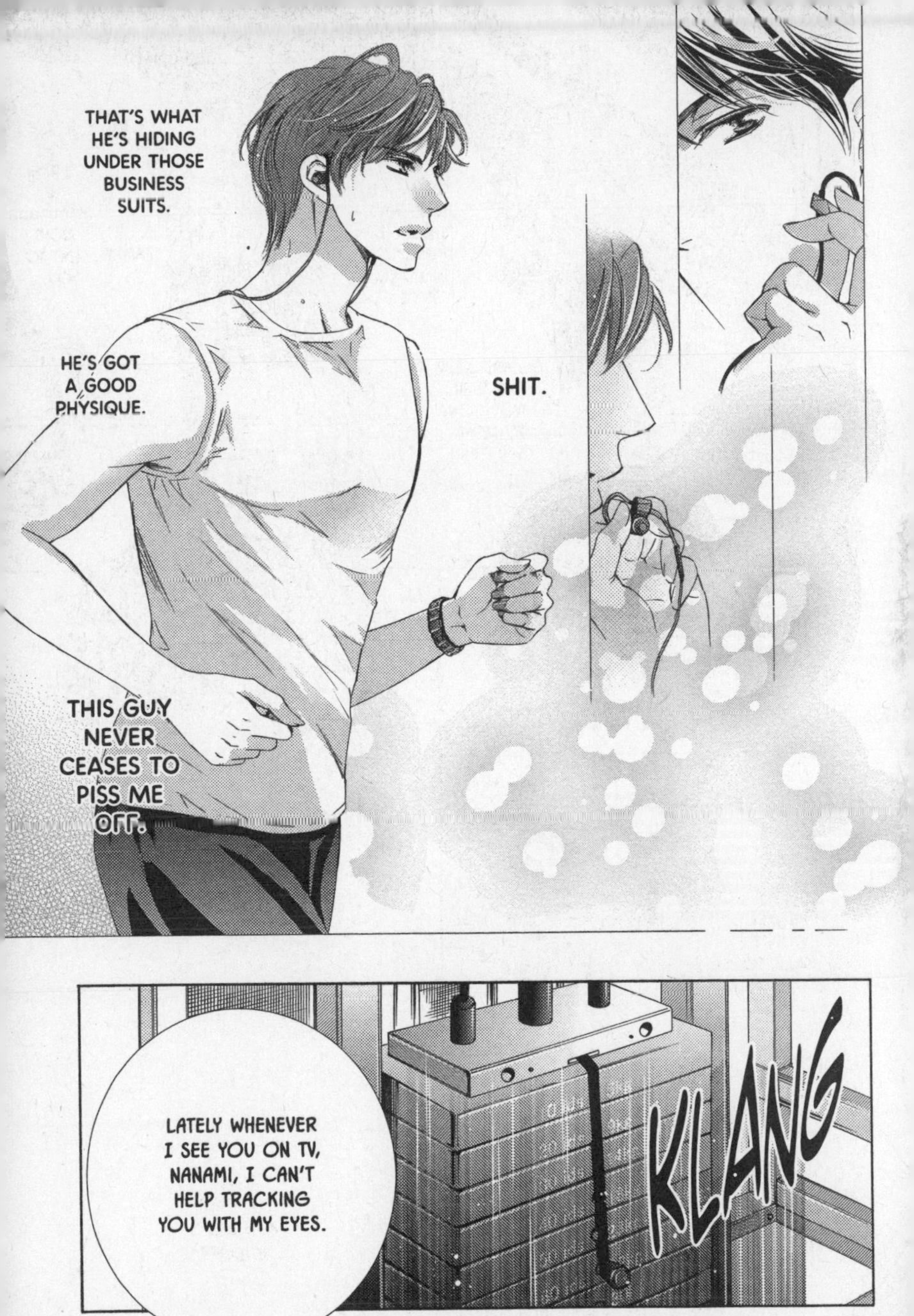
SHIT.
THAT'S WHAT HE'S HIDING UNDER THOSE BUSINESS SUITS.
HE'S GOT A GOOD PHYSIQUE.
THIS GUY NEVER CEASES TO PISS ME OFF.
KLANG
LATELY WHENEVER I SEE YOU ON TV, NANAMI, I CAN'T HELP TRACKING YOU WITH MY EYES.

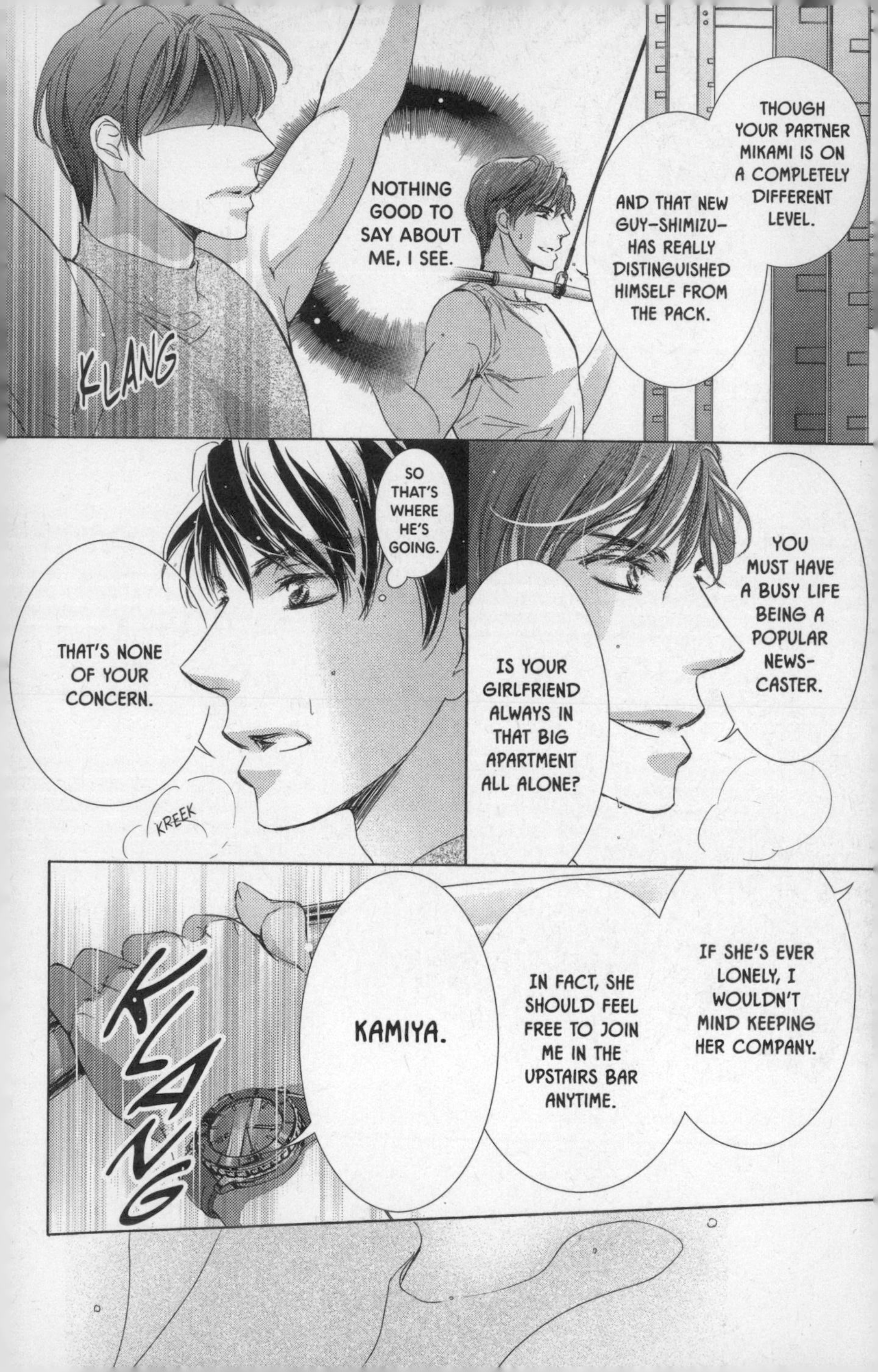
THOUGH YOUR PARTNER MIKAMI IS ON A COMPLETELY DIFFERENT LEVEL.
AND THAT NEW GUY—SHIMIZU—HAS REALLY DISTINGUISHED HIMSELF FROM THE PACK.
NOTHING GOOD TO SAY ABOUT ME, I SEE.
KLANG
YOU MUST HAVE A BUSY LIFE BEING A POPULAR NEWS-CASTER.
IS YOUR GIRLFRIEND ALWAYS IN THAT BIG APARTMENT ALL ALONE?
SO THAT'S WHERE HE'S GOING.
THAT'S NONE OF YOUR CONCERN.
KREEK
IF SHE'S EVER LONELY, I WOULDN'T MIND KEEPING HER COMPANY.
IN FACT, SHE SHOULD FEEL FREE TO JOIN ME IN THE UPSTAIRS BAR ANYTIME.
KAMIYA.
KLANG

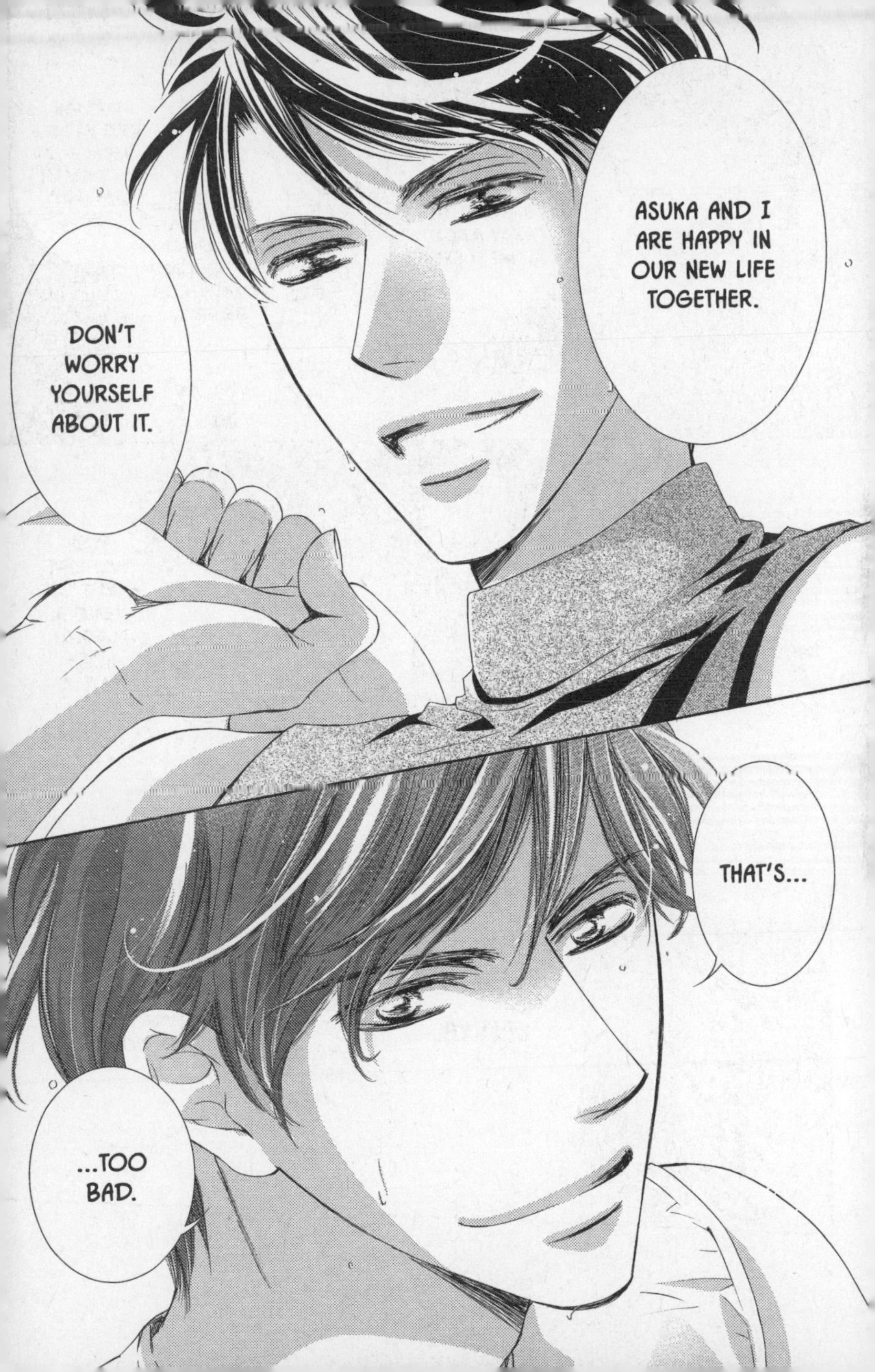
ASUKA AND I ARE HAPPY IN OUR NEW LIFE TOGETHER.
DON'T WORRY YOURSELF ABOUT IT.
THAT'S...
...TOO BAD.

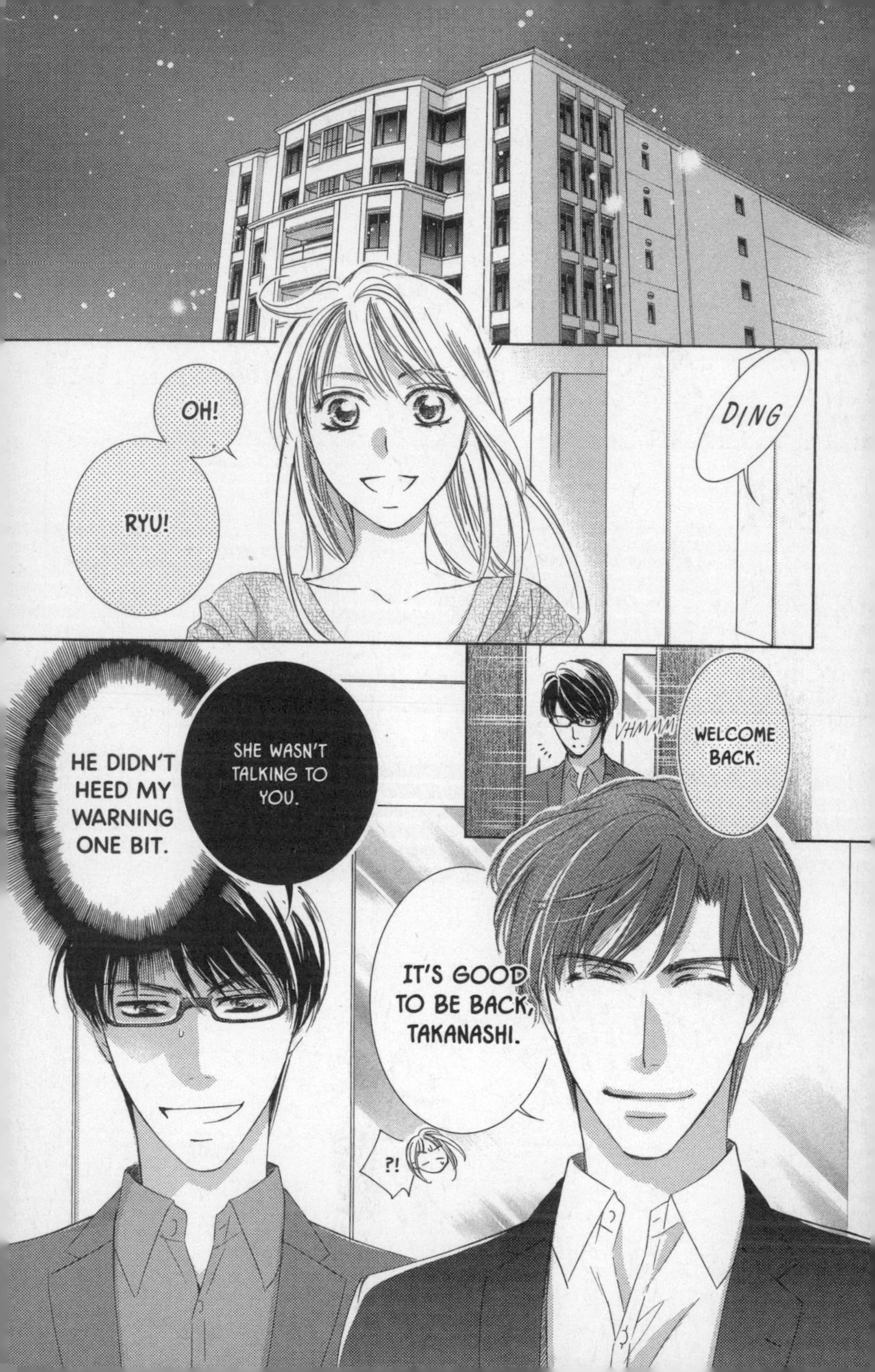
DING
OH!
RYU!
WELCOME BACK.
VHMMM
IT'S GOOD TO BE BACK, TAKANASHI.
?!
SHE WASN'T TALKING TO YOU.
HE DIDN'T HEED MY WARNING ONE BIT.

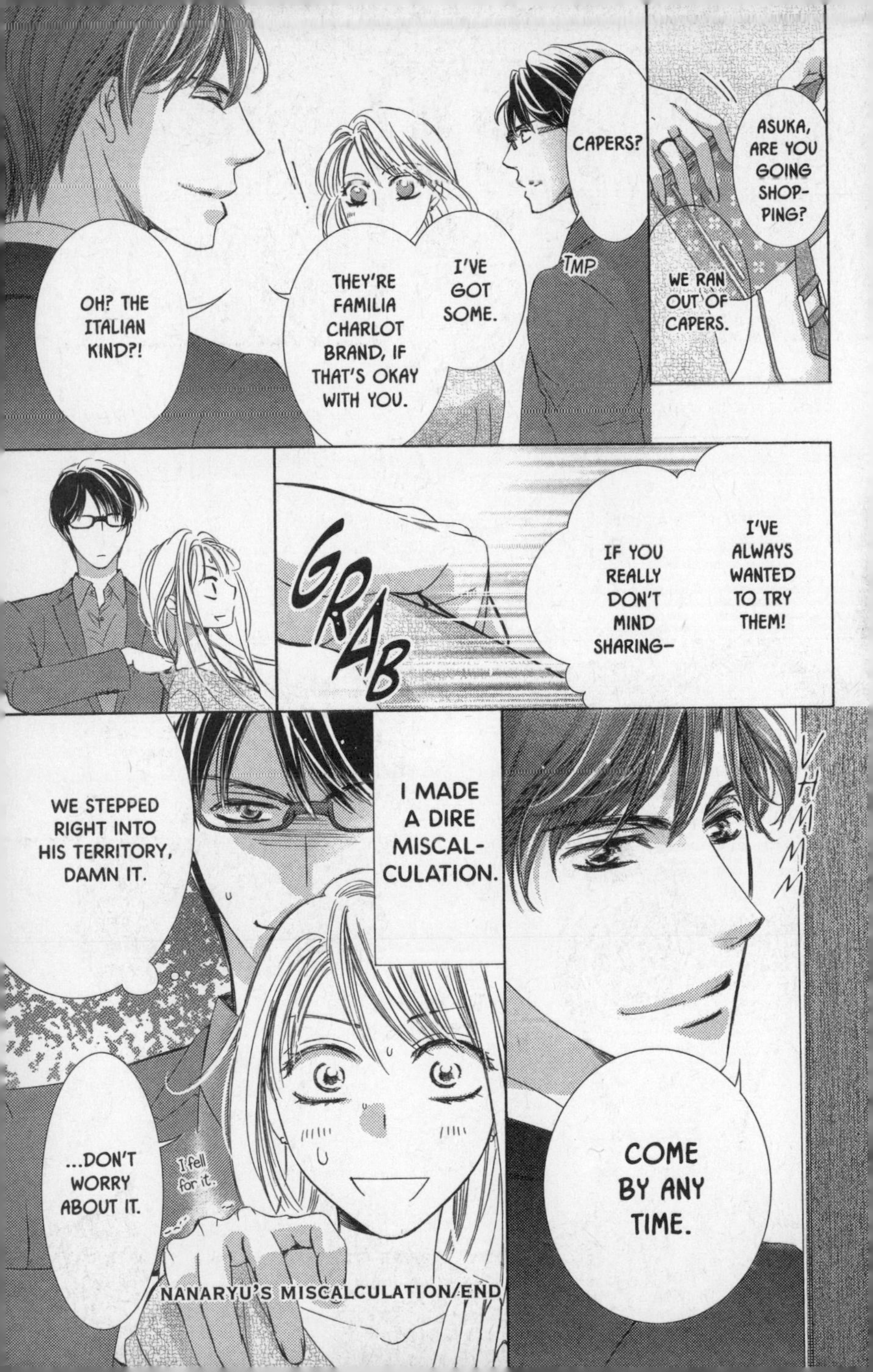
ASUKA, ARE YOU GOING SHOP-PING?
WE RAN OUT OF CAPERS.
CAPERS?
TMP
I'VE GOT SOME.
THEY'RE FAMILIA CHARLOT BRAND, IF THAT'S OKAY WITH YOU.
OH? THE ITALIAN KIND?!
I'VE ALWAYS WANTED TO TRY THEM!
IF YOU REALLY DON'T MIND SHARING–
GRAB
VHMMMM
COME BY ANY TIME.
I MADE A DIRE MISCAL-CULATION.
WE STEPPED RIGHT INTO HIS TERRITORY, DAMN IT.
I fell for it.
...DON'T WORRY ABOUT IT.
NANARYU'S MISCALCULATION/END

Hi, I'm Kanade.

This is Kanade. He appeared in the last volume in name only. On the back cover of volume 6, I drew Kamiya and Kanade together because I really like the two of them. I want to draw them in color again.

IZUMI MIYAZONO

IZUMI MIYAZONO is from Niigata Prefecture in Japan. She debuted in 2005 with *Shunmin Shohousen* (A Prescription for Sleep). In 2014 she began serializing *Everyone's Getting Married* in *Petit Comic*. This series was also adapted for a live-action TV drama in Japan.

Everyone's Getting Married (6)

SHOJO BEAT EDITION

STORY AND ART BY IZUMI MIYAZONO

TOTSUZEN DESUGA, ASHITA KEKKON SHIMASU Vol. 6
by Izumi MIYAZONO
© 2014 Izumi MIYAZONO
All rights reserved.
Original Japanese edition published by SHOGAKUKAN.
English translation rights in the United States of America, Canada,
the United Kingdom and Ireland arranged with SHOGAKUKAN.

ORIGINAL COVER DESIGN Kaoru KUROKI, Saaya NISHINO + Bay Bridge Studio

TRANSLATION Katherine Schilling
TOUCH-UP ART & LETTERING Inori Fukuda Trant
DESIGN Alice Lewis
EDITOR Nancy Thistlethwaite

The stories, characters and incidents mentioned
in this publication are entirely fictional.

Printed in Canada

Published by VIZ Media, LLC
P.O. Box 77010
San Francisco, CA 94107

10 9 8 7 6 5 4 3 2 1
First printing, September 2017

PARENTAL ADVISORY
EVERYONE'S GETTING MARRIED is rated
M for Mature and is recommended for
mature readers. This volume contains
mature themes.
ratings.viz.com

www.viz.com

www.shojobeat.com

Happy Marriage?!

Story & Art by **Maki Enjoji**

Can two strangers living together find their way to a happy marriage?!

In order to help her father, Chiwa Takanashi agrees to an arranged marriage with the company president, Hokuto Mamiya—a man she doesn't know—at the request of Hokuto's grandfather. Chiwa believes the arrangement isn't binding, but her new partner seems to think otherwise...

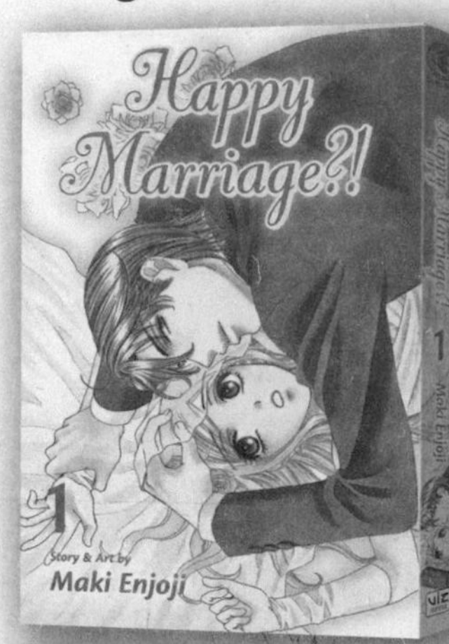
Happy Marriage?!
1
Story & Art by
Maki Enjoji
Happy Marriage?!
1
Maki Enjoji
VIZ

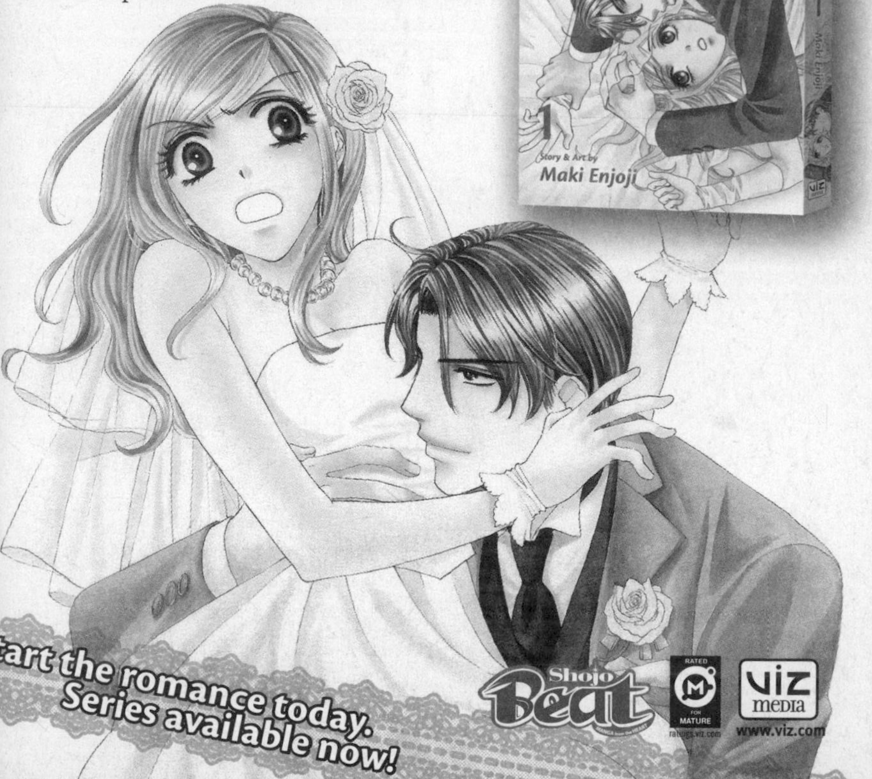

tart the romance today. Series available now!

Shojo Beat

RATED M FOR MATURE ratings.viz.com

VIZ media www.viz.com

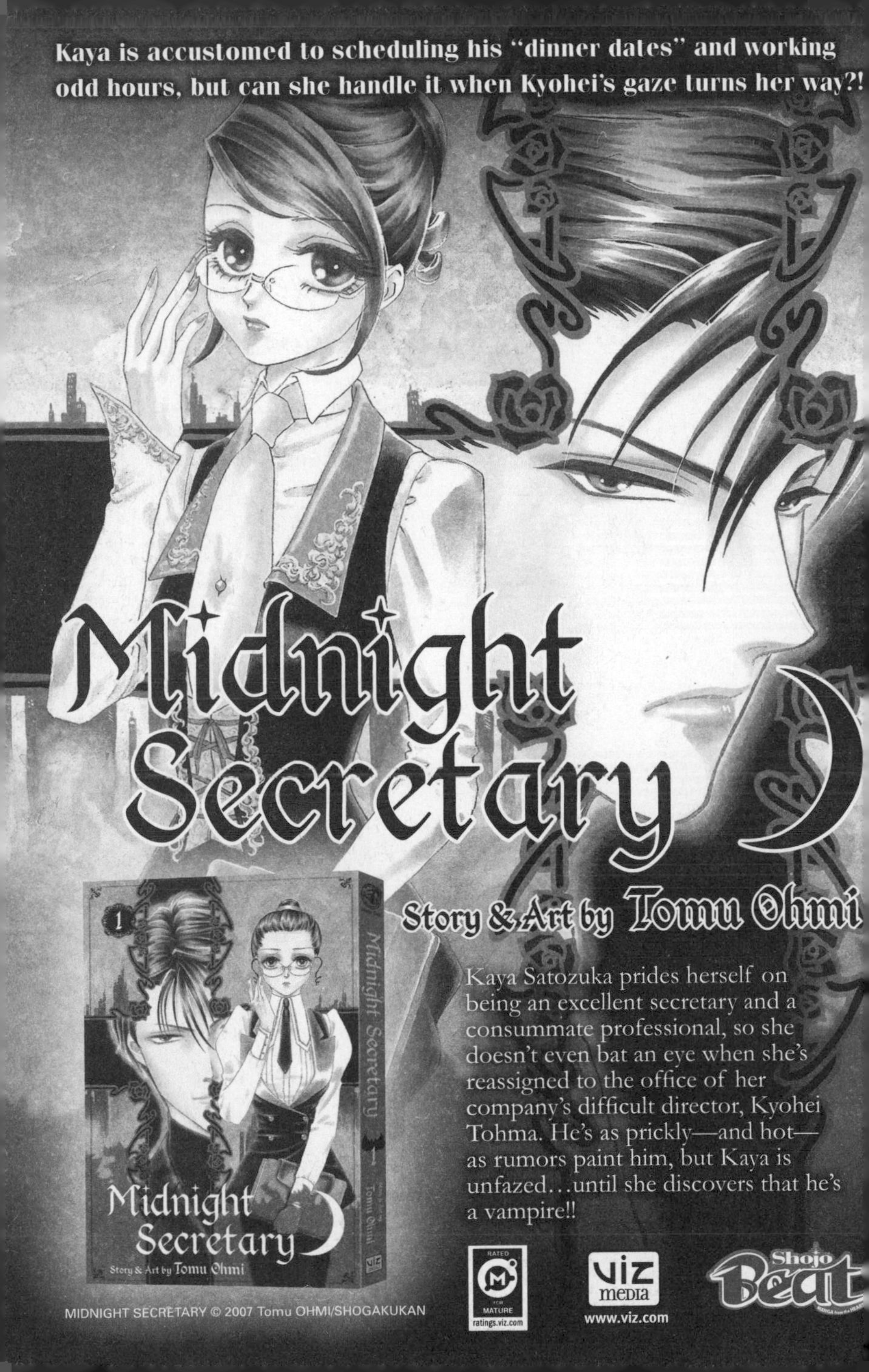
Kaya is accustomed to scheduling his "dinner dates" and working odd hours, but can she handle it when Kyohei's gaze turns her way?!
Midnight Secretary
Story & Art by Tomu Ohmi
1
Midnight Secretary
Story & Art by Tomu Ohmi
Kaya Satozuka prides herself on being an excellent secretary and a consummate professional, so she doesn't even bat an eye when she's reassigned to the office of her company's difficult director, Kyohei Tohma. He's as prickly—and hot—as rumors paint him, but Kaya is unfazed…until she discovers that he's a vampire!!
RATED M FOR MATURE
ratings.viz.com
viz media
www.viz.com
Shojo Beat
MIDNIGHT SECRETARY © 2007 Tomu OHMI/SHOGAKUKAN

STOP!

YOU MAY BE READING THE WRONG WAY!

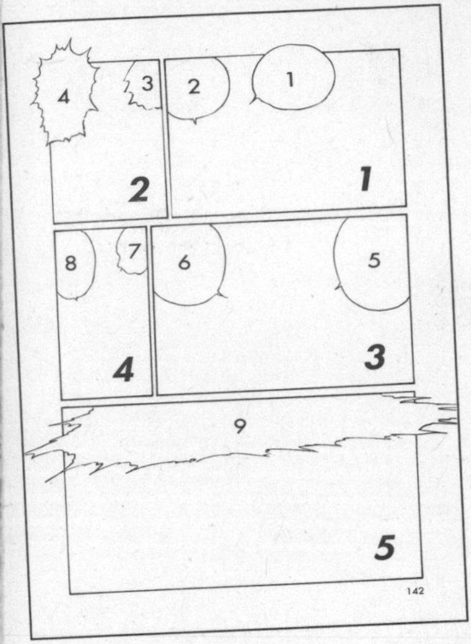
1
2
3
4
5
6
7
8
9
1
2
3
4
5
142

In keeping with the original Japanese comic format, this book reads from right to left—so action, sound effects and word balloons are completely reversed to preserve the orientation of the original artwork.

Check out the diagram shown here to get the hang of things, and then turn to the other side of the book to get started!

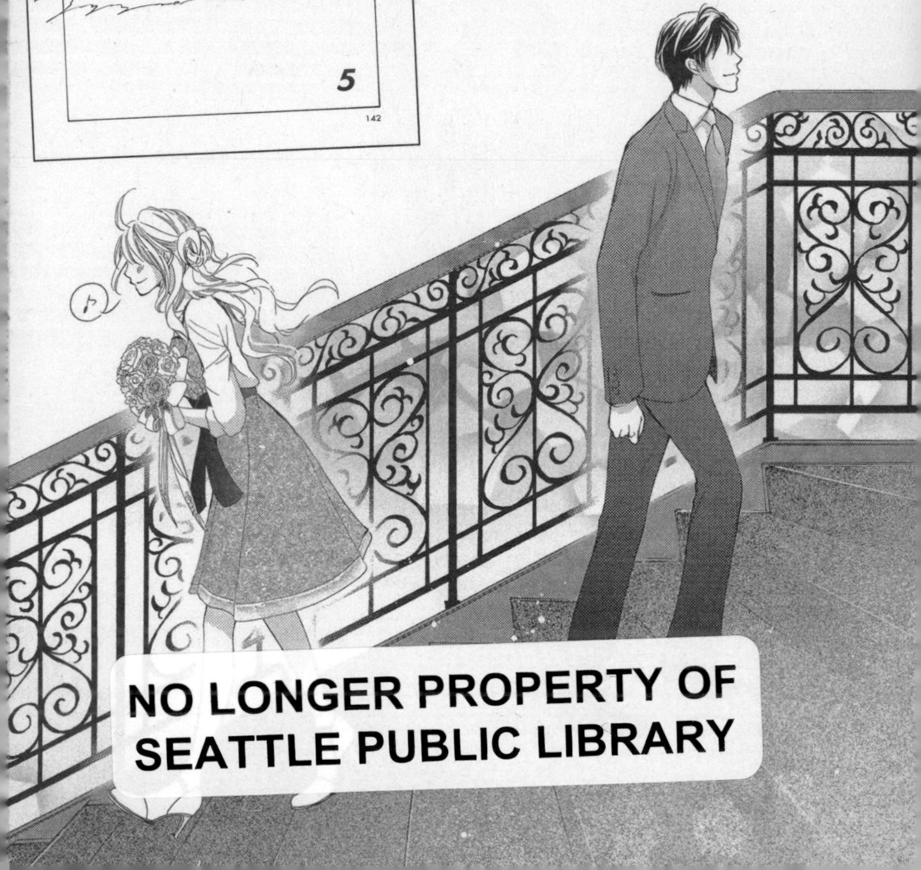